D0734264

INNOVATIVE BEHAVIOR AND COMMUNICATION

Editors' Series in Marketing

Paul E. Green, Philip Kotler, advisors

THOMAS S. ROBERTSON *Wharton School*
University of Pennsylvania

INNOVATIVE BEHAVIOR
AND COMMUNICATION

730572

HOLT, RINEHART AND WINSTON, INC.
New York Chicago San Francisco Atlanta
Dallas Montreal Toronto London Sydney

TO DIANA

Editors' Foreword

The Advisory Editors of the Holt, Rinehart and Winston Marketing Series are pleased to publish this scholarly and timely study of innovation diffusion and communication processes in marketing. Innovation diffusion has been a subject of major interest to students in a variety of disciplines, among them sociology, economics, geography, technology, and business. Until now, no one has systematically examined what this growing and scattered literature has to say to marketing practitioners who seek to develop new products that have a reasonable chance of gaining customer acceptance.

Thomas S. Robertson has done a superb job of synthesizing the relevant portions of this literature and of creating a framework designed to maximize understanding of what is known, what is tentative, and what is still unproven about the diffusion of new products. His work is an excellent blending of theory, research, and implications, which should be basic reading for business executives, as well as for students of innovation and communication. We are proud to publish this as the first book in the Holt, Rinehart and Winston Editors' Series in Marketing.

Paul E. Green
Philip Kotler

Preface

This book is an attempt to place diffusion theory within a marketing context and within a management decision-making framework. It provides a review and structuring of the far-ranging diffusion literature—from communication research, sociology, anthropology, economics, and, most importantly, marketing.

Diffusion research is currently a major concern within the marketing field, and the results of this research are of a high level of interest among marketing managers. Hopefully, this book will advance the theoretical development of the new product diffusion topic and provide a conceptual framework for further research and a rationale for applications of such research to new product marketing programs.

The idea for this book was a natural outgrowth of my thesis research as a doctoral student at Northwestern. Sidney Levy and Ralph Westfall were instrumental in stimulating my interest in the diffusion topic, and Philip Kotler encouraged me to consider writing a "new product diffusion" monograph. The initial version of this book was envisioned as an expansion of my thesis and a report of further diffusion research I was conducting while on the UCLA faculty from 1966 to 1968. As my involvement with the book grew, however, its focus changed to a more general literature treatment and to an attempt to conceptualize the diffusion perspective in marketing terms.

The book is divided into three parts and reflects the wide scope of diffusion theory. Part One takes "innovative behavior" as its primary focus and examines individual adoption processes and social diffusion processes. Part Two is essentially communication theory and reflects my view of diffusion as a communication process. Primary concerns here are personal influence and opinion leadership as well as the structure and functioning of communication variables. Part Three reflects a growing sophistication within the diffusion perspective and considers attitude theory and generalized mathematical models of new product acceptance.

The preparation of this book has benefited from the critical inputs of a number of people. Paul Green, of Wharton, and Philip Kotler of Northwestern, were the general editors and offered much valuable help and critique. Gerald Zaltman (Northwestern), Harold Kassarjian (UCLA), Raymond Bauer (Harvard), and Lyman Ostlund (Columbia) also provided review and critique. Scott Ward, of Harvard, provided me with a continuing stream of meaningful feedback throughout the several phases of manuscript preparation. The book must surely bear the imprint of their insightful critiques and ideas, and I gratefully acknowledge their contributions. Philip Kotler was of help in a direct way, because Chapter 11, "Models of New Product Acceptance," was written by him for his book *Marketing Decision Making: A Model Building Approach* (New York: Holt, Rinehart and Winston, Inc., 1971), and is presented here with some modifications with his permission.

It has also been my good fortune to have excellent research help. James Koch, at UCLA, and Christopher Lovelock, Cheryl Nash, and George Apostalicas, at Harvard, served as research assistants in various diffusion projects. My secretary, Bonnie Green, deserves my continuing gratitude. Financial assistance has been generously provided by the Division of Research, UCLA, and the Division of Research, Harvard Business School, as well as by the Shell Companies Foundation, Inc.

Philadelphia   T. S. R.
July 1971

Contents

PART TWO

Communication and Social Influence

PART ONE

Innovative Behavior

CHAPTER 1

INNOVATION IN THE
AMERICAN ECONOMY

Product innovation is critical to survival and essential to growth for American firms in the 1970s. The pace of technological advances, coupled with the American consumer's receptivity to progress and "newness," is shortening the life cycles of established products and placing a premium on new products.

Product obsolescence rates, of course, continue to vary among industries and across product groups. In general, the less the commodity nature of the product group or, alternatively, the more the opportunity for product differentiation, then the more rapid is innovation and obsolescence.

The flow from innovation to obsolescence is shown in the familiar product life cycle model (see Figure 1.1). This concept is analogous to the life process in organisms; the product also moves through a sequence of stages—introduction, growth, maturity, saturation, decline—and ultimately "dies" when it ceases to be profitable and is withdrawn from the market. Profit margins, as shown, increase throughout the product's growth phase and then reach a maximum and decline as maturity is reached.

Figure 1.1   Basic Life Cycle of Products

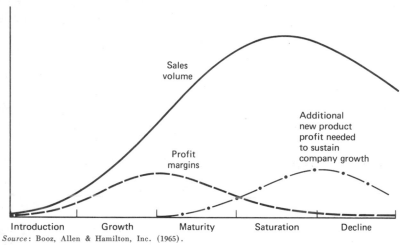

Source: Booz, Allen & Hamilton, Inc. (1965).

Change is generally thought to be inevitable. The nation's most successful companies are those that can create change in the form of product innovations and gain consumer acceptance of these innovations. A company's ability, however, to create new products usually far surpasses its ability to secure consumer acceptance, even when these new products are superior to existing products on the market.

The concern of this book is essentially the process of new product acceptance among consumers.

WHAT IS A NEW PRODUCT?

An initial difficulty is in defining what a new product, or product innovation, is. Four definitional criteria frequently have been used: (1) newness from existing products, (2) newness in time, (3) newness in terms of sales penetration level, and (4) consumer newness to the product.

Newness from Existing Products

Many authors argue that a "new product" must be very different from established products, although there is little attempt to make such a definition operational. One writer (Collier, 1964), for example, argues that "Pumpernickel or peaches don't change with the introduction of . . . snap-top, tear-open, flip-top, transparent, opaque, rigid or flexible packaging. True innovation means thinking big and acting big" (pp. 243–244). What "thinking big" means is not made explicit, and no operational guidelines are given for classifying products as "true innovations," or as "untrue innovations."

The Federal Trade Commission (1967) has rendered an advisory opinion that a product may properly be called new "only when [it] is either entirely new or has been changed in a functionally significant and substantial respect. A product may not be called 'new' when only the package has been altered or some other change made which is functionally insignificant or insubstantial" (p. 1).

E. B. Weiss (1965) argues that over 80 percent of new products are not "new," but "simply modifications" of existing products (p. 101). Again, however, guidelines are not established for distinguishing such modifications from new products. By extending this argument, it is possible to view all new products as modifications or recombinations of existing items. Barnett (1953), an anthropologist who has studied innovation and its effects on cultural change, states that "no innovation springs full-blown out of nothing; it must' have antecedents . . ." (p. 181). This viewpoint, which is quite prevalent in sociological thinking, examines innovation as the outcome of an evolutionary sequence. For example, an innovation such as the computer would be considered the result of a recombination of existing elements coupled with a measure of technological insight.

William E. Bell (1963) defines innovations as strategic and functional. A *strategic* innovation generally involves a product alteration and requires little change for either the firm or the consumer. As examples of this form of innovation, Bell offers color television and stereophonic equipment. A *functional* innovation involves the performance of a previously fulfilled consumer function in a new way and generally requires "more change for both the firm and the consumer" (p. 86). Examples are dishwashers and airconditioners. These definitions, while seeming to make good sense, are difficult to work with, since they combine degrees of change for both firm and consumer; and these perspectives need not be consistent in the amount of change involved.

Newness in Time

Length of time on the market is a second criterion in defining a new product. There has been a pronounced tendency for firms to promote a product as new for as long as two to three years after introduction under the assumption that the word *new* in advertising or on the package is a positive and desirable sales appeal. The Federal Trade Commission (1967) advisory opinion limits the use of the word *new* to six months after the product enters regular distribution after test marketing.

In opposition to the FTC point of view is the thinking of Nourse (1967). He addresses the issue of how long a product remains new and concludes, "only as long as its performance differs substantially from that of other acknowledged, mature products in the same category" (pp. 4–10). He suggests that in the food industry, a product may be considered new during its first two years of regular distribution. Using Nourse's definition, however, could lead to considering a product new for many more years. For example, the Polaroid camera, some twenty years after its introduction, could still be considered substantially different in performance from other cameras.

Newness in Terms of Sales Penetration Level

Another new product definitional criterion is the sales level which the item has achieved. William E. Bell (1963) and Robertson (1966), for example, have arbitrarily called products innovations if they have not yet secured 10 percent of their total potential market.

Consumer Newness to the Product

Yet another criterion for defining a new product is that the consumer must *perceive* it as new. Everett M. Rogers (1962 *b*) in *Diffusion of Innovations*, a summary volume in the rural sociology tradition, defines an innovation as "an idea perceived as new by the individual" (p. 13). Given this definition, an item can be new without being substantially different in function, without being a very recent market introduction, and while possessing a significant sales penetration level. The critical factor is *consumer perception*, and invariably there is some consumer who is new to the product. On the other hand, a newly introduced and functionally changed item need not be perceived as new—especially if the change is not obvious or significant to consumers. Thus, if a gasoline could be refined which improved performance by 10 percent, the company or the objective observer would feel justified in labeling the product new. The consumer, however—especially since gasoline ingredients are not "inspectable"—might not consider the product new.

Placing the burden for a new product definition upon the consumer is consistent with a marketing philosophy that looks to the satisfaction of consumer needs as the economic and social justification for the firm's existence. The firm is challenged to be consumer-oriented in its actions, including its new product strategies. However, talking in terms of any individual consumer is not particularly useful, since the *aggregate consumer* is generally what the marketer has in mind. Perhaps a product could be defined as new when a majority of consumers perceive it as new, but this certainly would be arbitrary.

These definitions, unfortunately, need not yield the same determinations of what products are new, as is illustrated by the examples in the preceding paragraphs. A further difficulty in the discussion to this point is the use of a simple dichotomy: a product either is new or not new. More logically, a range of newness should be the case.

NEWNESS IN TERMS OF CONSUMPTION EFFECTS

The critical factor in defining a new product should be its effect upon established patterns of consumption. A continuum may be proposed for classifying new products by how continuous or discontinuous their effects are on established consumption patterns. Or it may be convenient to think in terms of (1) continuous innovations, (2) dynamically continuous innovations, and (3) discontinuous innovations.

1. A *continuous* innovation has the least disrupting influence on established consumption patterns. Alteration of a product is almost always involved, rather than the creation of a new product. Examples include fluoride toothpaste, menthol cigarettes, and annual new-model automobile changeovers.
2. A *dynamically continuous* innovation has more disrupting effects than a continuous innovation. Although it still generally does not involve new consumption patterns, it involves the creation of a new product or the alteration of an existing one. Examples include electric toothbrushes, electric haircurlers, and the Mustang automobile.
3. A *discontinuous* innovation involves the establishment of new consumption patterns and the creation of previously unknown products. Examples include television, computers, and the automobile.

This definitional framework, while recognizing that innovations are not all of the same order of newness, unfortunately does not distinguish new products from products that are not new. It is the opinion of this author that this decision is always arbitrary. Perhaps it is possible to agree that new sizes, new flavors, and new packages are not new products. Does, however, the addition of sugar to corn flakes or raisins to bran flakes constitute a new product? Is an instant oatmeal a new product or a variation of the old one? No definition of innovation satisfactorily answers these and similar questions unless we rely on consumer perception and, as suggested, accept majority consumer opinion of what is and what is not an innovation.

DIMENSIONS OF NEWNESS

It may be of value to specify in what ways a product can be new. Innovations may be new in (1) a functional sense, (2) a technical sense, or (3) a stylistic sense.

Function

Products which are functionally new perform either a previously unful-filled function or an existing function in a new way. Most such products tend toward the discontinuous end of the innovation continuum; the automobile, contact lenses, and the computer are appropriate examples.

Technical Characteristics

Products new in technical characteristics employ new materials, new ingredients, and sometimes new forms. Most of these products tend toward the continuous end of the innovation continuum and sometimes are not noticeably new to consumers. Examples here are permanent press clothing, nylon, and freeze-dried coffee.

Style

It is in the category of style that so much disagreement occurs as to whether a product is new. Most style innovations are continuous in nature; fashions in clothing and new models in automobiles and appliances provide good examples. Frequently, stylistic innovations are intended to create in the consumer a *perception* of newness and are consequently centered on features, generally exterior ones, which will be most obviously different.

OBSOLESCENCE

The natural outcome of new product introductions is that the established products they seek to replace tend toward obsolescence. This innovation-obsolescence turnover is indicated in data for grocery items from A. C. Nielsen Company (1967). It is reported that a total of 33,000 grocery items was available in 1965. In the period 1965–1966 about 7300 "new items" (not necessarily new products) were introduced and 5543 items were discontinued. The Nielsen data further showed that over a fifteen-year period for foods and drugs, 40 percent of the leading brands faltered and were replaced by new leaders. The basic reason given by Nielsen is that these brands were replaced by either radically new or substantially improved brands.

An examination of *Fortune's* list of the top fifty industrial corporations indicates similar effects for companies which fail to innovate and instead cling to established forms of business. Analysis by sales trends from 1960 to 1970 indicates the fall of steel, rubber, and meat-packing companies and the rise of computer, electronic, and conglomerate firms.

ADAPTATION

Established products need not be replaced by superior new products if they themselves adapt to changing conditions. Tide detergent, for example, has successfully incorporated technological improvements over a number of years and has maintained its market leadership. Gross (1968) likens product evolution to species evolution and talks of the survival of the fittest. The survival and success of a product is dependent upon its adaptability to changing environmental needs and tastes and its responsiveness to competitive advances.

There are often strong pressures upon successful organizations, however, to be nonadaptive. A company tends not to significantly change a best-selling brand; and not until a new brand makes serious competitive inroads is change likely. But by then, serious damage may have occurred, and sales leadership may even have been lost.

NONADAPTIVENESS: A CASE EXAMPLE

The Coca-Cola Company provides an excellent example of an organization which was not adaptive to changing consumer tastes nor responsive to competitive strategies. In 1950, Coca-Cola's share of the domestic soft drink market was 60 percent. Its product line consisted of one item, Coke syrup, which was supplied to soda fountains and bottlers for distribution in six-and-a-half-ounce bottles. Then in the early 1950s, competition became more aggressive and appealed to a greater variety of consumer tastes and desires with various flavors, bottle sizes, and advertising approaches. By the late 1950s, Coca-Cola's share of the United States soft drink market had fallen to 40 percent (a decline of one-third in market share).

As might be imagined, today Coca-Cola has a very different philosophy— an innovation and diversification philosophy in tune with market desires. The soft drink line has been vastly expanded to include such new offerings as Fresca, Sprite, Tab, and Fanta flavors and to include multiple sizes and types of containers. The firm's market definition has been expanded beyond soft drinks to beverages in general with the purchase of Minute Maid citrus products and Butter Nut coffee products. It is interesting that despite such strong innovative strategies, Coca-Cola's share of the soft drink market is still just over 40 percent. Once market share is lost, it is indeed difficult to regain (Slocum, 1965; *Forbes Magazine*, 1967).

TYPES OF OBSOLESCENCE

It is possible to apply the same framework to a classification of forms of obsolescence as was used for innovation. We may think of functional, technical, and style obsolescence.

Functional Obsolescence

Functional obsolescence occurs when new products render existing products inferior in terms of functional performance. The jet aircraft, for example, made the piston-engined plane functionally obsolete. Very often, the established product may continue to exist or perform more specialized functions, but it will tend to be in the decline of its life cycle. For example, commercial air travel has had this effect on the railroad industry; and oral contraceptives have had this effect on the sale of other contraceptive devices.

Technical Obsolescence

New products may render existing products obsolete in terms of materials, ingredients, and form. Nylon had this effect on silk, just as instant oatmeal is having this effect on regular oatmeal. Again, however, the established product need not disappear, but may fulfill more limited or specialized purposes or may appeal to a more limited market segment.

Style Obsolescence

Style changes may cause existing products to be perceived as out-of-date. This, of course, is often a desirable marketing strategy, as in appliances, clothing, and automobiles. This type of obsolescence is also an area of considerable controversy, since the old-style product by no means need be functionally or technically deficient.

PLANNED OBSOLESCENCE

Planned obsolescence is a favorite target of social critics, such as Vance Packard (1960), who labels companies engaging in such activity as "waste makers." There is an important difference, however, between "planned obsolescence" and "planned substitution of a better product for existing products." The introduction of Maxim freeze-dried coffee by General Foods was a competitive ploy to enlarge its share of the coffee market; *but* this product was also (by many objective standards) a superior substitute for existing instant coffees.

Even planned obsolescence may be beneficial in its long-run effect. The 1970 automobile was superior to the 1960 automobile as the result of cumulative minor improvements over time. Furthermore, consumers may prefer stylistic changes and, therefore, the company which fails to change the esthetics of its product offerings may suffer obsolescence.

It also has been suggested that planned obsolescence is necessary to our economy due to its stimulation effect on consumer demand. Says economist Eva Mueller (1966) of the University of Michigan Survey Research Center:

> In an affluent society, and one interested in building up its savings, saturation might easily set in. Or at least, the acquisition of more and more consumer goods might become uninteresting and unexciting. Innovation, product change, and variety play a crucial role not only in maintaining demand, but also in leading people to upgrade their possessions (p. 34).

MOST INNOVATION IS CONTINUOUS

Most innovation in the American economy is of a continuous nature and, especially in the consumer sector, is the result of an attempt to differentiate products in order to increase market share. Few and far between are innovations of a discontinuous nature which significantly alter or create new consumption patterns. The image of innovations resulting from the inspiration of the occasional genius does not fit the typical occurrence; and even discontinuous innovations are increasingly the result of planned team research. Most innovation today results from programmed, systematic research efforts.

If we continue the analogy between human life cycles and product life cycles, we find similar continuities in mutations. Most mutations cause only minor morphological changes, and biologists seem to reject the idea that major changes in species result from single large mutations (Gross, 1968). In product as in species categories, most change seems to be minor, although the cumulative effect over time may be substantial.

SOME CASE EXAMPLES

If the first detergent on the market represented a fairly discontinuous innovation, then the succeeding proliferation of brands would have to represent highly continuous innovations. One brand may be a low sudser, another contain bleach, another contain disinfectant for baby clothes, and another possess cold water attributes; but all are essentially minor variations on the basic product and thus are *programmed innovations.*

The automobile industry is the leading example of programmed, continuous innovations. New products appear on schedule each year, and, as a rule, major design changes occur every three years. This planning and programming of innovation occurs across almost all industries.

When a major aircraft manufacturer was considering its next venture into the commercial market, it plotted the various offerings then available in terms of such variables as runway requirements, flying range, seating capacity, and cost of operation and found the gaps in the market. These gaps were in short-range jets and high-seating-capacity jets. The company then planned to innovate in one of these areas and did so.

THE IMPORTANCE OF INNOVATION TO THE FIRM

Innovation, according to a variety of sources, occurs because of (1) shrinking profit margins for established products, (2) shorter lives for established products, and (3) excess capacity. In addition, Schumpeter (1939) has attributed innovation to (4) a search for profit; Brown (1957), in an empirical study of the machine tool industry, found that innovation there resulted from (5) a search for increased demand; and Barnett (1953) has emphasized (6) the pressure of competition and the search for product differentiation as factors leading to innovation.

These reasons for the occurrence of innovation overlap considerably. Analysis of their content also reveals their all-inclusive nature. Innovation, it would appear, is the solution to all business problems. Perhaps Schumpeter's view of innovation as a search for profit summarizes all the other reasons, although corporate marketers generally cite growth or forward momentum as the most important factor encouraging new product development.

MAINTAINING MOMENTUM

New products are basic to company growth and to profitability. It is seldom possible in today's economy to maintain momentum or even stability without innovations. Mattel Toymakers, for example, grew rapidly with the acceptance of Barbie doll; but such growth could not be continued without other new products, since Barbie soon reached maturity in its product life cycle. It is also difficult to maintain profit margins when a product reaches maturity, since competition intensifies and product advantages are neutralized. Figure 1.1, (p. 4) for example, shows that profit margins decline while sales are still increasing and that the company must look to other new products for continued profit performance.

EMPIRICAL DATA

The effects of innovation upon established product groups are shown in Figures 1.2 and 1.3. In Figure 1.2 it can be seen that the increasing sales levels in the cereal industry are a result of two product innovations: presweetened and nutritionally enriched cereals. Regular cereal sales have been fairly constant since 1947 (probably as a result of the other product innova-

Figure 1.2   Ready-to-Eat Breakfast Cereal Sales, 1947–1963

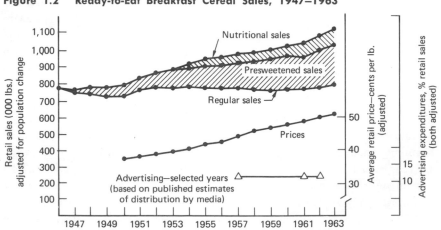

Source: Reprinted from Buzzell in *Proceedings of the American Marketing Association* (1966, p. 60).

Figure 1.3   Margarine Sales, 1952–1964

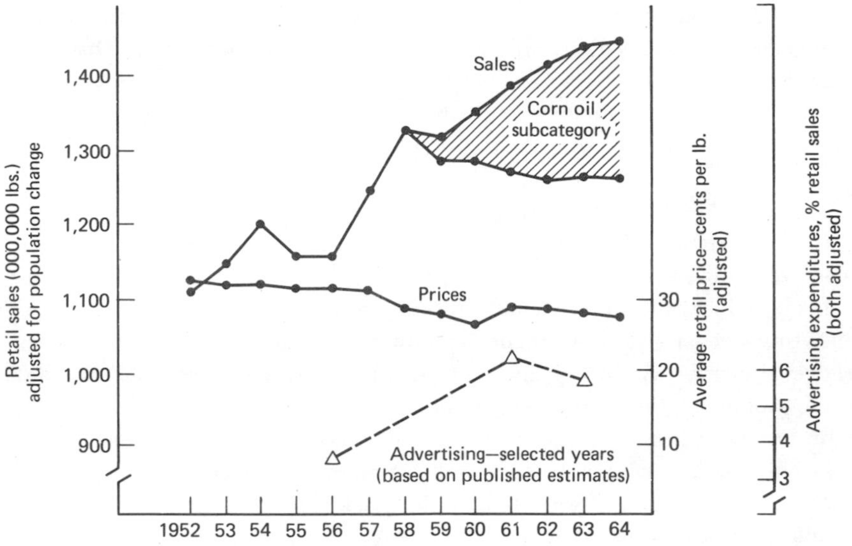

tions). In Figure 1.3 it can be seen that new corn oil margarine sales comprise the growth in the margarine product group. In this case, the new product is not only expanding product group sales but also is causing a decline in regular margarine sales.

The contribution of new products to the sales growth of various industries has been researched by Booz-Allen & Hamilton, Inc. (1965). Expected growth from new products varied from 46 percent to as much as 100 percent, with an average of 75 percent. Innovating industries were also found to be high-growth industries. Chemicals, electrical machinery, and textiles were among the industries showing highest growth from new products.

The effect of new products upon growth is further demonstrated in data from the food industry. High-growth food-processing companies achieved 73 percent of their sales increases from new products, while moderate-growth companies secured 47 percent of their sales increases from new products (Buzzell and Nourse, 1967, p. 146). Product innovation was found to be the most important growth factor.

Data from the Nielsen Company retail index (1967) reveal that new "items" (which are not limited to new products, but may include new sizes and additions to product lines) introduced in 1966 accounted for 12 percent of total 1966 grocery sales. Established items showed only a 1.1-percent increase in dollar sales volume, or an actual decline in sales on a real per capita income basis.

The value of technological innovation to the growth and profitability of *individual firms* is demonstrated by Mansfield (1962). His concern was with acceptance of capital goods' innovations by firms of comparable initial size in the steel and petroleum refining industries. He concludes that "In every interval and in both industries, the successful innovators grew more rapidly than the others, and in some cases, their average rate of growth was more than twice that of the others" (p. 1036).

INNOVATIVE COMPETITION

The importance of successfully marketing product innovations is being recognized now as never before. This is evidenced in the focus of the marketing trade magazines and the academic journals, as well as in the proliferation of consulting agencies devoted to new products and the establishment of new product divisions within existing agencies. Innovative competition may well be the modus operandi of business today.

But as more firms become committed to innovation, new product advantages exist for shorter time periods, and the monopoly power of new products is soon overcome. When General Electric quickly followed Squibb into electric toothbrushes, for example, it added innovation to innovation by marketing a cordless version, which was then a new usage concept. The new product marketplace is subject increasingly to fairly simultaneous innovations and imitation is rapid indeed. Many firms, such as Mattel Toymakers, prefer to go from product tests to national marketing, since test marketing would be very risky in terms of speeding imitation.

Concurrently, however, many authors argue that consumers increasingly expect and prefer new products. This is implicit in Ogilvy's recommendation (1963) that "The two most powerful words you can use in a headline are FREE and NEW. You can seldom use FREE, but you can always use NEW—if you try hard enough" (p. 105). This point of view is further reflected by Zaltman (1965), who states that "Today, more than ever before, the flow of goods and services consists of innovations. Consumers not only expect a constant change in the items available to them, but they have come to consider such change desirable" (p. 3).

These statements summarize a considerable amount of thought in marketing circles that consumers "prefer" new products. This assertion, however, is open to question and may lead some marketers to believe that new products are inevitably successful. The facts are that most new products are unsuccessful—a point we will develop shortly, after first assessing consumer views on innovation.

NEWNESS AS A PURCHASE MOTIVATION

New products may also possess symbolic importance for consumers simply *because they are new.* Today's American consumer seldom keeps his car until it no longer runs or his clothes until they are worn out. More commonly, these products are replaced by new products for the sake of newness. There are a number of consumption areas where, despite criticisms of deliberate obsolescence, consumers desire newness. It is also probably true that new product purchases are seen by some as a path toward status, recognition, and the esteem of family and friends. To the extent that new products are visible to others, they are also a means of conspicuous consumption and subject to imitation. Witness the clusterings of swimming pool purchases in many neighborhoods or in an earlier day, the nonrandom distribution of window air-conditioning units (Whyte, 1954).

Bauer and Marple (1968) have studied consumer perception of *value* in food products and have found new products to be less favorably rated. Consumers do not believe they are getting as much value per dollar as from established food items. Indeed, a consequence of the growing "consumerism" movement may be greater consumer skepticism and cynicism over the merits of so-called new and improved products, especially when their distinguishing characteristics are not readily apparent.

Many consumers reject newness, so that the marketer must not be misled by the acceptance patterns of a visible minority. Consumer *innovators*, that is, the first people within a community to buy new products, reflect more favorable new product attitudes and are more swayed by newness appeals than later buyers. But even consumer innovators maintain they will not buy an item just *because* it is new, but that they must "need" the item. One of our society's values would seem to be that consumption should be "rational"; and although on occasion consumers may buy on the basis of newness, they will not admit this in reconstructing their purchase decision.

Norms in regard to new product purchases are illustrated in research by Robertson (1966) with consumer innovators and noninnovators for a new small home-appliance product. Note the generally unfavorable attitudes toward buying on the basis of *newness*, particularly among noninnovators.

Question:

"Among the women you know, how would you describe those women who are usually first to buy new things?"

Innovator answers:

"I don't have anybody that I can think of that is always first on these things. Most are like we are. If they are in need of something they will replace it with a new item."

"Whatever I am—interested in progress, want convenience and comfort, can afford them."

"Some of the few I know, you're never quite sure if they're buying them because they really want them, or if they are going to make an impression by having them."

Noninnovator answers:

> "Compulsive. They just have to have what's new. Whether they need it or not doesn't matter."

> "They have rather poor judgment. I can only think of one person who goes out and buys everything new that she sees, whether she needs it or not."

> "I don't know, because they're all about like me. We kind of wait until things have been out a while and come down in price" (p. 132).

The range of responses is rather interesting. On the whole, whether one *needs* the product is the critical issue. Buying for newness' sake is not an acceptable purchase motivation, or, at least, it is not acceptable to *say* so!

The following comment by Mueller (1966) seems an appropriate summary to the newness issue:

> The fact that more appealing, more serviceable, and genuinely better consumer goods can stimulate demand should not be confused with the notion that the American consumer wants change for change's sake only, that he falls for every silly fad, or embraces every highly advertised gimmick (p. 37).

RISKS IN NEW PRODUCTS

Commitment to new products is not without serious problems and associated risks. Research and development expenditures for 1971 are estimated at $22.4 billion (*Business Week,* 1968). The largest spenders on R&D are high technology industries. Thus, the leader in R&D expenditures is the aerospace industry, followed by electrical machinery and communications.

Most research and development funds are spent on *unsuccessful* new product ideas. Based on responses from fifty-one prominent companies, Booz-Allen & Hamilton, Inc., (1965), report that it takes almost sixty *ideas* to result in one commercially successful new product. Most ideas do not survive initial screening, and there is a subsequent drop-off throughout the process of business analysis, development, testing, and actual market introduction. Minnesota Mining and Manufacturing estimates that out of every one hundred laboratory starts there will be an average of thirty-three technical successes out of which will come three commercial successes (Weiner, 1964).

It is estimated that three-fourths of new product expense funds are spent on unsuccessful products and that two-thirds of this "waste" is in the development stage (Booz-Allen & Hamilton, Inc., 1965). These figures must be treated as estimates only, especially since this is a sample of prominent companies and we can probably assume greater sophistication in the research and development process. It may be, for example, that in less sophisticated companies more ideas survive screening and more new products are judged (and quite often harshly) by the market rather than by the company. Results may also vary by industry.

Buzzell and Nourse (1967), in an extensive study of product innovation in the food industry, report that of every 1000 new product ideas,

> 810 are rejected at the idea stage, about half by informal means and about half on the basis of formal consumer tests;
>
> 135 are rejected on the basis of product tests, either formal or informal;
>
> 12 are discontinued after test marketing;
>
> 43 are introduced to the market on a regular basis (p. 105).
>
> 36 remain on the market after introduction (p. 124).

According to these figures, food-processing companies would appear to better the across-industry average reported by Booz-Allen & Hamilton of 1 successful new product for every 58 ideas. Buzzell and Nourse's figures suggest that more than 2 successful new food products result from every 58 ideas.

NEW PRODUCT FAILURES

The greatest risk in new products and the greatest potential monetary loss comes at the market introduction stage. Estimates of new product failures run from 10 percent to 80 percent, for reasons which we shall discuss shortly. Research by the National Industrial Conference Board, Inc., (Cochran and Thompson, 1964, p. 11) indicates that 30 percent of the new products introduced to the market fail. Research by New Products Action Team, Inc. (Angelus, 1969) classifies 80 percent of new supermarket items as failures because they did not meet sales goals. Booz-Allen & Hamilton, Inc. (1965), however, in its study of prominent companies, reports that of 366 new products "marketed," only 10 percent, or 37, were clear failures; 23 percent, or 84, were possible failures; and the remaining 67 percent or 245 products, were successful. Buzzell and Nourse (1967, p. 124), in their study of the food industry, report that 22 percent of product innovations were discontinued after test marketing and 17 percent were withdrawn following regular introduction.

Discrepancy in these new product failure figures is due largely to three reasons: (1) definition of what constitutes a new product, (2) measurement of what failure means, and (3) the sample of companies chosen.

New Product Definition

It could be hypothesized that the more strictly new product is defined— that is, the greater the discontinuity level required from established products— the higher the new product failure ratio is likely to be. An entirely new product concept, requiring changes in consumption patterns, is probably more likely to "fail" or to be unprofitable for a longer period of time while consumer learning occurs, than a new product incorporating only minor changes.

However, at the other extreme, it could be argued that if a new product is defined too loosely and highly continuous innovations involving only minor alterations are included, that again the new product failure ratio could be expected to be high. In this case, if research and development costs are minor and if the risk in market introduction is small, especially since the new product is likely to be only an addition to the established product line, then the company may be inclined to let the market judge product success or failure and may be inclined to tolerate a higher "new product failure rate."

Measurement of New Product Failure

The measurement criteria employed by various researchers are, of course, an obvious reason for reported discrepancies in failure rates. While one study may include test market or regional introduction failures, another may include only failures at the national market level. Similarly, one study may include only product withdrawals, while another may include all unprofitable or marginally profitable products. While one study may limit itself to measurement within one or two years of introduction (when the product may yet be unprofitable), another may choose a longer time span.

The ambiguity in measurement is well illustrated in a set of figures from Buzzell and Nourse (1967, p. 126). Companies in food processing were asked to rate each of their "distinctly new products" (note the emphasis on discontinuous innovations in definition) as to success. Based on responses for 123 such products, these results were obtained:

Highly successful	18%
Moderately successful	40
Moderately unsuccessful	33
Extremely unsuccessful	9
	100%

The decision here is whether to assign 9 percent or 42 percent of these new products to the "failure" category. The firms studied actually *discontinued* 39 percent of these products, and this is perhaps the best indicator for assessing new product failure rates.

The Sample of Companies

As already argued, large companies are likely to market fewer failures than small companies and sophisticated, market-oriented industries are likely to market fewer failures than unsophisticated, production-oriented industries.

While it is difficult, therefore, to provide an average new product failure ratio which will apply uniformly, documentation has shown this failure rate can be quite high. To say that a *majority* of new products fail is probably fair, although it would be more meaningful to present standardized figures by *industry* if such figures could be obtained.

WHY DO NEW PRODUCTS FAIL?

New product failures seldom are due to basically unsound products. A fairly extensive National Industrial Conference Board study (1964) suggests the following reasons in order of frequency:

1. Inadequate market analysis	32%
2. Deficiency in the product	23
3. Higher costs than anticipated	14
4. Poor timing	10
5. Competition	8
6. Weaknesses in marketing efforts	13
	100%

While only 23 percent of product failures are attributed to product deficiencies and only 14 percent of failures are attributed to higher costs than anticipated, 63 percent of the reasons given for product failures are basically weaknesses in marketing—inadequate market analysis, poor timing, failure to anticipate competition correctly, and faulty distribution efforts.

In accounting for new product failures, executives in the companies involved blamed poor forms of *organization* for new product marketing, and failure to adequately *research* the market (less than 6 percent of R&D dollars were spent on marketing research). Thus, while considerable sums are spent on product development, very little is spent to adequately research potential market acceptance of the item and to test the most appropriate marketing programs of action.

Reasons for new product discontinuances in food are provided in Table 1.1, taken from Buzzell and Nourse (1967). The paramount reason, of course, is that sales did not reach anticipated levels, but this is, in turn, a function of the other reasons indicated. Poor timing, insufficient marketing efforts, and unexpectedly severe competition are again important. Failures because of deficiencies in the product occur in only a limited number of cases—15 percent of the products failed because of design and quality. These results are not dissimilar to those of Angelus (1969), who conducted interviews with company executives involved in seventy-five major packaged goods new product failures. He found product performance to account for only 12 percent of failures, the main reasons apparently being the lack of meaningful product differences to consumers, and poor product positioning.

Analysis of the marketing trade literature provides countless examples of basically sound new products failing upon market introduction. General Foods failed to succeed with a Birds Eye line of frozen baby foods and rejected Brim, a forerunner of Instant Breakfast, in test markets. Ford Motor Com-

Table 1.1   Stated Reasons for Discontinuance of Forty-eight "Distinctly New Products" after Test Marketing or Regular Introduction

Reasons for Discontinuance	% of Products Discontinued after Introduction
MISJUDGED MARKET CONDITION:	
Sales did not achieve anticipated levels	77%
Poor timing	21
Insufficient marketing effort	19
Unexpectedly severe competition	15
Failure to achieve adequate distribution	13
PRODUCT DIFFICULTIES:	
Development and production costs higher than anticipated	13
Problem with product design and quality after introduction	15
OTHERS	
Company withdrew from all activities in this area	13
Because of multiple reasons, the figures shown add to:	186%

Source: Buzzell and Nourse (1967, p. 125). Used by permission.

pany's Edsel is now a classic example of a new product failure. Campbell proved unsuccessful in marketing fruit soup as well as a Red Kettle line of dry soup mixes. Coca-Cola, despite its strong consumer franchise in cola beverages, was initially unsuccessful in marketing a diet cola.

While reasons for new product failures could be elaborated, the foremost problem is in marketing. More tightly controlled test market and market experimentation procedures are necessary as well as a greater volume of marketing research in advance of introduction. Sophisticated models for predicting new product sales levels should be encouraged. The primary focus of this book, however, is not on these concerns. It is the thesis of this volume that the probability of new product success can be increased by an understanding of the factors governing the *diffusion* and *adoption* of new products by consumers.

THE DIFFUSION PERSPECTIVE

Diffusion is the process by which something spreads. Anthropologists have studied the diffusion of language, religion, and methods of farming, fishing, and hunting *among* tribes and societies. Sociologists have studied the diffusion of new values and styles of life *within* societies. The principles and theories which these investigators have developed sometimes apply with equal force to the diffusion of new goods and services from producers to consumers. Marketers have studied diffusion implicitly for many years as they sought to guide and control the spread of new products. Only minor research and conceptual thinking, however, has been directed toward an understanding of the diffusion process and toward a specification of the major behavioral variables operating.

The diffusion literature, as developed across a number of disciplines, offers for consideration a fairly well-developed theoretical framework which applies to the flow of information, ideas, and products. It is the integration of this framework with the traditional marketing framework that may advance our understanding of how new products disseminate and gain consumer acceptance and which may suggest means of improvement in new product marketing strategies. The conceptual foundations to be applied in the study of diffusion are those of the behavioral sciences—psychology, sociology, social psychology, and cultural anthropology. These behavioral foundations emphasize the basic consumer point of view. Our attempt is to understand *how* consumers behave and to probe the issue of *why*. Meaningful marketing strategies can then be suggested with greater confidence in their probability of effectiveness.

This concern is ambitious enough, so we will assume that the new product is developed and ready to be marketed. Considerations of product development, concept testing, test marketing, and other basic preintroduction concerns will be left to other writers. While a sizable body of new product marketing literature exists, there is not a single volume focusing exclusively on the diffusion and acceptance of new products by consumers.

TRADITIONS OF DIFFUSION RESEARCH

Although diffusion has not, until recently, been a major area of concern within the marketing discipline, traditions of diffusion research exist in other disciplines. As mentioned, anthropologists have been concerned, over a considerable period of time, with how new ideas and practices diffuse from one society to another. Rural sociologists have studied the spread of new agricultural technology among farmers. Educationalists have studied school adoption of new teaching methods and equipment. Economists have been concerned with the imitation process by which firms adopt new technological and production processes. Communication researchers have focused on the diffusion process to better understand the dynamics of persuasion and propaganda.

A current inventory of diffusion research is maintained under the direction of Everett M. Rogers, whose book, *Diffusion of Innovations*, has brought diffusion research to the forefront as a subject of inquiry and as a generally applicable theoretical framework. As of August 1968, some 1126 publications were available on the diffusion of new ideas, practices, technologies, and products. The number of studies by research tradition is as follows (Rogers, 1968):

410 in rural sociology
 98 in communication
 71 in anthropology
 71 in general sociology
 95 in extension education
 83 in medical sociology
 76 in education
 70 in marketing
 39 in agricultural economics
113 "others" not classifiable into these
    major research traditions

According to Rogers (1968), the number of diffusion publications has doubled in the last five years. However, the rate of growth is even more dramatic within marketing. In his first inventory of research, Rogers (1962b) does not even list marketing as a diffusion research tradition. He dismisses it on the grounds that "there are relatively few research studies available in this field" (p. 23) and, in fact, he cites only four marketing studies (as best as can be determined). If a research tradition is to be defined as a series of studies concerning a specified topic, in which later studies are influenced by, and built upon, previous studies, then Rogers was correct in not recognizing a marketing diffusion research tradition.

This situation has changed and a marketing tradition of diffusion research is clearly recognizable today. The cumulative growth of marketing publications focusing on some aspect of the diffusion process is approximately as follows:

 19 publications in 1966
 45 publications in 1967
 70 publications in 1968
115 publications in 1969
155 publications in 1970

The first three figures are based on Rogers' annual *Bibliography on the Diffusion of Innovations* (1966, 1967, 1968). The 1969 and 1970 figures are estimates by the present author based on examination of the marketing literature. In many ways, "diffusion of innovation" is becoming a fad in marketing circles and there is some apprehension that the present high growth rate in publications may reach the saturation and decline stages—as in the product life cycle—unless meaningful research is done, applications to the business community are sought, and findings are integrated. Hopefully, this book will be a step toward integration and an expression of the theoretical value of the diffusion perspective.

It should be cautioned that some of the growth in publications is due simply to more intensive compilation procedures by Rogers and his colleagues, who have only recently become familiar with the marketing journals. In the present author's opinion, for example, the 1966 figure is understated. Furthermore, number of publications is by no means synonymous with number of *separate* research studies conducted. The cumulative growth in number of separate empirical diffusion studies conducted by marketers is approximately as follows:

> 13 studies in 1966
> 27 studies in 1967
> 41 studies in 1968
> 57 studies in 1969
> 71 studies in 1970

While these figures again use Rogers' annual bibliographies (1966, 1967, 1968), some discretion has been used in arriving at the number of studies per year. Only *separate* studies have been included, instead of all reports on any given study. Furthermore, only *new* empirical studies have been included, thus excluding reinterpretations of existing data. There is also some question whether certain of Rogers' entries actually pertain to diffusion. Finally, the number of studies would be even more restricted if it were limited to published reports in professional marketing journals.

OTHER DIFFUSION RESEARCH TRADITIONS

It would not seem particularly appropriate to present any in-depth discussion of the variety of other research traditions from anthropology to extension education. However, the marketing tradition, which has emerged so late, has been particularly dependent on the concepts and methodologies of both rural sociology and communications research. Thus, some background in these areas is probably in order.

The rural sociology research tradition, which has been most productive of findings (some five hundred studies as of 1969), dates, according to Rogers (1962*b*), back to the 1920s when the United States Department of Agriculture Extension Service instigated research programs to evaluate the effectiveness of extension agencies. The most famous study in this tradition is the hybrid corn study conducted by Ryan and Gross (1943). Among the significant findings, which were to have considerable impact for future research, were the following:

1. A relatively normal distribution of hybrid seed adoption occurred over time.
2. On the basis of this distribution, adopters were classified into four categories by time of adoption.
3. An adoption process was recognized from awareness to trial to adoption.
4. Salesmen were the most important *original* source of information about the seed, but neighbors were the most *important* source in the adoption decision.

The communications research diffusion tradition has its roots in the Columbia University Bureau of Applied Social Research. It began with the Albany voting study of the 1940 elections (Lazarsfeld, Berelson, and Gaudet, 1948) from which was formulated the "two-step flow-of-communications" hypothesis, and continued with the Katz and Lazarsfeld (1955) study of personal influence in the areas of grocery products, movies, fashion, and public affairs. More recently, researchers of Columbia background (James S. Coleman, Katz, and Menzel, 1966) have completed a study of the diffusion of a new drug among physicians. This work serves today as the major study of innovative behavior from the communications research tradition and is concerned largely with the interpersonal aspects of adoption. The study centers on a particular drug innovation and examines its pattern of diffusion and the characteristics of the doctor innovators.

A COMPARISON OF THREE TRADITIONS

It may be of value at this point to compare the rural sociology, communications, and marketing traditions of research in order to understand their similarities and differences. This will be done by reference to the leading studies in the rural sociology and communications traditions and to a recent study in the marketing tradition. An excellent article comparing the rural sociology and communications studies already has been published by Elihu Katz (1961).

The rural sociology study is that of Ryan and Gross (1943) on the adoption of hybrid corn among Iowa farmers and is the classic research piece in this field. The communications study is that of James S. Coleman, Katz, and Menzel (1966), which was conducted in the 1950s and accounts for the adoption of a new miracle drug, "gammanym," among physicians in four midwestern communities. The marketing study is that of Robertson (1966) and deals with the diffusion of a new telephone product among homeowners in a midwestern suburban community during 1965 and 1966.

The dimensions on which these studies will be compared are (1) the characteristics of the innovation, (2) the time involved in diffusion, (3) the channels of communication available, and (4) the social structure in which diffusion occurs. Table 1.2 provides a summary of this material.

The Characteristics of the Innovation

All three studies were concerned with the diffusion of a single innovation. Elihu Katz (1961) provides a listing of the basic similarities between the hybrid corn and miracle drug innovations as follows:

1. Both products "came *highly recommended* by competent scientific authority."
2. The effects of both products could "be measured with a rational yard-

Table 1.2   A Comparison of Studies in Three Diffusion Research Traditions

	Farmer Study	Physician Study	Consumer Study
Specific innovation	Hybrid corn	"Gammanym" (a miracle drug)	Touch-Tone® telephone
Time	Farmers classified according to own reports on year of first use	Doctors classified according to date of first prescription on file in pharmacies	Consumers classified according to date of installation from company records
Channels of communication	Farmers' reports on the channels that influenced their decisions to adopt; farmers' reports on their general communication behavior	Doctors' reports on the channels that influenced their decisions to adopt; doctors' reports on their general communication behavior	Consumers' reports on the channels which influenced their adoption behavior plus their reports of general media and interpersonal exposure
Social structure	All farmers in two midwestern farming communities; individuals classified in terms of age, size of farm, and so on, and in terms of their own reports concerning formal and informal social integration	All doctors in four midwestern communities; individuals classified in terms of age, type of practice, and so on, and in terms of relative formal and informal integration measured sociometrically	All consumers in a midwestern suburban community of some 14,000 population. Innovators and noninnovators categorized on a series of demographic, attitudinal, social interaction, and predispositional factors

Source: Based in part on Elihu Katz (1961).

stick which enables users to *see for themselves*, more or less, whether the innovation serves better than its predecessor."

3. Both products "could be accepted in installments. . . . This is quite different, obviously, from take-it-or-leave-it innovations, like an air conditioner or a new car."

4. Both products "were essentially modifications of products with which farmers and doctors, respectively, had had considerable experience."

5. Both products were such that "differentials in wealth, or in *economic profitability*, do not seem, *a priori*, to be of major relevance in determining response to the innovation" (p. 71).

The consumer telephone innovation, it should be obvious, bears more differences than similarities to the hybrid corn and miracle drug innovations. The telephone product was not "highly recommended by competent scientific authority"; its effect could not "be measured with a rational yardstick which enables users to see for themselves"; and the product could not be accepted in installments. The similarities are that Touch-Tone, too, was a modification of an already familiar product and "wealth" was not a major prerequisite for purchase.

Such will be the pattern for most new consumer products. Seldom is a product highly recommended by objective scientific sources. Endorsements, such as that of Crest toothpaste by the American Council on Dental Therapeutics, are indeed rare. It is also infrequent for consumer products to be objectively and "rationally" measured as to performance. Because consumers cannot test many products by "physical reality checking" (Festinger, 1950), opinions of other people become highly important. Of course, frequently consumer products can, in effect, be adopted in installments, as in the trial of a new food item. This is not the case for durable goods. As has already been argued, most consumer innovations are highly continuous and are essentially "modifications of existing products." Finally, the prerequisite of "wealth" may not be generally relevant in consumer adoption of new products, but "income" is often positively related to adoption. Of course, consumers simply are not concerned with the "economic profitability" of adoption decisions.

Time

Katz (1961) again compares the hybrid corn and drug studies and concludes that "both studies *can assign a date* to initial acceptance and that it is the element of time, perhaps more than any other, which makes the study of diffusion possible" (p. 72). The consumer telephone product study can also assign a date for initial acceptance. In fact, as in the physician study, the date can be determined objectively through company records. However, since it is not usually possible in consumer research to objectively determine date of adoption, consumer estimates often must be relied upon. Furthermore, for many products where trial takes place (as, for example, food items), it is difficult to determine "adoption" in the sense of commitment to the product and repeat purchase behavior.

Channels of Communication

This is a dimension of major consideration in almost all diffusion research and across all research traditions. In the studies of hybrid corn, the miracle drug, and the new telephone, the researchers attempted to reconstruct the adoption situation and to assess the impact of the various communication channels. Such research, unfortunately, relies almost exclusively on respondent report of channel importance.

The channels which are relevant are not the same in the three studies under examination. In the farmer situation, communication sources used were salesmen, neighbors and relatives, farm journals, radio advertising, and the Agricultural Extension Service. In the physician situation, the sources used were salesmen, colleagues, direct mail, drug-house periodicals, journal articles, and professional society meetings. For consumers, information sources can be considered to be marketer-controlled—including salesmen, advertising, direct mail, and product demonstrations—and consumer-controlled—basically interpersonal communication (word-of-mouth advertising). The importance of these sources is discussed at length in Chapter 5.

The Social Structure

Social structure defines the boundaries within which innovations diffuse. Within a given structure, individuals may also be characterized and "located" in terms of their social status, relative integration within the social system, and on demographic, attitudinal, and other variables. The farmer and physician studies were conducted within defined communities (social structures), as was the telephone study. In all three studies, it is possible to characterize and compare individuals (adopters and nonadopters) within these social structures. It is especially significant that social status and social integration of community members can be traced.

Most marketing studies, however, are not limited to a defined social structure, since sociological variables are of less concern. The marketing executive is more interested in data which is not bound to a single community and prefers data which is generalizable to entire market segments. The unit of analysis in marketing studies is almost always the individual and not the social system. Unlike the hybrid corn and miracle drug studies, marketing diffusion studies, including the telephone study, are principally concerned with establishing the profile of adopters versus nonadopters, or early adopters versus late adopters. This is true for studies of both ultimate consumers and of industrial buyers. Whereas this book reports mainly on the diffusion of consumer innovations, the diffusion of industrial products, processes, and technologies is also of concern. Findings in the industrial area are reported when applicable, although extremely limited research has been conducted to date.

SUMMARY

Technological change and consumer receptivity to newness cause a premium to be placed on product innovation if the firm is to survive and grow. Although various definitional criteria can be applied in determining what products are "new," the emphasis in this book is in terms of the *product's effects on established patterns of consumption*. Most innovation is highly continuous in nature—representing only minor change in consumption patterns. A very limited amount of innovation is of a discontinuous nature, in which entirely new forms of consumption are established.

The rapid pace of innovation in the United States economy has generally brought about significant changes and improvements in living standards and life style. Concurrent with these changes has been the demise of previously established products, although some firms may successfully adapt to changes in technology and consumer needs and thus extend the lives of existing products.

It would be tempting to conclude that consumers prefer new products, but the majority of new products fail and are withdrawn from the market. "Newness" alone is not a sufficient reason for purchase, although some consumers— particularly product innovators—may respond well to this appeal.

New product development and introduction often entails considerable risks and problems for the innovating company, and most R&D dollars are spent on new product ideas which prove unsuccessful. However, the greatest risk in terms of monetary loss comes at the market introduction stage, at which a significant proportion of new products fail. Technically unsound products account for a minority of such failures, and basic marketing weaknesses—inadequate analysis, poor timing, underestimation of competition, weak promotional efforts, and improper product positioning—are responsible for failure in the majority of instances.

The thesis of this book is that an improved understanding of the diffusion process by which consumers accept new ideas and products should lead to more effective new product marketing programs.

CHAPTER 2

THE DIFFUSION PROCESS

The business firm, in general, wishes to achieve *maximum new product diffusion*, that is, the greatest possible number of adopters or the largest possible market share in the *shortest possible period of time*. Successful diffusion, in terms of these criteria, is critically dependent upon the matching of new product, promotion, pricing, and distribution attributes with the characteristics of the social system and the individual consumer.

NATURE OF THE DIFFUSION PROCESS

The diffusion process concept can be meaningfully related to the more familiar concept of the product life cycle. The essential difference is that diffusion refers to the percentage of potential adopters within a social system or market segment who adopt the product over time, whereas the product life cycle is based on absolute sales levels over time. Two forms of the diffusion process are depicted in Figure 2.1. In Figure 2.1 (a), the cumulative percentage of adopters within a market segment is plotted over time, whereas in Figure 2.1 (b), the percentage of adopters within each time segment is plotted. Both curves assume 100-percent adoption—either 100 percent of all potential adopters or an adjusted curve in which 100 percent represents the highest penetration level achieved, which might be, for example, only 5 percent of the total potential market.

The cumulative diffusion curve resembles an S-shaped growth pattern, which is familiar to most marketers as the postulated shape of the product life cycle. The close relationship between these two curves would be expected to the extent that sales are proportional to cumulative adoption. The logistic pattern of the cumulative diffusion curve suggests that at least the following stages can be distinguished:

> *Introduction*—The product is placed on the market and sales increase slowly.
>
> *Growth*—The product enters a period of rapid growth.
>
> *Maturity*—Sales growth continues, but at a declining rate. Sales eventually reach a plateau.
>
> *Decline*— Sales begin to decrease.[1]

The noncumulative diffusion curve partitions diffusion into categories of adopters over time and has been found to be a fairly normal distribution. Rogers (1962b) states that of eight adopter distributions which he tested, all were bell-shaped and "approached" normality (p. 158). The cumulative distribution function, when derived from such a normally distributed density function, tends to exhibit a logistic pattern.

A classification of "adopter categories" from innovators (first to adopt) to laggards (last to adopt) is based on use of the mean and standard deviation, assuming a normal distribution (see Figure 2.1). Innovators, for example, are those lying beyond two standard deviations to the left of the

---

[1] This is not the only sequence of stages proposed in the literature. Booz-Allen & Hamilton, Inc., (1965), for example, have proposed an additional "saturation" stage between maturity and decline (see Figure 1.1 in this book). Pessemier (1966) has proposed the following sequence: introduction, growth, competition, obsolescence, termination.

Figure 2.1   Generalized Cumulative and Noncumulative Diffusion Patterns

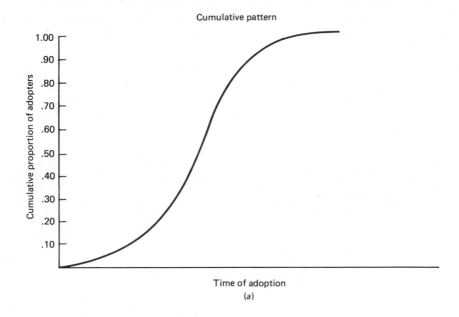

Cumulative pattern

(a)

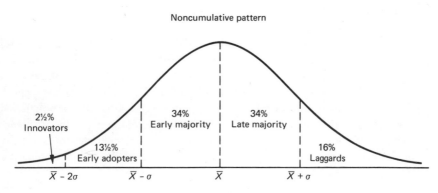

Noncumulative pattern

(b)

Source: North Central Subcommittee (1961, p. 3).

mean year of adoption (2.5 percent of adopters); laggards are those falling beyond one standard deviation to the right of the mean year of adoption (16 percent of adopters). This categorization is, of course, arbitrary and has been found meaningful so far mainly in studying the diffusion of agricultural innovations.

COMPONENTS OF THE DIFFUSION PROCESS

Diffusion is (1) the adoption (2) of new products and services (3) over time (4) by consumers (5) within social systems (6) as encouraged by marketing activities.

Adoption refers to the use and continued use of a new item; it involves commitment rather than purchase trial. The *adoption process* refers to the mental sequence of stages through which the consumer progresses from first awareness of the item to final acceptance. These concepts (adoption and adoption process) should be clearly distinguished from diffusion, or the diffusion process, which refers to the spread of an item from producer to consumer. The adoption process is an individual phenomenon, whereas the diffusion process is a social phenomenon.

New products and *services* will be considered in the broadest sense from highly continuous to highly discontinuous innovations. The *time* dimension distinguishes early adopters from later adopters and is the essential underlying factor in the diffusion concept. The *consumer adoption unit* may be the individual consumer, or a family or buying committee, or even a city of consumers, as for ecological systems.

Social systems constitute the boundaries within which diffusion occurs. In a broad sense, the entire market segment can be viewed as a social system, or, in a narrower definition, the consumer's friendship group can be considered his social system. Within these systems, communication—both marketer-initiated and consumer-initiated—occurs. *Marketing activities* are defined as the mix of product, price, promotion, and distribution plans and strategies.

These several aspects of the diffusion process are interdependent. For example, the attributes of the new product will affect the rate of adoption over time, the types of consumers who will adopt, the kinds of social systems within which diffusion will take place, and the marketing efforts which will be needed to achieve diffusion. Alternatively, successful new product diffusion is critically dependent upon the communication of relevant product information and the matching of new product attributes with social system and individual consumer characteristics.

PATTERNS OF DIFFUSION

The idea of an **S**-shaped diffusion process seems to have originated with the sociologist Gabriel Tarde (1903), who proposed that new ideas are accepted in such a pattern. Evidence for such a generalized pattern has since been found in a number of contexts including the diffusion of a new drug among physicians (James S. Coleman, Katz, and Menzel, 1966), the diffusion of new agricultural technology among farmers (Rogers, 1962b), the diffusion of new food products among consumers (Buzzell, 1966), the diffusion of promotional games among supermarkets (Allvine, 1968), and the diffusion of new manufacturing technology among firms (Mansfield, 1961).

There is also contrary evidence regarding the shape of the diffusion curve. Pessemier (1966) eliminates the initial period of slowly growing sales during introduction and proposes an exponential rather than a logistic pattern. Polli (1968) believes this modification to be appropriate for product improvements and model changes. Figure 2.2 shows the essential differences between the more traditional **S**-shaped pattern, which may be characterized by a logistic curve, and the exponential pattern.

Figure 2.2   Logistic and Exponential Life Cycle Patterns

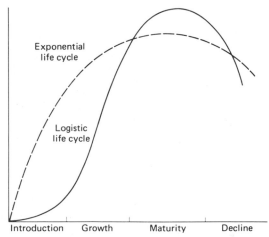

Data from Quaker Oats Company (1968) also suggests the absence of an initial period of slow growth in the ready-to-eat cereal market. Combined sales levels of four new cereal products were charted over the first year of their market introductions based on Nielsen data. The following pattern was obtained:

Months	Sales
0–2	$8.6 million
2–4	$9.2
4–6	$9.8
6–8	$9.7
8–10	$8.5
10–12	$8.2

This pattern, which Quaker considers typical for the industry, suggests a very quick buildup in sales levels rather than a process of slow growth, and further suggests that maximum sales may be achieved within a very short period of time and that a subsequent leveling-off may occur.

The validity of the product life cycle has been studied as part of a research program at Marketing Science Institute (Buzzell, et al., 1969; Polli and Cook, 1967, 1969). The model has been tested against actual data for 140 categories of nondurable goods and 50 categories of durable goods. Percentage changes in real sales for each item over time were compared with expectations based on the product life cycle model. The general rule, derived from fairly elaborate statistical techniques, was that if there were no inconsistent observations, then the model was in agreement with the data; and if inconsistent observations were less than 10 percent to 20 percent, then there was "quite good" fit between the model and data.

Their general conclusion is that the product life cycle is often a valid model of sales behavior, although this varies by industry and product type. Polli and Cook (1969) conclude:

> . . . we believe the product life cycle has proven to be a surprisingly good model of sales (market acceptance) behavior . . . one of our initial objectives was to show that the product life cycle should not be accepted at face value because it was simply too naive to explain much . . . we were unable to support that belief with research (p. 35).

CONTROL OVER THE DIFFUSION PROCESS

A central issue is the extent to which the product life cycle follows "its own natural pattern" and the extent to which it is shaped by marketing programs. The general tenor of the literature is that marketing programs should be "adjusted," or should "respond to" the product's stage in its life cycle. Thus, Joel Dean (1950) suggests that pricing policy should vary by life cycle stage and Levitt (1965) encourages new product managers to "foresee the profile of the proposed product's cycle" (p. 84). Cook and Herniter (1969) suggest that marketers lack substantial control over the product life cycle; in these authors' opinion, marketing programs may accelerate or retard consumer acceptance, but "they will not alter it in a significant way" (p. 124).

The question is whether there is any reason that a logistic, exponential, quartic, or any other diffusion pattern must occur. Green and Carmone (1968) emphasize that "Current use of the product life-cycle approach appears to emphasize empirical curve fitting procedures, rather than theoretical formulations . . ." (p. 1). To the extent that theoretical justification for a life-cycle model is given, reliance is placed on "diffusion theory" (for example, see Polli, 1968), which proposes an "interaction effect" leading to an S-shaped growth function. The thesis to be developed here is that the specific shape of a product's diffusion process is a result of both interaction effect and marketing and competitive strategies.

THE INTERACTION EFFECT

The *interaction effect* refers to a process of influence and imitation among consumers by which adopters of a new product lead others to purchase. The interaction effect is often posited to account for the rapid-growth stage in the diffusion process. It is reasoned that if every consumer considered adopting on an individual basis, without social influence, then the probability of his adopting in any given time period would be the same (no account is taken of the impact of marketing activities over time). If, however, consumer adoption decisions are based on social influence, then a "snowball," or rapid-growth, process will occur, since the probability of a consumer's adoption in any one time period is a function of the number of consumers who have already adopted. (These relationships are developed further and expressed mathematically in Chapter 11.)

It has been documented extensively that consumers go beyond promotional information sources and that other people often may be the most important information source in the purchase process—varying, of course, by product type. (The occurrence and functioning of such "personal influence" is explored in Chapter 8.) Suffice it for the present to generalize that personal influence gains in importance with higher price, greater product conspicuousness, greater product complexity, and a lack of objective standards by which to evaluate the product. Under such conditions we would expect the interaction effect to be most pronounced.

EMPIRICAL EVIDENCE FOR THE INTERACTION EFFECT

Perhaps the most convincing evidence for the effect of interaction upon the diffusion process is offered by James S. Coleman, Katz, and Menzel (1966) in their study of the diffusion of a new miracle drug among physicians. They were able to compare the diffusion processes for socially integrated and isolated doctors using information on the number of friendship choices received. As indicated in Figure 2.3, more socially integrated doctors introduced the new drug sooner than more isolated doctors. Since the socially integrated doctor's "receptivity" to adopt was not found to be particularly different from his more isolated colleague's receptivity, the authors attributed the difference in diffusion rate to greater interaction and resulting influence: the diffusion curve of the socially integrated doctors approximates a "chain reaction," or snowball process, while the diffusion curve of the isolated doctors approximates an ideal curve based on "individual" adoption decisions.

Subsequently, Arndt (1967a) assessed the effect of consumer social integration on the adoption of a new coffee product available only to residents of an apartment complex. His results (see Figure 2.4) bear considerable resemblance to the drug study diffusion patterns. More socially integrated individuals are likely to adopt sooner and in greater concentrations, attesting to

Figure 2.3   Choices Received as Discussion Partner and Adoption of New Drug

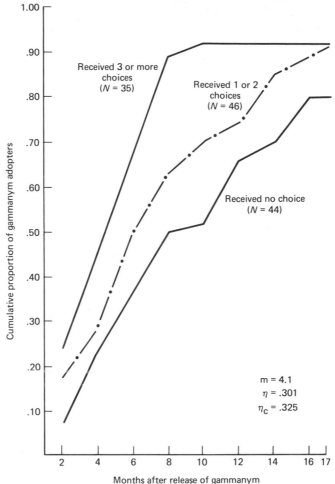

Source: *Medical Innovation: A Diffusion Study*, by James S. Coleman, Elihu Katz, and Herbert Manzel, copyright © 1966 by The Bobbs-Merrill Company, Inc., reprinted by permission of the publisher.

the powerful effect of social interaction. Arndt also recorded the number of comments each person received about the coffee and found that more socially integrated persons were more likely to receive information by word of mouth and were especially more likely to receive favorable comments about the new product.

Diffusion of technological innovations among firms in the bituminous coal, iron and steel, brewing, and railroad industries has been studied by Mansfield (1961). As exhibited in Figure 2.5, **S**-shaped growth patterns are again obtained. Basically, Mansfield found that the proportion of firms already using an innovation would increase the rate of adoption, or that competitive pres-

Figure 2.4   Relationship between Time of Purchase of New Coffee Product and Number of Choices Received as "Relatively Close Friend"

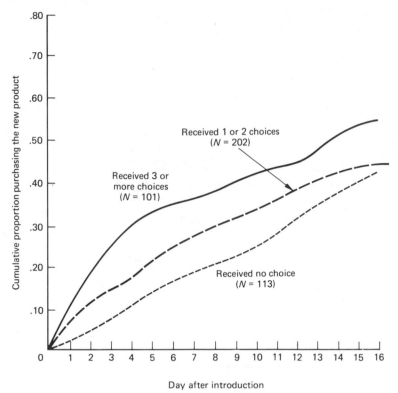

Source: Reprinted from Arndt in *Journal of Marketing Research* (1967a, p. 293).

sures would create a "bandwagon effect" (interaction effect). Considerable variability in the diffusion rate was found and, on average, it took 7.8 years for half of the firms to accept an innovation (such as the by-product coke oven, the diesel locomotive, or the high-speed bottle filler). The range in diffusion rate for half of the firms to adopt was from 0.9 to 15 years.

Allvine (1968) has studied the acceptance by supermarket chains of games, a traffic-building sales promotion device. Because of the highly competitive nature of the supermarket industry and the difficulties in establishing meaningful product or service differentiation, firms take on such games as a means of seeking a competitive edge. Diffusion of the games among other firms is then largely governed by a process of imitation as a counterstrategy to neutralize competitive advantage. Under such conditions, the interaction effect seems to lead to an S-shaped diffusion pattern. Because of the limited number of chains in any one market area, it is difficult to meaningfully plot a regional diffusion curve, but Figure 2.6 shows the acceptance of games by chains as the percentage of each chain's divisions adopting. The growth patterns, although far from an ideal series of **S**-curves, do tend to suggest a generalized **S**-shaped diffusion process.

Figure 2.5   Diffusion of Technological Innovations among Firms

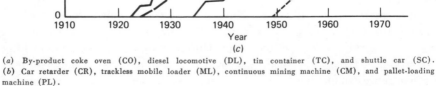

(*a*) By-product coke oven (CO), diesel locomotive (DL), tin container (TC), and shuttle car (SC).
(*b*) Car retarder (CR), trackless mobile loader (ML), continuous mining machine (CM), and pallet-loading machine (PL).
(*c*) Continuous wide-strip mill (SM), centralized traffic control (CTC), continuous annealing (CA), and highspeed bottle filler (BF).

Source: Reprinted from *Industrial Research and Technological Innovation*, by Edwin Mansfield, by permission of W. W. Norton & Company, Inc. Copyright © 1968 by W. W. Norton & Company, Inc.

Figure 2.6 Adoption of Games by Nine Multiple Market Chains

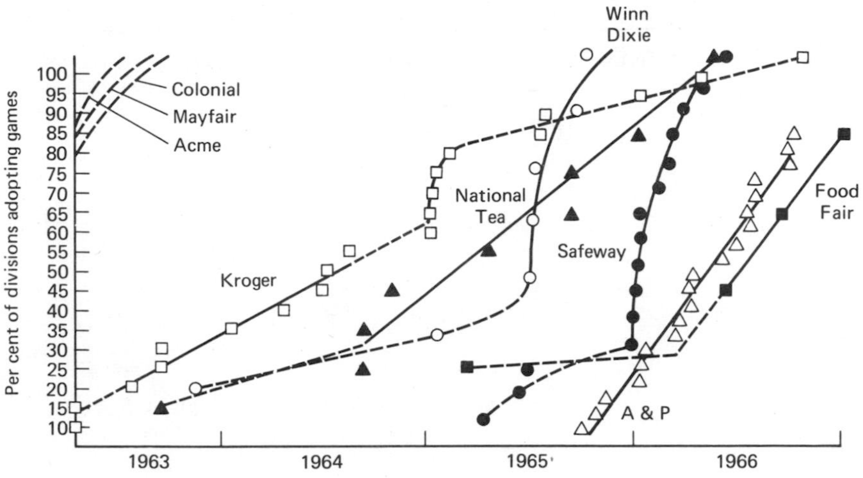

The least squares method was used to fit a straight line, an exponential curve, and a second degree polynomial to the data. The function having the minimum variance was used to plot the data. Discontinuous lines were drawn freehand.

Source: Reprinted from Allvine in *Proceedings of the American Marketing Association* (1968, p. 347).

Allvine found that in some market areas the diffusion process for games was completed in less than a year, while in other areas it took three years to complete. A key factor seemed to be the relative importance of the innovating firm. If the first adopter had a relatively small market share, then diffusion would be much slower than if the first adopter was a major factor in the market. This would, of course, also affect the slope of the diffusion curve.

The Allvine data further suggest that an **S**-shaped growth pattern among a firm's divisions is more characteristic of an earlier adopter, which experiments with games before adopting rapidly in all market areas. In contrast, a linear growth pattern seems to be characteristic of later-adopting chains, which must adopt quickly as a defensive strategy. It was found that Kroger and Safeway were often early adopters *in their market areas* and exhibited **S**-shaped diffusion patterns, whereas A&P and Food Fair were generally later adopters and exhibited linear diffusion patterns (see Figure 2.6).

MARKETING AND COMPETITIVE STRATEGY EFFECT

Marketing and competitive strategies also have considerable effect on the nature of a product's diffusion process. Table 2.1 summarizes the typical patterning of marketing strategies and competitive reactions by stage of the product life cycle. These factors may also help account for an **S**-shaped growth pattern.

Table 2.1   Summary of Changing Marketing Patterns and Competitive Reactions by Product Life Cycle Stage

Stage of Product Life Cycle	Marketing Patterns and Competitive Reactions
Introduction	High unit production and marketing costs High prices Negative profits Promotion designed to make the product known among consumers and distributors Poor technical performance of products Spotty distribution
Growth	Unit costs and prices decline Profits are positive and at their highest level Technical performance of products improves; marked technical and design differences among products Promotion aimed at establishing brand preference Opening of many distributive channels; distributors are eager to handle the product and promote it vigorously Factory shipments often rise more than retail sales Competing manufacturers' and distributors' brands enter massively into the market Consumers are very interested in the product and develop preferences that will last in future periods
Maturity	Profits are still positive, but lower than in growth stage Prices are at the same level or slightly lower than in growth Promotion aims at creating a distinct image for the product, stressing minor differences Some writers argue that the advertising effort will increase, but others disagree Performance of products is good and competing brands have almost the same technical and design characteristics; they are distinguished from one another by minor features and ingredients; some brands emphasize quality or special attributes that appeal to specific segments of the market Some writers see the development of severe price competition, but others disagree Market shares and price structures are stable Consumers are more knowledgeable about the product and demand excellent performance

Table 2.1—Continued

Stage of Product Life Cycle	Marketing Patterns and Competitive Reactions
Decline	Unit administrative and production costs rise; marketing costs drop to their lowest level Prices are at their lowest level Profits are depressed Severe price competition develops Many firms leave the market Consumers are no longer interested in the product and gradually withdraw from the market

Source: Polli (1968, pp. 30–31).

PROMOTIONAL EFFORTS

If we assume what seems reasonable, that consumers engage in a learning and decision-making process before purchasing, then it follows that a rush to purchase should not be expected, for the consumer must first obtain product information. Some advertising repetition may be necessary before the consumer becomes aware of the new product, gains sufficient knowledge about it, and exhibits some interest in it. The cumulative efficiency of promotional efforts over time can help account for the growth stage in the product life-cycle model. Advertising coupled with sales efforts, in-store displays, and other promotional efforts can provide the consumer with several kinds of information necessary to make a purchase decision. These sources may be mutually reinforcing, but it may take some time before complete promotional exposure occurs.

THE DISTRIBUTION AND PRICING SYSTEM

As Table 2.1 indicates, distribution is generally incomplete throughout the product's introduction phase and builds over time. This may be a limiting factor on initial sales. Quaker Oats Company (1968) data for the ready-to-eat cereal market suggest that a new item achieves only 60 percent distribution by the end of its first two months on the market. Distribution increases to approximately 90 percent by the end of its first year on the market. It is the company's conclusion that a different sales picture (very high initial sales) would result if distribution were at its peak from the beginning.

Prices also tend to decline over the range of the product life cycle, which suggests that sales will increase over time if the elasticity of demand is positive. Whether pricing is used to achieve maximum initial penetration or to skim the cream off the market also influences the diffusion process. This issue will be developed in the next section.

PRODUCT CHARACTERISTICS

Initial sales growth may be hampered if products have technical problems or if consumers believe this to be the case. Levitt (1965) suggests that the length of the introductory period depends upon the "newness" of the product concept, its complexity, the availability of substitutes, and its match with consumers' needs. He fails, however, to provide confirming evidence.

In turn, the almost inevitable decline in the diffusion curve results as consumers discontinue adoption, primarily because of the development of subsequent new products possessing superior attributes. Sales of evaporated milk, for example, have been declining steadily for twenty years due to the introduction and greater availability of new fresh milk products, powdered coffee creamers, and improved baby formula products, among other factors. Sales of regular margarines have fallen concurrently with the introduction of corn oil margarine and particularly "soft" margarine. Sales of regular toothpastes have declined with the introduction of fluoride and high-brightener products. Within product categories, established brands decline over time as new brands rise to challenge and replace them.

In fact, Buzzell (1968) identifies three kinds of "maturity" for food products, depending largely on whether new product subcategories have been introduced (see Figure 2.7). *Stable maturity*, as in cake mixes, is represented by a constant sales level from year to year. *Growth maturity*, as in peanut butter, is represented by somewhat increasing sales from year to year. *Innovative maturity*, as in ready-to-eat cereals, is represented by increasing sales due to the introduction of new product subcategories.

THE MARKETER'S DIFFUSION PROGRAM

At this point we may conclude the following:

1. The diffusion pattern for a new product may frequently be represented by a logistic (**S**-shaped) curve.
2. Such an "ideal" pattern need not occur on strictly theoretical grounds, and evidence has been found for other patterns, particularly exponential ones.
3. The diffusion pattern which a product will achieve is influenced not only by the interaction effect but also by marketing strategies and competitive responses.
4. The marketing executive should not passively respond to the diffusion pattern for his product, but should actively shape his product's diffusion pattern. The product life cycle model may be a valuable aid in adjusting marketing strategies consistent with life cycle stage, but such strategies may also change the nature of the product life cycle.

Figure 2.7   Sales Patterns during Maturity Stage of Product Life Cycle

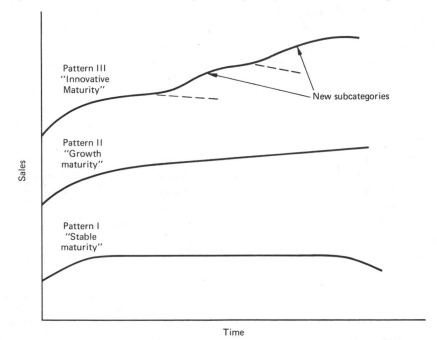

Source: Reprinted from Buzzell in *Proceedings of the American Marketing Association* (1966, p. 53).

The remainder of this chapter will be devoted to a discussion of the marketer's role in shaping the new product's diffusion pattern. The opportunities for so doing can be summarized in terms of the four components of the diffusion process: social system, consumer adoption, product meaning, and time.

SOCIAL SYSTEM

The social system refers to the boundaries within which an innovation diffuses. In the James S. Coleman, Katz, and Menzel (1966) drug study, the social system was the set of physicians within particular cities. In most farming studies the social system is defined as a farming community, often a county. It is also possible to think of the social system in terms of age, income, social class, or other criteria of market segmentation.

The characteristics of a social system highly influence diffusion patterns for new products, as has been demonstrated in a study by Graham (1956), on the diffusion of five innovations—television, canasta, supermarkets, hospital insurance, and medical service insurance—across social class levels. His research revealed that no single social class was consistently innovative in adopting all five innovations. Television, for example, diffused more quickly among lower social classes, while the card game canasta diffused more quickly among upper social classes.

Graham argues that the critical factor in diffusion is the extent to which the attributes of the innovation are compatible with the attributes of the culture of the receiving social system. The "cultural equipment" required for the adoption of television, according to Graham, included an average education, a minimum income, and a desire for passive spectator entertainment. This cultural pattern coincided with a lower social class level.

A distinction made by Rogers (1962b) and other rural sociologists is between communities exhibiting modern versus traditional norms. The modern-oriented community is receptive to innovations, while the tradition-oriented community relies on established ways of doing things. The norms in effect in a social system may have a sizable bearing on diffusion rates. Robertson (1968d) also has found that the norms of informal neighborhood groups are significantly related to the innovativeness of group members.

Innovations also may diffuse at different rates within particular spheres of a social system. For example, data already presented from the drug study, has shown that an innovation diffuses more quickly among socially integrated members of a social system than among socially isolated members. This same study also found that "profession-oriented" doctors adopted the new drug sooner than "patient-oriented" doctors. Similarly, internists adopted the drug sooner than general practitioners.

"Trickle-Down" or "Horizontal" Diffusion?

The "trickle-down" theory of diffusion was formulated to account for the acceptance of fashion with the notion that lower social classes look to and strive toward the way of life of the upper classes. Fashion, therefore, is hypothesized to move down the social class hierarchy one step at a time. This model has been propounded by a variety of scholars and is probably still the implicit model in many quarters. Perhaps the sociologist Simmel (1904) was the leading advocate of a trickle-down model. The upper classes were seen to be the first to adopt new fashions and then the first to abandon these styles as soon as the lower social classes prepared to adopt them.

The validity of such a trickle-down, vertical flow model has recently been subjected to critical examination—in particular by Katz and Lazarsfeld (1955) and King (1963). Katz and Lazarsfeld found influence regarding foods and household goods to flow most often horizontally, that is, people of similar status were used as a reference. When influence did cross status lines, no discernible direction was found; it was just as likely to flow from a lower-status to a higher-status person as vice versa. Furthermore, influence traveling outside a status level went almost exclusively to an adjacent level. This same finding held for clothing and movies; and only in public affairs was there some tendency for influence to flow from higher- to lower-status women. King (1963) focused on the fashion arena and found that the "vast majority" of influence transfer was among individuals of the same social status.

These findings, of course, do not suggest that vertical transfer of influence does not occur, but that vertical transfer is fairly infrequent and in many cases influence is as likely to trickle up as to trickle down. Many recent fashions, in fact, such as tight-fitting clothes and bright colors, have apparently emanated from the lower instead of the higher social classes.

The marketer has at his discretion the choice of social systems in which to market his product or in which to place heaviest support behind his product. This decision must be based on a matching of the attributes of the new product and the social system. Should segmentation be on the basis of social class, ethnic groups, age, or race? Given the most relevant social systems, what are the most appropriate promotional, distribution, and pricing strategies to reach them? Finally, is it possible to initiate strategies to reach the most likely buyers within a social system?

CONSUMER ADOPTERS.

Ultimately, diffusion is dependent upon the individual consumer. He must decide whether *adoption* of the new product is the appropriate course of action for himself. Is the expected utility worth the cost?

Whereas the diffusion process occurs within a social system, the *adoption process* occurs within the mind of the individual and is defined as the mental sequence of stages through which the consumer passes in arriving at an acceptance (adoption) or rejection decision. The adoption process can be conceptualized as awareness, liking, evaluation, trial, and adoption, although other similar conceptualizations have also been proposed.

Considerable research evidence indicates that communication sources are not equally effective at different stages of the adoption process. *Advertising* generally has greatest impact in the earlier stages of awareness, knowledge, and liking; then as the consumer seeks more objective and evaluative information at the later stages of preference and conviction, *personal influence* (word of mouth) often becomes the dominant communication source. This, of course, varies by product and is most likely when the consumer perceives a good amount of risk in buying. The important point is that as a purchase decision results from the cumulative impact of a number of communication sources, marketing strategies must attempt to move consumers through an entire sequence of information needs.

Not all consumers within a social system have an equal initial propensity to buy a new product. The earliest buyers, or innovators, have generally been found to possess different characteristics from later adopters. (A profile of innovator characteristics is provided in Chapter 4.) An initial goal before marketing a new product should be to establish the profile of the most likely consumer innovators. Then, as much as possible, marketing activities should be designed in line with this profile. As the innovator level of diffusion is achieved, marketing strategies should be reoriented to reach later buyers.

PRODUCT MEANING

The extent of a new product's diffusion and its rate of diffusion are, of course, largely functions of the attributes of the particular product. The emphasis given particular attributes and the overall brand image created are critical areas in the marketing decision.

There are several attribute classification schemes to account for differential diffusion rates. Rogers (1962b) proposes five characteristics of innovations which he believes to be conceptually distinct and generally relevant. These characteristics are (1) relative advantage, (2) compatibility, (3) complexity, (4) divisibility, and (5) communicability.

Relative advantage is the degree to which an innovation is superior to the product it supersedes or with which it will compete. While the addition of fluoride to toothpaste yielded extra value in that product, many other ingredients had previously been added to toothpaste without the consumer attaching relative advantage to the resulting "new" product. An important marketing management function often is to create product differentiation in order to encourage the consumer to perceive greater value in one brand than in another. This may involve, in the case of gasoline, for example, the addition of nickel, boron, platformate, a "final filter," or a detergent or antismog additive. Perception of relative advantage is a factor encouraging diffusion of a new product.

Compatibility refers to how consistent the new product is with existing ways of doing things. Television, for example, diffused more quickly at lower-social class levels because it was more consistent with the lower-class value system and way of life (Graham, 1954). The greater the need for potential adopters to restructure their thinking and to engage in new forms of behavior, the less quickly the item will generally diffuse.

Complexity refers to the degree of difficulty in understanding and/or using the new product. In general, the more complex the item, the slower its rate of diffusion and the narrower its potential market. *Divisibility* refers to the extent to which a new product may be tried on a limited scale. In-store sampling of a new food product takes account of the divisibility factor. Being able to purchase small packages of a new product may encourage diffusion. A related dimension might be "reversibility"—how readily the innovation can be discontinued without disruption. It might be hypothesized that reversibility would correlate positively with rate of diffusion.

Communicability is the degree to which word of the new product may be communicated readily to others. Conspicuous products, such as clothes, are highest in communicability. It is only necessary to see the item for information to diffuse. Products which can be demonstrated to friends, such as a new cartridge stereo or television, are also high in communicability.

The important point, according to Rogers (1962b), is how these characteristics are *perceived* by consumers, since this is what governs response. In summary, it can be hypothesized that rate of diffusion is related positively to relative advantage, compatibility, divisibility (and reversibility), and communicability, but related negatively to complexity.

Available evidence from the agricultural tradition of research (see Table 2.2) confirms a strong tendency for relative advantage, compatibility, and communicability to be related positively to innovative behavior. For the divisibility factor, however—with only fourteen generalizations categorized— the relationship is not clear-cut, although a tendency in a positive direction is indicated. Similarly, for the complexity factor—with just sixteen generalizations categorized—only some tendency toward a negative relationship with innovative behavior is shown.

Table 2.2   Research Generalizations Relating Perceptual Factors to Innovative Behavior

Perceived Characteristic of the Innovation	Relationships (Percent)					Total Number of Generalizations
	Positive	None	Negative	Conditional	Total	
Relative advantage	79	15	3	3	100	66
Compatibility	86	14	0	0	100	50
Divisibility	43	43	14	0	100	14
Communicability	75	25	0	0	100	8
Complexity	19	37	44	0	100	16

Source: Based on Rogers and Stanfield (1968, p. 243).

Within the same rural sociology research tradition, Lionberger (1963) has suggested a gradient of complexity affecting diffusion rate. At one end, an innovation may involve changes in materials and equipment, but no change in farming technique. This form of innovation, suggests Lionberger, will be adopted most quickly. In the middle range are changes in technique which need not involve changes in materials and equipment. These innovations will tend to diffuse more slowly because behavioral technique or habit patterns are not readily reoriented. At the other end, an innovation may involve change in the total enterprise, such as a shift from crop to livestock farming. Such a change will tend to diffuse most slowly. Lionberger's results suggest that rate of diffusion will be related positively to the continuity of the innovation in terms of established behavioral patterns. Continuous innovations will diffuse more quickly than discontinuous innovations.

Diffusion rates of technological innovations among firms have been studied by Mansfield (1961) and Sutherland (1959). Mansfield hypothesizes as follows:

1. Profitability of an innovation relative to others that are available will increase the rate of adoption.
2. The larger the investment required, assuming equally profitable innovations available, the slower the rate of adoption.
3. The type of industry will affect the rate of adoption depending on its aversion to risk, market competitiveness, and financial health.

Sutherland (1959), in a paper dealing with the diffusion of innovation in cotton spinning, adds to this list of factors affecting diffusion rate. According to his research,

4. Uncertainty about the future of an industry will retard rate of adoption.
5. The greater the potential cost reductions, the greater the rate of adoption.

Within the marketing literature there has not been much attention given to systematic accounts of innovation characteristics and diffusion effect. Wasson (1960) has suggested, in part, that product attributes may encourage, retard, be ambivalent, or neutral in effect upon diffusion. Positive attributes, he believes, are lower price, greater convenience, better performance, greater availability, opportunity for conspicuous consumption, and easy credibility of benefits. Attributes having a negative effect are new or unfamiliar methods of use, unfamiliar benefits, or costliness. Attributes having ambivalent effects are new appearance, different services, and new markets; whereas new construction or composition is neutral in effect. Such a series of generalizations, not based on a theoretical framework or good empirical evidence, is subject, of course, to considerable question.

A promising technique which relates new product perceptions to innovative behavior is "cognitive mapping." Stefflre (1968), for example, has attempted to build a technology for structuring a "cognitive map" of how consumers view a given product category and brands within it along dimensions which they identify as being specifically relevant to that product category. The basic assumption is that an individual will behave toward a new object or product in a manner similar to the way he behaves toward other objects he perceives in the same way. This is a simple and interesting behavioral prediction.

The proposition advanced by Stefflre based on this assumption is that behavior toward a new product can be predicted by determining where the item fits in the cognitive map of an individual or set of individuals. This "mapping," or "structuring," is done in relation to existing known products. Thus, if a product category consists of brands A, B, and C, and if a marketer is introducing brand X to this category, prediction of sales can be made if its positioning relative to existing brands is determined. For example: If X is similar to A but unlike B and C, then X should attain a significant proportion of A's sales but insignificant proportions of B and Cs' sales. A marketer, by using this technique, may be able to position his new product entry where the largest sales volume occurs or where a "gap" exists in consumers' cognitive maps and a new product is suggested.[2]

On a more specific empirical basis, it is suggested that the risk perceived by consumers in buying a new product is negatively related to innovative behavior (Arndt, 1967a; Cunningham, 1966). This perceived risk factor has been suggested by Sheth (1968) and Ostlund (1969) as a major factor in accounting for consumer response to new products. In a study of the diffusion of stainless steel blades, Sheth found a rapid diffusion rate which he attributed to the product's low risk and high relative advantage.

Ostlund (1969) has conducted research relating product perceptions to willingness to adopt a series of new items taken from test markets in other areas of the country. The product perceptions tested represented a combination of Rogers' factors (1962b) with perceived risk. Highly significant results were achieved which almost uniformly indicated that relative advantage, compatibility, divisibility, and communicability were positively related to innovative willingness for six product innovations, while complexity and perceived risk were negatively related.

Fad and Fashion Products

Fads and fashions constitute an interesting product phenomenon and involve their marketers in diverse problems of growth patterns, life cycles, and diffusion strategies. Perhaps the most essential distinguishing feature of fads and fashions from other new products is that their adoption is related largely to the perception of *newness* rather than to relative advantage or better functional performance. Sociologist Georg Simmel (1904), in his treatise on fashion, emphasizes that as fashion spreads, it goes to its doom: "As soon as the social consciousness attains to the highest point designated by fashion, it marks the beginning of the end for the latter" (p. 547).

Can fads be distinguished from fashions? Fashions are of a cyclical nature and typically exhibit a diffusion process resembling an S-shaped pattern, although more pronounced and more condensed in time. Fads, in contrast, tend not to repeat themselves and to exhibit much more rapid growth followed by generally complete collapse, although adoption can sometimes stabilize at a lower residual level. Figure 2.8 shows generalized diffusion patterns for a new consumer product (such as instant coffee), a fashion item (such as a clothing style), and a fad (such as the hula hoop).

[2] For a comprehensive account of cognitive mapping as related to new products, see Silk (1968).

Figure 2.8   Generalized Diffusion Patterns for a New Product, a Fashion, and a Fad

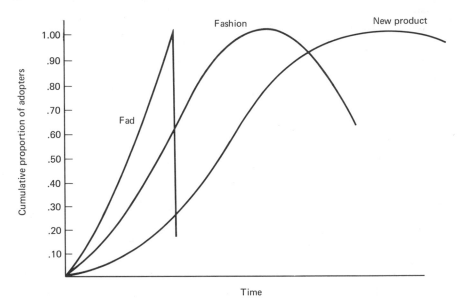

Simmel (1904) explains the adoption of fashion (and, it seems, fads also) in terms of *imitation* for social acceptance and, at the same time, *differentiation* from other people. Fashion, says Simmel, represents a means by which "we seek to combine in uniform spheres of activity the tendency toward social equalization with the desire for individual differentiation and change" (p. 543).

The concept of fashion used by Simmel refers to a much shorter time span and to much more specific styles than the concept of fashion used by Carman. Carman (1966) has used mathematical time-series models to study fashion trends in women's clothes from 1786 to 1965. The predictive accuracy of his models is good, based on two cyclical theories. One of these posits three cycles lasting approximately one hundred years: a bell, or full-skirt, cycle; a bustle cycle; and a tubular, or sheath, cycle. The other theory suggests shorter cycles of thirty to fifty years.

THE TIME DIMENSION

At times it may be desirable to gain maximum short-run penetration for a new product, while at other times a more deliberate segmentation strategy, often on the basis of price, may be followed. This may depend largely on the likelihood of other firms manufacturing a similar product. Thus, in the case of electric toothbrushes, maximum short-run penetration was sought because of the expected entry of other firms into the market, whereas in the case of the Polaroid camera, due to patent protection, it was possible initially to seek the most profitable market segments at a higher price. The diffusion strategy also will depend upon the availability of production facilities. In view of the order backlog for some time after introduction, Ford Motor Company may have wished Mustang off to a somewhat slower sales start.

A specific case of varying diffusion strategies occurs in the promotion of movies by film distributors. If the movie is good, it is usually placed in a small number of theaters and not distributed on a mass basis for a considerable period of time. This results in a fairly slow process of diffusion which often relies heavily on personal influence. If the movie is bad, it is shown in multiple runs in neighborhood theaters, with heavy advertising in order to secure as much "adoption" as possible before word spreads among moviegoers as to the film's true merits (Katz and Lazarsfeld, 1955, p. 180). This results in an extremely compressed diffusion process.

Marketers, of course, need no introduction to the fact that profits are a function of both diffusion levels and dollar margin per sale. A strategy of maximum diffusion need not be the most profitable. It is probably a fair generalization, however, that maximum diffusion (often equated with market share) is the goal for most new products. This is especially true for continuous and dynamically continuous innovations and less true for discontinuous innovations. It is also especially true for product categories where price is not an important competitive weapon. Where price lining occurs, this goal can be restated as maximum diffusion within each market segment. A second generalization is that maximum diffusion is most often sought within the shortest period of time possible.

The competitive situation is one factor encouraging the firm to speed the diffusion process. Sales must be gained before other product alternatives are available and in order to establish brand loyalty. There is a natural desire to recover research and development costs as quickly as possible. In fact, the speed with which a new product is likely to gain market acceptance and a resulting cash inflow for the firm is often an important determinant of investment decisions. Advertising efficiency will require a sufficiently high volume of sales. Furthermore, in line with our discussion to this point, it seems desirable to rapidly move the product through the introductory phase in order to reach the growth phase. Such early efforts on the part of the firm should reap benefits in terms of cumulative promotional effect and the interaction effect.

Penetration Strategy

In a penetration strategy, maximum diffusion is sought as quickly as possible. Price tends to be set relatively low; promotion leans heavily toward mass advertising; and intensive distribution is used. This strategy is most necessary if little product differentiation exists for the new product and, therefore, demand is highly elastic. This strategy is also necessary if competitors are likely to introduce similar new product offerings within a fairly short period, despite the continuity or discontinuity of the innovation. Rapid diffusion may discourage competition, although it can also have an encouraging effect when high sales are noted—especially if the estimated potential market is large. More importantly, however, rapid diffusion would lead to a large and brand-loyal consumer franchise which is crucial to continuing sales success given the subsequent entry of competition. It will also be documented (in Chapter 4) that consumer innovators are influential in advising other consumers about new products and will encourage further diffusion in many cases. A penetration strategy has additional advantages, therefore, in reaching these innovators before competition does so.

A penetration strategy has implications for the shape of the diffusion curve and encourages a high acceleration curve. In the presweetened cereal market and in the detergent market, for example, a new brand (because of concentrated advertising and deal activity at introduction) may attain its maximum life cycle sales within a few months and then settle down to a lower maturity level of sales. It is critical to remember that a varying proportion (sometimes very high) of beginning sales may be for *trial* purposes and need not represent *adoption*, that is, acceptance and commitment to the brand as reflected in repeat purchases. A company must quickly determine its trial-adoption ratio, or it can be misled into expanding production for never-to-be-realized repeat sales.

A penetration strategy for a new convenience brand generally does not show much of an interaction effect in the growth phase. Promotional efforts, combined with appropriate pricing and distribution, carry the sales generation burden. In many ways this is desirable, since personal influence is so difficult to take into account in a marketing program. This situation is possible only because the consumer can engage in trial without risking much of the family's resources. In many product categories of convenience goods, a considerable amount of brand switching occurs and trial of a new brand may not involve much commitment.

Sales-Staging Strategy

In a sales-staging strategy, the typical progression is from generally high, skim-the-cream pricing to relatively lower prices, from selective distribution to intensive distribution, and from limited promotion to expanded or mass promotion. Such a strategy is more likely for specialty and shopping items and is generally dependent upon a differentiated product and one which competition cannot duplicate readily. The somewhat discontinuous innovation allows, in effect, a certain degree of monopoly power. A staging process may be possible because demand by innovators quite often is inelastic and because such products may require a fairly high level of income. Higher price and higher margins may also be necessary to convince the trade to handle the new product, because the firm does not have high-volume production facilities available or because its investment must be recovered as quickly as possible.

DuPont's "Corfam" shoe material was marketed using the sales-staging strategy. It was deliberately introduced to manufacturers of quality shoe products before being made available on a mass basis. Management apparently felt that maximum long-run diffusion for the product would be gained if it were perceived not as a cheap substitute for leather but as a quality improvement over leather (Lawson, Lynch, and Richards, 1965). Therefore, DuPont, by choosing the manufacturers to whom it made the product available, was governing the intensity of distribution and pricing and the extent of manufacturer advertising.

The manufacturer's diffusion strategy, therefore, has an impact on the shape of the diffusion curve. But, by the same token, the selection of a strategy is also a function of the type of product and the competitive situation. A penetration or sales-staging strategy must be based on accurate assessment of future market acceptance. Wasson (1968), for example, argues that color television marketers unsuccessfully followed a penetration strategy for a number of years in the 1950s, when sales to support such a strategy were not forthcoming. They misjudged rate of market acceptance and should have been following a sales-staging strategy with selective distribution, relatively high price, and limited promotion until the growth segment of the diffusion process was attained. We must also recognize that while a dichotomy of ideal types makes for expository efficiency, a considerable range of strategies between staging and penetration is available in practice to the firm.

SUMMARY

Diffusion, or the process by which something spreads, has been studied by researchers across a number of disciplines including anthropology, sociology, medicine, and education. Marketing's interest in diffusion relates to the flow of goods and services from producer to consumer. While marketing focuses on the performance of business activities to direct this flow, diffusion theory focuses on the nature of the flow and offers a theoretical framework to explain the dissemination of information, ideas, and products. Integrating this framework with existing marketing theory may advance our understanding of how new products disseminate and gain consumer acceptance and may suggest means of improving new product marketing strategies.

As conceptualized for marketing purposes, the diffusion process is *the adoption of new products and services over time by consumers within social systems as encouraged by marketing activities*. These several aspects of the diffusion process are interdependent. The concept of diffusion is related to the product life cycle, which traces adoption over time. This pattern often follows an **S**-shaped curve as the product moves from *introduction* to *growth*, to *maturity*, and into *decline*. In diffusion, however, the emphasis is on the percentage of *adopters* for a product within a social structure or market segment, rather than on absolute *sales* levels.

The "interaction effect," whereby adopters of a new product influence others to purchase, is often posited to account for the rapid-growth stage in the diffusion process. And to the extent that the product is subject to social influence, the interaction effect is one valid explanation. Marketing strategies, however, also influence the pattern of the diffusion process; and the marketer shapes the diffusion curve as a function of pricing, distribution, and promotion decisions.

Specifically, the marketer has the following opportunities by area of the diffusion process:

1. *Social System.* Marketing decisions can select the social systems (market segments) in which diffusion is most likely to be successful for a new product. Promotion, pricing, and distribution strategies can then be combined to reach specified social systems.
2. *Consumer Adopters.* Marketing decisions can establish the consumer profile most likely to adopt the new product. Promotion, pricing, and distribution strategies can be oriented toward this consumer profile. Marketing strategies can vary by penetration level in order to reach specific kinds of consumers. For example, advertising strategies to reach first adopters usually should be different than strategies to reach later adopters.
3. *Product meaning.* Marketing activities can help define product meaning and can encourage diffusion by emphasizing the most relevant product attributes. For example, should promotion for a new dessert emphasize taste, convenience, low cost, or low-calorie content?
4. *Time.* Marketing activities can affect *rate* of diffusion and rate of adoption. A low price penetration strategy, a high level of promotional expenditures, free sampling and deal activity, and intensive distribution will generally encourage fast adoption and diffusion rates.

The extent and rate of diffusion are strongly influenced by the attributes of the product including relative advantage, compatibility, complexity, divisibility, communicability, and perceived risk. Social system characteristics also have a strong influence on the diffusion patterns of most products, constituting the boundaries within which diffusion occurs. The norms in effect within a social system may have a sizable bearing on diffusion rates. Early theories of diffusion positing a trickle-down model—in which adoption of innovations moves vertically down through the social class structure—have been questioned in recent years. Research findings now suggest that influence for many product categories tends, in fact, to move horizontally among people of similar status.

Most new product introductions are based on a *penetration strategy*, where maximum diffusion is sought as quickly as possible in order to preempt competitors. This tactic is chosen because most innovations are of a continuous nature, only slightly differentiated from competition and, therefore, relatively easily duplicated. New products of a discontinuous nature are more likely to be protected by patents or technical expertise. In these circumstances, it may prove more profitable to employ a *sales-staging strategy*, which is characterized initially by high pricing, selective distribution, and limited promotion; subsequently, the strategy moves toward lower prices, more intensive distribution, and mass promotion.

CHAPTER 3

PRODUCT ADOPTION PROCESSES

This chapter will examine several formulations dealing with product adoption processes. All of these formulations are concerned with specifying the mental and behavioral sequence through which consumers must progress if *adoption*—that is, the acceptance and continued use of a product (or brand)— is to occur. Thus, these formulations assume that consumer adoption of a product is not an instantaneous or random event, and they attempt to specify the antecedents of adoption. Such specification may result in better understanding of consumer actions or inactions and may suggest marketing strategies to increase product adoption, to speed the process, or to minimize nonadoption.

Several adoption and purchase decision models have been postulated. These models are similar in their conceptualization of a flow of events rather than an "instant metamorphosis." And all of these models postulate a series of "stages" to represent the sequence of mental and/or behavioral events assumed to be antecedents of adoption. But there is considerable difference in the number of stages and in the nature of these stages; and there is controversy over whether the notion of stages is appropriate at all. However, it should be recognized that all such schemes are conceptual frameworks only and, therefore, neither true nor false. They are scaffoldings erected by social scientists for the construction of generalizations toward an explanation of perceived reality and must be evaluated in terms of their utility.

A distinction should be made between the terms *product adoption* and *product purchase*. The adoption process concept has been devised strictly from literature dealing with innovations, while the purchase decision process has been used in a variety of contexts, not necessarily related to new product adoptions. More importantly, the adoption process, which generally has been postulated for new items, usually refers to the possible acceptance and continued use of an item, while discussions of the purchase process usually refer to a single buying decision. Purchase of a product is a necessary but not a sufficient condition for adoption, since adoption includes a sense of product commitment, involving acceptance and use over time. Not every purchase results in adoption, nor is every purchase evidence of a consumer's decision to *adopt* a product or brand.

Distinguishing between product purchase and adoption is frequently difficult. Often the distinction depends on the product category under consideration. For an appliance, for example, the adoption process and the purchase process would be practically synonymous, since purchase of large-ticket items is dependent upon a sense of commitment and since the low extent of purchase frequency makes the concept of acceptance and continued purchase questionable.

For a product such as detergent, where a high rate of purchase frequency exists and there is reasonable brand switching, the question is what number of repeat purchase decisions should be considered adoption: three in a row, three out of four, or what? What determines adoption will also vary for heavy versus light users of a product. Nakanishi (1968) has distinguished between two modes of adoption: that of the "regular user" and that of the "occasional user." The regular user purchases the product at regular intervals, exclusive of available alternatives, whereas the occasional user makes occasional purchases of the product and purchases substitutes at in-between times.

THE ADOPTION PROCESS SCHEME

The adoption process, as first defined in the rural sociology literature in the mid-1950s, consists of five sequential stages. These stages and their commonly accepted definitions are as follows:

1. *Awareness.* The individual knows of the new idea but lacks sufficient information about it.
2. *Interest.* The individual becomes interested in the idea and seeks more information.
3. *Evaluation.* The individual makes a mental application of the new idea to his present mode of consumption and makes the decision either to try it or not.
4. *Trial.* The individual uses the innovation on a small scale to determine its utility for him.
5. *Adoption.* The individual accepts the innovation and commits himself to its use.

No provisions are made in this scheme for the individual to skip stages, nor are any feedback loops provided. For example, after trial the individual could return either to an interest stage and seek further information or to an evaluation stage (which would seem to be implicit in trial) and continue to weigh the item's utility. Or he might skip evaluation and go directly to trial, especially if a trial purchase were inexpensive and would yield a high level of information. The model does allow the innovation to be *rejected* at any stage in the process. Furthermore, individuals may proceed through these stages at varying rates of speed.

The possibility of *rejection* as well as *adoption* might suggest that we refer to an adoption *decision* process rather than simply the *adoption process*, since the latter terminology implies only an adoption outcome. Whereas it should be kept in mind that consumers may or may *not* adopt a product or brand, we will not refer to an adoption decision process, since *decision* implies purposive behavior or deliberate cognitive activity. In reality, consumers may adopt products with little deliberate cognitive activity; the notion of adoption is really only the investigator's attempt to represent processes leading to product acceptance and continued use. The term *decision* may imply considerably more than really goes on as consumers adopt products and brands.

THE HIERARCHY-OF-EFFECTS SCHEME

A hierarchy-of-effects scheme has been proposed in the marketing literature by Lavidge and Steiner (1961) and named by Palda (1966). This conceptualization consists of six steps to purchase which are related, according to Lavidge and Steiner, to three basic psychological states: *cognitive, affective,* and *conative*. The cognitive dimension is the realm of thoughts; the affective dimension is the realm of emotions; and the conative dimension is the realm of motives.

Definitions of stages in the hierarchy-of-effects model are as follows:

1. *Awareness*. The individual is aware of the product's existence.
2. *Knowledge*. The individual knows "what the product has to offer."
3. *Liking*. The individual has favorable attitudes toward the product.
4. *Preference*. The individual's favorable attitudes have "developed to the point of preference over all other possibilities."
5. *Conviction*. Preference is coupled "with a desire to buy" and confidence "that the purchase would be wise."
6. *Purchase*. "Attitude" is translated into actual buying behavior.

In elaborating upon this model, Lavidge and Steiner have pointed out that the stages are not necessarily equidistant. The difficulty and time involved in moving up each step in this hierarchy will depend upon both product and consumer characteristics. Thus, they offer the hypothesis that "The greater the psychological and/or economic commitment involved in the purchase of a particular product, the longer it will take to bring consumers up these steps, and the more important the individual steps will be" (p. 60).[1] They have pointed out further that a buyer may sometimes move up several steps simultaneously, for example, in an impulse purchase. Thus, they are arguing that each stage is necessary and that any apparent skipping of stages reflects a collapsing of the hierarchy into a shorter time interval. Again, in this model, there are no feedback loops to earlier stages; and a unilateral and continuous process is envisioned.

The hierarchy-of-effects model is perhaps the first such model to explicitly rely on an information-attitude-behavior theory of communication effect. It has been assumed for some time (see, for example, Hovland, Janis, and Kelly, 1953) that communication functions by providing information (awareness and knowledge), forming or changing attitudes (liking and preference), and thus inducing behavior (conviction and purchase). In fact, Lavidge and Steiner have specified the hierarchy-of-effects model as a framework for measuring advertising effectiveness. Their basic thesis is that while the end objective of advertising is to produce sales, immediate sales results do not constitute a valid measure of advertising effectiveness. Yet "if something is

[1] While this statement is probably generally true, there may be some interesting exceptions. For example, Katona and Mueller (1954) suggest that the relationships may invert. For example, a poor person may have more time to deliberate over a sports shirt than over a refrigerator, if he has continued to use the latter until it falls into disrepair. *Psychological* and/or *economic commitment* really refer to terms which may be relative for different kinds of people.

to happen in the long run, *something* must be happening in the short run, something that will ultimately lead to eventual sales results" (Lavidge and Steiner, 1961, p. 59). It is their contention that the short-run effects of advertising can be measured in terms of movement on the purchase decision process. However, even if we may specify consumers who are at one stage in their purchase decision process, this does not necessarily mean that they will continue along the process. For example, "liking" may not be a sufficient condition for the consumer to "prefer" the product.

OTHER PURCHASE PROCESS SCHEMES

A variety of other schemes has appeared in the literature, such as that advanced by Hovland, Janis, and Kelly (1953). Although these authors were concerned with communication and persuasion, not with purchase behavior specifically, they extended learning theory notions and posited a three-step model: attention, comprehension, and acceptance. More recently, Janis and Mann (1968) have proposed a five-stage conflict theory approach to attitude change and decision making: appraisal of a challenge, appraisal of alternatives, selection of best alternative, commitment to a new policy, and adherence to the new policy despite negative feedback.

The most familiar scheme in marketing and advertising texts is the AIDA scheme: Awareness, Interest, Desire, Action. These four stages are suggested as an invariate model of audience response. The AIDA model has been applied to personal selling efforts as well as to advertising (Tosdal, 1925). A comparison of the AIDA model with the adoption process and hierarchy-of-effects models is shown in Figure 3.1.

As stated, examination of adoption processes should not be restricted to instances in which deliberate cognitive activity is involved. However, in

Figure 3.1   Alternate Models of the Purchase Decision Process

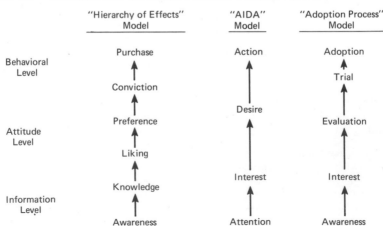

some cases, the adoption process may be viewed in terms of a basic problem-solving model as follows (Usher, 1929):

1. *Perception of the problem.* In order for adoption to occur, a problem must first be felt to exist. (This would assume that perception of the problem precedes awareness of the innovation. It could also be argued that awareness of the innovation induces perception of a problem.)
2. *Setting of the stage.* Some particular configuration of information and solution alternatives (including the innovation) is brought together.
3. *The act of insight.* The solution is found, and the innovation is chosen over other alternatives or it is rejected.
4. *The critical revision.* The innovation is analyzed by the consumer to determine how practical it is (cost, availability, and so on).

This decision-making sequence is basically similar to that of Dewey (1910), who proposed the following framework: (1) a felt difficulty, (2) definition of the problem, (3) data collection and suggestion of possible solutions, (4) evaluation and reasoning about these solutions, and (5) testing of the solution on a trial, or experimental, basis.

A major difficulty of the problem-solving model is that adoption need not be based on such behavior. The consumer could be "playing the psycho-social game" (Bauer, 1967) and adopting a product by a process quite different from that outlined. That is, consumers can decide to adopt a product on the basis of "what others will think," rather than in terms of which product will best solve the problem (Ward and Gibson, 1969).

A further difficulty is that consumers are not likely to engage in much data collection, except for important purchases; and the information they use is usually far from complete. Furthermore, the beginning stage of adoption behavior need not be problem perception by the consumer, as the model assumes. Instead, the beginning stage may be perception of a potential solution to a problem not yet specified. The hierarchy-of-effects model, among others, seems to avoid most of these difficulties.

CRITIQUE OF ADOPTION PROCESS MODELS

The discussion now summarizes several critiques of either adoption process models or the hierarchy-of-effects model. In general, these critiques apply equally to both models.

Mason (1962) challenges the notion that five discrete stages are necessary to account for adoption. Using the Guttman technique of scalogram analysis, he found that the sequence of stages proposed by rural sociologists did not occur and that several forms of an adoption process were to be found, depending on the practice being studied and the individual farmer. There was no single process of adoption for all the items studied, except that awareness preceded adoption (and there was even one exception to this).

Mason also found that evaluation apparently occurred before interest and that adoption was not the terminal stage, but was followed by interest and information seeking. This finding is suggested by some studies of cognitive dissonance which have observed information-seeking or selective exposure following decisions (Ehrlich, Guttmann, Schonbach, and Mills, 1957). However, this finding is still being debated (Freedman and Sears, 1965).

A consistent adoption process conceptualization seems unlikely across any range of consumer goods. For inexpensive, low-risk products, deliberateness in purchase may not be as necessary as for expensive, high-risk products. Important differences also seem to exist in the adoption processes for continuous versus discontinuous innovations.

Campbell (1966) has presented a paradigm of the adoption process which differs in two important respects from earlier schemes. His first point is that the adoption process may not be as rational as commonly assumed. The model has an inherent rational bias in that it suggests deliberate information seeking and "evaluation" of alternatives and consequences. Campbell's second point is that the adoption process may not start at awareness, which assumes a passive consumer. Instead, the beginning of the adoption process may be perception of a problem (as in problem-solving models). As has been noted, whether consumers are relatively active or passive at beginning stages probably depends on the situation, for example, whether the products involved are expensive, infrequently purchased items or inexpensive, frequently purchased ones.

Based on these two distinctions, Campbell specifies four forms of the adoption process. The first of these he calls *rational/problem solving*. The consumer becomes aware of a problem, looks for a solution, and carefully evaluates any product which potentially solves his problem. The adoption stages are (1) problem (defined by Campbell as synonymous with interest), (2) awareness, (3) evaluation, (4) rejection, or (5) trial followed by adoption or rejection. The second adoption process distinguished by Campbell is *rational/innovation*, in which the consumer becomes aware of the innovation before the problem. This corresponds to the traditional specification of the adoption process, that is, awareness, interest, evaluation, trial, and adoption. Rejection may follow evaluation, or the consumer may try the product and then reject it.

The third form distinguished by Campbell is *nonrational/problem solving*, in which the problem is perceived in advance of product awareness, but "in seeking a solution, the consumer impulsively accepts the innovation without careful consideration or evaluation" (p. 463). Adoption stages are (1) problem (interest), (2) awareness, (3) adoption or rejection, and (4) resolution.

The resolution stage may reduce dissonance if it exists. It is debatable, however, that a resolution stage would be unique to nonrational adoption. The fourth adoption process form is *nonrational/innovation,* which occurs when the individual "sees something new and impulsively adopts the item without deliberation as to its utility" (p. 464). In this process the stages are (1) awareness, (2) adoption or rejection, and (3) resolution.

Palda (1966) has been the leading antagonist of the hierarchy-of-effects model. As discussed earlier, since adoption process models and hierarchy-of-effects models are related, Palda's criticisms are relevant to both. His basic premise is that he finds no *evidence* for a hierarchy of effects as such. Even if one assumes a hierarchy of effects, Palda asserts that no evidence exists which clearly demonstrates the relationship between each step on the hierarchy and final purchase of the product; he further argues that there is no logical necessity for awareness of a brand to precede purchase by any significant amount of time, particularly in today's self-service stores. He further discounts research evidence that buyers of a product are more exposed to product advertising on the grounds that (1) buyers may be better rememberers, since all product stimuli may then be more salient; and (2) buyers may selectively expose themselves to ads in order to reduce cognitive dissonance.

Palda further argues that there is no documented connection between attitude and behavior toward a brand—a point to be taken up in greater depth shortly. Furthermore, research which shows buyers to possess more favorable attitudes than nonbuyers is unsound methodologically, since the before-and-after conditions could create the differences in results, rather than the buyer-nonbuyer predispositions.

Palda's basic contention is that only sales results can be used as a meaningful measure of advertising effectiveness. The marketer who chooses advertisements to move consumers along the purchase decision process may be using a suboptimal strategy if other criteria would be more relevant to ultimate product purchase. Palda does not, however, specify conditions to measure sales effect due to advertising. While his thesis represents a valuable point of view, lack of proof for an adoption process does not, of course, refute the existence of such a process. Moreover, the fact that cognitive and affective changes are difficult to measure does not mean that these changes do not occur; and the fact that cognitive-affective effect on purchase cannot be documented does not mean it does not exist. Even if these changes did not occur in every instance, they might occur frequently enough to make the model useful.

THE INFORMATION-ATTITUDE-BEHAVIOR RELATIONSHIP

All of the various adoption process models assume, either implicitly or explicitly, that information must precede attitude and that favorable attitude toward the product must precede behavior. However, empirical research has not clearly specified these relationships. In fact, some research, such as that on source effects, has demonstrated opinion change with little information retained (Hovland, Janis, and Kelley, 1953). And Festinger (1964) notes that whereas many studies examine attitude change, little research exists to document the relationship of attitude change and behavior change. Thus, since adoption process models posit certain orderings of these variables, it is important to examine in detail the relationship between information, attitude, and behavior.

Most persuasive attempts are unsuccessful. The operation of selective processes prevents most messages from getting through. As we have noted, however, research suggests that even a message which gets through, in terms of acceptance of factual material, need not invoke attitudinal change. As related to adoption process models, these research results suggest that because a person has been moved to a given stage does not necessarily mean he can be moved further. Thus, the consumer may gain knowledge that a deodorant product contains XZ_7 and lasts longer than 90 percent of all other deodorants on the market, but still hold the opinion that another product is better.

Perhaps the most completely documented study showing the communication of facts without opinion change is that of Hovland, Lumsdaine, and Sheffield (1949), who exposed groups of American soldiers during World War II to a film entitled *The Battle of Britain*. The purpose of this film, and of the series of which it was a part, was (1) to communicate facts about the war (2) in order to encourage soldiers to hold more favorable attitudes relative to American participation, which (3) would increase their motivation to fight. The film was found to be highly effective in communicating factual information, but almost entirely ineffective in eliciting attitude change regarding British or American participation in the war and totally ineffective in changing motivation to serve in the war, "which was considered the ultimate objective of the orientation program" (p. 65). The authors note one other interesting phenomenon, the so-called *sleeper effect*: that opinion changes tended to show an average increase with the passage of time.

The relationship between attitude change and behavior has been subject to considerable debate recently. Cohen (1964), in a summary volume on attitude change, pointedly concludes:

> Most of the investigators whose work we have examined make the broad psychological assumption that since attitudes are evaluative predispositions, they have consequences for the way people act toward others, for the programs they actually undertake, and for the manner in which they carry them out. Thus attitudes are always seen as precursors of behavior, as determinants of how a person will actually behave in his daily affairs. In spite of the wide acceptance of the assumption, however, very little work on attitude change has dealt explicitly with the behavior that may follow a change in attitude (pp. 137–138).

Festinger (1964), in an article prompted by Cohen's conclusion, states that he was at first skeptical; but after prolonged search, he found only three relevant studies which focused on the relationship between attitude *change* and behavior *change*. He points out that it is not the attitude-behavior relationship which is being questioned, but only the attitude change–behavior change relationship.[2] Upon examination of these studies, Festinger found that the "obvious" relationship between attitude change and behavior change did not hold. This led him to suggest that when attitudes are changed on the basis of persuasive communication, this change "is inherently unstable and will disappear or remain isolated unless an environmental or behavioral change can be brought about to support and maintain it" (p. 415). This almost seems to put us in the awkward position of having to change behavior in order to change behavior. But Festinger's main point is that unless environmental change to support the new opinion occurs, "the same factors that produced the initial opinion and the behavior will continue to operate to nullify the effect of the opinion change" (p. 416). Thus, attitude change may not serve as a sufficient condition for behavioral change.

Festinger's point may be well taken. If an advertising campaign successfully changes a person's attitude toward a brand, there is still no guarantee that the consumer will move along the adoption process and eventually purchase that brand—unless it is socially acceptable, fits the person's definition of self, is economically feasible, and so on. Volkswagen advertising could change an individual's attitude from highly negative to positive, without gaining a purchase response. The car just might be perceived as unsuitable to the person's station in life; or the person might feel he or his family would be uncomfortable in such a small car; or other attitudes, such as buying American products, could dominate. It seems reasonable that the probability of behavioral change would be greater as environmental circumstances also change. Thus, environmental changes such as the car's becoming a reverse status symbol (as it has in some quarters), or the company's introducing larger models could encourage behavioral change.

It has been suggested further that behavior change can occur without attitude change preceding it. Instead, attitude change can follow behavioral change. This has been most clearly suggested to marketers by Cox (1961), who argues that a person could see an advertisement, buy the product, and then shift his attitude in line with the advertisement. He cites evidence from several dissonance experiments to back up the behavior change–attitude change possibility. In one experiment by Brehm (1956), for example, young women were asked to rate eight products by desirability; were then offered a choice between two of these products, and were asked again to rate them. Brehm's

[2] Documented evidence for the relationship between attitudes and behavior is readily available en masse. See, for example, Day (1970).

results indicated that after making the choice, subjects showed a marked increase in preference for the product chosen and a marked decrease in preference for the product not chosen. Commitment to a decision apparently sets in motion attitude change which results in cognitive consistency. In a later study by LoSciuto and Perloff (1967) involving a similar experimental design, the same form of results was obtained. These results suggest that the exact order of stages in adoption process models may be questioned.

Attitude change occurring after a behavioral response has also been noted by Krugman (1965). In accounting for the impact of television advertising, he attributes much of its effect to "learning without involvement." This learning tends to be incidental, much as the learning of nonsense syllables and other meaningless material. Constant exposure to low-involvement television advertising, coupled perhaps with a lack of perceptual defense, may lead to learning and alteration in cognitive structure regarding a product, but not to attitude change. When the individual is faced with the item in a purchase situation, he may see it "in a new, 'somehow different' light although nothing verbalizable may have changed *up to that point*" (Krugman, 1965, p. 354), and purchase may be the result. Attitude change may then follow product purchase.

In Krugman's thinking such postpurchase attitude change is not a form of "rationalizing" purchase. His explanation, therefore, is not in terms of dissonance theory. He argues instead that attitude change is "an emergent response aspect of the previously changed perception" (p. 354). Attitude change following behavior may give meaning to the behavior. Moscovici (1963), for example, has recognized the dual direction of attitudinal and behavioral change:

> When attitude is changed first, the aim is to cause a change in behavior. On the other hand, if behavior changes first, a change in attitude is involved and serves to give a meaning to the already achieved behavior. Attitude may thus be viewed either as a mechanism directing behavior, or as a modality which confers on behavior its meaning (pp. 249, 250).

Krugman expects the typical attitude change–behavior relationship under high-involvement conditions and the behavior-attitude change relationship under low-involvement conditions. If this is in fact the case, it would suggest different forms of the adoption process.

Bauer (1966) has argued that the way in which some writers have talked about "behavior change without attitude change" is misleading; it appears that for many writers the concept of "attitude" has taken on some specific meaning such as "an explicit shift in brand preference." The concept of attitude as originally introduced into psychology was so broad as to refer to *any* intervening state of the organism that preceded and presumably accounted for a change in behavior. It is difficult to conceive of a change in behavior occurring without *some* prior change within the organism. The danger of dismissing the matter by saying that behavior can change without a "change in attitude"—meaning a shift on some conventional measure of brand preference or the like—is that this view diverts the researcher from the business of searching out what *did change* prior to the change in behavior.

Bauer's comments have at least two implications for adoption process models: (1) it may be difficult to adequately *measure* changes in intervening states which precede behavior change in adoption processes; and (2) it is necessary to specify the conditions in which being in one stage is a necessary and/or sufficient condition to progress to the next (that is, whether attitude change must precede behavior change, and/or whether attitude change will always lead to behavior change).

ADOPTION PROCESS MODELS: A SUMMARY

In the abstract, the adoption process concept makes sense. If a behavioral act is to occur, it must have antecedents. As a conceptual framework, the adoption process can be of value in focusing attention on such antecedents. It can also perform a disservice for marketers to the extent that it specifies an order of antecedents which does not hold universally or even generally. Even with these limitations, however, the concept appears able to increase our understanding of consumer behavior.

Several refinements of the adoption process concept can be made in order to increase its utility. These refinements are based on the following three observations:

1. There is no single *form* to which the adoption process must conform. It may be useful to suggest at least three alternate forms: the *rational/ decision-making* form, the *nonrational/impulse* form, and the *nonrational/ psychosocial* form.
2. There is no specified *number* of stages that will always occur. The minimum number of stages seems to be two, while a maximum number has never been specified. The upper limit would probably be more a function of our ingenuity in drawing distinctions than of the state of the real world.
3. There is no specified *sequence* of stages which must occur. Any such model must allow consumers to skip stages and must also provide feedback loops, since the adoption process is not necessarily linear and unidimensional.

ALTERNATE FORMS

Most adoption process models have a rational, problem-solving bias. The consumer is seen as securing, processing, and evaluating information. The assumption is that he makes his decision in the rational manner of an "economic man," based on the intrinsic qualities of the information obtained. This is one form of the adoption process and approximates reality for certain classes of decisions. This form is closest to the problem-solving models outlined earlier and can be referred to as the rational/problem-solving form. The consumer may also, however, make decisions in a manner that is non-rational, *in the sense of not securing, processing, and carefully evaluating all available information.* He may make adoption decisions on impulse, or he may make decisions to ingratiate himself with other people.

The nonrational model, in contrast with the rational/problem-solving form, implies different amounts of information-seeking behavior and different strategies regarding kinds of information seen as useful in making product choices. Two alternate forms of the nonrational adoption process are suggested: the nonrational/impulse form and the nonrational/psychosocial form. These models do not follow the same stages nor truly resemble the rational/decision-making form. Both models will be noted for their lack of information seeking and evaluation.

The form of the adoption process will vary with (1) the importance of the decision, (2) the extent of meaningful product differentiation, (3) the extent of product conspicuousness and the consumer's desire for social approval, (4) the extent to which the consumer can afford to take risks, and (5) the decision-making ability of the consumer. For example, it would be expected that the more important the decision, the more likely the adoption process will approximate the rational/decision-making form; and the less the amount of meaningful product differentiation, the more likely the consumer will decide on impulse or on the basis of psychosocial influence. Product conspicuousness would be considered more likely to lead to a nonrational/ psychosocial adoption process. Some evidence for this expectation is provided by Ward and Gibson (1969), who found that housewives who most desired social approval used different amounts and kinds of information in making decisions about purchases of products varying in physical visibility.

Finally, it would be expected that the more risks consumers are able to take financially and socially, the more the adoption process will depart from a rational/decision-making form to a nonrational/impulse or psychosocial form. And the more able consumers are to engage in rational decision making (which is a learned problem-solving approach), the more likely such an adoption form. Thus, Fliegel, Kivlin, and Sekhon (1968) found that American Pennsylvania farmers were considerably more likely to review factors such as expected payoff and saving of discomfort in arriving at adoption decisions, while Indian Punjabi farmers were considerably more likely to use such factors as social approval and clarity of results.

NUMBER OF STAGES

Adoption, if anything, is the outcome of a *flow* of psychological and mental processes. It is convenient and meaningful for the social scientist to divide this flow into stages. Such stages, however, are arbitrary and no specified number of stages can be considered right or wrong, just as no specified number of periods in history can be considered right or wrong.

Mason (1962) has argued that only two stages are necessary in the adoption process: awareness and adoption. This can be accepted as the minimum number of stages, since it hardly seems possible that a person could adopt a product without being aware of its existence. In contrast, it is conceivable that the maximum number of stages could be vast. For example, the following decision sequence might be suggested. The adoption process could begin with *perception of a problem* which could cause the individual to engage in *information seeking*, resulting in *awareness* of the new product and subsequently *knowledge* about it. A favorable *attitude* could then occur, followed by *legitimation* leading to *trial*. The consumer would then engage in *evaluation*, which could lead to further *information seeking*. *Adoption* (which could lead to *dissonance*) or *rejection* would be the outcome with *discontinuance* perhaps at some future time.

SEQUENCE OF STAGES

Whatever adoption process conceptualization is used, allowance must be made for consumers to skip stages and for the occurrence of feedback. In a comprehensive study of the adoption of new grocery products, Nakanishi (1968) has argued that the sequence of stages used by consumers is a function of the product category's attributes. The most significant attributes for new grocery products are (1) low unit prices, (2) divisibility into small sizes allowing trial, and (3) reversibility of decisions. These attributes, argues Nakanishi, "contribute to a striking characteristic of their acceptance process, namely, the integration of the interest, evaluation, and trial stages" (p. 36). Because trial for grocery products is inexpensive and easily conducted, consumers tend to skip from awareness to trial and gain product knowledge and evaluate the product this way, rather than seeking information in advance of purchase. Figure 3.2 is a flow diagram for the adoption of new grocery products. The arrow from evaluation back to trial takes into account the possibility that one trial purchase will not provide sufficient information for the consumer to make an adoption decision.

Consumer attributes also govern the adoption sequence. For example, to the extent that a consumer already possesses product category knowledge and holds attitudes about products in that category, he is more likely to skip from awareness to attitude to adoption or rejection. To the extent that the consumer is venturesome (a risk taker), he is more likely to go from awareness to trial without any intervening stages.

RESPECIFICATIONS OF THE ADOPTION DECISION

A number of marketing scholars have recently proposed more comprehensive explanations of the consumer decision-making process. These descriptions—particularly those of Andreasen (1965), Howard and Sheth (1968),

Figure 3.2   Simple Flow Diagram for the Adoption of New Grocery Products

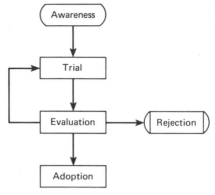

Source: Based in part on Nakanishi (1968).

and Nicosia (1966)—account more fully for the dynamics of consumer decision-making and attempt to specify the operating variables and their interrelationships.

The Nicosia model is shown in Figure 3.3. The basic assumptions are that the firm is introducing a new product or brand and that the consumer has no prior attitudes toward either the brand or its product class. The decision flow consists of the firm's sending out an advertisement, the consumer's possible exposure to it, the interaction of consumer attributes with message content, the resulting possibility of attitude formation, the possibility of this attitude's invoking search/evaluation procedures leading to motivation, the possibility of motivation converting into purchase behavior, and the feedback of purchase information to the firm and to the consumer which may lead to modification of the consumer's predispositions toward future purchase and perhaps to modification of the firm's future communication strategy.

The model, as proposed, is in the form of a summary flow chart indicating major fields, but Nicosia has also specified several subfields to each major field and the possible outcomes, besides elaborating on the purchase decision flow. Subfield 1 of field 1, for example, considers the factors determining exposure. Whether or not exposure occurs is seen as a function of the firm's attributes (communicator characteristics), the attributes of the message and the product, the attributes of the promotional channel used, and, of course, the attributes of the audience member, including his social-environmental characteristics.

Several important differences between this model and the earlier adoption process accounts can be noted. Perhaps the most important difference, according to Nicosia, is that this conceptualization is amenable to simulation techniques, since the process is in the form of a computer flow diagram. Thus, hopes Nicosia, using computer simulation, the interactions among the large number of variables can be explored and perhaps specified, resulting in a

Figure 3.3   The Nicosia Conceptualization of the Purchase Decision Process

Field 1: From the source of a message to a consumer's attitude

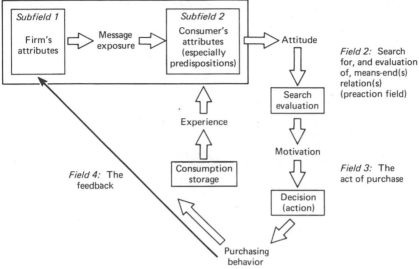

Source: Nicosia (1966, p. 156).

model with dynamic properties. This may be possible, since specific variables are defined and their overall interrelationships discussed. Further advantages of this model are that it indicates the occurrence of feedback and successfully integrates communication input and response output variables, unlike the original adoption process or hierarchy-of-effects specifications.

But Nicosia's model and others like it—including those to be discussed—are not without their faults. Ehrenberg (1968) has criticized the Nicosia model for consisting mainly of "long listings of variables that might possibly enter into such a [consumer behavior] model with little, if any, explicit treatment of how they are interrelated" (p. 334). He also levels the complaint that such models should be derived from empirical knowledge rather than from concepts. In defense of Nicosia, we may note that little systematic empirical knowledge exists, and, more importantly, that all researchers work with concepts in mind. Both empirical research to test theories and models and theoretical elaborations and systematizing of empirical knowledge are necessary.

Andreasen (Figure 3.4) has proposed another conceptual scheme of the adoption process. Again, innovative behavior is assumed on the part of the consumer, since the product will be either a new product or a new product for the specific individual. Thus, suggests Andreasen, "marketers should distinguish between items which are new to a given cultural inventory and items which, although old to a culture, may be new to given individuals" (p. 2).

The process begins with a consumer in a state of unawareness about a product or brand and, therefore, holding no attitude toward it. *Information,*

Figure 3.4   The Andreasen Conceptualization of the Purchase Decision Process

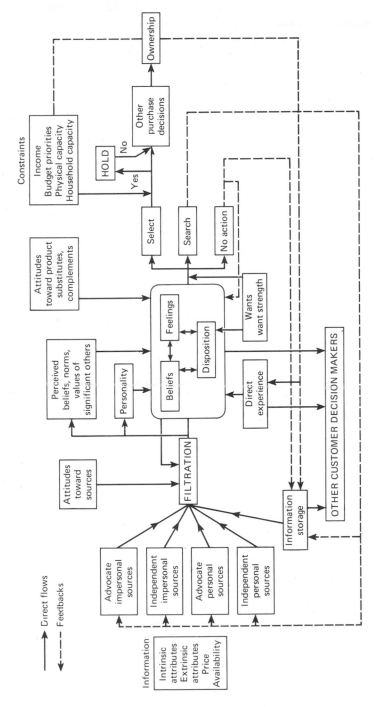

Source: Andreasen (1965, p. 12).

communicated by one of a number of *sources*, reaches the consumer and is *filtered* by him (selective processes). Such information then has an effect on the consumer's *attitude*, defined in terms of belief, feeling, and disposition components. Attitude may result in a decision to *select* the product, *search* for more information, or take no *action*. A "select" decision will be mediated by certain *constraints*, and other *purchase decisions* (store, quantity, and so on) will have to be made before *ownership* is final. In Andreasen's model, appropriate mediating variables are also indicated and feedback flows are traced. This model contains almost all of the advantages of the Nicosia model over traditional models as well as the faults of even more incomplete specification of variable interrelationships and lack of firm empirical footing.

Howard and Sheth (1968) have recently presented a theory of buyer behavior, as summarized in Figure 3.5. Unlike the preceding models, theirs focuses on repeat purchase behavior and has four major components: stimulus inputs, hypothetical constructs, exogenous variables, and response outputs. The *inputs* to the buyer's internal state are stimuli from the marketing and social environments, including "significative" stimuli, communicated by the brand itself, and "symbolic" stimuli, communicated by information channels. The *hypothetical constructs* are enclosed within the large rectangle, which represents the consumer's internal state. These constructs include perceptual constructs (for information processing) and learning constructs (for concept formation). The perceptual constructs include sensitivity to information, perceptual bias, and search for information; whereas the learning constructs include motives, evoked set, decision mediators, predispositions, inhibitors, and satisfaction. The *exogenous variables*, shown at the top of the diagram, influence the hypothetical constructs and provide for adjustment for interpersonal differences. The *response variables* are in the form of outputs which closely resemble the hierarchy-of-effects model, but take account of feedback.

It is difficult to do justice to the Howard-Sheth model in such a short description. Each of these variables and constructs, for example, is defined at length and its interrelationships are approximately specified.

The three models summarized here represent a significant step forward from the original adoption and purchase decision process specifications. As Howard and Sheth observe, "We hope that our theory will provide new insights into past empirical data, and guide future research by instilling coherence and unity into current research, which now tends to be atomistic and unrelated" (pp. 486–487).

A SUMMARY MODEL

Without an attempt to present a "new" or "improved" or "modified" adoption process model, Figure 3.6 is offered as an outcome of the discussion so far. Several features of the model should be emphasized.

Figure 3.5   The Howard-Sheth "Theory of Buyer Behavior"

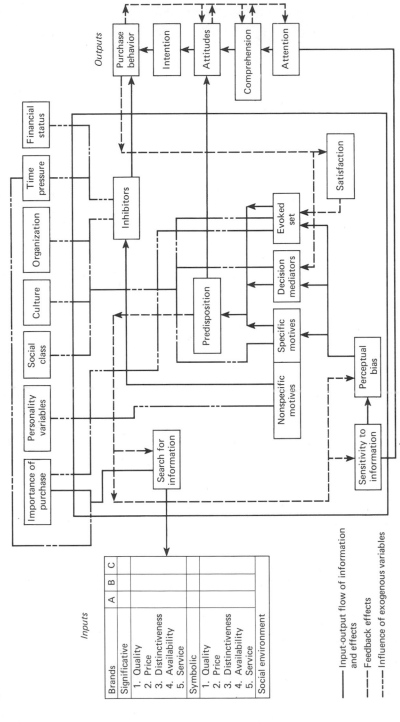

Inputs

Brands	A	B	C
Significative			
1. Quality			
2. Price			
3. Distinctiveness			
4. Availability			
5. Service			
Symbolic			
1. Quality			
2. Price			
3. Distinctiveness			
4. Availability			
5. Service			
Social environment			

———— Input-output flow of information and effects

– – – – Feedback effects

–·–·– Influence of exogenous variables

Source: Figure 1, "A Theory of Buyer Behavior" by John A. Howard and Jagdish N. Sheth, from *Perspectives in Consumer Behavior.* Copyright © 1968 by Scott, Foresman and Company. Reprinted by permission of the publisher and the authors.

Figure 3.6   A Summary Adoption Process Model

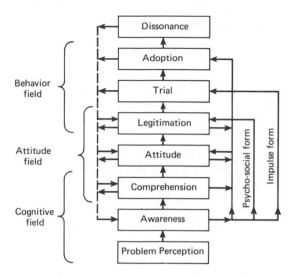

1. The information-attitude-behavior relationship is conceptualized as in previous models, since this is felt to provide a meaningful format for viewing adoption. It is directly related to the common understanding of how advertising functions.
2. It is possible to trace the different *forms* of the adoption process. The rational/decision-making form follows the full sequence of stages, while the nonrational/impulse form goes from awareness to trial; and the nonrational/psychosocial form goes from awareness to legitimation to trial or, possibly, to adoption without trial.
3. Feedback effects are noted by dotted lines. Thus, adoption affects legitimation and attitude (as argued earlier by Palda, 1966) and also adds to knowledge and heightens product awareness. Other feedback effects could be similarly detailed.
4. Problem perception (as proposed by Campbell, 1966) and dissonance are added as two basically new stages to the process to account more fully for the possible *sequences* which may occur.

EXPLANATION

It should be noted initially that *rejection* can occur at any stage after the individual is aware of the innovation. Many adoption process models have included an *interest* stage, but it is felt here that interest is not a useful, distinguishable stage. Instead, interest is considered a prerequite for the occurrence of every stage of the process. Similarly, *evaluation* has been discarded, since it also does not appear to be a useful and distinguishable stage.

Rather, evaluation occurs throughout the process and not at any one time. The consumer first evaluates the item on the basis of initial awareness and knowledge, then as part of attitude formation, then in legitimating trial, and, of course, in considering the trial experience.

DEFINITION OF STAGES

Problem Perception

At times the adoption process will begin with the consumer's perception of a problem. The natural result should be a search procedure whereby the person evaluates his existing knowledge and set of alternatives and turns to his environment for further information and alternatives. It is in this environmental search that the innovation alternative can become available to him.

Awareness

The common start of the adoption process is awareness, whereby the product stimulus registers with the consumer, having passed his filtration process. Awareness assumes only that the consumer knows of the product's existence.

Comprehension

Comprehension is based on knowledge and represents the consumer's conception of what the product is and what functions it can perform. Differential comprehension occurs in the abilities of consumers to handle and reason with information. Some consumers, for example, characteristically may simplify and assimilate information into a small number of categories, whereas others may complicate and contrast information into a large number of categories. Thus, some consumers can perceive a product as basically the same as all other offerings, while other consumers can take note of individual differences and perceive the product as new.

Awareness and comprehension are the information-processing stages. Together they comprise the cognitive field of the purchase process. Comprehension, however, overlaps with the attitude stage, since knowledge (defined in terms of beliefs) is recognized as an attitude component.

Attitude

Attitude is defined as an interrelated system of beliefs, feelings, and action tendencies toward an object (Krech, Crutchfield, and Ballachey, 1962). It goes beyond comprehension in terms of the feeling and action tendency components. An attitude most generally is thought of as the predisposition of the individual to evaluate an object of his environment in a favorable or unfavorable manner. In almost all cases, a favorable evaluation is necessary for the adoption process to continue.

Legitimation

If the individual realizes a favorable attitude, he will be disposed to purchase the product on a trial basis. However, whether or not trial will occur depends largely upon the result of the legitimation stage. Legitimation means that the individual becomes convinced that purchase is the appropriate course of action. He may reach this decision using the information which he has already accumulated, or he may turn to his environment for further information. Such questions as "Do my friends buy this product?" or "Is the cost in line with similar products?" are relevant here. The legitimation stage may often stand as a barrier between favorable attitude toward the product and actual purchase.

The comprehension, attitude, and legitimation stages may be considered to comprise the attitude field of the adoption process. As noted, comprehension is also part of the cognitive field; and legitimation can also be considered part of the behavioral field, since the individual is, in a sense, acting toward goal achievement.

Trial

In trial, the consumer uses the product on a limited scale. Trial may represent a commitment toward adoption or a means of evaluating the product by experience.

Adoption

In adoption, the consumer accepts the product and continues to purchase and/or use it. The legitimation, trial, and adoption stages comprise the behavioral field in the adoption process. The process is now complete unless the occurrence of cognitive dissonance is considered.

Dissonance

As adoption implies, commitment to a decision tends to place the individual in a state of cognitive dissonance, since he has adopted a certain product, but may believe that other products also have desirable features. Because dissonance is psychologically uncomfortable, the individual will work to reduce it and to obtain consonance, for example, by seeking social support or by selectively perceiving advertisements for the product purchased in order to justify his own behavior. This may mean, in effect, that the individual will repeat the legitimation stage or, if dissonance is not successfully reduced, discontinue use of the product.

CONCLUSION

It should be emphasized again that alternate forms and sequences of the adoption process are possible and that there is no set number of stages which must be covered. This summary model has taken into account alternate model forms, has provided for skipping stages, and has provided for feedback effect.

USING THE ADOPTION PROCESS MODEL: A CASE EXAMPLE

It may be useful at this point to illustrate how the adoption process model may be used. In the following example, adoption *progress* rates are traced for a hypothetical innovation.

THE ADOPTION "PROGRESS" CONCEPT

The new product marketer may often be hampered in the early stages of a product's life cycle in arriving at meaningful sales predictions because the sales data base is so small and, frequently, unpredictable. Thus, early heavy sales rates may indicate either a large potential market or a small potential market that is highly interested in the product and highly motivated toward trial. Slow beginning sales rates may be due to the complexity or lack of communicability of the product and may not reflect long-run sales potential. In other words, *sales* figures in the short run need not be the best indicator of long-run adoption rates.

A more reliable and potentially more usable form of data may be to measure *adoption progress*. In this approach, as proposed by Klonglan, Coward, and Beal (1968), the focus is on the classification of consumers in the defined market segment at stages on the *adoption process*, instead of merely classifying consumers as buyers or nonbuyers. Thus, consumers will be distributed along the various stages of the adoption process.

A hypothetical example of the utility of the adoption progress approach is given in Table 3.1. Let us assume that a new product has been introduced to the market on January 1, 1971. Using adoption rates only, it is evidenced that 3 per cent of the potential market has adopted by June and 10 percent has adopted by December. At this point, management may be plotting sales figures and noting what appears to be the takeoff point on the traditional S-shaped curve (see Figure 3.7). The product manager may be a strong contender for a bonus.

Table 3.1   Classification of Consumers by Stage of the Adoption Process for a Hypothetical Innovation

Adoption process stage	Cumulative percentage of consumers* June 1971	December 1971
Awareness	55	85
Comprehension	45	70
Favorable attitude	25	30
Legitimation	16	18
Trial	10	14
Adoption	3	10

* 100 percent is assumed to represent the entire market potential for the product.

Figure 3.7   Adoption Progress Rates (based on Table 3.1)

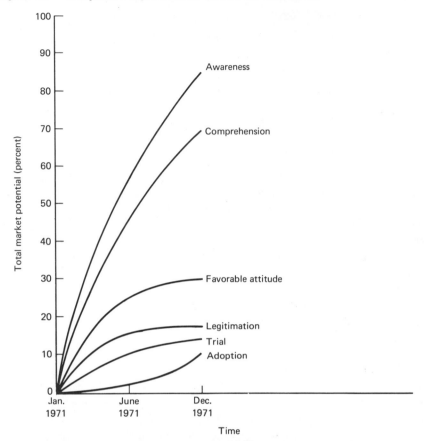

Time

If adoption *progress* rates are used, however, quite a different picture is seen. Although awareness and knowledge levels have shown significant gains, the relative percentage increase in number of consumers holding favorable attitudes toward the product is indeed small and an even smaller relative percentage increase is shown in number of consumers advancing as far as legitimation. This is clear in Figure 3.7. According to this additional data, sales levels will soon stabilize rapidly, since other consumers in the population are not progressing toward adoption.

This data would suggest either that the market share for this product is limited and has been quickly cornered or that promotional efforts are not successfully gaining attitude change—perhaps because they are still focusing on informational messages for the new product despite the fact that 85 percent of the consumers are at or beyond the awareness level. Using the adoption progress index, the marketer would be able to check these hypotheses out in December 1971 and not many months later when adoption had stabilized after production had been expanded. It would also be possible to attempt to modify the promotional campaign to correct the indicated difficulties.

INNOVATOR–LATER ADOPTER DIFFERENCES IN REGARD TO THE ADOPTION PROCESS

What distinguishes innovators from later adopters is that the former advance to adoption more quickly. It is also possible that innovators and later adopters can be distinguished at earlier stages of the adoption process. This possibility will now be examined.

PRODUCT INFORMATION

The question may first be raised whether later adopters adopt late because of lack of information about the new product. In a review and comparison of the Coleman, Katz, and Menzel (1966) physician drug study and the Ryan and Gross (1943) hybrid corn study, Elihu Katz (1961) concludes that lack of information cannot account for different adoption rates. In the hybrid corn study, over 90 percent of the farmers had heard of the new product at a certain point in time, but only 20 percent had tried it. Within four months of the new drug's availability in the other study, 67 percent of the doctors had heard of it, but only 33 percent had adopted it.

In a direct test of this hypothesis in the consumer realm, Robertson (1968c) measured awareness and knowledge levels among nonadopters of a new telephone product one year after it was introduced to the market. It was found that 95 percent of the nonadopters had awareness of the product, that is, they knew of its existence. A breakdown by degree of knowledge showed that 75 percent of the nonadopter respondents could describe the product well; 15 percent could give a fair account; 5 percent could state only that they had heard of it; and, as noted, 5 percent were unaware of the product's existence. Product knowledge, therefore, does not seem to distinguish innovators from later adopters.

ATTITUDE CHANGE

If innovators and nonadopters (who may in time become later adopters) generally cannot be distinguished by information level, can they be distinguished in terms of their attitudes toward the product? A comparison was made by Robertson (1968b) of the extent of attitude favorability of innovators versus nonadopters toward the telephone innovation. As might be expected, innovators were significantly more favorably inclined toward the product—87 percent reflected a favorable to highly favorable attitude as compared to 45 percent of the nonadopter sample.

It can be argued, however, that the more favorable innovator attitude *after* purchase does not constitute a valid comparison with nonadopter attitude *before* purchase. Most desirably, innovator attitudes should have been measured before purchase was made. After purchase, innovators must justify their action to maintain cognitive consistency, and, therefore, unfavorable responses are less likely.

Although they are not directly comparable, a strong parallel may exist between the results of this study and the earlier experiment by Hovland, Lumsdaine, and Sheffield (1949) who showed American servicemen the *Battle of Britain* film. These authors concluded that this movie was highly effective in imparting factual information, but was entirely ineffective in attaining attitude change. This conclusion seems to apply also in the present case, where 90 percent of nonadopters could render at least a "fair account" of the product, although only 45 percent of nonadopters reflected a favorable attitude toward the product.

It seems, furthermore, that information and attitude are not always discrete stages *from the consumer point of view*. Information and ideas seem to be immediately processed by the individual in line with his value system, and positive or negative feelings result. This is illustrated in the following non-adopter responses, which tend to reveal each person's opinion of the product.

Question:

Are you familiar with the Touch-Tone telephone? If so, how would you describe it to me?

Answer:

"I've used them in pay phones. It's a luxury. I can't see that much trouble in dialing. It's like an electric typewriter. You just push buttons and as fast as you touch them, they register."

Answer:

"Yes. I think it is a pain with the push buttons. My fat mother-in-law has it."

Answer:

"Yes. My girlfriend has it. I just think it's fascinating. I never knew they sounded musical" (p. 49).

This mixing of opinion when level of knowledge was being measured, may, of course, be a function of the respondent's being interviewed at a point where attitudes toward the product had already been formed. Perhaps discrete information and attitude stages would be apparent if the consumer could be interviewed immediately as she gained product knowledge.

It appears that innovators and nonadopters may be differentiated at the attitude stage, although methodological difficulties render this generalization less conclusive than otherwise might be the case. If an advertising campaign were to be instituted in the community of this study at this time, it would seem reasonable to suggest that its emphasis be at an affective (feelings) level rather than at a cognitive (informational) level.

ADOPTION INTENTION

Innovators and nonadopters are, of course, clearly differentiated at the adoption stage. Using the telephone data, however, it is possible to gain some insight as to whether nonadopters are likely to become adopters. These nonadopters were asked whether or not they would consider buying the new telephone product. Respondents voiced the following purchase intentions:

Would consider buying	20 percent
Might consider buying	10 percent
Would not consider buying	63 percent
Undetermined	7 percent

Thus, while 45 percent of nonadopters held favorable attitudes toward the product, only 30 percent of nonadopters would or might consider purchase.

It might be suggested further that nonadopters have difficulty legitimating purchase, which might help account for the low purchase intention rate despite a higher percentage of favorable attitudes and a very high percentage of adequate knowledge. It was found in this study that innovators most often used interpersonal communication as a means of legitimating purchase. Nonadopters, however, were found to be less socially integrated and, therefore, perhaps less likely or less able to turn to other people for legitimation.

CONCLUSION

One important reason for examining differences between innovators and nonadopters is that comparison data may suggest ways of speeding up adoption processes. Different marketing activities may be called for to reach optimum adoption rates within both groups.

Both innovators and later adopters seem to have comparable amounts of product information. However, these two types can be distinguished in terms of their attitudes toward a product innovation.

Both innovators and nonadopters perceive and process product information in terms of their own predispositions, values, past experiences, and so forth. Therefore, different advertising strategies may be suggested for innovators and nonadopters. Promotional efforts should, perhaps, assist noninnovators in obtaining legitimation by simulating the interpersonal legitimation process. Advertising could, for example, stress the "social correctness" of adoption, refer to the notion that "everyone is buying," or emphasize a testimonial approach.

SUMMARY

In this chapter, adoption process models and related notions have been critically examined.

Adoption models grew out of sociological studies of the diffusion of innovations. Other schemes, such as AIDA and the hierarchy of effects, are conceptually quite similar. All of these models posit somewhat different kinds and numbers of stages, but all provide a conceptual framework for the study of processes by which consumers purchase, try, and adopt or reject products.

Limitations and conceptual difficulties attending the various schemes have been discussed. A central conceptual difficulty concerns the relevance of *stages* in examining different purchase situations. For example, quite different processes may occur for frequently purchased, low-cost items versus infrequently purchased, high-priced items.

Another major difficulty is that empirical research has not yet adequately demonstrated relationships between information, attitude, and behavior, the essential elements in adoption process schemes. That is, we cannot specify precisely when being in one stage is a necessary and/or sufficient condition to move to another stage. Some adoption process models attempt to avoid this difficulty by including feedback loops or the possibility of skipping stages.

Whereas adoption process models are not without these shortcomings, it should be kept in mind that their utility must be measured in terms of how well they help us to understand certain consumer processes. An example was presented in which specifying adoption progress suggested different marketing strategies during new product introduction. Hopefully, refinement of these models will aid marketers in optimizing strategies—for example, speeding up the adoption process, tailoring different and more effective advertising appeals to innovators and later adopters, and, possibly, minimizing product rejection.

CHAPTER 4

PROFILING CONSUMER INNOVATORS

Innovators are the individuals within a population who are the first to adopt a new idea, technology, service, or product. Five adopter categories are defined in the rural sociology literature based on time of adoption (see Figure 4.1. These are: innovators (the first 2.5 percent of the population to adopt), early adopters (the next 13.5 percent), early majority (the next 34 percent), late majority (the next 34 percent), and laggards (the remaining

16 percent). This schema, while arbitrary, is based on a normal curve of diffusion which has often been found to occur (see Rogers 1962*b*, pp. 156–157).

Extensive research evidence in rural sociology reveals that each of these adopter categories possesses distinguishing characteristics (see Table 4.1). The farmer innovator is venturesome (willing to take risks), youngest, highest in social status, wealthy, in close contact with scientific information sources, and very cosmopolitan. He shows greater interaction with other innovators and greater use of impersonal information sources; and he exercises some opinion leadership. The laggard, in contrast, is tradition-oriented, oldest, semiisolated, and lowest in social status and income. He has the smallest farming operation, with little specialization; and he makes greater usage of neighbors, friends, and relatives of similar values as information sources; he shows very little opinion leadership.

This comparison suggests that differential promotional programs would be appropriate to these two farming groups. But will differences be this pronounced in consumer goods marketing? Will this same adopter categorization be meaningful? Are research findings available to characterize consumer adopters?

DIFFERENCES BETWEEN FARMERS AND CONSUMERS

One of the most essential differences between the realms of the farmer and the consumer is the extent to which most innovations diffuse. In farming the assumption is generally that 100 percent of the population will eventually adopt the innovation, but this does not hold in consumer goods, especially if each brand of a product innovation is considered a separate innovation. Thus, it is necessary to base the definition of a consumer innovator on a percentage of the expected number of adopting units who do adopt rather than a percentage of the total population. If the expected number of adopting units (based on sales forecasts) is 100,000, then in line with the rural sociology adopter category conceptualization, innovators will be defined as the first 2500 units to adopt.

The 2.5-percent innovator definition is, of course, arbitrary and may not be meaningful for marketing researchers and practitioners. In fact, diffusion research by marketers has shied away from this percentage definition and has used a variety of percentages—a 10-percent innovator definition perhaps being most common (William E. Bell, 1963, and Robertson, 1966). This, of course, creates serious problems in attempting to generalize the results of these studies. It becomes very difficult to compare results defining innovators as the first 10 percent to adopt a new product with results using a 35-percent innovator figure, such as King (1963), or with results from the rural sociology literature where the 2.5-percent innovator definition has been maintained quite consistently. There is an immediate need within the marketing tradition

Table 4.1 Summary of Characteristics of Adopter Categories

Adopter Category	Salient Values	Personal Characteristics	Communication Behavior	Social Relationships
Innovators	"Venturesome," willing to accept risks; scientific	Youngest age; highest social status; largest and most specialized operations; wealthier; high level of education; farming practices may not be accepted	Closest contact with scientific information sources; use more impersonal sources; interact with other innovators	Some opinion leadership; very cosmopolitan
Early Adopters	"Respect," regarded by many others in the social system as a role model	High social status; large and specialized operations; slightly above-average education	Greatest contact with local change agents; leaders in local organizations	Greatest opinion leadership of any category in most social systems. Very localite
Early Majority	"Deliberate," willing to consider innovations only after peers have adopted	Above-average social status; average-sized operation; slightly above-average education	Considerable contact with change agents and local adopters; many informal community contacts	Some opinion leadership
Late Majority	"Skeptical," overwhelming pressure from peers needed before adoption	Below-average social status; small operation; little specialization; small income; slightly below-average education	Secure ideas from peers—mainly late or early majority; less use of mass media; little activity in formal organizations	Little opinion leadership
Laggards	"Tradition" oriented; agricultural magic and folk beliefs; fear of debt	Little specialization; lowest social status; smallest operation; lowest income, oldest	Neighbors, friends, and relatives with similar values are main information source; semi-isolates; few memberships in formal organizations	Very little opinion leadership; little exchange with neighbors

Source: Rogers (1962b, p. 185) and North Central Rural Sociology Committee for the study of Diffusion of Farm Practices (1961, p. 9).

of diffusion research to standardize definitions for innovators and other critical concepts being measured.

In the final analysis, whether the innovator concept is operationally useful in the design of marketing programs must be tested. Innovators may constitute a meaningful form of market segmentation if their characteristics are significantly different from later adopters and if they can be reached efficiently as a specific market segment. The definition of the consumer innovator should be based on practical marketing considerations, that is, what categorization will be most usable by marketers.

DIFFICULTIES IN DEFINING INNOVATORS

A considerable number of difficulties are involved in arriving at a practical and workable innovator definition. These difficulties are summarized in the following paragraphs.

As discussed, it is indeed a rare occurrence when a consumer product innovation achieves complete diffusion within a social system. It has been argued, therefore, that a definition of innovators must be based on some percentage of the *expected* number of adopting units. This assumes that expected diffusion can be predicted, although many, if not most, sales forecasts are considerably off target.

If this is to be the definitional basis, an obvious difficulty is to decide upon an appropriate percentage. The most meaningful definition would be at the point of a "natural" break in the diffusion curve—if such a break occurred. Thus, if adopter characteristics seem to change at a 10-percent diffusion level, this would provide a highly useful definitional form. It is doubtful, however, that such a natural break occurs and especially doubtful that it would occur at the same point across a number of product categories. This places us in the position, therefore, of establishing a logical breaking point between innovators and later adopters. Rural sociologists have done this using standard deviations and assuming a normal curve of diffusion over time. For marketing purposes, any definition should include enough innovators to constitute a worthwhile market segment. A 2.5-percent figure is not a good definition if it does not provide a sufficient number of innovators.

Some problems in the innovator concept depend upon the innovation under consideration. If we loosely define innovations to include new brands, then can the characteristics of innovators (given, say, a 10-percent definition) for the third fluoride toothpaste on the market be compared with the characteristics of innovators for the first fluoride toothpaste on the market? The innovator concept is undoubtedly more meaningful for product innovations than for brand innovations. The marketer of the third fluoride toothpaste on the market should probably assume that diffusion is beyond the (product) innovator category and should market in accordance with the characteristics of later adopters.

Should the innovator definition be on a national or local basis? Should account be taken of ethnic groups or age groups or social classes? It may well be that diffusion rates vary with such dimensions. Then, is a person an innovator when he adopts after 30 percent of his fellow community members have adopted, although diffusion on a national level has only reached a 5-percent level? Is an individual an innovator if he is in the first 10 percent of blacks to adopt a new product, despite the fact that diffusion among whites is at a considerably more advanced level? These questions depend in considerable measure on how the marketer is segmenting his markets. It may be wise to trace diffusion rates on the basis of a number of segmentation criteria and to reach separate innovator groups for these segments.

Innovators can also be defined on the basis of adoption time regardless of percentage diffusion rates. An innovator for a new fashion item might be defined as a buyer within the first three months in which the item is available. The Federal Trade Commission (1967) has issued a guideline that products are new only for the first six months of their life history. Innovators could be defined as persons who buy within this period when the product is new.

Until this point, innovator definitions have been considered in terms of adoption of a single product. The marketer may, however, find a definition of innovators to be more meaningful in terms of adoption of a set of products. He may be less concerned with the characteristics of one food product's innovators than with the characteristics of innovators across a range of food products. It may be of limited value to study the innovators for a single product a firm has introduced, since it would be too late to appeal to them with the knowledge gained. But if the general characteristics of innovators for a product category are known, then the firm is in a position to appeal to these innovator traits as a new product is introduced. This assumes, of course, that product category innovators exist—an issue to be discussed shortly.

MEASURING INNOVATIVENESS[1]

There are essentially four measures of innovativeness which have been developed for locating innovators and later adopters. These are

1. ratings by judges or sociometric choices
2. self-designated measures
3. longitudinal measures
4. cross-sectional measures.

JUDGES OR SOCIOMETRIC METHOD

Ratings by judges or experts are sometimes used in the rural sociology realm, but have not been noted in the marketing literature. This method could

[1] The discussion here is based largely on Rossiter and Robertson (1968).

be of value if the social system were small and members well known to each other—as is sometimes the case in industrial marketing. Problems with the method reside in its judgmental nature: it presumes competence of the judges and high interjudge realiability; it allows a subjective definition of innovators; and its validity depends on how well the judges know the individuals they are rating. An extension of this technique is to use sociometric measures where every group member rates every other member on innovativeness. Sociometric measures also have been used in rural sociology, but not in marketing.

SELF-DESIGNATED METHOD

In the self-designated method the individual is asked to indicate whether he perceives himself to be an innovator. Summers (1968), for example, asked individuals to rate themselves as "earlier," "about the same time," or "later" when buying new fashion items relative to "most people" and to "friends." The correlations between actual fashion ownership and these perceived measures were quite low (averaging approximately 0.17), which would suggest caution in using perceived innovator measures as a substitute for behavioral measures for defining innovators. Robertson (1970), in a study using multiple measures of innovativeness, found that a semantic differential measure of self-assigned innovativeness ("How willing are you to buy new products?— very willing to very unwilling") was significantly related to actual new product purchases ($x^2 = 12.6$, $N = 72$, $p < .02$).

LONGITUDINAL METHOD

The longitudinal method is the most widely used for classifying innovators based on the first x percent of individuals to adopt a new product over time. Its difficulties now have been discussed at sufficient length. Two forms of this method have been used: (1) consumer report of adoption date and (2) records to establish adoption date. The consumer report may suffer from unreliability in conveying actual behavior, much as may the self-designated method. Menzel (1957), for example, has found discrepancies in doctor reports of adoption date and the actual adoption date as established by prescription records. He reasons that individuals tend to claim earlier adoption than is actually the case when social system norms favor innovativeness and tend to claim later adoption than is actually the case when social system norms oppose innovativeness.

It is highly recommended, therefore, to use recorded adoption dates whenever available, as in the case of physicians prescribing drugs (James S. Coleman, Katz, and Menzel, 1957), consumers ordering telephones (Robertson, 1966), or consumers adopting large-ticket items, or ordering new products by mail order or by charge account. Warranty records may also provide accurate adoption dates.

CROSS-SECTIONAL METHOD

The cross-sectional method employs an instantaneous categorization along a continuum of number of items purchased (rather than a time continuum). Such an approach is applicable only when a number of innovations exists within a given consumption category, as is frequently the case for consumer products and much less so in the farming realm where the longitudinal method was developed. This cross-sectional method would seem to be more reliable in arriving at general innovator profiles, since it allows some latitude for consumer preference.

Figure 4.1   Adopter Categorization Based on Relative Time of Adoption

Time of adoption

Innovators	2.5%	Late majority	34.0%
Early adopters	13.5%	Laggards	16.0%
Early majority	34.0%		

Source: North Central Subcommittee (1961, p. 3).

A graphical comparison of the longitudinal and cross-sectional approaches is given in Figure 4.2. The cross-sectional adoption distribution is also assumed to approach normality with valid and sufficient selection of innovative items. Inclusion of too many well-adopted items would, of course, produce skewness of one sort, while inclusion of too many limited-adoption items would produce skewness of another sort. It becomes necessary, therefore, to rigidly define products for inclusion in terms of diffusion levels.

Rogers and Rogers (1961) suggest that if such a cross-sectional scale is used, then credit should be given for relatively earlier adoption as well as the number of items adopted. The time-of-adoption dimension could be added to the cross-sectional method and a weighting system derived to give credit for earlier adoption. However, it also may be expected that at a given point in time, individuals who are typically among the first to adopt will also have adopted more items. Rossiter and Robertson (1968), in using a cross-sectional method to measure fashion innovativeness, found only minor differences in the classification of individuals by adopter category when the time factor was incorporated with total ownership of fashion items. Items chosen which vary

Figure 4.2   Comparison of Longitudinal and Cross-sectional Methods for Defining Innovators

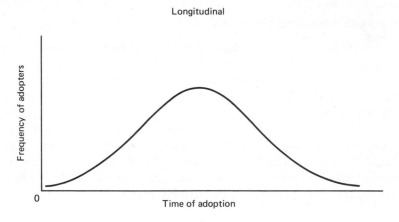

Longitudinal

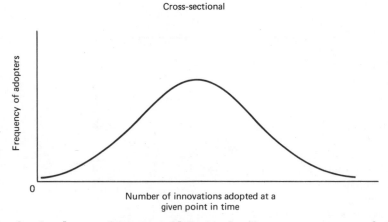

Cross-sectional

somewhat by degree of newness (diffusion level) may operate as a built-in control for the cross-sectional method.

The cross-sectional method seems to have inherent pragmatic validity to the extent that past innovative behavior is indicative of continuing innovative behavior within the product category. In contrast, lack of such validity is a serious drawback to the one-item, longitudinal method. The reliability of the cross-sectional method can be tested across individuals but not on a test-retest basis, since, by its very nature, the measure is an instantaneous one. Perhaps in a retest new items meeting the same criteria of innovativeness could be used (but variability would be expected), or the same list of items could be retained and an upward adjustment allowed for in the retest situation. The question of scale discriminability resolves to adequate and sufficient selection of items, since measure and criteria appear to be largely colinear.

THE FARMER INNOVATOR PROFILE

Although the farmer innovator is not expected to have identical or even highly similar characteristics to the consumer innovator, the logical first step in arriving at a consumer innovator profile is to assess the farmer innovator profile, since this is where the most extensive documentation of innovator characteristics has occurred and where many consumer studies have borrowed characteristics for testing. Table 4.2 is a review of factors related to farming innovativeness showing the number of studies conducted and the direction of the relationships. The table is arranged so that the first four categories list factors which also have been tested in marketing studies, while the last two categories list factors unique to the farming system.

Table 4.2   Factors Related to Innovativeness in Farming

Factor	Number of Studies Showing Significant Relationships		
	Positive	None	Negative
Demographic Factors			
Education	24	1	0
Social status	21	0	0
Age	2	4	2
Communication Behavior			
Extent of information exposure	20	2	0
Social Interaction Factors			
Social participation	9	2	2
Opinion leadership	5	0	0
Cosmopolitanism	5	3	0
Community norms on innovation	5	0	0
Attitudinal and Personality Factors			
Venturesomeness	1	0	0
Self-perception of innovativeness	2	1	0
Personality:			
Rigidity trait	0	0	2
Dogmatism trait	0	1	0
Attitude:			
Toward change	2	0	0
Toward innovations	3	0	0
Value Factors			
Religion:			
Affiliation	1	2	0
Church membership	2	1	0

Table 4.2—Continued

	Number of Studies Showing Significant Relationships		
Factor	Positive	None	Negative
Values:			
Conservatism	0	0	3
Protestant ethic	0	0	2
Belief in science	2	1	0
Efficiency	1	1	0
Individualism	1	1	0
Familism	1	4	0
Progress	0	2	0
Achievement	0	1	0
Farming as way of life	1	0	0
Security	0	2	1
Material comfort	1	0	0
Farm Management Factors			
Size of farm operation	27	3	0
Usage of management practices	4	0	0
Rationality	2	0	0
Attitude toward credit	3	0	0
Years of farming experience	0	2	1
Farm specialization	3	0	0

Source: A modified version of Havens (1962).

A difficulty should be noted at this point. Factors related to *innovativeness* can differ to some extent from *innovator* characteristics, although the two would be imagined to be fairly synonymous. For example, in some cases the innovator is reported to be a deviant—low on social participation—although innovativeness in general is positively related to social participation (Rogers, 1962b, ch. 7). Only studies which look at the specific characteristics of adopter categories, rather than using correlation techniques, can identify the innovator profile accurately. This difficulty, while suggesting a more cautious interpretation of Table 4.2, is not particularly serious, since most studies of adopter category characteristics have found a "linear" profiling (see, for example, Rogers, 1962a).

DEMOGRAPHIC FACTORS

Innovativeness has been conclusively shown to be positively related to *education* level and to *social status* (Table 4.2). *Age* has been shown to vary in its relationship with innovativeness from study to study. Income can be inferred from social status and size of farm operation (Table 4.2) and is positively related to innovativeness.

COMMUNICATION BEHAVIOR

Innovators are found to have greater *exposure* to sources of information in general and particularly to sources of information about innovations. They are found to have more mass media contact, more extension and scientific agricultural contact, and more farm bulletin and magazine contact. Rogers (1962a) finds that 42 percent of innovators have direct contact with agricultural scientists, while laggards have no contact whatsoever.

SOCIAL INTERACTION FACTORS

Innovativeness most often bears a positive relationship to *social participation,* although exceptions occur. This seems to suggest that the farming innovator can, in certain cases, be a deviant. Innovativeness and *opinion leadership* are positively related; that is, the innovator will tend to be more influential than the average member of the social system. *Cosmopolitanism,* that is, orientation beyond the local community, most often is positively related to innovativeness. *Community norms on innovation* are positively related to the innovativeness of community members, although the innovator sometimes has been found to violate existing norms—especially if they oppose innovation (Marsh and Coleman, 1956).

ATTITUDINAL AND PERSONALITY FACTORS

Venturesomeness has often been used as a summary concept to characterize innovators, although it has seldom been operationally defined and tested. In Table 4.1, for example, the innovator is described in summary form as venturesome, or willing to accept risks. The innovator in farming is found to be prone (two cases out of three) to *perceive* himself as an innovator. This can be important in terms of promotional appeals. *Personality* has not been researched in any comprehensive fashion, and the only suggestion is that "rigidity" as a personality trait may be negatively related to innovativeness. *Attitudes* favoring change and favorable attitudes toward innovations have been found to be positively related to innovativeness.

VALUE FACTORS

On the whole, only limited research has been conducted on the association between *values* and adoption of innovations. It appears, for example, that belonging to a church may be positively associated with innovativeness, perhaps in relation to the social participation finding reported earlier. "Conservatism" and "belief in the Protestant ethic" are negatively related to innovation adoption, but "belief in science" appears to be positively related.

FARM MANAGEMENT FACTORS

It has been found generally that the larger the *farm operation,* the more likely the acceptance of innovations. Usage of *management practices* (such as cost accounting), a *rational decision-making orientation, favorable attitude toward credit,* and *specialization* in farming operations have also been found to be positively related to innovativeness. *Years of farming experience,* much like age, is inconclusively related to innovativeness.

A BRIEF PROFILE OF THE PHYSICIAN INNOVATOR

Characteristics of the physician innovator for a new miracle drug are detailed by Coleman, Katz, and Menzel (1966). This profile is based on one study only and, therefore, cannot be accepted with the same confidence as the farming profile, where multiple studies were conducted using similar variables in a variety of settings and using a number of research designs. In fact, Winick (1961) found an inconclusive profile of the physician innovator in his study of the diffusion of another prescription drug in a large city. The drug which he studied seemed not to be as discontinuous an innovation as that studied by Coleman, Katz, and Menzel; and it did not achieve as successful a diffusion level.

DEMOGRAPHIC FACTORS

The physician innovator for the new drug product was unlikely to be old, but equally likely to be middle-aged or young. Few of his patients were low-income, and he was more likely to be a specialist than a general practitioner. These are surrogate measures which suggest that the physician innovator was of higher income than the average physician. Higher education and social status would also be associated generally with a medical specialty.

COMMUNICATION BEHAVIOR

The physician innovator was much more likely to subscribe to a large number of medical journals and to attend meetings of specialty societies. He was also more in touch with out-of-town medical institutions.

SOCIAL INTERACTION FACTORS

Doctors who were rated high on social participation with other members of the medical community were likely to adopt the new drug sooner than doctors with less social participation. Physician innovators were higher than average on opinion leadership and more cosmopolitan, in that they attended more out-of-town medical meetings and visited more out-of-town medical institutions. The innovator could be considered to be abiding by medical social system norms by supporting a progressive and scientific orientation (Elihu Katz, 1961).

ATTITUDINAL FACTORS

"Scientific orientation" was found to be positively related to early adoption of the drug. "Profession-oriented" doctors were considerably more likely to be innovators than "patient-oriented" doctors.

OTHER FACTORS

The attribute showing the strongest relationship to innovativeness was level of use for this category of drugs. The innovator was most often a heavy user (prescriber) for other similar drugs.

THE INDUSTRIAL INNOVATOR PROFILE

Relating the characteristics of the industrial innovator is not without problems, mainly because of the relative paucity of conceptual thinking and research in this area. Nor is an innovation so clearly defined as in other traditions of diffusion research.

There are at least three forms which innovation may take in an industrial or commercial setting. These may be categorized as (1) *product* innovations, (2) *process* innovations, and (3) *organizational* innovations. The distinction between product and process innovations may be somewhat blurred at times, but briefly, product innovation refers to the employment of a new product as opposed to the application of a new method. Adoption of a new process may occasionally involve no expenditure of funds, but just a redeployment of existing resources with a view to increasing productivity or reducing costs. Organizational innovations generally refer to the adoption of new structural forms or new managerial techniques. These three categories of innovation sometimes may be closely interrelated. Thus, automation of a plant will require adoption of new machines, new production methods, and a new organizational structure reflecting the firm's revised labor and managerial needs. However, the extent to which this is so will depend on the nature of the innovation (continuous or discontinuous) and its impact on the total operations of the innovating firm.

Industrial innovators must be categorized along two fronts. One relates to the characteristics of the innovating *firm*, the other to those of the *decision-making group* within the firm. Most of the research to date in this field has focused on the nature of the firm, and little evidence exists on the characteristics of the innovating group. Furthermore, industrial innovation has tended to be studied by economists examining the diffusion of new technology, whose findings consequently are centered on the adoption of new products and processes directly related to the production function. Thus far, relatively little work has been done by behavioral scientists studying the adoption of new organizational structures and managerial techniques.

One of the pitfalls faced in examining the characteristics of industrial innovators lies in determining which factors are conditional and which are causal. For instance, Carter and Williams (1957) find a rapid increase in profits to be correlated with what they term "technical progressiveness"; but they subsequently comment that "it is not proven that technical progressiveness is the cause of fast-rising profits; it may be that the profits are the stimulus or the necessary means for the progressiveness" (p. 185). It is also necessary to draw a distinction between, on the one hand, the characteristics of the *innovations* which are most likely to be successful and the *circumstances* in which this may be so and, on the other, the characteristics of the *innovator*. Thus a study by the National Institute for Economic and Social Research (1969) concluded, predictably enough, that a very important characteristic of industrial process innovations was "the advantage of the new process in terms of overall profitability" (p. 83). However, we should also be concerned with identifying the type of firm most likely to perceive these advantages and to act accordingly at an early date.

THE RATE OF INDUSTRIAL DIFFUSION

Various studies have pointed to the slow rate of diffusion for industrial innovations. Mansfield's evidence (1968) indicates an average lag between invention and acceptance of about ten to fifteen years. The 1969 National Institute for Economic and Social Research study—which covered six European countries—pointed to wide variations in rate of diffusion among different countries. Sometimes existing laws and regulations in one country affected the adoption of new techniques there, relative to other countries where the relevant regulations were less restrictive. Patents are another factor in that some companies which have developed a new product or process are reluctant to license potential competitors, while other companies do so freely with a view to maximizing royalty revenues.

From the research which has been undertaken, a number of factors which may affect the rate of industrial diffusion have been identified. Mansfield (1968) proposes the following relationships:

1. Profitability of an innovation, relative to others that are available, will speed the rate of diffusion.
2. The larger the investment required, assuming equally profitable innovations available, the slower the rate of diffusion.
3. The type of industry will influence the speed of diffusion, depending on its aversion to risk, market competitiveness, and financial health.

Sutherland (1959), in a paper dealing with the diffusion of innovation in cotton spinning, adds to the list of adoption determinants as follows:

4. Uncertainty about the future of an industry will retard diffusion.
5. The greater the potential cost reductions, the faster will be diffusion.

CHARACTERISTICS OF THE INNOVATING FIRM

In examining the characteristics of the innovating firm, a significant consideration is the *size* of the innovator. Mansfield (1968) found little support for the allegation that the largest firms are the early adopters. The National

Institute for Economic and Social Research (1969) concluded that their six-nation study of ten innovations in nine industries

> . . . provides no definite evidence for saying that large companies have always been in the forefront of technical progress in the sense of being leaders in innovation and the adoption of new techniques. The leading role which they often play in research and development, their generally more sophisticated managerial set-up, and their easier access to new capital are likely to give them a lead over smaller firms: some of the case studies do indeed point to the outstanding part played by large companies. But in other cases it has been the opposite way round (p. 83).

Other factors may be more significant than absolute size. Two factors which are often, but not necessarily, related to size are the firm's *growth rate* and the *availability of capital.* Thus the Carter and Williams (1957) study found a high growth rate to be linked to early adoption of innovations by firms. Subsequently, the National Institute for Economic and Social Research (1969) study identified "access to capital"—that is, a company's ability to finance costs associated with the adoption of an innovation—as a leading factor in diffusion.

Webster (1969) perceptively suggests several reasons why research into the relationship between size of firm and innovativeness has so far proved largely inconclusive. He posits that "one cannot specify the influence of size without also specifying the investment required, the ability of the adopting firms to tolerate risk, the value of the information that the seller can provide to potential buyers, and the complexity of the organization" (p. 38). He goes on to argue that early adopting firms are those:

1. For whom the innovation offers the greatest *relative advantage,* as measured by expected incremental profit
2. That can best tolerate the *risk* in adoption, as measured by the amount of investment required and the maximum possible loss
3. That have the highest *level of aspiration,* as indicated by recent profit-ability trends and market shares
4. For whom the *information* about the innovation which is provided has the greatest value

These propositions, while intuitively interesting, have not been subjected to empirical testing.

Underlying all of these studies is the perceived profit potential (or cost reduction potential) of an innovation and the firm's ability to raise funds to secure such an innovation. The characteristics of the innovating firm are bound to vary by industry and type of innovation.

Within retailing, Allvine (1968) has studied the acceptance of promotional "games" as a product innovation among supermarket chains. The innovators, he found, could be characterized as "offensive" in their marketing strategy and as operating under a less "provincial" (or more "cosmopolitan") business philosophy. Curhan (1969) has examined innovation of a much more discontinuous nature in retailing—the diffusion of new organization forms, for example, supermarkets and soft goods discount stores. His major conclusion is that the innovators were entrepreneurs from outside the dominant, conventional distributive channels. Star (1969) has found that executives in large-scale retail operations are significantly more innovative in regard to new operating *methods* than in regard to new institutional forms of retailing or new products.

This raises the interesting question of how often the early adopters of a new product, process, or organizational structure are nontraditional industry members. It was not A&P or the Kroger Company which innovated by the adoption of supermarkets. It was not Marshall Field or J. L. Hudson which established the first discount software store. It has been the chemical companies and not the textile companies which have developed new miracle fibers. The "steam car" as well as the "electric car" are not being developed by firms in the automobile industry. Neither can the role of government in industrial innovation be ignored, for federal agencies are increasingly sponsoring the application of innovative techniques, products or services which the private sector might otherwise dismiss from consideration because the perceived benefits would be outweighed by the attendant costs, risks, and problems of implementation. This is particularly true of innovations promising national prestige, military security, or social benefits, which might be difficult to quantify in dollar terms.

Thus, the Anglo–French supersonic airliner, the Concorde, is an innovation which confers prestige on the two sponsoring countries. Meantime, social benefit is exemplified in the development of new rapid transit systems aimed at combatting the problems posed by increasing automobile traffic. One such case is the gas turbine–powered TurboTrain, developed by United Aircraft (not a traditional manufacturer of railroad equipment) and operated under contract for the Department of Transportation by Penn Central on the Boston–New York route. It seems unlikely that this innovation would have been developed or introduced without government sponsorship.

Viewed overall, the factors characterizing industrial innovators are certainly diverse, disorganized, and incomplete. In contrast to rural sociology, no conceptual framework has been developed to account for diffusion; and this is, therefore, a challenging field for further research and theorizing.

CHARACTERISTICS OF THE INNOVATING DECISION-GROUP

Nearly every study of industrial diffusion cites the attitude of management as a critical factor in the adoption of innovations. However, insufficient research has been done in this area to provide any useful and more specific generalizations. Mansfield (1968), for example, infers that noneconomic variables are sometimes more important in determining a firm's time in adoption; he states, "The personality attributes, interest, training, and other characteristics of top and middle management may play a very important role in determining how quickly a firm introduces an innovation" (p. 205).

Hypotheses as to the characteristics of people within innovating firms have been proposed, but few have been convincingly tested. Carter and Williams's findings (1959) point to factors such as cosmopolitanism (high quality of outside contacts and willingness to share knowledge), good communications internally and externally coupled with effective coordination, a positive attitude to science and technology, and the application of sound management techniques (modern methods, cost and profitability consciousness, forward planning, and so on) as primary characteristics of the management of innovating firms. Green and Sieber (1967) find that the overwhelmingly important variables describing innovators are "heavy buyers with low brand loyalty" (p. 253).

Again, this evidence is incomplete and only enough to suggest some variables for more comprehensive research. We will now proceed to an examination of the consumer innovator, on whom a body of literature is being developed and consistent findings are beginning to appear.

THE CONSUMER INNOVATOR PROFILE

Evidence regarding the characteristics of consumer innovators is provided in twenty-one studies within the marketing tradition of diffusion research. This research spans a wide range of product categories, sampling populations, and research methodologies. Unfortunately, it also spans a wide range of definitions of innovators.

A summary of consumer research findings, listing the most important variables studied and relationships found, is provided in Table 4.3, which combines results across product categories. Tables 4.4 and 4.5 focus on the appliance innovator and the grocery products innovator. These are the product

Table 4.3   Factors Related to Consumer Innovativeness across Product Categories

Factor	Number of Studies and Relationships Shown*		
	Positive	None	Negative
Demographic Factors			
Age	1	6	4
Education	7	3	0
Income	9	4	0
Occupational Status	6	5	0
Number of Children	1	8	1

Table 4.3—Continued

Factor	Number of Studies and Relationships Shown*		
	Positive	None	Negative
Communication Behavior			
Print Readership	7	2	0
Television Viewership	1	3	1
Social Interaction Factors			
Social Participation:			
Informal	6	6	0
Formal	4	3	0
Opinion Leadership	10	3	0
Cosmopolitanism	1	3	0
Social Mobility	4	0	0
Norm on Innovation	6	0	0
Attitudinal, Perceptual, and			
Personality Factors			
Venturesomeness	5	0	0
Perceived Risk	0	4	5
Self-Perception of Innovativeness	2	0	0
Personality:			
Inventories†	2	3	0
Other-Directedness	1	5	0
Generalized Self-confidence	1	1	0
Attitude Toward Innovations	8	0	0
Value Factors			
Religious Participation	0	1	1
Values	1	0	0
Consumption Patterns			
Product Category Usage Rate	7	1	0
Number of Stores Shopped	1	0	1
Willingness to Try New Products	4	1	0
Brand Loyalty	0	1	3

* In the derivation of this table, a number of judgments had to be made. Not all studies reported significance levels of results, and a variety of statistical techniques was used when significance levels were reported. Certain definitional difficulties were also involved, since what appeared to be equivalent concepts were not always presented as such; or, operational definitions did not always suggest equivalent concepts.

† By personality "inventories" is meant administration of instruments measuring a variety of traits. Other studies discussed in this chapter have sometimes shown specific variables to be related to personality.

Source: Based on research as reported by Advertest Research, Inc. (1958); Andrus (1965); Arndt (1968); William E. Bell (1963) and Lazer and Bell (1966); Bylund (1963); Cunningham (1966); Engel, Kollat, and Blackwell (1969); Frank and Massy (1963) and Frank, Massy, and Morrison (1964); Gorman (1966); Graham (1956); Gruen (1960); King (1964); Opinion Research Corporation (1959); Pessemier et al. (1967); Popielarz (1967); Robertson (1966); Robertson (1968d) and Robertson and Myers (1969); Rossiter and Robertson (1968); Sheth (1968); Tigert (1969); and Whyte (1954).

Table 4.4   Factors Related to Consumer Innovativeness for Appliances

Characteristic	Number of Studies and Relationships Shown*		
	Positive	None	Negative
Demographic Factors			
Age	0	3	2
Education	5	0	0
Income	6	0	0
Occupational Status	5	1	0
Number of Children	0	4	1
Communication Behavior			
Print Readership	2	1	0
Television Viewership	1	1	0
Social Interaction Factors			
Social Participation:			
Informal	4	1	0
Formal	2	1	0
Opinion Leadership	4	0	0
Cosmopolitanism	0	2	0
Social Mobility	1	0	0
Norm on Innovation	2	0	0
Attitudinal, Perceptual, and			
Personality Factors			
Venturesomeness	2	0	0
Perceived Risk	0	1	0
Personality:			
Inventories†	1	1	0
Other-Directedness	0	1	0
Generalized Self-confidence	0	0	0
Attitude toward Innovation	3	0	0
Value Factors			
Religious Participation	0	0	0
Values	0	0	0
Consumption Patterns			
Product Category Usage Rate	3	0	0
Number of Stores Shopped	0	0	1
Willingness to Try New Products	2	0	0
Brand Loyalty	0	0	0

* In the derivation of this table, a number of judgments had to be made. Not all studies reported significance levels of results, and a variety of statistical techniques was used when significance levels were reported. Certain definitional difficulties were also involved, since what appeared to be equivalent concepts were not always presented as such; or, operational definitions did not always suggest equivalent concepts.

† By personality "inventories" is meant administration of instruments measuring a variety of traits. Other studies discussed in this chapter have sometimes shown specific variables to be related to personality.

Source: Based on research as reported by Advertest Research, Inc. (1958); Andrus (1965); William E. Bell (1963) and Lazer and Bell (1966); Gorman (1966); Robertson (1966); Robertson (1968d) and Robertson and Myers (1969); and Whyte (1954).

Characteristic	Number of Studies and Relationships Shown*		
	Positive	None	Negative
Demographic Factors			
Age	0	2	1
Education	1	2	0
Income	1	2	0
Occupational Status	0	3	0
Number of Children	1	3	0
Communication Behavior			
Print Readership	1	1	0
Television Viewership	0	0	0
Social Interaction Factors			
Social Participation:			
Informal	0	3	0
Formal	1	1	0
Opinion Leadership	2	2	0
Cosmopolitanism	0	0	0
Social Mobility	2	0	0
Norm on Innovation	2	0	0
Attitudinal, Perceptual, and			
Personality Factors			
Venturesomeness	0	0	0
Perceived Risk	3	0	0
Self-Perception of Innovativeness	1	0	0
Personality:			
Inventories†	0	1	0
Other-Directedness	1	1	0
Generalized Self-confidence	0	1	0
Attitude toward Innovation	3	0	0
Value Factors			
Religious Participation	0	1	0
Values	0	0	0
Consumption Patterns			
Product Category Usage Rate	3	1	0
Number of Stores Shopped	1	0	0
Willingness to Try New Products	2	0	0
Brand Loyalty	0	1	2

* In the derivation of this table, a number of judgments had to be made. Not all studies reported significance levels of results, and a variety of statistical techniques was used when significance levels were reported. Certain definitional difficulties were also involved since what appeared to be equivalent concepts were not always presented as such; or operational definitions did not always suggest equivalent concepts.

† By personality "inventories" is meant administration of instruments measuring a variety of traits. Other studies, as discussed in this chapter, have sometimes shown specific variables to be related to personality.

Source: Based on research as reported by Arndt (1968); Bylund (1963); Cunningham (1966); Frank and Massy (1963) and Frank, Massy, and Morrison (1964); Pessemier et al. (1967), Robertson (1968*d*) and Robertson and Myers (1969); and Sheth (1968).

categories where the greatest amount of research evidence is available.[1] Many of the variables used in the consumer research tradition are taken from the rural sociology tradition, although some variables are unique to consumer research.

DEMOGRAPHIC FACTORS

Among the demographic factors, *income* most often is found to be associated with innovativeness. In the thirteen studies where this variable is examined, nine show higher income level to be associated with higher innovativeness, while four show a lack of relationship. The positive association between income and innovativeness is uniformly the case for appliances (see Table 4.4), whereas other product categories show weak relationships.

Where the income-innovation relationship is positive, it may not be entirely linear. Frank and Massy (1963), for example, suggest that they found non-linearities for the income variable as related to new product adoption. Cancian (1967) has brought to bear data to show that a curvilinear relationship is to be expected (at least in farmer adoption), since middle-income people are less willing to take risks and tend to be the more conservative element in a society.

Level of *education* also shows a pronounced relationship to innovativeness. On an across-product category basis, seven out of ten studies show higher education level to coincide with greater new product adoption. Again, this relationship is due primarily to results for appliance innovativeness, while the other product categories show inconclusive patterns. The same holds with regard to *occupational status*. Of the six studies showing a positive relationship with innovativeness (Table 4.3), five are studies of appliance adoption (Table 4.4), while occupational status appears unrelated to innovativeness in other product categories such as grocery products (Table 4.5).

Age tends to show a lack of relationship to innovativeness, although some evidence points to a younger innovator. This finding is consistent across product categories. The *number of children* in the family is unrelated to innovativeness in eight out of ten cases.

COMMUNICATION BEHAVIOR

It appears that greater *print readership* is associated most often with higher innovativeness, while *television viewership* is generally unrelated to innovativeness. Again, this finding would have to be examined more closely on a product category basis, and not enough research has been conducted within product categories to provide definitive conclusions. For example, it might be expected that television viewership would be related to grocery

[1] The number of consumer studies by product category follows: appliances, 7; grocery products, 7; fashion, 3; mixed, 7. One of the twenty-one consumer studies provided results for more than one product category.

product innovativeness, but this had not been tested. It also might be expected that print readership (in this case, magazines) would be highly related to fashion innovativeness, and the two studies testing this relationship report such a finding.

There has been a tendency, in line with the two-step flow-of-communication hypothesis, to expect innovators to be more exposed to mass media. In general, however, such a relationship should not be expected, since by their very nature, such media are mass and pervasive. Differences are only found when exposure to media relevant to a product category is examined; for example, fashion innovators do read more fashion magazines, but are not more exposed to mass media in general.

SOCIAL INTERACTION FACTORS

The innovator is sometimes higher on both *informal social participation* (friends and neighbors) and *formal social participation* (organizational memberships). This finding is again most pronounced for the appliance product category and a lack of relationship is common for the other product categories. It has been argued by Elihu Katz (1961) that the greater the risk in adoption, the more the need for social legitimation. Socially integrated members of a community will, of course, be in a better position to secure legitimation and to innovate in product purchase. Thus, it can be argued that social integration should be closely related to innovativeness only for risky product categories, such as appliances; and the relationship need not hold to the same extent for other, less risky product categories.

There is no evidence, however, to suggest that the innovator may sometimes be a "marginal man," or a socially nonintegrated member of society. This position has been suggested sometimes by rural sociologists, including Rogers (1962b), who states, "Agricultural innovators were perceived as deviant by other members of the social system. Innovators perceive themselves as deviant from the norms of their local social system . . . innovators *are* in step with a different drummer" (p. 107). Such a conclusion may be valid in the agricultural arena (although this possibility is not supported by Table 4.2) when the norms are traditional and against change. Such a conclusion may also occur when innovators are defined strictly as the first 2.5 percent of a social system's members to adopt. In consumer research, we have never analyzed this initial small percentage of adopters.

An association between *opinion leadership* and innovativeness is shown in ten out of thirteen studies. This is a critical relationship because so much of diffusion theory is built around the influencing role of the innovator. The extent of the innovativeness-influential relationship will be related again to the risk involved in adoption and to the conspicuousness of the product. Thus, if there is a high risk in adoption, greater advice is likely to be sought by later adopters. We would expect, therefore, a stronger relationship between innovativeness and opinion leadership for durables than for convenience items, which are subject to trial at nominal cost. Furthermore, if the item is conspicuous, such as clothing, the innovator is in a position to be more influential, although he need not be *most* influential within the social system.

The *cosmopolitanism* variable has not been subject to much research and the only report of a positive association is in the "Tastemaker" studies (Opinion Research Corporation, 1959). Based on the evidence to date, however, a lack of relationship is probably to be expected, except for such "cosmopolitan" products as car rentals and credit cards. It would appear that, in general, consumer information sources are so diffuse that the individual need not look beyond the local community. How cosmopolitan does the consumer have to be to learn of a new food product? It will be advertised on national television and in shelter media, and there really is no cosmopolitan source of information.

Only four studies have assessed the impact of *social mobility* upon innovativeness, and all have shown a positive relationship. This variable seems to deserve further research. People moving up in social class may innovate to indicate their having arrived or to provide a means of conspicuous consumption. Or, perhaps the socially mobile person is going through new life experiences and is therefore more accustomed to newness and more drawn to new product experiences.

Finally, innovators reflect a more favorable *norm* toward buying new things. This is an expression of how the individual consumer perceives the relevant standards regarding innovative behavior within his social system. Interestingly, there is a tendency for both innovators and noninnovators to reflect some cautiousness toward new purchases, although, of course, noninnovators reflect considerably greater caution. The norm is that one must have a "need" for a new product before buying it.

ATTITUDINAL, PERCEPTUAL, AND PERSONALITY FACTORS

Venturesomeness refers to willingness to take risks—both in product performance and psychosocial implications—in the purchase of new products. Rogers (1962b) has referred to venturesomeness as the major value of the innovator; and in the five consumer studies examining this variable, it has been found to be uniformly related to high innovativeness. Robertson (1966) found venturesomeness to be the leading predictor of consumer innovativeness toward a small appliance innovation. Popielarz (1967) found "breadth of categorization" to be related to innovativeness. A broad categorizer is a person who places a wide range of stimuli in the same class and under a common label. According to Popielarz, the broad categorizer is willing to run risks of buying some products which may not prove satisfactory—he has a high tolerance for type-I errors. The narrow categorizer, in contrast, restricts his purchases to familiar brands and runs the risk of missing some products that would be better than his present loyalties—he has a high tolerance for type-II errors.

Related to the venturesomeness, or risk-taking, concept is *perceived risk*. It is not known whether the venturesome consumer sees less risk in a new product or whether the risk does not concern him. There may even be purchase occasions where risk is sought, as for fashion merchandise. There undoubtedly is an interdependence between venturesomeness and perceived risk which deserves study.

In a majority of studies it has been found (see Table 4.3) that perceived risk is negatively related to innovativeness. In the nine studies testing this relationship, mostly among grocery products, five report such a negative relationship and four report a lack of relationship. The innovator, for the most part, therefore, is likely to be a risk taker and is likely to perceive less risk in purchase as well.

A finding with considerable potential for advertising strategy is that *innovators perceive themselves to be innovators*. Only two studies have examined this relationship, but it seems to hold promise in that there may be a self-selection of innovators in response to innovative communications.

Personality as a predictor of innovativeness does not produce particularly meaningful results. In the administration of personality inventories such as the Thurstone Temperament Schedule and the California Personality Inventory, two studies have reported positive findings, while three studies have reported a lack of relationship. Other-directedness, or orientation toward other people, is related to innovativeness in only one case, while five cases show a lack of relationship. Generalized self-confidence has been found to be associated with innovativeness in one out of two studies. There also have been some incidental personality findings, not reported in Table 4.3. King (1964), for example, found early buyers to be higher in "achievement/competitiveness" and higher in "change orientation" than later buyers or non-buyers. Bylund (1963) found innovators for food products to be more "optimistic."

Brody and Cunningham (1968) have recently argued that personality should not be expected to relate to all conditions of consumer behavior. They show preliminary evidence that personality can be a useful predictor of behavior under conditions of high brand loyalty (assuming conditions of high specific self-confidence and high perceived performance risk). Innovators, who are not brand-loyal and are generally low in perceived performance risk, would not be expected to show distinguishing personality traits in accordance with the Brody-Cunningham conceptual framework. Furthermore, a number of authors question the use of standardized personality tests, which measure generally developed tendencies, and argue for the development of personality measures more closely related to purchase behavior. A recent study by Tigert

(1969), which measures psychometric variables closely related to purchasing, finds some significant relationship between those variables and innovativeness.

Attitude toward innovations, as would be expected, is considerably more favorable for innovators. This has been found to be consistently true and is illustrated in innovator versus noninnovator comments such as the following (Robertson, 1966):

Question:	How do you feel about buying new things that come out for home?
Innovator response:	"I'm very interested in trying them. The minute I see new things advertised I try to find them in the stores."
Innovator response:	"I'm all for this. For me, the thing is they've brought them out because there's a need. A lot of work and thought goes into new products. Most new things are time savers. I'll pay more money for anything that saves time."
Noninnovator response:	"We're not real anxious to buy new things. We're quite conservative about what we buy and think a long time before we do."
Noninnovator response:	"I am very conservative. I'm very slow when it comes to buying new things" (p. 111).

VALUE FACTORS

The subject of *values* has not received much attention in consumer diffusion research. Only one study—the Opinion Research Corporation's "Tastemaker" research (1959)—has intensively assessed the effect of value factors upon consumer innovative behavior, and this study did find certain distinguishable patterns. High-mobile early adopters tended to be more committed to travel, intellectual and cultural pursuits, social life, political matters, and various recreational forms (p. 89). *Religious participation* has been studied as an incidental variable in two studies; and while one study found no relationship to innovativeness, another study found less frequent church attendance to coincide with higher innovativeness.

CONSUMPTION PATTERNS

It has been documented in seven out of eight studies that innovators for a new product are *heavy users* of that product or similar products. The innovator for a new kind of coffee is likely to be a heavy coffee drinker. The innovator for a new telephone product is likely to have a larger monthly telephone bill. This, of course, makes it particularly crucial to secure innovator adoption, since innovators may account for a disproportionate amount of product category sales.

The findings on *number of stores shopped* are entirely inconclusive. The rationale for why innovators should shop a greater or a lesser number of stores has never been presented. Innovators are found to be higher on *willingness to try new products*, but this is almost tautological.

It would seem logical that innovators be *nonbrand-loyal*, and three out of four studies find this to be the case. The innovator is an experimenter, and it may well be that he is also the first to *discontinue* use of a once-new product and to adopt succeeding new products.

SUMMARY OF FACTORS

It is not possible to cite the relative predictive ability of individual factors or sets of factors. The analysis to this point only allows us to talk of the "importance" of factors, based on the number of studies showing positive, negative, or lack of relationships. Even this is deceiving because while some factors, such as opinion leadership, have been assessed in a significant number of studies, other factors, such as brand loyalty, have been assessed in a very limited number of studies and results must be viewed as fairly inconclusive.

A summary table, such as Table 4.3, must also be cautiously interpreted, since as will be discussed next, innovativeness is not a generalized across–product category phenomenon. If a marketing program is to be oriented toward innovator characteristics, it must be focused on the relevant characteristics for that product or product category. As shown in Tables 4.4 and 4.5, the characteristics of the appliance innovator and the grocery products innovator are not identical. There is a serious question, in fact, of how usable the grocery products innovator profile is, due to the large number of nonsignificant relationships found and due to the small amount of evidence when significant relationships are found—for example, in regard to social mobility and brand loyalty.

A further caution may be in order because of the natural tendency for positive research findings to be reported, resulting in the list of nonsignificant or negative findings being somewhat understated. If a researcher arrives at a set of nonsignificant findings, he is less likely to submit his work for publication and, if submitted, it is less likely to be published. There is an inherent bias toward the reporting of significant positive relationships.

No available study has measured all of the sets of factors summarized in Table 4.3. It appears that the social interaction factors and consumption factors possibly might be better predictors of innovativeness than demographic, communication, attitudinal, and value factors. This, however, is indeed a tenuous generalization and cannot be supported. It would also be expected that the impact of each set of factors varies by product category. Thus, while demographic factors are of significance in appliance innovativeness, they are almost entirely unrelated to grocery product innovativeness.

Some studies have, of course, looked at the relative impact of specific factors contributing to innovativeness. Arndt (1968) assessed the relative importance of twelve factors, using discriminant analysis techniques to separate innovators from noninnovators for a new coffee brand. Four of these factors explained 84 percent of the difference in innovativeness between the two groups. In descending order of importance these factors were lack of brand loyalty, deal proneness, high usage rate of coffee, and low perceived risk.

Frank, Massy, and Morrison (1964) also used discriminant analysis to separate adopters and nonadopters for a new coffee brand. The set of explanatory factors which they used was, however, different from that of Arndt. While they do not provide the relative percentage differences in innovativeness explained, they do rank the variables contributing most to innovativeness. The six most important variables, in order of importance, are (1) average number of purchases per shopping trip, (2) low brand loyalty, (3) a nonworking wife, (4) high average pounds of coffee purchased per shopping trip, (5) high proportion of shopping trips on Friday, and (6) high proportion of purchases of beverages. These variables obviously are highly purchase-situation-specific.

A similar discriminant procedure has been used by King (1964) to distinguish early buyers of hats from other consumers. Using twenty-one variables, he was able to classify correctly 74 percent of his sample into early buyer and nonbuyer groups. The six most important variables were (1) frequency of hair permanents, (2) social visiting with other women, (3) family income level, (4) frequency of changes in hair style, (5) attendance at spectator sports, and (6) a psychological characteristic of change orientation.

As a final example, Robertson and Kennedy (1968) used discriminant analysis techniques to test the relative importance of a number of factors in the adoption of a new telephone product and to assess the predictive value of the set of characteristics. Seven factors were used in the research and were found to significantly discriminate between innovators and noninnovators while correctly classifying 75 percent of the respondents. The factors making the greatest contribution in discriminating between the two groups and the relative "difference" explained by each are as follows: (1) venturesomeness, 35 percent; (2) social mobility, 29 percent; (3) financial privilegedness, 11 percent; and (4) social integration, 11 percent. In other words, these four factors accounted for an 86-percent "contribution" toward innovative behavior.

IS THERE A GENERAL INNOVATOR?

There has been a tendency in the popular marketing literature, and even among some serious researchers, to talk of the innovator as a "superinnovator." Many people implicitly assume that if an innovator for one product can be identified, then he can be sold a host of other new products as well. Rogers (1962b) raised the issue of consistency of innovativeness, but was only able to conclude that "There is no clear-cut evidence as to whether or not innovating behavior is completely consistent," but he did postulate that "it is doubtful whether an individual who is an innovator for one idea is a laggard for another idea" (p. 187).

A rigorous examination of this issue within the consumer diffusion research tradition leads to the conclusion that *consistency of innovativeness cannot be expected across product categories, but can be expected within product categories and, sometimes, between related product categories*. The paragraphs to follow will document this conclusion.

INNOVATIVENESS ACROSS PRODUCT CATEGORIES

Very few consumer studies have examined innovativeness in more than one product category. Graham (1956) studied diffusion of five diverse innovations including Blue Cross insurance and television and found that no one social class was consistently innovative in responding to all of these innovations. Opinion Research Corporation (1959) has suggested that the "high mobiles" in the population which it identified were earlier to adopt a host of products from yachting club memberships to stereo equipment to ballet slippers. The documentation for this is inadequate for us to assess this finding.

Robertson and Myers (1969) examined the relationship of innovativeness between product categories for appliances, clothing, and food products. Correlation analysis revealed that appliance and food innovativeness were significantly related at the $p = .01$ level, as were appliance and clothing innovativeness, while clothing and food innovativeness were related at the $p = .05$ level. These interrelationships of innovativeness by product categories, though statistically significant ($r = .20$ to $.28$), are pragmatically low; and these authors dispute the notion that innovativeness is a general trait possessed by the individual.

While not presenting data to support his view, King (1964) also disputes the idea of a general innovator. His argument is that innovators are active in product contexts which are consistent with their psychosocial makeup. If they do innovate across product categories, it is likely to be in complementary categories.

INNOVATIVENESS WITHIN A PRODUCT CATEGORY

It has been documented in a number of studies that innovativeness is consistent within a product category, although minor disconfirming evidence is also available. Whyte (1954), for example, found that the innovator for airconditioners was also likely to own such other appliance innovations as a freezer and a dishwasher. Consistency of innovativeness within the appliance product category was the conclusion. Similarly, Robertson (1966) in a diffusion study for an appliance innovation, found that the innovators for this new product were significantly more likely to own other appliance innovations as well. Andrus (1965) parallels this finding and finds consistency in the adoption rates for consumer durable purchases.

The confirming evidence cited is from research on appliance innovativeness and this constitutes most of the research which addresses this question. Arndt (1968) in a study of food innovativeness concludes that "within the 'food consumption system,' [food] innovators possess a generalized receptiveness to new products" (p. 83). From Frank, Massy, and Morrison (1964), however, it can be interpreted that the "product category" may have to be as narrowly interpreted as beverages, rather than food, before consistency of innovativeness occurs.

INNOVATIVENESS BETWEEN RELATED PRODUCT CATEGORIES

Relative consistency of innovativeness may extend beyond one product category to related product categories or related parts of the consumption system. In farming, for example, equipment and practices are often interrelated, so that an innovator for one practice is also a likely innovator for related practices. This may also be true among ultimate consumers, where an innovator for high fashion items may also innovate in the related area of cosmetics and personal care products.

It is, furthermore, difficult to define a product category. We have tended to classify food or appliance or clothing products as categories. However, a more relevant classification scheme might be based on a dimension such as "convenience" or "visual display" and we might find considerable consistency of innovativeness for products high on these attributes.

WHY REACH INNOVATORS?

The importance of the innovator in the diffusion process stems essentially from three reasons.

1. Innovators account for initial levels of penetration.
2. Innovators influence later adopters.
3. Innovators influence retail product offerings.

These reasons suggest that the innovator can speed diffusion of the new product and lower the chance of new product failure.

INITIAL PENETRATION

That innovators account for initial levels of penetration is true by definition. The implications for marketers are, however, in terms of how quickly and efficiently such innovators are converted into product users. Most product failures never gain innovator adoption. If innovators do, in fact, possess distinguishing characteristics from later adopters, then market segmentation would seem to be in order as a strategy. A marketing program to gain new product diffusion would be varied as penetration is achieved to appeal directly to the characteristics of each adopter category.

Thus, if innovators for a product area are found to be essentially venturesome, that is, willing to take risks and to engage in daring behavior, and especially if they also perceive themselves as such, then advertising strategies focusing on this trait may be appropriate. It may also be possible to select media to maximize exposure to venturesome individuals. Alfred Politz (1956), for example, has suggested on the basis of his program of media research that some magazines have larger proportions of venturesome readers than others. The advertising strategy appropriately would be changed when innovator penetration had been attained and when it then became necessary to appeal to more cautious potential adopters.

A rapid product takeoff, whereby innovator penetration is soon achieved, may yield several advantages for the firm. An obvious advantage is a quicker return on investment. If initial diffusion can be achieved quickly, other benefits may accrue to the firm. Word-of-mouth advertising may recommend the product, thus supplementing the firm's advertising program and leading to continued rapid adoption. This may be tied largely to the interaction, or snowball effect, discussed in Chapter 2, whereby future adoption is a function of past adoption.

INNOVATOR INFLUENCE OF LATER ADOPTERS

It has been documented fairly extensively that innovators influence later adopters. Such influence may be direct, as in discussions between innovators and potential adopters whereby product evaluations or recommendations are made. Such influence may also be indirect, whereby the innovator provides exposure for the innovation. King (1964) describes the fashion innovator as "the earliest visual communicator of the new season's styles for the mass of fashion consumers" (p. 325). If the innovator does not perform this visual display function, then other consumers are less likely to be aware of the item's existence and, even if aware, are less likely to feel that adopting the item is socially acceptable.

The innovator, then, provides *social display* leading to awareness; he may provide *legitimation* for other consumers that the item is an acceptable purchase; and he may directly *encourage* others to buy. The social display and legitimation functions are most relevant to the extent that the item is, in fact, visible (clothing, for example, but not laundry detergent) and to the extent that the item requires legitimation, which is largely a function of perceived risk. The consumer may require social legitimation for fashion items but may buy a new laundry detergent and use her experience with it to secure legitimation for future purchase of the same brand.

Social Display

Innovator performance of the social display function is evidenced in research by Robertson (1966), in which 77 percent of the innovators for a new telephone product either directly or indirectly influenced visitors to their homes in regard to the new product. Furthermore, most of this influence seemed to come via *social display* of the item. Thus, 47 percent of in-home visitors noticed it or used it and 13 percent of the visitors asked to be shown it, whereas only 17 percent of the respondents took the initiative in showing or mentioning the new product.

A couple of fairly typical comments for innovators reflect the dynamics involved in the social display function.

Question: Do people know you have a Touch-Tone telephone, or, if they don't, do you show it to them?

Answer: "I don't think I point it out on purpose, but people who use the phone are fascinated with it if they don't have it themselves."

Answer: "Those who come in and use it seem impressed with it. I don't show them unless they ask how it works" (p. 155).

Legitimation

King (1964) has observed that "the innovator's early selections and reactions to the fashion inventory often give certain styles 'legitimacy' in the mass consumer market" (p. 325). Whereas the innovator may be willing to take new product purchase risks and may even achieve satisfaction from such avant-garde behavior, later adopters seem to seek risk minimization by late purchasing and may seek more legitimation than innovators. Later adopters often reflect a wait-and-see attitude whereby they wish to gain from the experience of earlier adopters.

Encouragement

Innovators may also verbally communicate encouragement to adopt by calling attention to the item or recommending its usage. William E. Bell (1963) found that approximately two thirds of the appliance innovators in his sample gave advice about the new products and that "Of the innovators who gave opinions or demonstrated the products, 68 percent asserted that their questioning friends then purchased the innovation" (p. 93). Robertson (1966) found that one third of the innovators for the Touch-Tone telephone could name at least one person who followed them in adopting the product and who credited themselves with at least partial influence in that adoption decision.

INNOVATOR INFLUENCE IN PRODUCT OFFERINGS

Initial market reaction to a product may often determine subsequent response within distribution channels. As explained by General Electric researcher Robert Igoe (1967), "the retailers see that the product is moving, and this encourages them to feature the item more prominently in their stores, to advertise it in newspapers and to build their stock of it by reordering." Therefore, initial penetration levels may encourage a snowball effect, based on innovator social display, legitimation, and recommendation functions, and on channel response to the item. Retailers may use new products, it is suggested, to enhance their own innovative images and, most basically, because new products frequently carry higher profit margins.

King (1964) has concluded similarly that innovators may influence retailer stocks and promotion. In the fashion realm he has also emphasized that the innovator may have major impact on the season's product lines, for the innovator provides early feedback on new offerings; and it is on this information that major style commitments often are made by manufacturers.

CAN THE INNOVATOR BE REACHED?

The critical advantages of quickly gaining innovator penetration raise the all-too-relevant question of whether innovators can be efficiently reached. It has been suggested, without elaboration, that media may be selected to reach individuals more likely to be innovators and, more importantly, that promotional appeals may be aimed at innovator characteristics.

On the basis of the research evidence summarized in this chapter, it does appear that the innovator *is* different from later adopters and that a distinguishable set of characteristics can be ascertained. The profile of the appliance innovator is particularly pronounced; and some profiling occurs for the grocery products innovator, although the latter category may well be too broad to produce a clear pattern. The more narrowly defined a product category—for example, frozen foods rather than grocery products in general— the more pronounced we would expect the profile of the innovator to be.

Based on a characterization of the product category innovator, such as that of the appliance innovator in Table 4.4, a number of marketing strategies can be initiated to secure rapid innovator adoption of a new product.

REACHING KNOWN INNOVATORS

It has been concluded tentatively that innovativeness is a generalized phenomenon for a product category. If this is the case, some manufacturers may be in the fortunate position of having records of innovators from previous new product offerings. Such records often are based on warranty files. General Electric, for example, has used warranty records to conduct research characterizing innovators (Igoe, 1967). These manufacturers may then be able to utilize direct mail to encourage adoption of subsequent innovations within the same product category.

Illinois Bell Telephone Company was provided with information that the most likely adopter of a new telephone product, such as the Picture-Phone, would be a consumer who previously adopted such new equipment as Touch-Tone telephones, extension phones, and color phones. It was then possible, based on available records, to determine in a community the households with the greatest probability of new equipment adoption.

USING APPROPRIATE MEDIA

The profile of the appliance innovator clearly suggests that print media will be more effective than television media. Choice of media, of course, will depend on the product category. Furthermore, it should be possible to select a media mix which will deliver an audience with traits similar to the innovator's. For example, in view of the higher educational and income levels of innovators, selective magazines, which deliver such a profile, should be chosen, rather than mass magazines.

USING RELEVANT APPEALS

The promotional campaign should be designed to appeal specifically to innovator characteristics. The appliance innovator is higher in income, education, occupational prestige, social interaction, opinion leadership, social mobility, venturesomeness, and other variables. He also perceives less risk in buying, perceives himself as an innovator, and expresses greater willingness to try new products.

Faced with a myriad of messages, the innovator is, of course, going to choose the messages most consistent with his self-image. Because innovators perceive themselves as such, promotional appeals can play directly upon this theme. The advertiser should probably focus on the newness of the product to achieve maximum attention. Innovators also have been found to perceive themselves as more venturesome, more popular, and more financially privileged. Thus, an advertising campaign providing symbols congruent with these characteristics would also match the actual self-concept of the innovator.

NEW PRODUCT ACCESSIBILITY

The greater the accessibility of the innovation, the better the chance for innovators to respond selectively. This may involve free sampling, demonstrations, or critical placement of the new product.

SELECTING APPROPRIATE DISTRIBUTION CHANNELS

The characteristics of the innovator should be taken into account in initial distribution channel placement. At a practical level, distribution might be sought in certain communities before others and even in certain areas of the country. Type of retail outlet for initial distribution—for example, department store versus specialty or discount store—might also be a relevant consideration.

OVERCOMING COGNITIVE DISSONANCE

The innovator will be susceptible to cognitive dissonance and will not have prior adopters to turn to in order to reduce such dissonance. If the dissonance cannot be resolved, the innovator is likely to dissuade fellow consumers from buying. This places an additional burden on marketing communications to provide dissonance-reducing information. For expensive consumer durables, a letter from the manufacturer confirming the wisdom of the purchase may be appropriate; but for most other products, advertising and package information must perform the dissonance-reduction task.

SUMMARY

The basic conclusion is that innovators tend to possess distinguishing characteristics from later adopters. This suggests that the innovator concept may provide a valid and meaningful form of market segmentation.

Findings from twenty-one studies assessing consumer innovator characteristics were synthesized, and an overall innovator profile was discussed. Among *demographic factors*, income, education, and occupational status were positively related to innovativeness whereas age and number of children were generally unrelated. Among *communication behavior factors*, print readership showed a positive relationship to innovativeness; whereas television viewership was generally unrelated. An analysis of *social interaction factors* showed that innovators tend to have somewhat greater formal (organizational) and informal (friendship) social participation. Opinion leadership, social mobility, and a favorable norm on innovation were all positively associated with innovativeness; but cosmopolitanism exhibited an inconclusive pattern.

Among *attitudinal, perceptual, and personality factors*, venturesomeness was uniformly related in a positive manner to high innovativeness, whereas perceived risk tended to be negatively related. On the basis of highly limited evidence, innovators tended to perceive themselves as such, although personality was not a meaningful predictor of innovativeness. *Consumption patterns* indicated that heavy usage within a product category is positively related to innovativeness, and that brand loyalty is generally negatively related.

The innovator, however, does not tend to be innovative across product categories; his innovativeness tends to be bound to one product category or to closely related product categories. Thus, if a marketing program is to be oriented toward innovator characteristics, it must be based on the characteristics relevant to that product category. A sharper innovator profile can be obtained on a product category basis.

The importance of the innovator in the diffusion process stems from the facts that he accounts for initial levels of penetration and that he may influence later adopters. Innovators potentially can speed the diffusion of new products and may help lower the risks of new product failure. A rapid product takeoff, following early achievement of innovator penetration, may yield advantages to the firm including a quicker return on investment. Later adopters may be directly influenced by word-of-mouth recommendations from innovators. Innovators may also exercise indirect influence by providing social display, which can stimulate awareness among other consumers and serve to legitimate purchase of the product by these individuals.

The research evidence clearly seems to indicate that the consumer innovator *is* different from later adopters. Given the advantages in quickly gaining innovator penetration, the key question remains whether these individuals can be reached efficiently. It was suggested that when innovators are known—as in the case of warranty records—a direct mail campaign may be appropriate. Alternatively, when the firm possesses only a profile of innovator characteristics for its product category, it may still be feasible to select appropriate media—probably print—which can deliver the required audience profile. By ensuring that the resulting campaign provides symbols and appeals congruent with the innovator's needs and self-image, the most effective message may be delivered. At the same time new products should be made easily accessible to innovators in order to encourage self-selection, and care should be taken in selecting appropriate distribution channels.

PART TWO

Communication and Social Influence

CHAPTER 5

COMMUNICATION PROCESSES

The diffusion process is, of course, critically dependent upon the communication of information to potential adopters. Part II, Chapters 5 through 9, examines concepts relating to human communication. The present chapter presents an overview of communication *processes* and the development of

* This chapter in particular has benefited from the insightful comments and suggestions of my colleague Scott Ward.

communication theory. Chapter 6 is a detailed account of communication *structure* and discusses the effects of source, message, and channel attributes on the outcome of a communication transaction.

The remaining three chapters in this part focus on interpersonal communication. Chapter 7 is a theoretical treatment of the occurrence and functioning of personal influence. Chapter 8 considers a model of personal influence and opinion leadership, and Chapter 9 presents marketing considerations to affect the personal influence process.

THE ONE-WAY MODEL OF COMMUNICATION

Historically, communication processes were defined in terms of the elements, actors, and inferred activities in a communication act. These include source, message, channel, audience, and response (see Figure 5.1). The essential nature of this early descriptive model is that communication is a one-way process, flowing *from* the source *to* the receiver. The burden of effort is clearly with the communication source, which, implicitly, *directly affects* the receiver. Consequently, this model is euphemistically called the "hypodermic needle" model.

From the point of view of the new product marketer, the *communicator*, or *source*, is the business enterprise or its designated agents. The *message* is a configuration of elements—words, pictures, sound, movement, facial expressions—which are interdependent and attempt to communicate meaning. *Channels* of communication are the means of information dissemination. Channels may be under the direct control of the marketer or beyond his direct control. Marketer-controlled channels include advertising, personal selling, and sales promotion, whereas nonmarketer-controlled channels include publicity[1] and interpersonal communication, or "word-of-mouth advertising."

The *audience* is that sector of the population to whom the message is

Figure 5.1   A Simplified Model of the Communication Process

Who — says what — by which channel — to whom — with what effect?

---

[1] What distinguishes publicity from other forms of marketing communication is that control is held by the media communicator, not by the marketer. Publicity can be the result of skillful public relations, such as news stories about company contributions to the community; or it can be totally unintended, such as publicity about a company's pollution problems. In neither case does the marketer have control over it, at least, not in the same sense as paid media advertising.

directed. *Response* is designated in this simplified model as purchase of the product and is also a form of *feedback* to the communicator about the success of the communication program.

CRITICISMS OF THE ONE-WAY MODEL

In reality, the "one-way" model is deceivingly simple and bears little resemblance to the evidence presented by communication researchers. It does not adequately account for the varieties and subtleties of possible consumer responses to communication. Two basic faults are involved:

1. The model suggests that most messages get through to consumers.
2. It further suggests that if a message does get through, the consumer will act in accordance with the communicator's goal; that is, he will make a purchase response.

Communication processes can rarely be understood in terms of this "stimulus-response" model. Few messages even reach the consumer, much less elicit some direct response.

Furthermore, if consumer response (product purchase) occurs, it cannot be inferred that this is due directly to the communication event. Sales are influenced by many factors other than communication (such as price, past purchase behavior, distribution, and so on); and usually it is impossible to use sales as a valid or reliable feedback measure.[2] Consequently, marketers use "communication measures" as feedback, usually in an attempt to assess the effectiveness of advertising campaigns or specific advertising messages. These include measures such as recognition of advertising and aided or unaided recall of advertising content. They may be used prior to the advertising campaign, in an attempt to predict the campaign's success, and following the campaign, in an attempt to assess its actual effectiveness.

The assumption underlying the use of communication measures as feedback is that communication precedes and is at least correlated with ultimate sales results. Hierarchy-of-effects models explicitly assume that consumers progress along a continuum of communication effects, such as product awareness and interest, to purchase response. Whereas these assumptions may be questionable, communication measures can provide some indications to marketers of communication effectiveness.[3]

The misleading nature of this simplified one-way model is not often recognized by the public, although it is acknowledged by communication

[2] Under some circumstances, with adequate controls, sales feedback measures are possible: for example, in direct mail and mail order advertising, using coupon returns as communication effectiveness criteria. See Wolfe, Brown, and Thompson (1962). Mayer (1965) also provides a comprehensive review of sales measures.

[3] Perhaps the most often-cited argument for communication measures as feedback is Russell H. Colley's *Defining Advertising Goals for Measured Advertising Results* (1961).

researchers and by any advertising account executive who has ever attempted to trace the impact of an advertising campaign! The image of Madison Avenue boys pulling strings to manipulate the public is part of our folklore, but far from an accurate perception of reality.

THE TWO-STEP FLOW-OF-COMMUNICATION MODEL

One response to the simplified "direct effects" model offered by communication researchers was to suggest that communication does not affect people directly, but works through a web of interpersonal networks. Katz and Lazarsfeld (1955), among others, have proposed that communication follows a "two-step flow." This model was originally derived in research during the 1940 presidential campaign from a study which documented the influence of the individual's "primary group" (family, close friends) on his voting behavior. Radio and the printed page were found to have "only negligible effects on actual vote decisions and particularly minute effects on *changes* in vote decisions" (p. 31); whereas the individual's primary group held the greatest influence over him. His voting decisions, particularly those involving a change in voting behavior, were found to be influenced most often by "other people."

Further analysis indicated that the individuals who were more influential in affecting voting behavior were more in contact and more influenced by mass media than those who were less influential. This is the basis of the "two-step" communication model. It implies basically that the mass media influence opinion leaders, who in turn influence a set of followers. Opinion leaders, according to Katz and Lazarsfeld, are to be found scattered throughout society at all social class levels, in all occupations, and in all communities.

The two-step model represents an improvement over the "direct effects" model, although it also represents an incomplete picture with its particular emphasis on group and opinion leader influence and its general disregard of other important mediating variables. The purpose of the two-step proposal, however, was not to set forth an encompassing theory of communication, so that its proponents cannot be blamed for emphasizing the point which they set out to develop.

At least two important benefits have been gained from the two-step proposal. The first has been to encourage marketers away from an atomistic model of society to a view which recognizes the mediating impact of interpersonal relationships on mass communications effects. The individual does not live alone in society. Instead, each individual is bound to other people by distinctive patterns of social interaction which affect consumption behavior. Mass media communication efforts are generally not a sufficient cause of effect, but instead work amidst mediating factors.

The two-step flow hypothesis has also challenged and changed the notion that ideas and influence flow down the status levels of society in a "trickle-down effect." For example: fashions were assumed to start at upper social class levels and to eventually reach the lower classes. Instead, influence has been found to move most often horizontally among members of similar status levels (King, 1963). Of course, this relatively high incidence of influence exchange within any social class is explainable because most interaction occurs among people in the same social class. The wealthy matron may learn about a new recipe from her cleaning lady, but this is the exception rather than the rule—for the most part she interacts with and is influenced by other upper-status people.

SOME DIFFICULTIES WITH THE TWO-STEP MODEL

Despite the benefits mentioned, the two-step model contains certain disturbing conceptual features and has not proven to be particularly useful in explaining communication processes.

The major shortcomings of the two-step model, as outlined by Rogers (1969), are as follows:

1. It implies that opinion leadership is a dichotomous trait. A given sample of respondents may often be dichotomized into opinion leaders versus followers, but in fact, opinion leadership is a continuous variable, and should certainly be conceptualized (even though not always measured) as such.
2. It implies a competitive rather than a complementary role for mass media and interpersonal communication channels. The two-step flow hypothesis ignores stages in the decision-making process about a new idea . . . Channel differences in the knowledge versus persuasion stage exist for *both* opinion leaders and followers; thus it is not only the opinion leaders who use mass media channels.
3. It ignores the so-called time of knowing. Maybe opinion leaders are simply early knowers of a new idea, who pass the innovation along to later knowers.
4. It implies active opinion leaders and a passive audience, while actually many opinions are actively sought by followers from opinion leaders (p. 222).

In short, the overall criticism of the two-step flow, as originally defined, is that it is oversimplified and does not tell us enough. Far more is involved in the communication process than just two steps.

The operational difficulties with the two-step model, for marketers and other communication sources, are in terms of

1. The identification of opinion leaders.
2. The means by which to influence opinion leaders to promote the product.

The initiative of the communication exchange in the two-step model rests with the communicator. This is noted by the direction of the arrows in Figure 5.2. Yet, *information seeking* also takes place, and the individual to

Figure 5.2   The Two-step Conceptualization

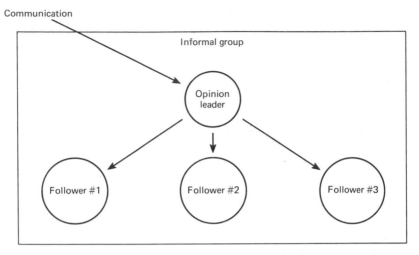

whom a communication is directed is also active in the communication event. The members of the audience, as we have seen, are not "passive patsies being pushed around by communicators" (Bauer, 1967, p. 6).

This tendency to view communication from the communicator's point of view is consistent with our managerial emphasis, but this selective and one-directional perspective can lead to suboptimal decision making. Bauer (1963a), in research on communication processes in the Soviet Union, found that the two most frequently cited information sources for news of what was going on were newspapers (an official source) and word of mouth (hardly an official source). Receiving scarcely any mentions were official information-dissemination sessions which respondents were frequently *required to attend.* The point is that "There was a difference between what the people wanted to know and what the regime wanted them to know. Apparently . . . respondents did not regard meetings as a place where *they* learned what *they* wanted to know" (Bauer, 1963a, p. 4). Much the same is the dilemma of the marketer: what he wants consumers to know may not be what they want to know.

There is an inherent difficulty in the concept of the "opinion leader." It suggests, much as would be the case in a formal organization, that an absolute leader exists for each informal group (see Figure 5.2). Yet *opinion leadership* resides to some extent in all group members. It is hard to believe that even the most uninfluential member does not have some influence—even if it is negative, so that when he recommends something, group members act in a contrary manner. Opinion leadership is a matter of degree, therefore, and some group members will be more influential than others. Moreover, opinion leadership is situation-bound. A group member may be an opinion leader on some matters, but not on others. To single out one member as an opinion leader seems not to reflect the true state of affairs, since he is only relatively more influential. It is necessary to specify how much more influential he is, regarding what topics, and how processes of opinion leadership vary across kinds of social groupings.

An additional conceptual difficulty with the opinion leader concept is that information is assumed to flow only from the mass media to opinion leaders and, in turn, to "followers" (Figure 5.2). Yet opinion leaders are only *more* in touch with mass media. Followers are also in touch with and influenced by mass media. Furthermore, there is no reason why a follower cannot receive the message first and act on it alone or initiate interpersonal communication about the message with others, perhaps including the opinion leader. The power of opinion leaders to influence is overstated, since they will be called upon for advice, formally or informally, in few cases and since their influence will be mediated by other factors. Instead of directly relaying mass media messages and accordingly influencing other group members, the function of the opinion leader is more in the order of editing and filtering mass media material and being in a position to offer advice, should he be requested to do so.

A final conceptual difficulty with the notion of opinion leadership concerns precisely *what* is transmitted interpersonally. In some situations it may be influence; in other cases it may simply be information transmission, relatively free of influence.

Even if the two-step model accurately depicted reality, the difficulties of instituting marketing strategies in line with it would remain enormous. The first problem is how to single out opinion leaders who are found at all status levels and within all informal groups. This is compounded by the fact (to be discussed in more detail later) that within any given group, different opinion leaders are likely to exist for different product categories and interest areas. Furthermore, the individual is likely to belong to more than one group where consumer information may be transferred and where opinion leaders exist. Finally, if it were possible to identify opinion leaders, how could the marketer appeal to them so that they would promote his product?

THE PHENOMENISTIC APPROACH: COMMUNICATION AS TWO-WAY TRANSACTION

Increasing dissatisfaction with the early direct effects model is illustrated by an observation of Bernard Berelson (1948) that "*Some* kinds of communication on *some* kinds of issues, brought to the attention of *some* kinds of people under *some* kinds of conditions have *some* kinds of effects" (p. 172). This statement is, obviously, a discouraging one. But it accurately reflects the paucity of real knowledge about communication processes generated by the one-way model. Berelson's statement attests to the fact that communication is a complex process which cannot be understood in terms of simply labeling elements of a stimulus-response communication act.

Researchers such as Bernard Berelson, Wilbur Schramm, Raymond A. Bauer, and Joseph T. Klapper were among the first to propose that communication can only be understood as a *transaction*, with the set of audience members as active, responsive participants in the ongoing communication process. These researchers argue for a "phenomenistic approach" to understanding communication processes. That is, they argue that communication can only be understood if we focus on the individual predispositions, social influences, personal experiences, and other factors which people *bring to* communication situations and which, in turn, shape their use of, and responses to, communication. Such a process is essentially *transactional* in that individuals are active participants in communication. The extent and nature of their "participation"is determined by their backgrounds and personal makeups. Such an approach represents a change from viewing mass communication as a "necessary and sufficient cause of effects," to a perspective that the media are pervasive influences, operating together with other influences as part of a total situation.

THE SELECTIVE PROCESSES

The host of "background factors" brought to a communication situation by an individual mediate the impact of communication because of the individual's active involvement in message reception. These processes of mediation are most clearly seen in selection processes of audience members. For example, selective exposure, perception, and retention result from the interaction of the consumer's attributes and predispositions with the characteristics of the communicator, message, and channel.

These selective processes are quite complex. For example, different processes are involved depending on whether one is talking about actual motivated behavior to "seek out" product information or motivated behavior to avoid some information—as is sometimes posited in selective avoidance behavior as a response to cognitive dissonance (see Ehrlich et al. 1957). The essential notion for present purposes, however, is that people are actively involved in the seletcion of what they will attend to in the mass media.

Selective Exposure

Consumers cannot attend to all possible messages emanating from all possible media. Since they cannot read all magazines, watch all television programs, or listen to all radio broadcasts, they must, of necessity, engage in selective exposure to media and to messages. Advertisers, too, since they cannot afford to cover all possible media, must selectively place messages. The probability of a consumer being exposed to any given advertising message is infinitely small.[4] Bauer and Greyser (1968), for example, estimate that the "average consumer" is *potentially* exposed to some 750 advertisements per day, which are contained in the media to which he attends. However, the consumer by no means "sees" all of these ads, and in fact, Bauer and Greyser estimate that the average American adult is exposed to or aware of only 76 advertisements a day (p. 176). This figure is based on respondent counts using a simple mechanical counter.

Unfortunately—and again testifying to the complexity of communication processes—the evidence for selective processes is not clear-cut. Freedman and Sears (1965) review several studies which report contrary and alternative findings.

Early research with voters (Lazarsfeld, Berelson, and Gaudet, 1948) seemed to demonstrate that selection favors messages in line with the individual's previous feelings, needs, and interests, whereas irrelevant or threatening messages tend to be avoided. Other studies seem to support the view that, to a large extent, communications which reinforce existing beliefs and attitudes will be selected (Mills, et al., 1959; Adams, 1961). Ehrlich, et al., (1957), for example, found that new car owners are more likely to select advertisements for their make of car rather than for other cars. The explanation is that exposure to other car ads might raise questions in the consumer's mind about the wisdom of his choice. The experience of "cognitive dissonance" (a postpurchase state of anxiety), it is hypothesized, leads the new car owner to select advertisements for the car he purchased, thus lending support to and reinforcing his choice.

Freedman and Sears (1965) argue that these findings may not be due to motivated selectivity; rather, they suggest that this selectivity could be an incidental effect of other factors and "might be entirely independent of any preference for supportive information" (p. 61). Such *de facto* selectivity could be due, for example, to the relative availability of supportive and discrepant information in the environment. If a town has predominantly Republican newspapers, then selective exposure to Republican information may be due not to motivated selectivity, but to the relative availability of Republican information. Atkin (1970), in research on political issues, has tested both the notion of motivated selectivity and the relative availability of information as alternative explanations for communication exposure. His results support the existence of motivated selectivity. The relative availability hypothesis seemed to be applicable only for "politically neutral" subjects.

Although the matter is complex and the evidence far from clear, there is

[4] There are difficulties involved in defining *exposure*. For a discussion, see Advertising Research Foundation, Inc., (1961).

certainly some justification for the notion of motivated selective exposure. For example, life insurance advertisements emphasizing death are likely to attain low exposure scores, since thoughts of death are threatening to most people and therefore may be repressed.

Conversely, there are circumstances under which people may pay greater attention to communications which are opposed to their beliefs than to those which tend to be reinforcing. Thus, a study by Ray (1968) found that although individuals were more interested in reading supportive than refutational material, defenses of *noncontroversial* beliefs discrepant with respondents' beliefs received higher interest ratings than did consonant defenses. While suggesting that this result might be explained by cognitive dissonance theory, Ray prefers the explanation offered by conceptual notions of "curiosity" or "novelty-seeking": "the opposition positions to 'cultural truisms' are so unusual as to be a novelty, thus creating greater interest" (p. 338).

Selective Perception

Consumers see communications in a selective and individualized manner. Perception can be thought of as a result of stimulus factors and personal factors (Krech, Crutchfield, and Ballachey, 1962). *Stimulus factors* refer to the nature of the physical stimulus, for example, the size, color, or actual wording of an advertisement. *Personal factors* refer to the nature of the individual perceiver—his needs, values, experiences, and personality. The interdependence of stimulus and personal factors can be illustrated by the fact that a beer ad is increasingly more likely to be seen by a man than a woman, a thirsty man, a man who habitually drinks beer, and so on. The stimulus remains the same, but is differentially interpreted by individual perceivers.

Some idea of how the perception process functions is given by Bauer and Greyser (1968). In their report and interpretation of a comprehensive research project concerning responses and attitudes of Americans toward advertising, they cite data concerning audience "reactions" to advertising messages. The research procedure was to give each respondent an "ad record card" to be filled out for each ad the respondent considered especially annoying, enjoyable, informative, or offensive of those to which he was exposed. Of the seventy-six ads that an average respondent noted per day, he was found to fill out cards for twelve, or some 16 percent of his total level of exposure. Thus, and this is a loose interpretation and not necessarily in line with the discussion by Bauer and Greyser, of the seventy-six ads consciously attended to daily, only twelve are of sufficient impact to "register" and be categorized by respondents. The process of registration and categorization is most akin to perception (p. 181). It is to be noted that different ads would register with different audience members and would also tend to be categorized differently.

Although some general agreement might exist among the population, considerable disparity could exist in which ads are perceived as annoying, enjoyable, informative, and offensive.

Selective Retention

People do not remember all they internalize. Product stimuli will be remembered if particularly essential to the individual's need-value system. Most communication messages, however, will be forgotten unless reinforced by follow-up communication. Experimental evidence reported by Hovland, Janis, and Kelley (1953) indicates that there is generally, following exposure to messages, an initial period of rapid forgetting of factual material and then a more gradual decrease occurs until an asymptote is reached, at which the rate of forgetting stabilizes (p. 245). This evidence suggests that some 50 percent of the material may be remembered in the very short run, that is, less than a day or two, and that retention tends to stabilize at about a 30-percent level over the longer run, that is, up to one hundred days.

However, this evidence was gathered in laboratory conditions where subjects *had* to attend to the message and where there were no competing messages. The situation in marketing is, of course, quite different in that the consumer may perceive the same advertising message a number of times over a hundred-day period, but he also may perceive advertisements for competing products as well.

It would seem apparent that to achieve exposure, or even perception, without retention, is to conduct an unsuccessful communication campaign. If the consumer does not retain the product message over time, there would seem to be little probability of a sales outcome.

Again, however, things are not so simple. Advertisers may assume that high levels of exposure and perception will lead to high retention, and, perhaps, sales outcome. The media abound with bathing beauties, dogs, children, and other attention-getters. Although the pretty girls may have initial appeal for men, and the dogs and children may appeal to women, the connection between the attention-getters and the selling message may be tenuous. Such attention-getters actually may distract the consumer from retaining sales points from the message.

A more basic problem in the relationships between exposure, perception, and retention is posed in research by Krugman (1965, 1970). Krugman suggests that, in some ways, television is a "low-involvement" medium (at least compared to magazines). This is not intended as a negative comment about TV, but as a suggestion that television has a particular *kind* of communication process—with its own properties and effects on audiences. Television communication may be as "effective" as magazine communication, though its processes may function differently. Specifically, Krugman suggests that consumer responses to television advertising occur gradually, without visible shifts in perception or retention. This is similar to the learning of trivia or nonsense syllables in psychological experiments:

> . . . as trivia are repeatedly learned and repeatedly forgotten and then repeatedly learned a little more, it is probable that two things will happen: (1) more simply, that so-called "overlearning" will move some information out of short-term and into long-term memory systems, and (2) more complexly, that we will permit significant alterations in the *structure* of our perception of a brand or product, but in ways which may fall short of persuasion or of attitude change. One way we may do this is by shifting the relative salience of attributes suggested to us by advertising as we organize our perception of brands and products (Krugman, 1965, p. 353).

An important implication of Krugman's very heuristic research is that it may be erroneous to assume that advertising must be perceived and retained in measurable ways. Such effects may not be valid indicators of advertising success. Actually, Krugman's research may suggest that the early one-way model may be correct in some ways—at least in regard to television communication processes. The essential notion of "low involvement" is that audience members are *not* particularly active participants in the television viewing situation. The communication effects are subtle, and Krugman suggests, perhaps persuasive.

SELECTIVE PROCESSES AND CONSUMER DECISION MAKING

Even assuming that the message gains exposure, perception, and some level of retention, consumer response is by no means automatic. Consumers are active in the purchase decision-making process and respond to communication in line with their particular needs, interests, motivations, and overall attributes—as discussed in Chapter 3. Moving consumers along the purchase decision hierarchy may involve different types of communication emphasis, appeals, and media.

Furthermore, it should be noted at this point that the communication process seldom is limited to one communication event. The marketer does not phrase his communication objectives in terms of one message getting through, but is concerned instead with the campaign's overall effect over time. It is rare that one advertisement would move a consumer to a purchase response, although the cumulative effect of several advertisements may do so. The communication system, therefore, should be seen as a recycling, in that information is being introduced continually from the environment and the long-run communication effect is what concerns the marketer. Thus, any one event taking place within the communication system has a low probability of resulting in a sales outcome. However, the communication event may move the audience member further along the message and purchase decision processes, so that as subsequent communication events occur, he is no longer in the same position and is more or less likely to buy.

THE PHENOMENISTIC APPROACH: SUMMARY AND CRITICISM

It has been stated that the phenomenistic approach to understanding communication processes is a desirable response to the overly simplistic direct effects, or one-way, model. The phenomenistic approach has forced marketers to focus on the individual audience member and the factors affecting his use of, and responses to, communication. In sharp contrast to the all-powerful image of communication in the direct effects model, the phenomenistic approach portrays individuals as *bringing something to* communication situations, that is, as being active participants in communication.

However, this view perhaps can be extended too far. The media can be portrayed as rather weak influences on human lives, merely reinforcing existing conditions. This reinforcement view is expressed by Klapper (1960), who observes quite accurately that the media rarely convert opinions or radically alter beliefs and who advances the following generalizations:

1. Mass communication is generally not a necessary and sufficient cause of effects, but operates through mediating factors—environmental conditions as well as audience predispositions and attributes.
2. Mass communication is most often a "contributory agent" in a process of reinforcing existing conditions. Communication, most simply, is much more likely to reinforce than to change.
3. When mass communication does serve to change, it is because the mediating factors are inoperative or are themselves favoring change (p. 8).

We have cited research evidence to support the first generalization—that selective processes serve to mediate the impact of mass communications. However, the latter two generalizations may be questioned. First, much of the evidence for these two points comes from laboratory persuasion experiments. The question arises about the extent to which these findings may be generalized to mass media communication, much less to advertising. Second, persuasion may be a straw man as far as the effects of television are concerned, since television rarely attempts to persuade, except in advertising. Thus it is hardly surprising that little evidence is found for persuasion in general television fare.

Proponents of the reinforcement view are not looking for the kinds of effects that may be typically expected in television programming (not advertising) ; rather, they are looking for effects which should not be expected of television. *Learning* effects probably are more appropriate to television than is persuasion per se (Ward, 1970). Children, for example, may slowly acquire views of the world through years of exposure to television programming.

Some social critics have suggested that this gradual learning process occurs as some children acquire socially dysfunctional views and behavior from programs that emphasize violence. No doubt television is not the sole cause of these potentially dysfunctional effects. Children from families in which aggression is sanctioned, to some extent, may be more influenced by television violence than children from homes in which aggression is disapproved. Although this illustration is far from the marketing context, the point is that the reinforcement view may overlook other, more subtle, kinds of effects. As Krugman (1965) suggests, "in the low involvement communication model . . . persuasion as such, i.e., overcoming a resistant attitude, is not involved at all and . . . it is a mistake to look for it in our personal lives as a test of television's advertising impact" (p. 353).

SUMMARY

Communication is basic to the process of diffusion of marketing information. In this chapter, an attempt has been made to describe the "state of the art" as regards our knowledge of human communication processes.

The early view of communication portrayed a one-way flow of effects from sender to receiver. This "direct effects" scheme posited messages being transmitted from communicator to audience and inducing some form of response. The audience was portrayed as a mass of essentially passive recipients of communication. In reality, most messages fail to reach consumers; and even when they do, a direct response rarely occurs.

An improvement over the direct effects communication scheme is to be found in the two-step flow of communication, which suggests that mass media first reach opinion leaders who subsequently pass on what they have learned to associates for whom they are influential. Although it is not without its failings, the two-step concept has served to move marketers away from an atomistic view of society to one which recognizes the social relationships present.

Among the problems associated with the two-step model are (1) its suggestion that an absolute leader exists for each informal group—when, in fact, opinion leadership resides to some extent in all group members; and (2) information is assumed to flow only from mass media to opinion leaders and then to followers. In practice, followers are also in touch with the mass media—although perhaps not to the same degree as leaders. More correctly, the opinion leader should be viewed as an *editor* of mass media material and an influential information source.

The phenomenistic approach to communications was primarily a reaction to the direct effects model, but is also a considerable refinement over the two-step model. Audience members are viewed as bringing various pre-dispositional background factors to communication situations. These individual factors mediate the impact of mass communications. A primary mediating mechanism is selectivity. An individual is selective in exposure, perception, and retention of media fare generally and advertising specifically. Thus the audience member is an active participant in the communication process in searching for and/or selectively receiving messages from his environment and in actively considering them.

Problems with the phenomenistic approach occur if one goes to the extreme that media are merely weak reinforcers of existing audience predispositions. Such a view may have arisen because some have assumed that since the media do not typically convert or persuade, they merely reinforce. Communication media may have more subtle, gradual, and pervasive effects than persuasion, however. This is strongly suggested by Krugman's research, in which the low-involvement medium of television may gradually alter perceptions and even persuade in a gradual and difficult-to-measure manner. Such an approach suggests that the one-way model may not be all wrong—at least for television communication.

The progression of research and conceptual development in understanding communication processes has occurred for the most part beyond the bounds of marketing and advertising research. If marketing-related models of communication are to be developed, research should be specific to advertising communication events. Advances in our understanding of communication processes would undoubtedly follow from clarifying the range of communication activities to which concepts are applied.[5] In this chapter, for example, much discussion was derived from research in areas outside advertising or marketing. Krugman's research points up the need to focus concepts specifically on the kinds of communication being investigated. His research suggests very different kinds of communication processes, depending on whether one examines television or print media.

A further need is to develop concepts specific to various *levels* of communication activity. That is, one level concerns the intraindividual processes which mediate the impact of mass communications (such as selective processes) or are a response to communication (decision making, dissonance, and so on). Another level of analysis of communication processes concerns interpersonal communication. However, adequate knowledge is lacking concerning the relationship of mass communication and related interpersonal communication in the environment.

[5] Further discussion of the need to develop concepts specific to kinds of communication is provided by Ray (1969).

CHAPTER 6

COMMUNICATION STRUCTURE

Communication effectiveness is a function of source, message, and channel attributes and the interaction of these attributes with the characteristics of the audience. In this chapter these elements will be considered as the essential aspects of communication structure.

136

SOURCE EFFECT

The *source* of a communication typically is considered to be its origination point. In most behavioral science research on the effect of source characteristics upon message acceptance and response, it has been fairly easy to identify the source. Most such research involves experimental conditions in which a speaker (source) orally presents a communication or a written communication is attributed to a specific person (source). In marketing, however, the source of a persuasive communication is not identifiable so readily.

The "origination point" of promotional communications is the business enterprise, although the message may be prepared or delivered by a designated agent or employee of the firm such as an advertising agency or public relations firm or sales agent. Consumers, however, sometimes are apt to identify the source of a promotional message as the channel (media or sales personnel) or the paid commercial announcer (who, from the firm's point of view, is an integral part of the message), as well as the firm itself. Since the ultimate criterion of source effect must be from the *consumer's point of view*, we are led to a complex definition of source based on the point of *validation*, rather than the point of origination. A source, then, is that person or agent who *validates* the message.

A lack of consumer distinction between source and channel is particularly likely to occur, since media often try to set themselves up as sources and since companies establish their sales personnel as sources. Magazines such as *Life, Readers' Digest, Good Housekeeping*, and *Parents' Magazine*, which claim to exercise discretion as to what advertising is accepted and use seals of approval or implied product endorsements, are, in effect, standing behind these products and recommending them in the capacity of a source. The sales agent, for all practical purposes, *is* the company or the source for most consumers. He is the officially designated representative and speaks for the company. Certain sales announcers, such as Arthur Godfrey and Bob Hope, have also been successful in gaining consumer confidence and are relied upon and looked to as a source of product information by a significant segment of consumers.

DIFFERENTIAL IMPACT

The success of a communication will depend, sometimes to a considerable extent, on how the audience perceives the source. An advertising message from a respected company such as IBM may gain greater acceptance than a similar message from a less respected company. An advertisement placed in what may be a respected publication, such as *Readers' Digest*, may gain greater acceptance than the identical advertisement placed in a less-respected publication, perhaps *True Confessions*. A sales message by one salesman may gain better acceptance than an identical message by another salesman. A public relations release in the form of editorial content (perceived as originating with that medium) may gain better acceptance than the same information communicated in the form of advertising.

Frequently, the attributes of the advertising medium and the attributes of the sponsoring company—to the extent that both are considered components of the *source*—may be expected to interact. Fuchs (1964) conducted an experiment to test the effects of these two sources components on attitudes towards little-known advertised products. It was found that the dependent attitudes changed generally as a linear function of the prestige of the two source components, so that the greatest positive shifts were obtained as a result of exposure to advertising in a combination of high-rated magazine and high-rated company, whereas little or no shift occurred from a combination of low-rated company and low-rated magazine.

The question becomes, "What characteristics of the source affect message acceptance and consumer response and what dynamics are involved?" The approach from this point will be to isolate the most important source factors and to specify effects. This will be done by reference to communication research findings.

SOURCE CREDIBILITY

The most frequent source characteristic investigated has been *credibility*. This is defined by Hovland, Janis, and Kelley (1953) to consist of two components: (1) expertness, or the extent to which the source is considered capable of making valid assertions, and (2) trustworthiness, or the extent of confidence in the source's actually making such valid assertions.

A research experiment by Kelman and Hovland (1953) illustrates how variations in source credibility lead to differences in communications impact. Subjects for the experiment were high school students who were exposed to a "radio broadcast" in which the speaker advocated extreme leniency in the treatment of juvenile delinquents. Three versions of the talk were given to three groups of students, differing only in the speaker introduction. In the *positive* (high-credibility) introduction, he was identified as a judge in a juvenile court and was described as well-trained, experienced, sincere, and having the public interest at heart. In the *neutral* (medium-credibility) introduction, he was identified only as a member of the studio audience, chosen at random. In the *negative* (low-credibility) introduction, he was presented as a member of the studio audience who had been a juvenile delinquent and who was at the moment out on bail after being arrested and charged with dope peddling.

Results from this experiment are summarized in the form of the five following conclusions.

Evaluations of Presentation

Despite identical messages, audience judgments of fairness of presentation measured immediately after the communication were more favorable to the high-credibility communicator and less favorable to the low-credibility communicator.

Attitude Change

Immediate attitude change in the direction advocated by the communicator was most pronounced for the high-credibility source and least pronounced for the low-credibility source.

Retention of Attitude Change

A follow-up measure of attitude change administered three weeks after the presentation indicated that the differences originally present had disappeared. There appeared to be a forgetting effect for the high-credibility communicator and a sleeper effect for the low-credibility communicator.

Retention of Attitude Change with Reinstated Source

As a further aspect of the experiment, part of each experimental group again heard the introductions in order to reassociate source with message. When the source was thus reinstated, the high-credibility communicator again achieved greatest attitude change and the low-credibility communicator achieved least attitude change.

Retention of Factual Material

Recall was significantly better for the medium-credibility source than for either of the other sources. The authors hypothesize that affective responses to high- and low-credibility sources may adversely affect learning and recall of factual information.

It can be suggested initially, therefore, on the basis of this experiment and others which have yielded fairly consistent results, that generally a high-credibility source can be most advantageously used by marketers, since short-term attitude change will be desired or, when long-term attitude change is desired, the source will be reinstated due to repetition. However, if long-term attitude change is desired and the source will not be reinstated after some period of time, or if considerable learning of factual material is necessary, then a high-credibility source may not be best.

COMPONENTS OF CREDIBILITY

A major difficulty with the credibility concept is in specifying the main components. Cohen (1964) asks, "Is it expertness or trustworthiness, perception of fairness or bias, disinterest or propagandistic intent, or any combination of these factors which is responsible for the effects of credibility on attitude change?" (p. 26). Bauer (1967) has recently argued that credibility may be something other than the "unitary" phenomenon which it has been regarded as and that high credibility may not always be a "good thing."

A major step forward in specifying the dimensions of credibility has been taken by Rarick (1963), who distinguishes between the *cognitive* and *affective* components of credibility. The aspects of the cognitive component are power, prestige, and competence, while the aspects of the affective component are trustworthiness and likability. Attitude change in Rarick's findings showed a positive relationship to both cognitive and affective components, but learning of factual material was related negatively to the affective component. Thus, the more intense the affective component (either liking or disliking), the less the retention of information.

Bauer (1967) elaborated and extended the Rarick findings by relating them to his own conceptions of the problem-solving and psychosocial games and to Kelman's conceptions (1961) of types of attitude change. (The work of Bauer and Kelman is discussed further in Chapter 8.) This is illustrated in Table 6.1. The consumer in a purchase decision situation, according to Bauer, will either play the problem-solving game—that is, he will engage in behavior appropriate to choosing the best purchase alternative by searching for and evaluating information to reach a decision—or he will play the psychosocial game—that is, he will come to a decision based on the behavior he sees as most likely to be rewarded by his peer group. In line with this reasoning then, competence and trust are relevant to the problem-solving game, since they involve assessments of whether the person is qualified to make assertions and whether he is likely to be honest in such assertions. Power and likability are relevant to the psychosocial game, since they involve assessments of whether a particular response will please another person or lead to group acceptance.

A distinction between problem-solving and psychosocializing may be especially meaningful for marketing, since it distinguishes between the two

Table 6.1   Components of Credibility and Their Relations to the Game Played and the Type of Attitude Change

Credibility Components		Game	Type of Attitude Change
Cognitive	Affective		
Competence	Trust	Problem-Solving	Internalization
Power	Likability	Psychosocial	Compliance or identification

contrasting consumer goals of product evaluation and the desire to emulate other persons or groups. Wilding and Bauer (1968) studied the relationship between the reaction of individuals with these different goals to a persuasive communication and their perception of the various components of the source of this communication. While pointing out the need for further research, they postulate that the consumer will display "a differential response to the several components depending on the goals with which the subject is concerned" (p. 76).

Attitude change based on problem-solving can be classified as *internalization* (see Table 6.1), since the changed attitude is a result of the congruence of the information accepted with the individual's value system. Attitude change based on the psychosocial game can be classified as either *compliance* (if the person accepts an opinion to gain a favorable reaction from another person) or *identification* (if the person accepts the opinion to establish or maintain a satisfying self-defining relationship to another person). Kelman (1961) has related these forms of attitude change to source effects. Internalization, he believes, will occur if the source is perceived as expert (or competent) and trustworthy. Compliance will occur if the source is perceived to exercise control (power). Identification will occur if the source is considered attractive (likability). Kelman has also specified under what conditions these forms of attitude change will result in consonant behavior. Attitude change based on compliance will result in behavior only under conditions of *surveillance*. Identification will lead to behavior only under conditions of *salience* of the person's relationship to the other person. Internalization will lead to behavior under conditions of *relevance of the values* which were initially involved in the attitude change.

FURTHER RESEARCH ON SOURCE CREDIBILITY EFFECT

The dynamics of source credibility when the individual is playing the problem-solving game have been further specified by Hilibrand (1964) and Bauer (1967). The relevant dimensions are competence and trust; the type of attitude change is internalization; and a behavioral result will occur to the extent that the values involved in the initial attitude change are relevant to the conditions present (see Table 6.1). In line with Rarick's results (1963), when a person is exposed to a highly competent, highly trusted source, he will show considerable attitude change, but not necessarily retain factual material. The affective component (trust) interferes with the cognitive component (competence) and causes the individual to accept the advocated opinion without sufficient critical evaluation; that is, if the source knows what he is talking about *and* I trust him, why should I examine the evidence? The individual exposed to a highly competent, not-so-trusted source should show less attitude change, but better retention of factual material. Over time it would be expected that as source and message become disassociated (unless reinstated), the advantage of the high-trust source would be overcome. Furthermore, it is hypothesized by Hilibrand (1964) that the individual exposed to the high-trust source will be particularly vulnerable to counterpropaganda, since he has not learned the arguments to support the opinion taken. These results and predictions are summarized in Table 6.2.

An experiment conducted by Hilibrand lends support to the counterpropaganda hypothesis. His subjects were state government employees who were exposed to a strong, pro–civil defense message, supposedly emanating from one of four sources: (1) high competence–high trust, (2) high competence–low trust, (3) low competence–high trust, and (4) low competence–low trust. The high-competence–high-trust source was depicted as a man of high technical competence who was fairminded and objective; the high-competence–low-trust source also was described as of high technical competence, but lacking in perspective because of his passionate advocacy of civil defense; the low-competence–high-trust source was described as a highly regarded lawyer lacking technical background; and the low-confidence–low-trust source was portrayed as a former politician who had slipped his way into a civil defense position. It is to be noted that competence is topic-bound.

Hilibrand's results (1964) may be summarized as follows:

1. The highly competent–highly trustworthy source provided the strongest short-run attitude change (p. 292).
2. To a limited extent, the sleeper effect was borne out, that is, the persuasive advantage of the highly competent–highly trustworthy source diminished somewhat over time (p. 294).

Table 6.2   Source Effect as Trustworthiness Is Varied with Competence Held Constant

Effect Under Conditions of High Competence	
High Trustworthiness	Low Trustworthiness
Greatest short-run attitude change	Least short-run attitude change
Little learning of factual material	Considerable learning of factual material
Decreasing attitude change over time unless source is reinstated	Increasing attitude change over time unless source is reinstated
Least vulnerable to immediate counterpropaganda	Vulnerable to immediate counterpropaganda
Vulnerable to counterpropaganda on a delayed basis	Less vulnerable to counterpropaganda on a delayed basis

Source: Based on Hilibrand (1964).

3. Greater knowledge and message understanding occurred when the message was attributed to a source other than the highly competent–highly trustworthy one (p. 296).
4. If exposure to counterpropaganda occurs immediately after initial message exposure, susceptibility to counterpersuasion is least for the highly competent–highly trustworthy source (p. 296).
5. If exposure to counterpropaganda occurs on a delayed basis (two weeks later), then "susceptibility is shown to be greater for the highly competent and highly trustworthy source than for any other source used" (p. 297).

These results are particularly significant in that they are consistent with the earlier Kelman and Hovland (1953) experiment in certain important respects, as well as with the findings of Rarick (1963), and yet go beyond these two earlier studies to show a most interesting result based on counterpropaganda. It can be concluded that a highly credible source is not necessarily a good thing and that high competence–high trust may fail to achieve the communicator's objective if counterpropaganda is likely to result after some period of time in which the original message has not been reinforced.

In the realm of marketing, counterpropaganda is the general occurrence unless the product is radically new. Repetition of promotional communications by the company, however, is also the general practice, so that source and message are continually reassociated in the consumer's mind. Therefore, research going one step further than Hilibrand's is necessary to test retention of attitude change under varying source conditions and in cases where both repetition of the initial communication and counterpropaganda occur. The marketer for the present is well advised to consider whether the additional cost of highly trustworthy sources (including media and commercial announcers) is worth the likely reward in terms of the communication objective. Such additional cost may be justified when immediate response is the goal or when a high frequency promotional campaign is planned but may not be justified under the opposite conditions or when the communication is subject to a high frequency of counterpropaganda.

MESSAGE EFFECT

The message in a persuasive communication event is generally only part of a larger campaign theme which attempts to communicate a certain *meaning* about the product. The communication objective is to create the most desirable meaning for the product and to arouse the individual's desire for it as well as to give him knowledge of how to satisfy this desire. It is necessary, therefore, to focus first on the desired product meaning and then to design messages accordingly.

The product is a complex stimulus containing a perceived set of want-satisfying attributes and a generally distinguishable symbolic character.

According to this rationale, a product is more than its physical properties. In fact, consumers quite often are unaware of a product's true physical properties. For example, few consumers know or care to know the chemical composition of gasoline or aspirin. Consumers buy these products because of their *want-satisfying attributes*, that is, for what they can do. Gasoline provides power for transportation, and aspirin relieves pain.

Especially to the extent that it is differentiated and not a commodity item, a product also possesses a more abstract, *social-symbolic meaning*, or what has popularly been termed *brand image*. According to Levy (1959), "people buy things not only for what they do, but also for what they mean" (p. 118). The car-buying consumer, for example, is buying more than transportation. "The Continental way of life" expresses quite a different social-symbolic meaning than "The car with continental elegance at a Plymouth price." Most American women no longer buy dresses primarily on the basis of utilitarian characteristics. Observation in a clothing store reveals that few women carefully evaluate the workmanship of a dress to assess how long it will last. Their dominant purchase motivations include buying the latest style, buying what will appeal to men, or, as has been maintained, buying what will win favor with other women.

Products vary in the degree to which social-symbolic meaning is important. Cars and clothing are both products which are high in visual display and recognized in our society as saying something about a person. For other products, such as canned vegetables or work tools, social-symbolic meaning is of less importance, although still present. LeSueur petits pois may still mean something different than brand X peas, and Black and Decker tools may say something different about a man than brand Y tools.

Products and brands, to the extent that each has a meaningful symbolic character, will be evaluated by the consumer for appropriateness to his way of life and self-conception. In this view, consumer behavior represents a decision-making process whereby products with the most desirable symbolic meanings are chosen. "In the broadest sense, each person aims to enhance his sense of self, and behaves in ways that are consistent with his image of the person he is or wants to be" (Levy, 1959, p. 119). Maintenance of self-consistency and presentation of self in the most becoming manner are recognized principles of human behavior. Product consumption, especially as visible to other people, is an important aspect of self-presentation and an opportunity for self-enhancement. Thorstein Veblen (1899) translated this principle of consumer self-enhancement into his concept of "conspicuous consumption," whereby he viewed consumer motivation, at least among the affluent, as "a race for reputability on the basis of an invidious comparison" (p. 32).

Symbolic product differences are especially crucial when technical product differentiation is limited or not possible. Moreover, in a modern mass-consumption economy, where competition is predominantly promotional rather than price-based, symbolic product meaning is of major significance in brand choice. Experimental research has found that a majority of consumers in blindfold tests cannot distinguish among brands of cola beverages and cigarettes, yet exhibit brand loyalties (Husband and Godfrey, 1934; Thumin, 1962). A study on beer drinking demonstrated that drinkers do not show a preference for their own brand when the labels are removed (Allison and Uhl, 1964). Research on retail outlets has also shown the value of symbolic distinctions. While many stores may appear outwardly similar, distinct store images are often created and consumers act upon such images in store selection (see, for example, Fisk, 1961–1962). In industrial goods, Shoaf (1959) recognized that products were becoming more alike objectively and that "the buyer's final decision is based more and more upon subjective emotional factors" (p. 128).

The message then, must be consistent with the desired brand image and must attempt to build, refine, and extend it. Seldom will an advertising message openly encourage an immediate sale. Instead, the underlying principle is that if the right meaning is created for the product, then long-run sales will be the outcome. Unfortunately, very little research evidence is available on message attributes under such campaign considerations. Most research has focused on the effects of specific message types in experimental settings.

CREATING IMBALANCE

A general principle of message design when change is the desired objective is to create a sense of cognitive imbalance within the receiver and then to gain acceptance for the message as the individual seeks a means of returning to a balanced state. The underlying assumption of such "balance" models, deriving from the field theory of Kurt Lewin (1936), is that individuals seek to achieve equilibrium, so that when tension is aroused leading to disequilibrium, forces will be set in motion to seek means to restore the balance. This process is noted by Hovland, Janis, and Kelley (1953) in their focus on threat appeals as a message type:

> While a person is paying attention to a communication, certain contents are presented (notably those evoking anticipation of a threat to the self) which induce unpleasant emotional reactions. Under these conditions the individual becomes highly motivated to try out various responses, both symbolic and overt, until the unpleasant emotional state is alleviated (p. 62).

The same principle should apply for messages which, instead of threatening the person, strengthen a positive definition of self-concept.

As formulated by Hovland, Janis, and Kelley (1953), a threat appeal—

that is, a message alluding to unfavorable consequences which will occur from failure to follow the communicator's recommendations—will lead to emotional tension which will cause the individual to seek means to alleviate this state, most likely by trying out potential responses in his mind. Of course, the communicator at the same time is providing an answer which he hopes the receiver will accept. Thus, a mouthwash advertisement alludes to social disapproval which, if meaningful to the audience member, induces tension. Tension being uncomfortable, the subject will seek to achieve balance by rehearsing certain responses and may find the communicator's recommendation best and accept it. He could, of course, return to balance by accepting the idea of purchasing any brand of mouthwash or using a stronger toothpaste or rationalizing that this problem is not really his or believing that bad breath is a copywriter's dream. Thus, he need not accept the recommendation of the communication and can even react against it.

It is hypothesized that a similar process occurs for messages alluding to positive, rather than negative, results. Thus, the perfume ad promising romance also may lead to tension (desire for romance), which the individual may reduce by buying that brand or in a number of other ways, such as scoffing at the reality depicted or buying a new outfit instead.

It is further hypothesized that strictly "factual" material will cause the same reaction. To the extent that a product is relevant to the person, an advertisement describing its features and uses also can induce tension—if the information is incongruent with his existing attitudes toward that type of product or if he uses another brand. Thus, the facts communicated that product X can perform at a given capacity may be incongruent with his attitudes that product Y is best. Again, the imbalance of facts and attitudes should lead the person to seek a solution—changing to the new product or perhaps discounting the performance claims made for it.

It is dangerous, however, to dichotomize between factual and nonfactual material or, relatedly, between rational and emotional messages. All advertising uses "facts" to make a point, and these facts support the conclusion of brand superiority or brand leadership. Recently, three of Chicago's four newspapers were claiming to be first in circulation based on the "facts." Of course, each was using different facts to make the same statement: first in weekday circulation, first in weekday-plus-Sunday circulation, first in growth of circulation, first in total circulation for a specified period, and so on. The point is that facts are relative in time, place, and perspective. The rational-emotional distinction is similarly relative. Rationality and emotionality are not necessarily competitive but often highly complementary.

Hovland, Janis, and Kelley (1953) have posited factors bearing on both the arousal of emotional tension and the acceptance of the message. They hypothesize that the arousal of emotional tension is a function of content factors, source factors, and antecedent communication experiences. As to *content* factors, they basically argue that the subject must be one to which the individual reacts emotionally, so that specific approaches can create more or less emotional tension. Appraisal of the *source* also can affect the arousal of emotional tension. His reputation, expertise, and perceived manipulative intent influence the audience's reaction. Finally, the audience's *communication history* is relevant. Emotional innoculation may occur if the audience has been previously exposed to similar messages. More emotional tension may be aroused by a vague threat than by a concrete threat. In a vague appeal the individual may well project his own exaggerated fantasies into the situation. This is illustrated by the tremendous impact of Orson Welles's famous radio broadcast on the "invasion from Mars," which was in the same format as a news story; thousands of listeners perceived the danger as real and fled their homes. More recently Chu (1967) has found that children exposed to vague threats of roundworms experience as much anxiety and show almost as much persuasiveness as children exposed to concrete threats.

Because a communication arouses tension does not mean that it will be successful. The audience member can adopt tension-reducing strategies other than the communicator's recommendations. This is one form of *interference*. The consumer may also consider the communicator's recommendations, but disregard them as irrelevant to the threat or impossible to institute. Or he may fail to pay attention to or actually reject the communicator and/or his recommendations.

MESSAGE ACCEPTANCE: THREAT APPEALS

Not all messages are successful in

1. Arousing tension.
2. Gaining acceptance of the communicator's recommendations.
3. Maintaining acceptance over time.

Over the years, conflicting findings have emerged concerning the effectiveness of fear and threat appeals in gaining message acceptance. The classic study in this field was conducted by Janis and Feshbach in 1953. Fear appeals were hypothesized to be effective if they aroused sufficient emotional tension to constitute a state of drive and if the acceptance of the action recommended was seen as leading to a reduction of tension. The experiment concerned the use of threat appeals to encourage good dental hygiene among high school students. Janis and Feshbach's findings indicated that a *strong* fear appeal was less effective than either *moderate* or *mild* fear appeals in producing reported adherence to recommended dental hygiene practices.

However, this negative relationship between level of fear arousal and acceptance of recommendations contained in the communication has not been supported by a number of subsequent studies. Unfortunately, marketing and advertising strategies have continued to emphasize the findings of the 1953 study, as Ray and Wilkie (1970) point out. They suggest that "the picture emerging from the more recent research on fear is that neither extremely strong nor very weak fear appeals are maximally effective. It seems that appeals at a somewhat moderate level of fear are best" (p. 55). In support of this position, Ray and Wilkie hypothesize that two types of effects occur as fear increases:

> First there are the facilitating effects that are most often overlooked in marketing. If fear can heighten drive, there is the possibility of greater attention and interest in the product and message than if no drive were aroused. But fear also brings the important characteristic of inhibition into the picture. . . . If fear levels are too high, there is the possibility of defensive avoidance of the ad, denial of the threat, selective exposure or distortion of the ad's meaning, or a view of the recommendations as being inadequate to deal with so important a fear. Marketing, in its examination of fear has unwittingly put all its emphasis on these inhibiting effects of fear (pp. 55–56).

It is suggested by these authors that if curves are plotted for facilitating and inhibiting effects (as shown in Figure 6.1) and a third curve derived from both of these, the resulting total effects will appear as a nonmonotonic curve indicating higher effectiveness for moderate fear appeals in gaining message acceptance.

Figure 6.1   Facilitating and Inhibiting Effects of Fear Appeal Messages

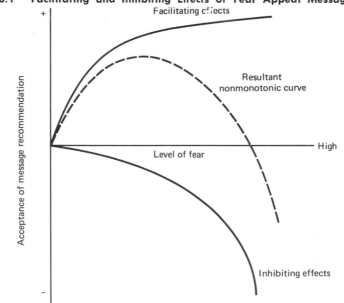

Source: Reprinted from Ray and Wilkie in the *Journal of Marketing Research* (1970, p. 56).

Ray and Wilkie reconcile the apparent discrepancy in findings among the many past threat appeal experiments by hypothesizing that different consumer segments and product categories possess different fear appeal response functions. In other words, a separate acceptance curve exists for each group, and these curves may be centered on different points along the level-of-fear axis. These authors feel that market segmentation techniques can be used to help assess the likely fear response functions of groups with specific socioeconomic, personality, and usage characteristics and, hence, to determine either the most appropriate level of threat appeal to employ or whether to use another form of appeal altogether. "In general," Ray and Wilkie (1970) report, "fear research mirrors marketing findings in that the segmenting characteristics which have discriminated best have been those most closely related to the product or topic" (p. 59).

MESSAGE ACCEPTANCE: PLEASANT VERSUS UNPLEASANT APPEALS

The pleasantness or unpleasantness of the message is perhaps the only other message format dimension to be studied systematically. Silk (1967), in a review of the literature, distinguishes between two competing views of the effectiveness of such messages. One view is that advertising which is seen as pleasant will be more effective than advertising which is seen as unpleasant. The reasoning offered in substantiation is that pleasant material is better *learned* than unpleasant material and that pleasant or unpleasant reactions to messages will be *transferred* to the products advertised. In contrast is the view that the determining factor is not the kind of message, but the intensity of reaction which the message achieves. Because memory is seen as most influenced by an intense emotional arousal, it is argued that either highly pleasant or highly irritating messages will have greatest effect. And it is reasoned that irritation facilitates attention and that any adverse reactions will be associated with the message and not transferred to the product. This tendency to disassociate the message and the product may not hold under message repetition, but this possibility has not been studied experimentally.

A frequent application of the pleasant appeal approach is the use of humor in advertising in order to attract attention and create a relaxed and receptive atmosphere for the transfer of information. However, humor is by no means a uniform variable. Research by Lynch and Hartman (1968) suggests that humor as employed in advertising may be categorized along several different dimensions and often may be sharply differentiated from the type of humor found in books, jokes, and gimmicks. Its function lies not so much in making the audience laugh as in making the message pleasanter.

In a preliminary experiment relating message pleasantness to effectiveness, Vavra (1967) exposed groups of college students to radio commercials for a shoe-care product. These commercials were specifically designed as pleasant, neutral, or irritating on the basis of the degree of hard sell, loudness, and background effects and music. Vavra's results on a one-time exposure basis suggested the following:

1. The irritating commercial achieved best recall on both an aided and unaided basis, while the pleasant commercial was lowest in recall.
2. The neutral commercial achieved a slight advantage on stated "willingness to buy."
3. The irritating commercial achieved an advantage in mentions on a "shopping list test," (the measure most closely approximating a behavioral indication).

While not conclusive, these results are among the few relating specifically to consumer purchasing. They suggest that the linear relationship posited between pleasantness and effectiveness is subject to doubt.

MESSAGE STRUCTURE

A body of experimental research is also available on the organization, or structure, of messages. This research emanated initially at Yale and has been conducted mainly by experimental psychologists. Researchers in marketing have been late to specifically consider attributes of message structure.

Conclusion Drawing

Should the communicator draw the conclusion for his audience or leave it implicit? The basic answer has been that it is more desirable to state the conclusion. However, the superiority of this approach may be reduced to the extent that (1) the communicator is perceived as untrustworthy, (2) the audience is more intelligent and less in need of conclusion drawing, and (3) the issue is simple or the matter is highly personal.

There is a certain danger in conclusion drawing in promotional messages, especially for new products. Conclusion drawing may limit unnecessarily the product's market and usage definitions. In fact, this leads to the broader issue of the advisability of concreteness versus ambiguity in new product promotion. The introductory campaign for Teflon focused on a concrete appeal that greaseless cooking had diet advantages. This appeal did not prove to be particularly popular, and Teflon did not really succeed until its ease of cleaning was emphasized. Mustang, while conceived as a youth car, was allowed to find its own market definition. Its advertisements did not draw conclusions as to its uses and potential users. At an early stage in Mustang's life history, Ford management considered comparing it to Corvair and emphasizing its superiority. This would have been a mistake, since most consumers did not define Mustang in the same category as Corvair.

Some authors such as Bullock (1961) have argued the advantages of relatively unstructured ads to reach both black and white consumers. These writers feel each consumer should be allowed to read whatever he wishes into an ad. In this case, however, the dangers of too much ambiguity soon become apparent, since consumers may read in product performance attributes not possessed by the product, and this could lead to consumer dissatisfaction. This possibility is a particular danger for new products.

Whereas conclusion drawing has been found most effective in experimental, nonproduct-related studies, certain dangers are involved in pursuing this strategy and a modified approach may be advisable. Conclusion drawing may be useful when the product is complex and performs specific and well-defined functions for a designated market segment. Conclusion drawing will probably be detrimental when the product is uncomplicated and when the functions it can perform and the markets it can appeal to are multiple and not fully defined. A dietetic product inadvisably may be defined as such and aimed at fat people. More advisably, it may be defined as a low-calorie product and aimed at weight-conscious consumers, both fat and slender. This is not to suggest, however, that a product should be offered as an all-purpose product for all consumers, since to appeal to everyone is often to appeal to no one; rather the product uses and market profile should not be unnecessarily limiting.

One-Sided or Two-Sided Arguments

The conditions favoring one- or two-sided arguments in messages are fairly well specified as:

1. *The initial position of the audience.* If the audience is initially favorably predisposed to the communicator's position, then he should present only one side of the issue, that is, positive arguments. If, however, the audience is initially opposed to his position, then he should present both sides of the issue, that is, positive and negative arguments.
2. *The educational level of the audience.* Presenting both sides of an issue is more effective with better-educated audiences, whereas presenting one side of an issue is more effective with less-educated audiences.
3. *Audience exposure to subsequent communication.* A two-sided message approach is better if the audience will be exposed subsequently to counter-propaganda.

The implications for the new product marketer are fairly clear. A two-sided message will be effective more often, but this conclusion deserves elaboration. Since most new products are modifications of existing products, the marketing objective generally is to gain market share at the expense of other brands already on the market and to which consumers already have varying degrees of loyalty—a condition in which the position of the audience is not in favor of the new brand (although not necessarily opposed). This suggests the superiority of a two-sided approach. If the new product is replacing another product on the market such as an electric toothbrush, the position of the audience again is not generally favorable or may reflect reluctance; and the superiority of a two-sided approach is suggested. If the new product will fulfill a need not previously met, then the audience may not have a ready position and this condition will, therefore, not be relevant in the selection of a one- or two-sided approach.

In a competitive environment, counterpropaganda is commonplace. The new product seeking market share through a modified appeal, the new product seeking to replace existing products, and the new product seeking to fulfill a need not previously met will all meet competitive reaction in time, and the benefits of a two-sided approach are again suggested. The long-run superiority of the two-sided approach seems to be explained in large measure by the concept of *innoculation*. By receiving a small dose of negative arguments, the audience member apparently becomes more resistant to a full play of negative argumentation at a later date.

Some consumers, of course, are favorably inclined toward new products. These people, we would imagine, are the innovators. Therefore, they may be more influenced by a one-sided approach in the short run and may be resistant when exposed to counterpropaganda for established products. To the extent that innovators for a new product can be specifically defined and appealed to, a one-sided approach seems recommended.

Educational level has also been identified as a determinant of the effectiveness of one- or two-sided messages. Marketers generally can select media in accordance with educational level, and some difference in degree of two-sidedness may be appropriately used. Less-educated audiences perhaps should receive a predominantly one-sided approach.

Bauer and Buzzell (1964) indicate how quantitative techniques may be used in formulating advertising strategy where one- and/or two-sided messages are to be employed. They suggest that a communications model can be built with the aid of market research. The audience is broken into segments according to its members' attitudes toward the product or service in question and the extent of their education; the probable conversion rates following one- or two-sided arguments for each of these sample segments are determined and the segments weighted by the probability of their exposure to the communication in the first place. Finally, the impact of successive communications is evaluated in the light of changes in the target population. If desired, additional factors also can be introduced into the analysis. Bauer and Buzzell argue that armed with this data (which must be derived through computer simulation because of the number of variables involved), the marketer may be able to determine such factors as the most appropriate appeals to employ, the segments of the audience at which to direct these appeals, and the number and frequency of messages to be transmitted.

A basic question at this point is what a two-sided message means in marketing. Does it imply giving equal time to the product's faults as well as its merits? Does it imply a *Consumer Reports* type of product evaluation? A marketing manager is not about to begin derogating his product on commercial time for which he is paying. The answer is in line with the innoculation theory. Only enough negative vaccine should be given to make the consumer resistant to counterpropaganda disease. Too much vaccine may well give the patient the disease.

A two-sided message approach in marketing is illustrated by Volkswagen, Avis, and Benson & Hedges advertising. Volkswagen to a certain extent spoofs the product on its size and looks, just as Avis has admitted that it's number 2, and Benson & Hedges—the first successful 100-millimeter cigarette —has pointed out that there are certain disadvantages to such a length. These ads are by no means objective, and the negative aspects of the product— while brought into the open—are treated in a humorous vein and most often neutralized; the positive aspects of the product dominate. It is interesting that in the case of Volkswagen and Avis these appeals have been directed to better-educated audiences, which may help account for their success.

Order of Presentation

The first question in regard to order of presentation is whether the communicator of a one-sided message should present his strongest arguments at the beginning (*anticlimax* condition) or at the end (*climax* condition). Neither order of presentation is found to be consistently superior. It is suggested that an anticlimax condition will be more successful when the audience has little interest in the product and that a climax condition will be more successful when the audience is interested. This further suggests that since there will be little existing interest for many new products, an anticlimax position is advisable for them. Conflicting findings are available on whether material is remembered better under climax or anticlimax conditions, but it is agreed that material in the middle of a message is retained least.

Another question is whether the communicator of a two-sided message should present his positive arguments at the beginning (*primacy effect*) or at the end (*recency effect*). This may depend on the level of interest that can be maintained in an advertisement. Since it has been found that opening copy of magazine ads and particularly headlines are better read than closing copy, then presenting positive arguments at the beginning is essential. Similarly, opening material in television commercials may receive better attention until the audience fully realizes that it is, in fact, a commercial. Again, therefore, the presentation of positive arguments at the beginning is recommended. Primacy or recency effectiveness may also depend on the initial position of the audience. If the audience is opposed initially, negative arguments with which it can agree are probably best presented at the beginning—in order to disarm the audience and to make it more susceptible to the positive arguments which will follow.

Another issue is whether messages will be more effective in an equal-interval sequence over time or in "flights" or "bursts" and whether messages will be more effective nearer the point of choice behavior. Wells and Chinsky (1965), in an experimental study on the effects of competing messages, found that the perceived salience of a message was increased by issuing it in flights and that this type of pattern was superior to an even distribution of messages. Perceived salience and increased choice also occur when a message is placed closest to the time of choice. Data relating specifically to advertising are not available, and the above results are far from conclusive enough to incorporate as fixed guidelines in the design of advertising programs.

Conclusion: Message Structure

Much research needs to be done on the effects of various forms of message organization with consumers in consumer settings. However, the evidence from the experimental studies cited suggests that message structure may have important implications for marketers and be directly related to message success.

CHANNEL EFFECT

Communication chanels have been classified by whether the marketer exercises direct control. *Marketer-controlled channels* include advertising, personal selling, and sales promotion. *Nonmarketer-controlled channels* include editorial or news material and interpersonal communication (personal influence).[1] The marketer can, of course, exercise some influence over nonmarketer-controlled channels and may institute strategies to encourage such channels to favorably review his products.[2]

Existing research evidence on the effects of communication channels upon message effectiveness leads to the following conclusions:

1. The various communication channels are not equally effective at all stages of the purchase decision process.
2. Channels often perform varying functions for the individual and provide different kinds of information.
3. Instead of competing with one another, exposure to more than one channel of information may increase the likelihood of purchase, due to the cumulative effect achieved.

---

[1] Cox (1961) has distinguished among "marketer-dominated," "consumer-dominated," and "neutral" information sources.

[2] The product itself also could be thought of as a communication form, or channel. The preference here has been to consider the product as part of the message.

4. Channel effectiveness varies by the amount of attitudinal or behavioral change necessitated for purchase of the product.
5. On the whole, interpersonal communication (personal influence) may be the most effective channel of communication.

PURCHASE DECISION STAGES

Marketer-controlled channels (particularly advertising) are most often mentioned by consumers as original and additional sources of information, whereas nonmarketer-controlled channels (particularly personal influence) are most often mentioned as the last source of information prior to purchase. This has also been the typical finding in rural sociological research regarding farmer adoption of new technology and practices.

Table 6.3 summarizes results on the usage of communication channels for three consumer product categories: food, clothing, and appliances. The data are tied to specific purchases just made by the sample of respondents (Robertson, 1968d) and indicate (1) how the item came to the respondent's attention for the first time, (2) how else she heard of it before buying, and (3) which *one* of the ways mentioned was the most important source of information in the purchase decision. In interpreting these and other such data, it must be remembered that the consumer is not always accurate in tracing her communication usage; and she may have a bias toward deemphasizing the importance of advertising, since the prevailing ethic dictates against being susceptible to advertising.

It clearly can be seen that the various communication sources are not equally effective at the different stages of the purchase decision process. Most notable is the position of advertising, which begins as the most likely source of initial information, then declines markedly as a source of additional information, and further declines as the most important source. Advertising is not a convenient information-*seeking* form; the consumer usually does not search through magazines for product information. In contrast, interpersonal communication is mentioned increasingly as we move from first to additional to most important source of information.

The point is that purchase occurs over time, and the functioning and usage of information channels varies with the consumer's position on the purchase decision process.

FUNCTIONS PERFORMED

Communication channels possess distinct structural and operational features and, as a result, tend generally to perform different functions and specifically to play different roles in the purchase decision process (Wilkening, 1956; Katz, 1961). Comparisons of communication channels in these regards are provided in Table 6.4. The *operational features* considered are whether the channel is personal or impersonal in nature, whether it is accessible to

Table 6.3   Usage of Information Channels in the Purchase Decision Process

Channels	Small Appliances			Clothing			Food		
	First	Else	Most Important	First	Else	Most Important	First	Else	Most Important
Marketer-Controlled									
Advertising	48	23	8	35	27	16	45	25	19
Salesmen	1	1	1	4	1	6	0	0	0
Sales Promotion*	9	7	9	19	14	32	26	16	27
Nonmarketer-Controlled									
Personal Influence									
Friends, neighbors, relatives†	23	41	53	27	29	33	16	19	29
Immediate family	8	7	11	2	4	0	12	12	21
Professional advice	6	8	13	0	0	0	1	0	0
Editorial and news material‡	1	0	1	6	6	6	0	0	1
No Mentions	4	13	4	7	19	7	0	28	3
Total (N = 99)	100%	100%	100%	100%	100%	100%	100%	100%	100%

Source: Based on Robertson (1968d).

Note: Three questions were asked:

"Could you tell me how this product came to your attention for the *very first time?*"

"How *else* did you hear about this product before you bought it?"

"Which *one* of these ways was your *most important* source of information in your decision to buy this product?"

* Includes sampling, displays, in-store shopping, packaging.

† Includes actual discussions as well as noticing the item or trying the item, for example, in the home of a friend.

‡ Includes *Consumer Reports.*

Table 6.4 Operational Features of Communication Channels, Functions, and Major Roles in the Purchase Decision Process

Communication Channel	Structural and Operational Features	General Functions	Major Roles in Purchase Decision Process
Marketer-controlled			
Advertising	Impersonal Easily accessible Content of general interest One-way communication	Providing information to a mass audience Inducing favorable attitude toward the product Encouraging sales	Awareness Knowledge Some level of attitude change or formation
Personal selling	Personal Not readily accessible Content of specific interest Two-way communication	Providing specific information to potential customers Closing sales	Instruction in product usage Some ability to persuade "maybe" buyers Closing sales
Sales promotion	Impersonal Sometimes accessible Content of specific interest One-way communication	Coordinating and supplementing advertising and personal selling	Awareness Knowledge Instruction in product usage
Consumer-controlled			
Interpersonal communication	Personal Not always accessible Content generally of non-product-related interest Two-way communication	Friendship Solidarity Mutual aid Social status Recreation	Knowledge Attitude change Instruction in product usage Help in decision making
News and editorial material	Impersonal Not readily accessible Content of general interest One-way communication	News of new products Evaluation of products	Awareness Knowledge Attitude change Help in decision making

Source: Based in part on Wilkening (1956).

consumers, what content of information it contains, and whether it is one-way or two-way.

Advertising is impersonal in nature and therefore, allows only one-way communication because the consumer can't talk back, although he can distort, misunderstand, and tune out. These controls indicate the *active* role played by the audience member. Perhaps advertising's major advantage as a communication form is that it is highly accessible to consumers, who, in return, become highly accessible to marketers through advertising. Many consumers, of course, resent the intrusive power of advertising and its obvious one-sided persuasiveness, which sometimes causes it to be low in believability. The consumer's cognitive defenses often can be set to ignore, distort, or forget advertising messages. Yet for many products advertising can and does provide considerable knowledge of a general content and in a form requiring very little effort on the part of the consumer.

Personal selling possesses features both superior and inferior to advertising. Because it is personal or face-to-face in nature, it allows two-way communication. The customer can inquire, question, bargain, and gain immediate feedback. This allows the communication content to be focused on the consumer's particular needs, rather than being general in nature. A major disadvantage of personal selling is its relative inaccessibility to the consumer. A salesman cannot be available at the flick of a switch, as in television advertising. The cost of personal selling on a per client basis may be very high. Generally the consumer must be fairly well advanced on the purchase decision process for personal selling to be effective. Finally, personal selling, like advertising, is perceived as biased and persuasive, which may reduce its effectiveness and cause consumers to avoid personal sales situations.

Sales promotion has many of the same qualities as advertising. It is impersonal, one-way, and persuasive, although not necessarily as accessible. It can, however, provide content of more specific interest to the consumer in the form of displays, product demonstrations, and package information.

Interpersonal communication is, by definition, personal and two-way. The content of such communication is not generally product-related, however, and securing specific product information may be difficult unless an informed communicator is known. Inaccessibility is a problem in many cases. Interpersonal communication does offer the considerable advantage of being objective, that is, the information source is not trying to sell anything and, therefore, should provide two-sided data.

News and editorial material as a communication channel is of comparatively minor importance to the consumer. It is impersonal, allows only a one-way flow of communication, and its content is of general interest to a mass audience. The volume of such material which is consumption-related is not particularly great and is not readily accesible to consumers.

Elaboration of the structural-operational features of communication channels helps explain why different channels are used at different stages of the purchase decision process. In the case of new product purchase, the "conviction" stage has been found to be perhaps the crucial one in distinguishing adopters from nonadopters. At conviction, the individual is considering purchase and must justify this behavior as the proper course of action. Risk in purchase is often perceived by the consumer. A major risk-handling tactic is information seeking to reduce uncertainty. Arndt (1967a), for example, found that women who considered buying a new coffee risky (high-risk perceivers) sought more information about the coffee than low-risk perceivers. Cunningham (1966), like Arndt, found that consumers who perceived high risk for a product were more likely both to participate in product-oriented conversations with fellow consumers and to initiate such conversations.

Risk reduction, they both suggest, is best handled by interpersonal communication, although neither Arndt nor Cunningham make any comparison of the relative advantages of communication channels for this purpose. Marketer-controlled channels are, by their very nature, deliberately persuasive and biased and do not discuss unfavorable consequences. Therefore, to the extent that he seeks to justify purchase, the consumer frequently turns to non-marketer-controlled channels—predominantly interpersonal—in order to gain objectivity and to test his purchase opinions against the opinions and experiences of others.

A contrasting function of interpersonal communications is as a means of "finding out what others will think." Some individuals may communicate with others to find out what consumption strategies will impress others. In some reference groups, two cars or a color television set may connote status, whereas in other reference groups the deliberate underconsumption of such conspicuous products may connote status. Communication may function, therefore, to guage reference group consumption norms.

The "phenomenalist," or "transactional," view of communication, furthermore, suggests that the background factors of individuals lead them to use the media in different ways. For example, individuals may select different kinds of communications in line with—or in some cases in opposition to—their preexisting attitudes or beliefs. Stephenson (1967) argues that much of the time the mass media perform the obvious function of providing enjoyment, or "play," for many individuals. McLeod, Ward, and Tancill (1965–1966) provide evidence that more socially alienated individuals use the mass media for vicarious, rather than informational reasons, to a greater extent than do less-alienated individuals.

CUMULATIVE EFFECT

Communication channels have been seen to perform varying functions throughout the purchase decision process. As such, they should be viewed not as competing information disseminators, but as complementary. Cox

(1961) posits that "Complementary reinforcement may occur when two or more media transmit different appeals or otherwise perform different functions for the same product on communications directed toward the same audience" (p. 160). He compares this to "mutual reinforcement," which may occur when two or more media transmit the same appeal to the same audience. Both forms of reinforcement may result in added effectiveness.

Consumer exposure to multiple communication channels, according to this rationale, may result in a cumulative effect, since channels complement rather than compete with one another. Thus, the marketer should establish a total communication mix in order to achieve maximum cumulative effect.

An example may serve to demonstrate this point of view. In the introduction of a new laundry detergent, various communication channels generally are used in focused promotions for a target market. In advance of consumer advertising, company salesmen must convince wholesalers and retailers to stock the product. This is done to a considerable extent using the argument, "You can't afford not to stock the product, since a national advertising campaign of x million dollars is scheduled as well as extensive sampling and couponing. Your customers will be up and down the soap aisle looking for it." Shortly thereafter, extensive sales promotion efforts start just as advertising is beginning to appear. Sales of the product are due to multiple channel usage—each channel performing a somewhat different function in moving the consumer along the purchase decision process.

VARYING CHANNEL EFFECTIVENESS

In general, the effectiveness of communication channels will depend upon the following:
1. The degree of attitudinal or behavioral change necessary for product purchase.
2. The newness of the product concept.
3. The degree of perceived risk in product purchase.
4. The degree to which existing attitudes for the product category are ego-involved.
5. The degree to which existing behavior for this product category is group-sanctioned

Degree of Attitudinal Change Required

Marketer-controlled advertising is found to function far more frequently as an agent of reinforcement than change. Advertising will have greatest potential effectiveness under conditions necessitating least attitudinal-behavioral change. According to Klapper (1960), "Minor change, short of conversion (of attitude), simply may not constitute a psychological threat sufficiently critical to bring all the defensive forces into full play" (p. 44).

Newness of the Product Concept

Although advertising is relatively ineffectual in changing attitude or behavior, it can be "quite effective in forming opinions and attitudes in regard to *new issues*, particularly as these issues are the more unrelated to 'existing attitude clusters' " (Klapper, 1957–1958, p. 462). Since most innovations are, however, of a continuous nature (involving only minor alteration), existing attitude clusters will generally be relevant and guide attitude formation in regard to the new product. A new soap or cigarette, for example, will be judged in line with individuals' opinions of all such products. It may be proposed that the more discontinuous the innovation, the less in line it will be with existing attitude clusters and, therefore, the more effective advertising is likely to be in bringing about *favorable attitude formation*.

Degree of Perceived Risk

The greater the level of perceived risk in purchase, the more information is sought and the greater the reliance on interpersonal communication. Evidence to support this hypothesis has been provided by Cunningham (1966) and Arndt (1967a). Lionberger (1963) reports that farmers turn more to friends and neighbors as the importance of the purchase increases. Robertson (1968d), in a study of informal neighborhood groups, found that the greater the aggregate level of perceived risk within the group, the greater the communication among group members about the product in question. This relationship was most pronounced for appliances and less pronounced for food and clothing.

Degree of Ego-Involved Attitudes

Ego-involved attitudes are particularly resistant to change, especially by impersonal means of communication (Klapper, 1960, p. 45). However, for large segments of the population, many attitudes in regard to consumption may not be ego-involved. This may be the basis of the "low-involvement" hypothesis of attitude change; that is, low salience may lead to attitude change, since the individual does not actively resist persuasion, that is, his defenses are not aroused. The less ego-involved the consumption of a certain product or brand, the more effective advertising is likely to be in gaining immediate change.

Degree of Group Relevance

Finally, channel effectiveness will vary with the degree to which consumption for a certain product type is group-sanctioned or group-related. The more formalized and rigid the group norm, the less effective marketer-controlled channels are likely to be.

Bourne (1957), in an article much-quoted among marketers, has focused on reference group effect, including influence not only from *belonging* to a certain group but also from *anticipating* group membership or *avoiding* it. His thesis is that reference groups influence behavior in (1) setting aspiration levels and (2) specifying appropriate forms of behavior. However, he recognizes that reference group effect is only one determinant of purchase behavior and that it may or may not be important in a given purchase situation. Some purchases are socially conditioned, whereas others have little social relevance. Furthermore, reference group influence varies in brand selection also. Thus, in some situations, reference group influence will be present in (1) product purchase and/or (2) brand purchase or (3) neither product nor brand purchase.

Cars are cited by Bourne as an example of high reference group influence in both product and brand decisions. Whether or not the person buys a car and what brand he buys are decisions affected by other people. Instant coffee, (at least in the early 1950s), was an item where the brand was not particularly subject to reference group influence, but whether a woman used instant coffee was subject to reference group influence, since instant was perceived as an inferior substitute for regular coffee. This has probably changed; and now, in the 1970s, at a later stage in the product life cycle and with more general consumer acceptance, the brand may be more subject to group influence than the product. Clothing is cited as an example of brand, not product, influence: everyone must wear the product, but the brand chosen is of social significance. This point is debatable, since other people seem to exert more influence regarding clothing styles, and there is little brand recognition. Salt is perhaps the best example where reference group influence is felt hardly at all either in product or brand selection.

These results are now some fifteen years old and must not be accepted as proven fact, but as indicative of the varying importance of interpersonal communication. These data have not been subject to empirical testing. It can be tentatively concluded that the less group-related the item, the more effective marketer-controlled communication channels are likely to be.

OVERALL EFFECTIVENESS

It has been concluded most often that interpersonal communication is more effective overall than any other communication channel. A substantial body of research documents this conclusion, although with differing methodologies and weights of evidence. The dominant importance of interpersonal communication, however, should cause us to lose sight neither of the cumulative effect of a sequence of communication sources nor of the fact that interpersonal communication, while powerful, seldom can act alone. Furthermore, since it is not under the marketer's control, his efforts to influence it may be more costly than the benefits to be gained.

The overall superiority of interpersonal communication is documented almost exclusively by postdecisional research which traces the consumer's usage of information channels and attaches effectiveness ratings based on his opinions of which source was "most important." Whereas such research may yield indications of channel effectiveness, it must be reiterated that consumers, in order not to appear gullible, are often reluctant to attribute advertising with any considerable degree of influence.

Evidence for interpersonal communication's superiority does come from research in a variety of consumption categories. Katona and Mueller (1954) concluded that personal influence was the major information means for buyers of durable goods. William E. Bell (1963) concluded that personal influence was more important than mass media advertising for buyers of new appliances. Ryan and Gross (1943) and Lionberger (1955) reported that interpersonal communication was the most important channel in the adoption of hybrid corn and other farming innovations. Rich (1963) found that interpersonal communication was used most by department store customers. Feldman and Spencer (1965) found that other people most often were used by new community residents in choosing a physician. Haines (1966) found interpersonal communication most important in decisions to adopt new food products. The data reported in Table 6.3, indicate that interpersonal communication was "most important" to consumers in recent purchase decisions for new small appliances, clothing, and food products. These results were most pronounced in the case of new small appliance purchases.

SUPERIORITY OF INTERPERSONAL COMMUNICATION

The documented superiority of interpersonal communication for many purchase decisions may be due to a number of reasons, including its nondeliberateness and corresponding trustworthiness, its ability to break down the selective processes, and its overall efficiency.

Nondeliberateness

Interpersonal communication attains much of its power because of its generally nondeliberate nature. Individuals are much less likely to raise cognitive defenses than in regard to advertising.

Breakdown of Selective Processes

The overall effectiveness of interpersonal communication is further explained in that the selective barriers of exposure, perception, and retention are less likely to be fully operative (Rogers, 1962, p. 225). In the course of discussion with another person, the opportunity to avoid *exposure* to certain topics does not exist. In fact, the topics discussed are most likely relevant to both parties, or communication will cease. Furthermore, the other person cannot be ignored as easily or tuned out; and, of course, to the extent that the topic and person are relevant, there may be little attempt to do so *(per-*

ception). Finally, a more conscious attempt to remember the content of the discussion may occur, since a response to the same person on the same topic may be necessary at a later point, and the other person can also act as a reminder at a later date *(retention.)*

This is not to suggest, however, that the selective processes are inoperative. The individual's mental predispositions and attitudes still act as a filter for information received, recorded, and remembered over time. Arndt (1967*b*), for example, suggests that respondents who were predisposed not to purchase a new product also were less likely to engage in interpersonal communication about it—the assumption being that lack of purchase interest acted against communication reception. There is considerable difficulty, however, in establishing whether lack of interest led to less communication participation or whether less communication participation led to lack of purchase interest.

Communication Efficiency

Communication is most efficient under conditions of immediate feedback. The two-way nature of interpersonal communication allows each participant to be actively involved—to ask questions and to seek clarification. Learning can take place most effectively under such conditions, since the information exchanged probably is of direct importance to each party.

DYSFUNCTIONALITY IN INTERPERSONAL COMMUNICATION

The superiority of interpersonal communication as reported is from the *consumer point of view.* Although it has generally been concluded that interpersonal communication increases the rate of diffusion, this result *applies only to products which diffuse successfully.* For many other products which never achieve a necessary level of diffusion—the majority of new products introduced—interpersonal communication may retard and prevent diffusion. From the marketer's point of view, interpersonal communication is not necessarily a good thing. Furthermore, since it is beyond his direct control, it cannot be the main channel by which to disseminate product messages.

Interpersonal communication can be dysfunctional in (1) recommending against adoption, (2) being unreliable in content, and (3) being unfavorably perceived.

Recommending Against Adoption

A recommendation against adoption can occur first when the norms of the groups to which the person belongs oppose certain forms of innovative behavior. This may have accounted for initial reaction against the "midi" in 1970. Similarly, a corporation president's friends may well talk against his buying a Volkswagen. Rejectors of innovations may also discourage others from buying. If an individual has undergone a bad experience with a product, he may often become an "active rejector" and have quite a disrupting effect on adoption by other members of his group.

Unreliability in Content

People do not necessarily communicate accurate information about a product. In fact, they tend to communicate opinions, that is, evaluative rather than factual information; and people who are not well informed may retard diffusion. A good deal of distorted communication may circulate especially for radically new products or products which are difficult to explain or demonstrate.

Being Unfavorably Perceived

Information disseminated may be unfavorably perceived if the communicator is unfavorably perceived or perceived as unreliable. John G. Myers (1966), for example, has found that adoption of a new product is more likely to occur when recommended by a leader rather than a nonleader. There is a tendency, of course, for many people to be negative in outlook and to convey such feelings about products and brands. And people tend to select other people who hold many of the same opinions. Thus, a person who feels that new products are generally worthless may choose others of this opinion, whereas a person who feels that new products are generally worthwhile may choose others of this opinion. A compounding effect is, therefore, likely to occur.

Evidence for the potentially dysfunctional nature of interpersonal communication is given by Arndt (1967a), who found that only 18 percent of those exposed to unfavorable word of mouth about a new coffee bought the product, compared to 54 percent of those exposed to positive word of mouth.

SUMMARY

The communication event consists of a communicator sending out a message using a given channel to a specified audience of consumers. The success of a communication in gaining exposure, favorable attitude, and ultimate response is the result of the interaction of source, message, channel, and consumer attributes.

Source Effect

The success of a communication depends, sometimes in considerable measure, on source effect, that is, how the audience perceives the communicator (or source). A critical element in a communicator's effectiveness is his perceived credibility. In a famous experiment by Kelman and Hovland (1953), three audiences were exposed to identical messages favoring extreme leniency in the treatment of juvenile delinquents. The first audience had the speaker identified as a juvenile court judge; the second audience heard the message as from a member of the audience; and the third audience was told its speaker was a juvenile delinquent. Despite identical messages, audience judgments of fairness of presentation were more favorable for the high-credibility communicator (the judge), and more immediate attitude change occurred in the direction advocated by the high-credibility communicator.

Bauer (1967), however, has since argued that credibility may be something other than the "unitary" phenomenon it has been regarded to be and that a high degree of credibility may not always be a good thing. Rarick (1963), for example, has distinguished between cognitive and affective components of credibility. The aspects of the cognitive component are power, prestige, and competence; the aspects of the affective component are trustworthiness and likability. Attitude change, in Rarick's findings, showed a positive relationship to both cognitive and affective components; but learning of factual material was negatively related to the affective component. Thus, the more intense the affective component (either in liking or disliking), the less the potential retention of information.

Bauer (1967) has elaborated and extended the Rarick findings, relating them to his conceptions of problem-solving and psychosocial games. The consumer in a purchase decision situation, according to Bauer, will either play the problem-solving game, that is, he will engage in behavior to choose the best purchase alternative by searching for and evaluating information to reach a decision, or he will play the psychosocial game, that is, he will come to a decision based on the behavior he sees as being most likely to be rewarded by his peer group.

In line with this reasoning, competence and trust are relevant to the problem-solving game, because they involve assessments of whether the person is qualified to make assertions and whether he is likely to be honest in such assertions. Power and likability are relevant in the psychosocial game, because they involve assessments of whether a particular response will please another person or lead to group acceptance.

Message Effect

The message is a total configuration of such elements as words, pictures, sounds, and movement which attempts to communicate a certain meaning. These elements are interdependent, and the meaning derives from the Gestalt. The issue is how message structure affects communication impact. A typical list of questions might be:

1. How "factual" should the message be?
2. How much of a "threat appeal" should the message use?
3. How entertaining or irritating should the message be?
4. Should conclusions be drawn or left implicit?
5. Should a one-sided or two-sided (pro-and-con) message be used?
6. Should the message rely on a climax or anticlimax technique?

These questions have not been answered definitively. The issue of how factual a message should be yields conflicting results—both factual messages and messages with very little factual information, seem to be effective under conditions not yet fully specified. Results on threat appeal suggest that moderate threat in advertising probably has best long-run effectiveness. Investigation of the entertaining-irritating issue, although highly preliminary, suggests that the kind of message is not the determining factor of its effect, but the intensity of reaction the message achieves. Thus, it is argued that either highly entertaining or highly irritating messages may have greater effect than more neutral messages.

Experimental research has demonstrated that conclusion drawing in a message is advisable. However, certain situations may mediate this finding. Conclusion drawing may be detrimental to the extent that (1) the audience is intelligent, (2) the issue is simple or highly personal, and (3) such an approach may unnecessarily limit the product's market and usage definitions. Conditions favoring one- or two-sided messages are fairly well specified and depend upon (1) the initial position of the audience, (2) the level of education of the audience, and (3) the audience's exposure to subsequent competing messages.

Finally, the issue of whether to use a climax or anticlimax message design has not been resolved and, in fact, the superiority of one or the other may depend upon individual situations. It is suggested, for example, that presenting the strongest arguments first (anticlimax) may be more successful when the audience has little interest in the product; or when the product is new. In contrast, a climax message may be superior when the audience is interested in the product. Although findings on the retention of climax and anticlimax messages conflict, it is agreed that material in the middle of a message is remembered least.

Channel Effect

Communication channels provide the means by which the message is disseminated. They can be distinguished on the basis of whether or not the marketer exercises direct control. Marketer-controlled channels include advertising, personal selling, and sales promotion. Nonmarketer-controlled channels include editorial or news material, consumer information publications, and interpersonal communication (word-of-mouth advertising). The marketer does, of course, exercise some influence over nonmarketer-controlled channels and may institute strategies to encourage them to review his products favorably.

Research evidence leads to a number of conclusions regarding channel effectiveness. First, the various communication channels are not equally effective at all stages of the purchase decision process. Marketer-controlled channels (particularly advertising) are most often mentioned by consumers as original and additional sources of information about products, whereas nonmarketer-controlled channels (particularly interpersonal communication) are most often mentioned as attitude determinants and as the last source of information prior to purchase. The point is that purchase occurs over time, and the function and use of information channels varies with the consumer's position on the purchase decision continuum.

Communication channels possess distinct structural and operational features and, as a result, tend to perform different functions for the individual and to provide different kinds of information. Thus, although advertising is highly accessible to consumers and provides a certain amount of factual information, its obvious one-sided persuasiveness and the desire of consumers to achieve more "objective" information often leads them to turn to fellow consumers for evaluative information.

A consumer's exposure to more than one channel may increase the likelihood of purchase response because of the cumulative effect achieved. Channels should, therefore, be viewed as complementary rather than competing.

Channel effectiveness varies by the amount of attitudinal or behavioral change necessitated for purchase of the product. Marketer-controlled advertising, for example, is likely to function far more frequently as an agent of reinforcement than of change. Advertising has greatest potential effectiveness under conditions requiring least attitudinal change.

On the whole, a number of researchers conclude that interpersonal communication (word-of-mouth advertising) may be the most effective channel of communication. This should not obscure the cumulative effect of a sequence of communication sources. The facts are that interpersonal communication seldom is effective alone, and that interpersonal communication, although powerful, is not under the marketer's control, and his efforts to influence it often may be more costly than the benefits gained.

CHAPTER 7

PERSONAL INFLUENCE AND OPINION LEADERSHIP

The marketing executive hardly needs an introduction to the concept of personal influence. The impact of this phenomenon is recognized at least implicitly, but the problem is its *control*. What strategies can the firm initiate to affect or take advantage of consumer networks of communication?

Personal influence is also a determining factor of consumer or market behavior in a number of sophisticated behavioral models. Some form of personal influence is basic to the Coleman, Katz, and Menzel (1966) and Bass (1969) epidemiological models, to the Nicosia (1966) and Andreasen (1965) buyer behavior models, to the SPRINTER (Urban, 1969) and NOMMAD (Cook and Herniter, 1968) new product decision models, and to such micro-behavioral adoption models as those of Alba (1967), Amstutz (1967), and Nakanishi (1968).

Despite its recognized importance in consumer behavior (and particularly innovative behavior), personal influence is one of the most elusive concepts in the marketing literature; and its complexity and functioning have not been well documented. The topic is often treated in simplistic terms, and there remains a belief in the two-step model of communication, that is, a flow of influence from the mass media to the opinion leader to his followers.

It is necessary to go beyond the two-step notion and to recognize it as only one mode of personal influence. It suggests a dominant opinion leader initiating influence contacts with followers. This model simply does not account for all the means by which personal influence may occur. (This chapter and Chapter 8 will present a rationale for the occurrence of personal processes of influence and a framework for viewing alternative influenced modes. Then Chapter 9 will present some considerations and guidelines for using personal influence in marketing programs of action.)

AN EXTENDED VIEW OF PERSONAL INFLUENCE

Personal influence refers to a change in an individual's attitude or behavior as a result of interpersonal communication. Personal influence is indeed a multidimensional phenomenon and can occur in numerous ways (see Table 7.1). Three basic distinctions must be made:

Table 7.1   Personal Influence Possibilities

Mode	Verbal		Visual	
Direction	One-way	Two-way	One-way	Two-way
Source-initiated	1	2	3	4
Recipient-initiated	5	6	7	8

1. Communication leading to influence may be initiated by the influencer or influencee. Influence, therefore, can be *source initiated* or *recipient initiated*.
2. Influence resulting from communication can be *one-way* or *two-way*. The individual can influence while being influenced.
3. Influence may occur through *verbal* or *visual* communication.

INITIATION OF INFLUENCE

At times it may be rewarding for the individual to communicate information to another person, and at times it may be rewarding for him to seek information from another. Cunningham (1966) found that approximately 50 percent of interpersonal communication involving household products was recipient-initiated, that is, information-seeking. Arndt (1968, p. 47) found that 22 percent of interpersonal communication about a new coffee product was also recipient-initiated.

A case example regarding the purchase of a car may serve to illustrate information giving and seeking. The person who has just purchased a new car may experience a need to talk about his purchase to other people and in the process may influence them. When, in contrast, the individual is considering the purchase of a new car, he often seeks information to reduce uncertainty. This tendency will be more pronounced, for example, to the extent that he lacks purchase experience.

Berlyne (1960) has proposed that the individual prefers, or at least deems satisfactory, an intermediate ambiguity (uncertainty) level. Under conditions of ambiguity beyond an intermediate level, the consumer actively seeks information to define the situation and to reach a decision. If ambiguity is increased too much, however, he tends to avoid information seeking and may resort to no decision or to any decision alternative ("One brand is as good as any other"). On the other hand, if ambiguity is too low, the individual may seek other alternatives.

Perhaps this can be illustrated by the case of a mattress buyer, who starts out under conditions of low ambiguity believing that one nationally advertised mattress is as good as another. Low ambiguity leads him to seek information to differentiate among mattress brands. Soon, however, he is in a position of high ambiguity because every mattress claims superior features and there appears to be no way to substantiate these claims because all the mattresses look and feel alike in a showroom trial. At this point, the consumer may return to his original position that all mattresses are the same and choose one intuitively.

DIRECTION OF INFLUENCE

It has been traditional to view personal influence as a one-way occurrence. This is reflected in the two-step flow hypothesis, where a change in attitude or behavior occurs only on the part of the *receiver*. This definition seems not to account for the many informal product-related conversations where a mutual give-and-take of information occurs and where either or both participants in the communication event may be influenced (assuming a two-person interaction event). An individual can influence (one-way) or influence and be influenced (two-way).

Returning to the automobile example, the possible occurrence of two-way influence can be noted under conditions of cognitive dissonance. One form of tension reduction is to seek confirming evidence that the right decision was made. Social support can provide such evidence and the new-car buyer may, therefore, talk about his car with others, thus rationalizing his behavior and gaining assurance that he acted wisely. Under these conditions he may influence others while being influenced himself.

Recent research findings support the occurrence of two-way as well as one-way influence. King and Summers (1967a, p. 29), in a study of fashion diffusion, found that 39 percent of those engaged in interpersonal communication mentioned participation as both a transmitter and a receiver. Furthermore, a majority of those who classified themselves as transmitters or receivers also reported playing the alternate role. King and Summers rightfully point to this data as questioning the two-step hypothesis. Robertson (1968d) in a study of innovative behavior and opinion leadership within informal neighborhood groups, asked each group member her best source of advice for food, clothing, and appliances. Results for a fairly typical group are depicted in Figure 7.1, and a reasonable amount of two-way influence is indicated.

Figure 7.1   Influence Sources for Food, Clothing, and Appliances within a Typical Informal Neighborhood Group

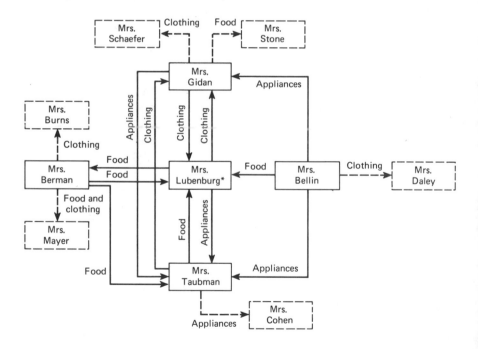

Zimmerman and Bauer (1956) give further evidence for the existence of two-way influence. Their findings show that an individual's image of his future audience can directly affect the way he perceives, structures, and communicates new information. For example, graduate students in journalism were given information for and against raising teacher salaries and later were told that they would address an assembly of teachers. When they were told of the possible speaking engagement, the students' retention of evidence *against* raising teacher salaries decreased significantly.

The fallacy of viewing all personal influence as one-way is tied to the highly questionable assumption that personal influence is most often *deliberate*. The proportion of cases in which communication is initiated with the objective of effecting change is probably small. When individuals are asked to relate incidents of communication preceding purchase of a product, they are quite likely to give replies such as the following: "We were all sitting drinking coffee when Eleanor asked if anyone had tried the new freeze-dried coffee being advertised on television. Nobody had, although we'd all seen the ads. Next time I was at the market I saw it and tried it."

The objective observer would probably say influence occurred in this situation, but it was not deliberate. The group discussion may well have served as a learning experience for a number of people, each of whom gave and received information, and in the process influenced and was influenced.

Newcomb (1953) hypothesizes that to the extent that two or more individuals interact with one another, their orientations toward each other and toward objects of the environment will be interdependent. This he refers to as his principle of "co-orientation." The minimal definition of such a system is schematically represented as follows:

Figure 7.2   Newcomb's "Coorientation" Model

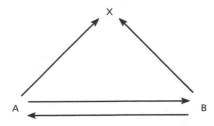

Accordingly, Newcomb argues that

There are few if any objects so private that one's orientations toward them are uninfluenced by others' orientations (p. 394). . . . And to be dependent upon the other, insofar as such dependence influences behavior, is to be oriented toward him (p. 395).

Newcomb also postulates that a strain toward symmetry of orientation will come about as persons modify their orientations toward items of the environment; this occurs over time as persons "exchange roles as transmitters and receivers of information" (p. 395).

MODE OF INFLUENCE

It is not necessary to talk to another person to be influenced by him. Seeing a neighbor wear a certain outfit may influence a consumer to do likewise. Such visual communication may, in fact, be as persuasive as verbal communication, particularly for goods high on visibility. The conspicuousness of room airconditioners may have been as important in accounting for diffusion patterns as the networks of conversation which were also operative (Whyte, 1954). Visual cues can be just as meaningful as verbal cues—a raised eyebrow or the failure of friends to mention a new dress may cause a woman to seriously wonder whether it is acceptable or not.

Personal influence can, in summary, be exercised in eight forms (see Table 7.1). It may be of value to consider each form briefly:

1. *Source-initiated/one-way/verbal* influence is most usually equated with the *two-step model* of communication. It is reflected in the following comment:

     "Jane Simpson told me about how good it was so I gave it a try."
2. *Source-initiated/two-way/verbal* influence occurs when the person who initiates the conversation influences the other person, but in the process she is also influenced:

     "I couldn't help showing her our new Touch-Tone telephone. She really wanted it and made me feel better about the higher cost."
3. *Source-initiated/one-way/visual* influence is very difficult to trace, yet highly prevalent. This form is reflected in a woman's showing off her new dress at a social function and thereby influencing another person.
4. *Source-initiated/two-way/visual* influence occurs when the woman shows off her new dress and influences others. Then, based on the feedback she obtains, she is influenced as to whether or not to wear the dress in the future. The feedback may be nothing more than a raised eyebrow, some flattering stares, or a lack of attention.
5. *Recipient-initiated/one-way/verbal* influence is the simple case of a person seeking advice from another person:

     "I asked Jean what she knew about blenders."
6. *Recipient-initiated/two-way/verbal* influence involves a mutual give-and-take of information whereby both parties may be influenced, although the conversation was initiated by a person seeking advice:

     "I asked Jean what she knew about blenders. Our conversation enlightened both of us."

7. *Recipient-initiated/one-way/visual* influence occurs as an individual, as part of his information-seeking efforts, observes the consumption behavior of others and is influenced in the process.

8. *Recipient-initiated/two-way/visual* influence may occur as the individual observes and is influenced. In turn, the very process of his observing may influence others. This is most obvious when a woman notices another woman's dress, thereby providing confirmation for the wearer.

OPINION LEADERSHIP

Consistent with the personal influence concept is the recognition that not all consumers wield equal influence. Those who are most influential are designated *opinion leaders*, that is, those to whom others turn for information and advice. This designation is unfortunate, since it suggests an absolute leader whom others seek to follow. Yet opinion leadership is a relative concept, and the opinion leader may not be much more influential than his followers.

The complexity of opinion leadership is illustrated in a comment by Coleman, Katz, and Menzel (1966) based on their research tracing diffusion of a new drug among physicians.

> Perhaps Dr. A., who had used the drug, advised Dr. B. to do likewise; perhaps Dr. B. copied Dr. A. without being told; perhaps Drs. A and B made a joint decision. Perhaps, in a more complex way, Dr. A. evaluated Dr. B's experience, whereupon Dr. B. accepted Dr. A's evaluation; and so on (pp. 111–112).

Marketers have long attempted to reach influentials, but these influentials were generally defined by high occupational status or by community position. A major value of Katz and Lazarsfeld's research (1955) and their two-step hypothesis was in pointing out that people are most often influenced by those with whom they are in everyday contact, by people most like themselves. The individual is not going to look to his congressman or doctor for advice on appliances, but to his closest friend or neighbor who has some expertise or opinions on the matter. There are opinion leaders, therefore, at every status level and within every informal group.

OPINION LEADER TRAITS

The first documentation of opinion leader traits is that of Katz and Lazarsfeld (1955), who analyzed the flow of influence in four areas of interest: marketing (in this case, food shopping), fashion, public affairs, and movies. Differing opinion leader profiles were obtained. The *food opinion leader* tended to be a married woman with a comparatively large family and of a gregarious or outgoing nature. She could be located on all status levels, and her influence was limited to the status level on which she was found. The *fashion leader* was more likely to be young and highly gregarious. She was also somewhat more likely to be of higher status. The *public affairs leader* was a high-status woman of considerable gregariousness. In public affairs influence did cross status boundaries, moving from high to low status. Finally, in the case of *movie going*, the leader was most often a young woman, often unmarried. Social status and gregariousness were not of significance.

Coleman, Katz, and Menzel (1966), in their study of physician adoption of a new drug, found that "social networks affected the [drug] adoptions of only those doctors who were well integrated into them; . . . the relatively isolated doctors tended to innovate by a more individualistic process" (p. 124). The process of personal influence functioned best, therefore, for doctors who were gregarious or socially integrated; and social integration was a primary determinant of the amount of opinion leadership exerted and received. The physician drug opinion leader was profiled as follows: attended a quality medical school; had more experience with out-of-town medical institutions; had a longer tenure of practice; was more often a specialist rather than a general practitioner; was more likely to be a native of the town in which his practice was located; was more likely to hold a senior staff position at a local hospital; was more likely to share an office with other physicians; attended more medical meetings; read more professional journals; was somewhat conservative in his attitudes toward therapy; and was more profession-oriented rather than patient-oriented (p. 148).

Rogers (1962b) has offered a general summary of opinion leaders which emphasizes three "traits": social participation, social status, and cosmopolitanism (p. 237). He concludes that opinion leaders evidence more social participation than followers, although the former "are not necessarily the powerholders or the formal leaders in their communities"; they also have higher social status than followers, "but not too much higher" (p. 241). And, opinion leaders are more cosmopolitan than followers, that is, they tend to be more oriented beyond their communities—attending more out-of-town meetings and having more friends outside the community.

The "Tastemaker" studies (Opinion Research Corporation, 1959) have suggested that the consumer influential is cosmopolitan as measured by a number of criteria. It seems, however, that cosmopolitan opinion leadership may be tied to cosmopolitan products; and many of the products studied were of this order—for example, car rentals and credit cards. Or, cosmopolitan opinion leadership may be tied to a basic lack of information at a local level. This would be true for many farming innovations, where information is available almost exclusively from out-of-community extension agents. For many, if not most, consumer products these conditions do not apply, and it would not be expected that the food opinion leader, for example, would be cosmopolitan.

It also has been found that opinion leaders deviate less from group norms than the average group member (Rogers and Cartano, 1962). Klapper (1960) states that opinion leaders "are usually supernormative [group] members" and that they are "especially familiar with and loyal to group standards and values" (p. 460). Elihu Katz (1957), addressing the same issue, talks of opinion leaders being "empowered" to act in this capacity by other group members.

Blau and Scott (1962), in their studies of formal organizations, have made the point that authority is vested in the leader by his subordinates and that unless he holds their respect, he will cease to be an effective leader. This concept of *vested* leadership seems particularly apt for the opinion leader. In order to attain and maintain an opinion leadership position, the individual has to reflect underlying norms and values for his area of consumption leadership. The clothing influential, for example, cannot be too far out or too far behind if she is to be accorded a position of leadership. She, among all group members, will most nearly reflect the existing norm in clothing.

A number of researchers (Rogers and Cartano, 1962) have found that opinion leaders are higher on innovativeness. It does not follow from this, however, that opinion leaders are innovators. King (1963), for example, in his study of fashion diffusion, found innovator and opinion leader functions to differ so that "The innovator is the earliest visual communicator of the season's styles for the mass of fashion consumers. The influential appears to define and endorse appropriate standards" (p. 124). Tigert (1969) has similarly concluded that the life-style patterns of the opinion leader and innovator differ in a number of important dimensions. Rossiter and Robertson (1968), in research dealing with the interplay of innovator and opinion leader roles in fashion, found a moderate relationship between innovativeness and opinion leadership, but differentiated innovator and opinion leader profiles. The opinion leader could be characterized as an editor of fashions, the innovator as an adventurer.

The correspondence between the roles of innovator and opinion leader and the persons playing them would seem to depend on the normative structure of the social system. Innovator and opinion leader roles coincide to a greater extent in the medical social system studied by Coleman, Katz, and Menzel (1966) than is generally the case in agricultural social systems. It may well be that urban medical norms are more progressive and, therefore, more conducive to new products than rural agricultural norms. Marsh and Coleman (1956) have pointed out that divergent results can also be obtained in farming. They found that opinion leaders in modern neighborhoods were mostly innovators, whereas in traditional neighborhoods they were just above average in innovativeness. This Marsh and Coleman attributed to the social system norms in operation.

Research with consumers by Nicosia (1964) indicated that auto insurance opinion leaders tended to know more about such insurance than nonleaders; he cautions, however, that "there can be respondents who influence others despite . . . their ignorance of that about which they are talking" (p. 355). This illustrates the potential unreliability of interpersonal communication. Although opinion leaders are generally found to know more about their area of interest, this is not always the case and the question could be raised whether opinion leaders sometimes occupy this position because of their higher gregariousness and, therefore, greater accessibility. This undoubtedly is a good part of opinion leadership, especially for product categories where technical knowledge is not required. It could also be asked whether opinion leaders achieve their positions on the basis of dominant personality traits. A research experiment by Robertson and Myers (1969), using a standardized personality test, suggests that this is not the case; in fact, these authors conclude, "One cannot say that any of the basic personality variables relates substantially to opinion leadership for any of the product areas studied" (p. 167).

Feldman and Spencer (1965) conducted research on how consumers select medical services and found that influentials tend to be somewhat older than advisees. In the Katz and Lazarsfeld (1955) study, age of the influential was found to vary with the interest area under investigation. Feldman and Spencer (1965) further found that most influentials were of the same social status as the persons they advised. King (1963), in a study of fashion diffusion, also found that influentials were generally of the same status level as those whom they advised (p. 39). Rogers (1962b), however, has concluded on the basis of his examination of agricultural research, that "opinion leaders have higher social status than their followers" (p. 241). Unfortunately, what these various researchers mean by "social status" is not clearly defined. Examination of the research evidence leads to the overall conclusion that opinion leaders are most often of the same or approximately same social class as their followers, although they might be of somewhat higher status within that social class. For example, Lionberger and Coughenour (1957) reported that farmers tended to seek advice from opinion leaders whose social status was slightly higher, but not "out of sight."

In an integrated, multivariable study of fashion opinion leaders, Summers (1968) found that "real differences" existed between transmitters and non-transmitters, but that "in the aggregate, these differences were not large" (p. 235). For example, opinion leaders were found to be younger, better educated, and with higher incomes and higher occupational status. Opinion leaders also showed tendencies to be higher on "organizational affiliation," "social communications," and "physical mobility." As for psychological factors, Summers found them of minor explanatory value and concluded that "This casts additional doubt on the applicability of the use of standard psychological tests for predicting market-oriented behavior" (p. 214).

A recent study by Tigert (1969) addresses itself to Summers's critique of the use of standardized personality tests as consumer research instruments. Tigert devised an Activities, Interests, and Opinions (AIO) scale based on three hundred questions concerning such topics as diet consciousness, sports, community affairs, and self-confidence. He concludes that although the opinion leader cannot be distinguished by demographic variables, she can be characterized by the AIO variables. The overall opinion leader profile drawn by Tigert (1969) is as follows:

> She tends to be a self-confident information seeker with a strong interest in the community and in new brands. In addition, she is price and fashion conscious, active in the PTA and charity work. She is strongly oriented toward the family and optimistic about the family's financial affairs. In general, one might summarize this profile by saying that the opinion leader is highly satisfied with life and an active participant in what this world has to offer (p. 30).

A summary profile of opinion leader traits in Table 7.2 indicates the tentativeness of existing results. Age varies by product category; social status is most often the same as that of advisees; high gregariousness is uniformly the case; cosmopolitanism, or orientation beyond the local community, is generally cited, but has not been tested explicitly for consumer goods; knowledge is generally greater; no distinguishing personality features exist; norm adherence is greater; and higher innovativeness is found.

Table 7.2   Summary Profile of Opinion Leader Traits

Characteristic	Findings
Age	Varies by product category
Social status	Generally same as advisee
Gregariousness	High
Cosmopolitanism	Limited evidence that higher than advisees
Knowledge	Generally greater for area of influence
Personality	No major distinguishing traits
Norm adherence	Generally greater than advisees
Innovativeness	Higher than advisees

A SITUATIONAL PHENOMENON

Lack of a clear-cut opinion leader profile or of specific opinion leader traits reflects much the same experience as in organizational behavior research. Cartwright and Zander (1960) conclude that, for the most part, efforts to discover the traits distinguishing leaders (within an organizational context) from nonleaders have been disappointing due to the contradictory findings obtained. Since standardized leader characteristics cannot be established, the process of leader identification is that much more difficult, as is the marketer's attempt to identify product opinion leaders. Cartwright and Zander, therefore, argue for a more "situational" approach to leadership (p. 490).

Although certain abilities and knowledge are required of a leader, these qualities also are widely distributed among his followers. And the abilities or knowledge which make a leader effective in one situation, such as food leadership, may be quite different from those required for another situation, such as automobile leadership. This is not to say that the marketer cannot study opinion leader traits for his product or product category; in fact, such research is an advisable course of action. But a standardized opinion leader profile does not apply across all product categories.

The requisites of such a situational approach are contained in a statement by Elihu Katz (1957) addressing the question, "What, if anything, distinguishes influential from influencee?" His conclusion is that influence is related to (1) *the personification of certain values* (who one is), (2) *competence* (what one knows), and (3) *strategic social location* (whom one knows). To the extent that an individual represents or personifies group values, he stands a better chance of leadership. Thus, if the group emphasizes an "in" manner of dress, the person who dresses most accordingly may well be influential. Again, to the extent that an individual is highly knowledgeable, he stands a better chance of leadership. Finally, to the extent that an individual is available and active in the everyday interpersonal communication process, the better his chance of leadership.

OPINION LEADERSHIP OVERLAP

A recurring question on the subject of opinion leadership is whether a "general" opinion leader exists. Is an opinion leader in one area also more likely to be an opinion leader in another area? The most frequently quoted finding on this issue is that of Katz and Lazarsfeld (1955), who conclude that

> The fact that a woman is a leader in one area has no bearing on the likelihood that she will be a leader in another. By and large, . . . the hypothesis of a generalized leader receives little support in this study. . . . Each arena, it seems, has a corps of leaders of its own (p. 334).

This conclusion has since been challenged by Marcus and Bauer (1964) after a reexamination of the original data. These authors employed what seems to be a more appropriate means of analysis and found that the number of two- and three-area opinion leaders was significantly greater statistically— but not importantly greater—than expected under conditions of independence among opinion leadership areas.

Wilkening (1956) found that different opinion leaders tended to exist for such different innovations as hog pasture and irrigation, but the same opinion leader tended to be used for *related* innovations. This suggests that a general leader does not exist for all farming operations, but one may exist within more limited confines.

Silk (1966) undertook research to determine the amount of overlap among self-designated opinion leaders in the limited area of dental products and services, including dentists, electric toothbrushes, mouthwashes, toothpaste, and regular toothbrushes. He concluded that there was no clear indication that overlap of opinion leadership was any greater than might be expected solely by chance. The Silk study raises the issue of not only whether there is an *across*-product category opinion leader but also a *within*-product category opinion leader. His results suggest that the latter does not exist. However, the spheres of activity for which Silk gathered data, while appearing to be related on common-sense grounds, actually may have involved quite different modes of consumption for different reasons and may have been, in fact, perceived as unrelated or even competing, so that to be an influential in one would preclude being an influential in another.

More recent research by Robertson and Myers (1969) has used peer selections to identify opinion leaders for three product categories—food, clothing, and small appliances—among ninety-five housewives within twenty informal neighborhood groups. Comparisons of pairwise correlations between the opinion leadership scores indicated hardly any overlap. These authors' conclusion was that opinion leadership is indeed monomorphic, at least in these three product categories and using a rather rigorous peer selection method of measuring opinion leadership.

In another study by the same authors (Myers and Robertson, 1970), however, a reasonable amount of overlap across product interest areas was found. This study used a self-designating opinion leadership item (rather than peer report as in the previous study) and was based on a mail sample of an ongoing (Haug Associates) consumer panel of housewives. Twelve product and interest areas (home entertainment, household furnishings, household appliances, home upkeep, recreation and travel, politics, children's upbringing, women's clothing, medical care, personal care, cooking and foods, and automobiles) were studied, and overlap was assessed on the basis of correlations between the opinion leadership scores for all possible pairs of areas. Of the sixty-six pairwise correlation coefficients, fifty-four were significant at or beyond the .05 level. Overlap was greatest among what appeared to be intuitively similar product areas.

The strongest evidence for opinion leadership overlap has been offered by King and Summers (1970), who studied opinion leadership overlap across a number of product categories: food products, women's fashions, household cleaners, cosmetics, large appliances, and small appliances. Their overall conclusions, based on probability and correlation analyses, are that a generalized opinion leader seems to exist and that overlap is greatest between similar product categories. Of the fifteen pairwise correlations on the opinion leadership measures, all were statistically significant beyond the .01 level. Furthermore, using the Marcus and Bauer (1964) test to compare generalized overlap, King and Summers found that overlap was "common": 46 percent of the sample qualified as opinion leaders in two or more product categories; 28 percent qualified in three or more categories; and 13 percent qualified in four or more categories.

Finally, Montgomery and Silk (1969) utilized data from 931 housewife members of MRCA's (Market Research Corporation of America) national consumer panel to test for overlap across self-designated areas of opinion leadership. The product and interest areas studied were household work, automobiles, food buying, food preparation, clothes, health, and home furnishings. Montgomery and Silk found significantly greater opinion leadership overlap than would be expected by chance "across most but not all of the categories studied . . . patterns of overlap in opinion leadership appeared to parallel the manner in which housewives' interest in these categories cluster together" (p. 18).

Recent evidence, therefore, although not completely consistent, suggests that opinion leadership overlap may occur and that, in some senses, a generalized opinion leader may exist. It should be cautioned, however, that evidence of statistically significant amounts of overlap does not mean that *one* opinion leader exists for all product categories. The overlap is only greater than would be expected assuming product category independence of opinion leadership. In the Montgomery and Silk (1969) study, for example, only about 3 percent of the respondents were opinion leaders in at least five of the seven product interest areas under investigation (p. 15). It can be concluded that opinion leadership is most common between or among closely related product interest areas.

Undoubtedly, a good amount of the inconsistency in opinion leadership overlap findings is due to methodological differences. Multiple sampling populations, measures of opinion leadership, definitions of opinion leaders, and analytical techniques have been used. Does a single-item opinion leadership measure give valid and reliable results? Does the self-designating measure yield results equivalent to the peer report measure? Defining opinion leaders as the upper one third of a sample on scores of opinion leadership is likely to give different results than defining opinion leaders as the upper 10 percent in opinion leadership scores. Greater rigor and caution should be exercised in research on this topic, and multiple measures of opinion leadership should be used where possible.

COMMUNICATION BEHAVIOR OF OPINION LEADERS

It has been concluded by Katz and Lazarsfeld (1955) and reiterated by Elihu Katz (1957), in his later restatement of the two-step hypothesis, that opinion leaders make greater use of mass media. Rogers and Cartano (1962) have further emphasized that opinion leaders tend to use "more impersonal and technically accurate" and more "cosmopolitan" sources of information (p. 437). Evidence has been cited by Rogers (1962b) that farmer influentials have more contact with county extension agents than do most other farmers (p. 238), as well as having more contact with agricultural scientists (p. 239). Physician opinion leaders have been found to visit more out-of-town medical institutions and teaching hospitals to acquire medical knowledge (Elihu Katz, 1961, p. 78). The problem exists as to the applicability of such generalizations to consumer marketing. Unfortunately, within the marketing literature there is little research which is directly relevant to test these assertions.

Nicosia (1964), in his analysis of auto insurance data, was able to derive an index of exposure to mass media (television, radio, newspapers, and magazines). He found that opinion leaders were somewhat *less* exposed to mass media. He also derived an index based on usage of "technical" personal channels (independent agents, direct writers, car dealers, lawyers, and bankers) versus "social" personal channels (friends, relatives, neighbors), with the result being that the opinion leader does, in fact, rely more on the "technically accurate" sources of information. Rossiter and Robertson (1968), in their study of fashion adoption among college coeds, found that the opinion leader had greater exposure to fashion magazines, though not as much as the innovators. It was believed that fashion magazines would be the critical mass media source and a "technically accurate" one. Summers (1968), in another study of fashion diffusion, also found opinion leaders to be more exposed to fashion magazines, although not to radio or television. Interestingly, however, almost one half of the fashion opinion leaders rarely or never read fashion magazines—a result further questioning the two-step flow hypothesis.

A general but tentative conclusion at this point is that the opinion leader can be expected to have greater exposure to *relevant* mass media, but not to mass media in general. Thus, the Nicosia (1964) finding assessing general mass media exposure may not be particularly meaningful, since insurance knowledge is not gained from a wide range of media sources. Similarly, Mason (1963, p. 460) has concluded that influentials for farming innovations are not more likely to expose themselves to mass media. It would help to know if they are more likely to expose themselves to *relevant* mass media, such as farm publications. Focused research is definitely needed to gather evidence regarding specific exposure to and usage of media by opinion leaders.

Elihu Katz (1957) has concluded further that despite the greater media exposure of opinion leaders, personal influence is the major factor in their decisions. Mason (1963) also finds this to be the most frequent case. The dynamics of influence exchange can be examined in Figure 7.1. As shown, twelve votes on influence were exchanged within the group. Of these votes, four were directed to one person, three to each of two other persons, and one vote each to the remaining two group members. Of the five *food* votes, three were directed to one person; of the four *appliance* votes, three were directed to one person; and of the three *clothing* votes, two were directed to one person. It can be concluded that opinion leaders, relatively speaking, exist. Now let us examine where the "opinion leaders" turn for influence. The food opinion leader (Mrs. Lubenberg) indicates that Mrs. Berman is her source of advice on foods, and a reciprocal relationship is found. Yet, no other group member mentions Mrs. Berman as a food influence source. The appliance opinion leader (Mrs. Taubman) is influenced by a person outside the group. The clothing opinion leader (Mrs. Gidan) cites Mrs. Lubenberg as a source of influence, as well as an influential beyond the confines of the group. Here again, no one else looks to the opinion leader's source of influence.

SUMMARY

A number of generalizations have been made regarding personal influence:

1. Personal influence refers to a change in an individual's attitude or behavior as a result of interpersonal communication.
2. Personal influence can result from a source-initiated or recipient-initiated communication event.
3. Influence resulting from communication can be one-way or two-way. The individual can influence while being influenced.
4. Personal influence can occur as a result of verbal or visual communication.
5. The "two-step hypothesis" is basically a source-initiated, one-way, verbal process of personal influence and is only one of eight possible modes of personal influence.

A number of generalizations have been made regarding opinion leadership:

1. The opinion leader is the person to whom others most often turn for information.
2. Opinion leadership is a relative concept. Opinion leaders are only "more" influential than their followers.
3. Opinion leaders do not always lead, nor do followers always follow.
4. The opinion leader is very much like the persons he advises.
5. Opinion leaders are generally most norm-abiding.
6. There is no clear-cut opinion leader profile.
7. Opinion leaders, while higher on innovativeness, are generally not innovators.
8. Opinion leaders and innovators generally possess different characteristics.
9. Moderate overlap of opinion leadership occurs across product categories. Overlap is most pronounced between related product categories.
10. Opinion leaders are more exposed to *relevant* mass media for their interest area.
11. Opinion leaders are most influenced by other people.

CHAPTER 8

THE ACCEPTANCE OF PERSONAL INFLUENCE

In line with the broader conceptualization of personal influence developed in the previous chapter, the acceptance of personal influence by the individual is tied directly to its satisfying a need for him. This is true both for communication in which the individual deliberately engages in information seeking and for communication directed to him, although not deliberately sought by him.

THEORIES OF PERSONAL INFLUENCE

THE KELMAN PARADIGM

A theory of particular importance regarding the acceptance of personal influence is that of Herbert C. Kelman (1961), who elaborates three processes by which persons respond to social influence. These are compliance, identification, and internalization. *Compliance*, according to Kelman, occurs when the person accepts influence in the hope of achieving a favorable reaction from another person or persons. He does not accept the influence because he believes in its content, but because of an anticipated gratifying social effect.

Influence based on *identification* occurs when the opinion or behavior accepted is associated with a "satisfying self-defining relationship" to a person or group. Identification is basically role imitation, whereby influence results from admiration of another person, or role maintenance, whereby acceptance is necessary to maintain a role-relationship with another person. The motivational basis for identification is different from that of compliance in that the person is not primarily concerned with pleasing the other person, but with meeting the other's expectations—or at least perceived expectations—for his own role performance. *Internalization* occurs when an individual accepts influence congruent with his particular value system. The content of the advocated opinion or behavior is of major concern and becomes integrated with the individual's existing values.

Table 8.1 outlines some of the crucial distinctions among the three processes of social influence. In this table are given the antecedents which determine the kind of social influence which is likely to occur as well as the consequents of the three kinds of social influence.

BAUER'S SCHEME

Bauer (1967) has argued that social processes need not lead to "influence" or "conformity" in the traditional sense. Bauer proposes that people engage in two different kinds of social "games," which he calls the *psychosocial game* and the *problem-solving game*. In the psychosocial game, the person attempts to gain group status or group acceptance and reward. In the problem-solving game, the individual uses information gained from other people as a reference point in defining his environment and in decision making. Both games are instances of influence, but the problem-solving game does not denote behavior in order to gain social rewards from others. Compliance and identification, in Kelman's sense, Bauer believes are clearly associated with the psychosocial game, but not with problem-solving. Internalization is related to the problem-solving game.

A similar distinction has been proposed by Cohen (1964) and by Deutsch and Gerard (1955). Deutsch and Gerard categorize *normative social influence* as an influence to conform to the positive expectations of others, and *informa-*

Table 8.1   Summary of Distinctions among Kelman's Processes of Social Influence

	Compliance	Identification	Internalization
Antecedents:			
Basis for the importance of the induction	Concern with social effect of behavior	Concern with social anchorage of behavior	Concern with value congruence of behavior
Source of power of the influence agent	Means control	Attractiveness	Credibility
Manner of achieving prepotency of the induced response	Limitation of choice behavior	Delineation of role requirements	Reorganization of means-ends framework
Consequents:			
Conditions of performance of induced response	Surveillance by influencing agent	Salience of relationship to agent	Relevance of values to issue
Conditions of change and extinction of induced response	Changed perception of conditions for social rewards	Changed perception of conditions for satisfying self-defining relationships	Changed perception of conditions for value maximization
Type of behavior system in which induced response is embedded	External demands of a specific setting	Expectations defining a specific role	Person's value system

Source: Kelman (1961, p. 67).

tional social influence as an influence to accept information contributed by others as evidence of reality.

Wilding and Bauer (1968) offer evidence on differing communication responses by individuals, depending on whether they are high in psychosocial or in problem-solving orientation. Those characterized as having psychosocial goals reacted to the communication in a way that their response was "dependent on their assessment of the source" (Wilding and Bauer, 1968, p. 76). Problem solvers, in contrast, reacted to the communication in a manner more independent of their assessment of the source. This would seem to suggest that messages directed to consumers whose goals are psychosocial should stress the power and likability of the source.

Much consumer influence is undoubtedly a mix of problem-solving and phychosocial influences. Much of what has been labeled conformity behavior is actually an attempt by the individual to establish a meaningful and valid frame of reference for purchase decision making. The group serves as a standard-maker, and the individual willingly participates in the process of establishing and adhering to group standards. Elaboration of the problem-solving game is particularly meaningful in that marketers and others too often have viewed group influence from a negative point of view. Conspicuous consumption, "keeping up with the Joneses," and status seeking have been viewed as essentially negative aspects of American society. However, the function of the group goes beyond providing status for its members.

WEBER'S SCHEME

Another conceptualization of relevance to personal influence is that of sociologist Max Weber (1947) in his treatise on bureaucratic organizations. Weber distinguishes among three forms of social influence: power, authority, and persuasion. He defines *power* as "the probability that one actor within a social relationship will be in a position to carry out his own will despite resistance" (p. 152). *Authority*, in contrast, is "the probability that certain specific commands (or all commands) from a given source will be obeyed by a given group of persons" (p. 324). It is distinguished from power in that (1) compliance is voluntary, (2) the source's exercise of control is considered legitimate, and (3) authority relations can develop only in a group context, since it is the group values which sanction the exercise of authority. *Persuasion* refers to the process by which one individual allows another to influence his attitudes or behavior on the basis of argument. It is distinguished from power in that it is voluntary and from authority in that there is no suspension of judgment to the communicator's commands (Blau and Scott, 1962, p. 28).

Persuasion is fairly equivalent to the narrow definition of personal influence offered earlier: one person successfully changing the opinions or behavior of another through verbal communication. The broader conceptualization of personal influence, however, recognizes that persuasion, authority, and power may all be forms of personal influence, although persuasion may be the most common case. Weber's scheme can also be approximately related to the Kelman scheme: persuasion involves internalization; authority involves identification; and compliance involves power.

FESTINGER'S SCHEME

Perhaps the most encompassing and meaningful theory of social influence is that of Leon Festinger (1954), who has elaborated a theory of "social comparison processes" which implicitly recognizes the psychosocial and problem-solving aspects of group influence. Festinger's basic assumption is that individuals seek to evaluate their opinions and abilities. He postulates that, to the extent that objective nonsocial means of evaluating opinions are available, individuals will use these means. To the extent that nonsocial means are not available, individuals will turn to other people for advice and information. This latter case would seem to be more frequent in marketing.

Social evaluation of opinions is not, however, conducted in a random manner. Rather, the individual tends to compare himself to, and gather information from, people who are fairly similar to himself. Thus, information seeking is selective and involves the choice of a relevant reference group. Given that group opinion on a matter is divergent, processes will be set in motion to reduce discrepancies and to arrive at a common norm. These processes also will tend to be binding upon the individual, thus encouraging his opinion to be similar to that of the group. The basic motivation for the individual to accept group opinion is his desire to maintain membership. Several experimenters, including Schachter (1959), have found that if a person's opinion becomes too discrepant from dominant group opinion, he tends to be rejected by the group and to become a social isolate.

Festinger, in this work (1954) and earlier work, has emphasized the forces toward uniformity within the group. Two basic forces are noted. The first of these is reliance upon the group to define *social reality*, which occurs when dependence upon physical reality for testing opinions and ideas is not possible. It then becomes important for the *group* to come to an agreement on the matter under consideration, that is, to define the environment for its members. The second force toward conformity is *group locomotion*, which occurs when uniformity is seen as desirable or necessary to the functioning of the group. This might be the case for a jury which must reach a unanimous opinion. Conformity behavior is positively related to the attraction of the group for its members. It is also found that the greater the group relevance of the opinion being considered, the stronger will be the pressure toward conformity within the group.

Not all groups are equally salient to the individual and not all groups are equally salient for any given opinion. The individual's "reference group" is the one to which he turns for attitudinal and behavioral guidelines. Yet different reference groups can exist for different decisions. In the realm of consumption, the group will be more salient to the extent that the item is conspicuous or high in perceived risk. The group also will be more salient to the individual to the extent that he values his group membership. Furthermore, the opinion area will be of relevance to the group only to the extent that a large number of members look to the group for attitudinal or behavioral guidelines in this matter.

The importance of the Festinger scheme is that it provides a rationale for an understanding of group influence. Throughout the Festinger model run the notions of psychosocial and problem-solving behaviors. The motivation for social comparison is at times the desire to gain social acceptance, but this is not always so. There are many cases when the individual, without a direct and physical reality check, is dependent on the group as a means of reaching or validating a decision.

RESISTING INFLUENCE

To this point we have talked in terms of the acceptance of communication through group influence. It is also possible to look at the rejection of communication on the basis of group influence. Hovland, Janis, and Kelley (1953), looking at social influence from this latter point of view, declared, "Our interest is the factors underlying the resistance to change of opinions which are held in conformity with the behavioral standards of a group to which the individual belongs" (p. 136).

From this point of view certain propositions can be derived. For example, the attractiveness of the group not only might cause the individual to adhere to its norms but also might cause him to reject information from other sources counter to these norms. In an experiment by Kelley and Volkart (1952), for example, boy scouts were exposed to communication counter to scout norms. It was found that subjects who most valued their group membership were least influenced in the direction advocated by the counternorm communication, which tended, in fact, to have an opposite, or boomerang, effect on them. In another experiment by Adams (1961), subjects were exposed to conflicting statements on a controversial issue emanating from spokesmen for two different nationalities. Opinion change was in the direction advocated by the spokesman of the subject's national reference group and against the direction advocated by the nonreference group spokesman.

The individual's status within a group may be a factor allowing him to deviate from its norms and to accept a countercommunication. It is felt that the leader of a group will be most valued by the group and, therefore, allowed the greatest freedom in his reaction to outside communications. However, it should be pointed out that in most studies the leader is one of the most conforming members, since he does not want to endanger his leadership position. Popularity, which generally depends upon conformity to social norms, is felt to be positively related to such conformance.

Hollander (1964), for example, suggests that an individual gains "idiosyncrasy credit" by conforming to the expectations of the group and by displaying competence in group activities. He postulates that "A person who exhibits both competence and conformity should eventually reach a threshold at which it becomes appropriate in the eyes of others for him to assert influence; and insofar as these assertions are accepted he emerges as a leader" (p. 329). Hollander also suggests that having gained idiosyncrasy credits and having emerged as a group leader, the individual is free to entertain counternormative communications and to change the norms of the group. Testing this hypothesis, Hollander did find that the leader had the power to change the group norms. When he was then placed in another group, it was found that he was unable to exert pressure toward normative change until he had again accrued a sufficient amount of idiosyncrasy credits.

Research has also been conducted on group *salience* and its effect on resistance to change. The general result is that as communication recommends opinions counter to the group norm and as the salience of the group increases, the less is the attitudinal change. In an experiment by Charters and Newcomb (1952), it was found that communication most clearly tied to a reference group would gain responses most in line with the norms of that group. In this experiment three groups of Catholic subjects were used, but each group reminded to a different extent of its affiliation. For example, in one group no mention was made of Catholicism, whereas in the other group the subjects were called together as Catholics and asked to discuss some of the basic assumptions of their faith. It was found that the more salient the religion was made to them, the more likely the subjects were to answer questions on a subsequent questionnaire in terms of their religious teachings.

THE OCCURRENCE OF PERSONAL INFLUENCE

When is personal influence most likely to be operative? Under what circumstances is it an important variable for consideration in marketing programs, and under what conditions should it be ignored? The occurrence of personal influence depends basically upon product, consumer, group, and social system attributes. These attributes now will be considered at length.

PRODUCT CHARACTERISTICS

Visibility of the product, as discussed previously, is one general attribute affecting the occurrence of personal influence. According to this rationale, clothing is more susceptible to personal influence than laundry detergents. Highly visible items such as swimming pools, color television sets, and room airconditioners have been noted not to diffuse randomly, but in clusters— presumably because of the functioning of personal influence.

Another product characteristic relating to personal influence is whether the product is subject to *testability*, that is, can it be tried and tested against some objective criteria? The merits of certain products, notably food items, can be physically tested in a convenient manner, while the merits of other products, such as appliances, cannot readily be judged by observation or physical testing, except in use over some period of time. When the individual can rely on physical reality in his purchase decision, he generally will not be as subject to the opinions and beliefs of others. On the other hand, when it is not possible to rely on physical reality, reliance upon social reality will be correspondingly high (Festinger, 1954). Along the same lines, to the extent that the product can be used on a *trial* basis, the less may be the consumer's reliance on other people.

Another product attribute related to personal influence is *complexity*. London and Lim (1964) conclude from experimental evidence that the "influence of one's peers over his decisions in a group problem-solving situation increases directly as the problem becomes more complex" (p. 83). This conclusion has not been tested with specific reference to product purchasing.

It has also been suggested by a number of researchers that extent of personal influence is dependent upon the amount of *perceived risk* which consumers associate with a product. Cunningham (1966), for example, found that more risk was perceived for headache remedies than fabric softeners and, correspondingly, more discussion occurred about the former item.

The product variables of visibility, testability, complexity, and perceived risk—although not representing an exhaustive list—do help to predict when personal influence will be most operative. The interdependency of these variables should also be realized. Ratings on these attributes are given below for food, small appliance, and clothing product categories. Although arbitrary, these ratings seem to lead to predictions that small appliances will be most subject to personal influence and that food products will be least subject to personal influence. These predictions are consistent with the findings from Robertson (1970) summarized in Table 6.3.

> Small appliances are frequently high on visibility, low on testability, relatively high on complexity and perceived risk.
>
> Food is frequently low on visibility, high on testability, low on complexity and perceived risk.
>
> Clothing is high on visibility, high on testability, low on complexity (except matching a wardrobe), and high on perceived risk.

CONSUMER CHARACTERISTICS

Consumers are not equally susceptible to personal influence. Logically, the most important determining factor of this variability would be extent of interpersonal *interaction*. The gregarious person simply is more likely to engage in conversation regarding products and brands and accordingly, to be more subject to personal influence. What, however, makes an individual interaction-prone and what encourages him to accept influence?

INNER- AND OTHER-DIRECTEDNESS

It might be expected that the "other-directed" person, who looks to others for behavioral guidelines, would be more subject to personal influence than the "inner-directed" person, who relies on his own value system as developed over time (Riesman, 1950). Some evidence to justify this hypothesis is available. Centers and Horowitz (1963) have found other-directed subjects to be more susceptible to personal influence; and Linton and Graham (1959) have found other-directed subjects to be somewhat more persuasible than average. Arndt (1966), however, has found a lack of evidence that other-directed individuals are more susceptible to personal influence.

In research as to preference for message formats in mass media, Kassarjian (1965) found that inner-directed people preferred inner-directed advertisements and that other-directed people preferred other-directed advertisements. Perhaps the same relationship may hold for message format in interpersonal communication, although this would have to be tested. The other-directed person may be more likely to respond to a message which promises social approval, while the inner-directed person may be more likely to respond to a message which is in line with his internalized belief system.

TRANSITIONAL LIFE STAGES

Individuals facing *new life experiences*, such as newlyweds or college freshmen, might also seem to be more susceptible to personal influence, advertising, and other forms of influence. In such states of life, habits for handling many situations are not established and the individual is open to information, if not actively seeking it. In studies of alcoholism, Bales (1946) proposed that the starting of the habit is largely a result of the individual's social milieu and that personal influence is an important determinant of habit adoption. The maintenance of the habit, however, is related more to the ability of the behavior to satisfy the individual's personal needs.

Individuals *aspiring to membership* in certain groups may be inclined to emulate the behavior of persons already in these groups. This has been referred to as "anticipatory socialization" (Merton, 1957, p. 265) ; that is, the person tends to adopt the attitudinal and behavioral characteristics of group members before he actually belongs. The MBA student, in anticipation of his forthcoming role, tends to look and think like a business executive. He dresses appropriately, carries an attache case, and reads the *Wall Street Journal*. Similarly, the medical student, at his first opportunity, dons the white coat of his profession and rushes to the college store to buy his symbolic stethescope. Such aspirational behavior is also seen in the social climber, who drives the "right" kind of car, joins the "right" clubs, and sends his children to the "right" schools. In all of these cases, the individual who lacks actual membership acquires the visible symbols of that membership.

PERSONALITY AND CONSUMER PERSUASIBILITY

Another factor bearing upon the individual's acceptance of personal influence is his general or specific *susceptibility to persuasion*. Research shows that some individuals are generally persuasible across a wide range of topics, while others are specifically persuasible on particular topics or for particular kinds of messages. Most of the research on persuasibility takes personality as the independent variable and deals with general rather than specific persuasibility.

In the earlier work on this subject, which is well summarized by Janis (1963), overall guiding hypotheses were established relating persuasibility to specific personality correlates. These hypotheses, which follow, refer to male subjects. Although females generally have been found more persuasible than males, it has been more difficult to relate women's persuasibility to specific personality correlates.

1. Men who openly display hostility toward others tend to be non-persuasible (p. 60).
2. Men who display social withdrawal tendencies tend to be nonpersuasible (p. 60).
3. Men who "respond with rich imagery and strong empathic responses to symbolic representations" tend to be high in persuasibility (p. 60).
4. Men who are low in self-esteem tend to be more persuasible than those of high self-esteem (p. 61).
5. Men who are other-directed in orientation tend to be more persuasible than those who are inner-directed (p. 62).

The most widely tested of these conclusions is that relating persuasibility to self-esteem or self-confidence. Janis (1963) and several fellow experimenters tested this hypothesis with varying groups of subjects including high school, grade school, and college students, and found the posited linear inverse relationship. Cohen (1964, p. 45) has found that individuals of low self-esteem tend to be more subject to persuasion from individuals of high self-esteem than vice versa and that individuals low in self-esteem also are less active in attempting to exert influence.

More recent research, however, has tended not to confirm the traditional relationship. Cox and Bauer (1964) report an experiment in which women were asked to choose between two brands of nylons which were, in fact, identical. After making their decisions, subjects then heard a salesgirl favor one brand and were asked to reevaluate their decisions. As expected, highly self-confident subjects were low in persuasibility. However, an unexpected finding was that subjects low in self-confidence were *low* in persuasibility. Those of medium self-confidence actually had the greatest opinion change. Cox and Bauer explain these findings in terms of a defensive reaction hypothesis; that is, low self-confidence individuals reacted in a defensive manner and, in order to protect "their selves," rejected the communication. In fact, these researchers show data that more subjects of low self-confidence changed in a direction contrary to the communication than subjects in any other group.

Since the Cox and Bauer experiment, other researchers have reported a similar curvilinear relationship between self-confidence and persuasibility. Gerald D. Bell (1967), for example, reports this relationship in a car-buying situation. Arndt (1968, p. 30) found that individuals low in generalized self-confidence tended to avoid exposure to interpersonal communication and, if exposed, tended to act in an opposite direction to that advocated. An experiment by Nisbett and Gordon (1967), however, found exactly the opposite relationship to that originally proposed: instead of individuals low in self-confidence being persuaded most easily, individuals high in self-confidence were found most easily persuaded.

Bauer (1967) attempts to reconcile these findings in terms of whether the motivation of the person is to gain social approval or to solve a problem. He distinguishes, therefore, between psychosocial and problem-solving, reasoning that when subjects are playing the psychosocial game, the traditional relationship between low self-confidence and persuasibility will be found; and highly self-confident individuals generally will be most reluctant to conform to the wishes of others. When individuals are trying to solve problems, however, the expected relationship is that individuals high in self-confidence will most readily accept evidence to help in the decision. It is Bauer's belief that the earlier experiments tended to have people play the psychosocial game, whereas later experiments tended to be designed for people playing the problem-solving game. Bauer also reasons that the Nisbett and Gordon (1967) finding arose when the message was self-sufficient and subjects were not source-reliant. Partial confirmation for Bauer's reasoning is provided in a thesis by Wilding (1966) which indicates that the direction of the self-confidence–persuasibility relationship depends upon the orientation of the experimental situation—whether problem-solving or psychosocial.

AFFILIATION AND INFLUENCE

The individual's susceptibility to *anxiety* has been found to be related to his communication behavior. Janis (1963, p. 57) reports that the chronically anxious person is more likely to reject the communicator's conclusions. Schachter (1959), in more extensive research on this subject, has demonstrated the "psychology of affiliation," that is, the arousal of anxiety in individuals produces a preference for social contacts. Affiliation with others is based upon a desire for anxiety reduction, which can be accomplished when others help to establish reality and to define the "appropriate and proper reaction" (Janis, 1963, p. 132).

The arousal of anxiety by the marketing communicator, therefore, may not be a desirable strategy, since consumers (1) may tend to reject the marketer's recommendations and (2) may tend to turn to other people instead. For example, it has not been found advisable for insurance company advertising to emphasize death, a strong anxiety-arousing stimulus. Other experimental evidence indicates that the higher the anxiety level, the more likely the subject is to "forget" things relating to the anxiety.

Schachter (1959), in the course of his research, also found that the level of aroused anxiety tended to be associated with the birth order of his subjects. Individuals who were firstborn and/or only children experienced higher levels of aroused anxiety than did second and later-born subjects when given an identical stimulus. *And* firstborn and only children were found to a greater extent to prefer the company of other people as a means of reducing anxiety. It was also found that earlier-born subjects were more susceptible to influence in order to obtain *social approval,* whereas later-born subjects were more susceptible to influence in order to *solve problems* (Deutsch and Gerard, 1955). Thus, earlier-born subjects were more likely to play the psycho-social game, whereas later-borns played the problem-solving game.

Anxiety in purchase may be due largely to the amount of risk which the individual perceives. Some persons may be high in generalized perceived risk and others may be high in perceived risk depending upon the product category. Cunningham (1967), however, cites a lack of significant findings in attempting to characterize the high-risk perceiver, and he contends that perceived risk is a "product-specific phenomenon," (pp. 102–108). It has been documented by a number of researchers that high-risk perceivers are most inclined to use interpersonal communication as a means of defining the situation and assessing the purchase consequences. Arndt (1967a) has found that high-risk perceivers for a new brand of coffee seek more word-of-mouth information. Robertson (1968d), in a study of informal groups, has concluded that members of groups in which high purchase risk is perceived engage in more communication about new products with one another than do members of groups in which low purchase risk is perceived.

It would also seem that perceived risk is greater—giving rise to greater anxiety and, hence, greater susceptibility to affiliation and personal influence—when the individual is in a transitional life stage. He may have difficulty defining appropriate behavior, since he has not fully learned the norms associated with his new role. Personal influence, in general, increases as uncertainty increases. This has been documented by Coleman, Katz, and Menzel (1966) in research on physician adoption of drugs. Bauer and Wortzel (1966) elaborate on this point in their study of the physician's usage of communication channels. They cite evidence that as the riskiness of prescribing a drug increases, physicians turn increasingly to fellow physicians and away from commercial drug information sources.

In an experiment by Radloff (1961), the affiliative tendency was extended beyond response to anxiety. He found that the drive to evaluate one's opinions was also an important determinant of affiliation. Under conditions of low information on the social correctness of his opinion, the individual was more willing to discuss his view than under conditions of high information. This is almost a direct test of Festinger's theory (1954) of social comparison processes—to the extent objective, nonsocial means of evaluating opinions are unavailable, the individual will turn to other people.

ADOPTER CATEGORIES

It has been concluded by Rogers (1962b), in his review of the diffusion literature, that impersonal and more technically accurate sources of information are more important for earlier adopters of innovations than for later adopters. He goes so far as to say that "Personal influence is evidently not as necessary to motivate the earlier adopters to accept a new idea as it is for the later adopters" (p. 179). This conclusion is based largely on agricultural research findings, however, and does not always hold in the marketing realm. Nor did this conclusion hold for physician adoption of a new drug (Coleman, Katz, and Menzel, 1966), where it was found that interpersonal communication was more important for earlier than later adopters, perhaps due to the perceived risk involved and the use of other doctors to legitimize adoption. It is difficult to find any distinguishable differences in communication behavior between early and late adopters of a consumer innovation; and early adopters, if anything, seem to engage more in interpersonal communication (Robertson, 1968b).

GROUP CHARACTERISTICS

REFERENCE GROUP EFFECT

Group membership and the characteristics of the group also affect degree of personal influence. The key to the existence of a group is continuing interaction among a set of people who perceive each other as constituting a distinguishable communality. This continuing interaction leads to the creation of a common sentiment, or group norm, which can influence individual behavior in certain situations. Robertson (1968d), for example, found that the favorability of a group norm on innovativeness was positively correlated with aggregate group innovative behavior. Group influence, as such, is a special case of personal influence.

The individual belongs to groups because they perform important and even vital functions for him. In almost all societies, for example, the individual belongs to a family group. The family has been found to be the most efficient means of propagating the human race, providing food and shelter for the helpless child, socializing him, and making him useful in his own right. In many societies, a majority of members belong to some form of religious group which may allay fears of death, provide some meaning to everyday life, provide a moral code, and, supplementarily, fulfill needs for ritual to mark important life stages or for social interaction with other people.

In American society, most people belong to many groups, not all of which hold the same meaning or importance for them. The individual's *reference group* is the group he most often uses as a point of reference in determining his judgments, beliefs, and behavior (Hyman, 1960). The individual may have more than one reference group and use different groups for different types of behavioral guidelines. Furthermore, his reference group need not be a group to which he belongs, but a group to which he relates or aspires to belong—or even an imaginary group. The social psychologist George Herbert Mead (1934) has developed the concept of the "generalized other," which views the development of the "self" as completed when the individual is capable of taking others' attitudes toward himself and acting in accordance with them. The individual then tends to behave in terms of how he views the generalized other viewing him. According to Mead, it is in the form of the generalized other that society influences the behavior of its members, since this is how society "enters" the individual's thinking process.

PRESSURES TOWARD CONFORMITY

In order to continue, the group must exert pressure on its members to conform to its beliefs, values, and norms; and it must assign them duties. In a work group, a binding set of rules may be imposed upon the worker and a specified set of duties extracted from him with severe sanctions (reprimand or dismissal) if he fails to perform. His motivation to conform is what he gets from his group membership—basically money, but also a sense of personal worth as a result of his work contribution.

The *informal group* also expects something from its members in order to maintain itself. Each person must act in accord with its rules or norms, which in this case are not explicitly stated, but learned from group members who communicate certain expectations of him in his group role. These norms may involve only a certain willingness to converse, avoid argument, and instigate interaction; or they may be much broader and include implicit guidelines on how to dress or decorate one's home. Norms in the informal group may be communicated as simply and casually as subtly making fun of a sloppily dressed member. Duties may involve a division of labor for coffee sessions or arranging theater parties.

The power of the group to extract conforming behavior from its members is shown in two famous social-psychological experiments. In one of these experiments, Sherif (1965) brought together subjects in small groups who were asked to judge the distance and direction a point of light appeared to move in a dark room. Actually, the light was stationary, but gave the appearance of movement due to an autokinetic effect. Results indicated that group members converged toward a common norm in their judgments; and when the group was dispersed and individual judgments made, the subjects held to the established group norm.

Asch (1965) also brought together small groups of subjects who were asked to match the size of a line on one card to one of three lines on another card. In cases where the individual made these judgments alone, there was virtually no error. In the group situation, however, Asch introduced confederates who deliberately announced wrong answers. Under pressure of being alone in an opinion or in a small minority, naive subjects often conformed to obviously incorrect group judgments. The extent of such conformity depended on the size of the group and the size of the incorrect majority; however, on an average basis, minority subjects accepted misleading majority decisions in 37 percent of the selections.

The experimental work of Asch was further developed by Crutchfield (1955), who designed an apparatus consisting of electrical panels on which up to five subjects could record responses. This apparatus allowed the researcher to control the information given to subjects. As part of the experiment, each subject recorded his judgment on certain issues with the understanding that his judgments would be communicated to the other subjects. However, the experimenter actually communicated a contrived series of standardized judgments which did not reflect the subjects' opinions and which left each subject with the impression that he was the last to make a decision. On the issue of matching lines, as in the Asch experiment, some 30 percent of the subjects conformed to incorrect group opinion. The Crutchfield experiment gets more interesting at this point, however, because stimuli of differential ambiguity were presented to the subjects. Under conditions of maximum ambiguity (given an insoluble number series to complete), 79 percent of the subjects conformed to a spurious group consensus choosing an irrational answer. Group influence was found to increase, therefore, as the ambiguity of stimuli increased.

The operation of psychosocial influence is illustrated in Asch's experiment. The naive subject conforms to the perceived expectations of other group members in order to gain group status or to avoid group punishment, that is, being isolated or rejected by other group members. The Sherif experiment illustrates the problem-solving game. Subjects used the group as a means of defining an ambiguous situation. The influence rendered yielded the individual a reference point from which to make his decisions. The Crutchfield experiment is actually a cross between the two kinds of games, and we commonly would expect to find both kinds of influence occurring simultaneously. In the unstructured situation, problem-solving behavior was undoubtedly operating in that no decision was readily available and the group served as a means of defining reality. In the structured situation, however, error was virtually impossible on an objective basis, and the errors made were due to the individual's need to conform to the perceived expectations of others.

CONSUMER RESEARCH ON GROUP INFLUENCE

A number of experiments focusing on group influence have been conducted on consumer topics. One of the first was conducted by Kurt Lewin during World War II and attempted to change meat consumption patterns to less desirable, but more plentiful, cuts such as kidneys and sweetbreads. In this study two experimental conditions were employed. In one, housewives heard a lecture on the benefits of these foods; in the other, a discussion was initiated among the women. The same information was relayed in both cases. Results gathered at a later date showed that 32 percent of the individuals participating in the discussion used the unfamiliar meats, compared to only 3 percent of the individuals who heard the lecture (Lewin, 1965). The explanation Lewin gives for this considerable divergence in findings is that in the discussion situation, a *group* came into existence as the individuals interacted with one another. Group processes thus came into play advocating the normative behavior desired.

A more recent study by Venkatesan (1966) was conducted along the lines of the Asch (1965) experiment. Students were asked to evaluate three identical suits and to choose the "best" one. The experimental situation involved a naive subject and three confederates of the experimenter. When subjects chose suits alone, the distribution of choices did not deviate significantly from chance. However, when placed in the group situation, the distribution of choices by the naive subjects deviated from chance, and it was concluded "that group pressure was effective and that individuals tended to conform to the group norm" (p. 386). This experiment is interesting because the students were faced with ambiguous, competing stimuli presented by the three identical suits. This is not unlike the situation facing consumers for many relatively nondifferentiated products, and it is not surprising that these individuals turn to other consumers and lean on group standards in making purchase decisions.

Another researcher, Stafford (1966), also presented consumers with identical, ambiguous, and competing stimuli. He identified in advance small informal groups of consumers who were individually asked to select a loaf of bread from four identical loaves marked with different letters of the alphabet. Selections were made over the course of eight weeks. Stafford's hypotheses were (1) informal groups would exert influence toward conformity of brand preferences; (2) the degree of such influence would be related to group cohesiveness, that is, the attractiveness of the group to its members; and (3) group leaders would be most influential in the formulation of brand preferences. He found that "the informal groups had a definite influence on their members toward conformity behavior" (p. 74). However, group cohesiveness did *not* appear significant in determining brand conformity. Informal group leaders did have the hypothesized brand preference influence.

In another such experiment, Myers (1966) identified informal groups, again in advance of the experiment, and opinion leaders within these groups. A new product was distributed to group members by either a confederate group opinion leader or a confederate who was not an opinion leader. Myers' findings suggested that resulting attitudes toward the new product were different under the two types of personal influence.

Cook (1967), in an experimental study based heavily on the pioneering work of Lewin, raised the issues of how effective group influence would be in homogeneous versus heterogeneous groups and what the effect would be of a presentation by a professional salesman versus group discussion. His results indicated the occurrence of attitude change resulting from *discussion* in both the homogeneous and heterogeneous groups. A significant change in attitude did not result from the presentation by a professional salesman. Cook concludes that group decision is relatively more effective in changing attitudes than a professional sales presentation, using this experimental design, at least for automobiles. Cook further found that in the homogeneous group a negative change in attitude occurred, whereas in the heterogeneous group a positive change occurred. Whether this would be the case always is, of course, in doubt. Cook offers the explanation that heterogeneous groups may tend to make positive decisions, since people with relatively dissimilar backgrounds tend to be more reserved and, therefore, less critical. They may also bring a wider range of experience to bear.

Finally, Robertson (1968d) has studied the effect of informal neighborhood groups on their members' innovative behavior. In general, the more favorable the group norm is on innovation, the greater the number of new products adopted by group members. Other variables relating to overall innovativeness are the level of intra-group communication about new products, the aggregate exchange of opinion leadership, and the overall level of risk perception. The specific nature of findings varied by product category. For example, level of intra-group communication and exercise of opinion leadership were positively related to innovativeness for clothing fashions, but not for new food products.

INDIVIDUAL RESPONSE TO GROUP INFLUENCE

The individual's particular relationship to the group determines the extent of the group's influence upon him. Some of the facets of this relationship have already been discussed, but it will help to briefly review them at this point. The individual's *social integration*, that is, his level of acceptance by other group members, will positively relate to the group's potential influence upon him. The individual's *role* within the group, that is, his expected behavior pattern based on his group position, will relate to degree of group influence. For example, the opinion leader will tend to reflect group norms most, although he often has the power, if he wishes to use it, to change group norms. The more *salient* the group to the individual, and particularly the more *attractive* the group, the more influence it can potentially exert upon the individual. It has been found by Festinger (1950) that the greater the difficulty of group entry, the more the individual is likely to value his group membership and to adhere to group norms.

Individual nonconformity to group expectations is demonstrated in two studies where the group is not the critical reference point for the individual. In one study by French (1960), highly productive salesmen were found most likely to violate sales-group norms by such practices as avoiding small sales, stealing sales, and rewriting exchange sales in their own names. Their ability to exist in this environment and reject its norms was due to their identification with another reference group. They named friends in other more highly regarded occupations and tended to reject and be rejected by other salesmen in their group.

This result is similar, in some senses, to a famous experiment conducted by Newcomb (1952) on the political attitudes of a class of Bennington College girls. He found that the college community served as the reference group for girls of nonconservative political attitudes, whereas the family served as the reference group for girls of conservative opinion.

The causal direction in the French and Newcomb studies seems to be reversed, however. French suggests that it is the reference group which affects behavior; Newcomb seems to suggest that existing attitudes affect the choice of a reference group. Undoubtedly, both factors are operative. Individuals initially choose groups on the basis of their own existing points of view, but they are in turn influenced by these groups.

Festinger (1950) has summarized the likely effect of group communication upon a recipient; the amount of change likely to result is seen a function of (1) the pressure toward uniformity within the group, (2) the strength of the individual's desire to remain in the group, and (3) the degree to which the individual's opinions and attitudes are anchored in limited group memberships (p. 276). Thus, the more the group finds it necessary to arrive at a common norm, the more effective a communication directed toward an individual member is likely to be. Again, the more an individual wishes to stay in a group—and particularly to the extent that other group memberships are not available to him—the more likely he is to conform to a group communication. However, to the extent the individual has multiple group memberships and interests, the less effective a group communication directed to him is likely to be.

THE FAMILY AS A DECISION-MAKING GROUP

For many purchases, the husband-wife dyad, or some other combination of nuclear family members, is the decision-making unit. The family is influential in most purchases and is often a readily available information source.

In fact, the family may be the most influential group, in terms of its implicit or explicit demands upon the actual purchase and because it serves as a low-cost information platform.

The family has not received much attention from marketers as to its decision-making *process*, although some research has been conducted focusing on family characteristics such as income level and size in order to predict decision-making *outcomes* (Ferber, 1962). Limited as it is, the available evidence from decision-making, process-oriented research, coupled with findings from sociology, can provide some generalizations on family communication and influence patterns.

Two overall conclusions can be made first: (1) there tends to be role specialization within the family, so that some purchase decisions are wife-dominant, and others are husband-dominant, and (2) influence of family members varies with the stage of the adoption process.

Role Specialization

Kenkel (1961) proposes that two basic kinds of behavior are exhibited in small groups: task, or goal-oriented behavior and social-emotional, or expressive behavior. Although individual group members may perform both forms of behavior, specialization generally occurs. In United States society, the man assumedly engages in task-oriented behavior, whereas the woman specializes in social-emotional behavior. This specialization has implications, claims Kenkel, for group decision making. It could be expected, for example, that the male would be more concerned with functional product attributes and would have more influence in actually "deciding" to buy and "concluding" the sale, since these are task-oriented behavioral forms. The female, in contrast, would be more concerned with esthetic product attributes and "suggesting" purchase, since these are expressive behavioral forms. These predictions, however, are dependent on the product category under consideration.

A study by Wolgast (1958) suggests that "important" consumer decisions most often are made jointly, although division of responsibility also occurs and either husband or wife may be dominant, depending upon the decision area. Thus, the husband was reportedly dominant in deciding when it was time to buy a new car, but the wife was dominant concerning money and bills. The wife also tended to be considerably more influential about savings and household goods and furniture.

Granbois (1964) concludes that role specialization is likely to occur when

1. A situation has been created in which it is desirable to reduce conflict and create a sense of autonomy or personal responsibility.
2. One of the family members has a recognized superior competence in certain fields.

In contrast, Granbois finds role integration (joint purchase involvement) is likely to occur as a function of

1. *The cost of the article to be purchased.* The more the good draws on family resources, the more each partner wants to play a role.
2. *Family income.* Joint participation is more prevalent in middle-class families.
3. *The degree to which each member is likely to use the product.* For example, television sets rate high on joint participation.

It seems logical that joint involvement in decision making would increase as the importance of the purchase to the entire family unit increased and as the monetary outlay increased. Specialization would be more likely to occur to the extent that purchase is related to particular knowledge or skills held by one or the other marriage partner and to the extent that the purchase is individual rather than family-related; for example, women's clothes.

Adoption Stage

The concept that family member influence in purchase decisions may vary by stage of the adoption process has not been well developed. Komarovsky (1961) has suggested that much of the confusion on family member influence could be due to the stage of the adoption process the researcher's questions suggested. Thus, the family member with dominant influence may be different at awareness than at evaluation. Some researchers have suggested that the influence of children is felt most in calling the parents' attention to products.

It also can be suggested that family influence will increase at later stages of the adoption process, much as personal influence in general is found to increase. Robertson (1966) found that personal influence was most important at evaluation and in the actual decision suggestion for a new telephone product. He also found that the immediate family was the most important communication source, amounting to 70 percent of mentions at evaluation and 92 percent at final purchase suggestion.

Further Determinants of Family Influence

It is possible to specify at length conditions which favor intra-family communication regarding consumption and other matters. Komarovsky (1961) has provided a fairly elaborate set of such conditions, but they are generally not of much practical value to marketers; for example, "the more rigid the institutionalization of marriage roles, the less communication" (p. 257). The question which this raises is under what measurable conditions will institutionalization of marriage roles occur? A series of practical determinants of family communication can, however, be abstracted from research by a number of authors.

Social Class. Joint involvement in decision-making is most frequent at middle social class levels, while autonomy in decision making is most pronounced at upper- and lower-class levels (Komarovsky, 1961). This may be due in large part to greater role integration (sharing of functions and activities) at middle-class levels and greater role segregation at working-class and upper social-class levels. It is further concluded that the wife has more decision-making responsibility at lower social class levels and less responsibility at upper social class levels (Komarovsky, 1961; Wolgast, 1958).

Social Mobility. Upward movement in social class, as well as locational mobility, tends to increase the level of intrafamily communication. Migration away from stable primary groups, according to Komarovsky, "throws the spouses upon each other" (p. 258). In contrast, continued residence in the same city means that marriage partners will maintain peer groups as competing information sources.

Life Cycle. Joint involvement in decision making decreases over the life cycle (Granbois, 1963; Wolgast, 1958). Wolgast has concluded that advancing age and tenure of marriage leads to greater specialization in decision making. Kenkel (1961) proposes that stability of the family as a social system leads husband and wife "to crystallize the conceptions that they have brought with them to marriage concerning what is appropriate behavior for them [and allows each] to develop expectations regarding the role behavior of the other" (p. 153).

Presence of Children. Kenkel (1961) suggests that the presence of children in a family will decrease the level of joint involvement in decision making. Additions to a family are likely to weaken an egalitarian, role-integration relationship, since the presence of the child necessitates the performance of certain role-specific functions and, in time, adds to the complex of interaction patterns.

Status Consistency. This concept refers to an individual's relative positioning on the attributes of status. If they "fit" together, then we would say that the individual is status consistent; and if they do no fit together, then we would call him status inconsistent (Lenski, 1954). The status attributes generally measured include occupation, income, education, and ethnicity. Thus, a person would be considered status inconsistent if he was high on occupation and income, but low on education and ethnicity.

In families characterized by status inconsistency, there should tend to be greater joint involvement in decision making. This is based on Lenski's reasoning (1956) that the status-inconsistent person occupies an ambiguous position in society and is likely to be subjected to unpleasant experiences in social interaction. Lenski, in fact, found that the status-inconsistent person more frequently showed social withdrawal and avoidance tendencies. Given greater difficulty in interaction, therefore, such families will be thrown back upon themselves instead of relying on extrafamily communication.

In families where only one spouse can be characterized as status inconsistent, however, there may tend to be less joint involvement in decision making. Blood and Wolfe (1960) have proposed the *relative contribution* hypothesis, that is, spouses who contribute greater resources (education, income, and so on) to the marriage are more dominant in decision making.

The Gatekeeper Effect

The purchaser of a product for the family is not always the user. Thus, the purchaser may act as a *gatekeeper* because he is in a position to make decisions binding on the consumption unit and can act to block certain purchases.

The gatekeeper effect was illustrated in a study by Berey and Pollay (1968) on the role of the child in influencing the family decision to purchase packaged cereals. Findings indicated that there was a strong tendency for the mother to disagree with the child on what brands of cereal to purchase and, thus, to act in a gatekeeper capacity. This gatekeeper effect has implications for many firms marketing child-oriented products. As Berey and Pollay state, "Given that the mother is not only a purchasing agent for the child but also an agent who superimposes her preferences over those of the child, it is clear that a lot of advertising would be well directed at the mother, even if the mother is not a 'consumer' of the product" (p. 72).

Conclusion: Family Influence

The family often will be the most important source of personal influence in the adoption process. The influence of the family will vary by product type, so that greater influence will be felt when the purchase involves a considerable monetary outlay and is family-related. The influence of the family also will be felt more at later stages of the adoption process. Other factors bearing on level of family influence have also been specified.

GROUP INFLUENCE IN INDUSTRIAL SELLING

In consumer buying, the purchase decision probably is made more often by a single person, although group influence can play a significant role for certain types of products. However, the majority of industrial purchases involve the participation of several people. Harding (1966, p. 76) cites studies that give widely ranging estimates of the average number involved in such decisions—from four to twelve people. Clearly, the nature of the purchase (cost, whether repetitive or nonrepetitive, intended use, and so on) plays a part; another consideration is how "involvement" in industrial decision making is defined. The man who only okays or rubber stamps a purchase order may be said to be involved, but does he exert any *real influence* on the purchase decision?

Harding's conclusion is that suppliers tend to underestimate the importance of middle management in industrial purchasing and to overestimate the impact of top management and of the purchasing department. There are, in addition, a number of discrete stages in the industrial purchasing process, much as in consumer purchasing. For many firms, the sequence of phases is approximately as follows:

1. Anticipation or recognition of a need.
2. Determination of the characteristics and quantity of the needed item.
3. Search for and qualification of potential sources.
4. Acquisition and evaluation of proposals.
5. Selection of suppliers.
6. Selection of an order routine.
7. Feedback and evaluation.[1]

Each of these stages may involve the participation of different individuals and varying degrees of influence.

For all but small repetitive purchases, it is unlikely that any one man has the technical expertise or skill to evaluate all products against the necessary criteria. Furthermore, the need for cost control (especially in large purchases) often requires purchase approval from members of the financial or accounting staff. Recognizing the multiplicity of industrial buying influences, Alexander, Cross and Hill (1961) conclude that

> It is apparent that buying influence is widely diffused among the officials and departments of the average customer firm and that in many cases a sale of industrial goods can only be made after the seller has convinced a considerable number of executives and supervisory officials of the buying firm. . . . Certain of these individuals are likely to be more influential than others. The purchasing agent in particular occupies a key position, because he generally selects the supplier and negotiates the terms of the contract. Consequently, he may be viewed as one of the "gatekeepers" of the industrial buying process (pp. 47–48).

SOCIAL SYSTEM CHARACTERISTICS

NORMS

The social system or community in which the individual resides will also affect the flow and content of personal influence. This has been demonstrated in a research project by Marsh and Coleman (1956) on the acceptance of agricultural innovations. Their results show considerable variation in the adoption of new practices among the neighborhoods of a single county and lend support to their hypothesis that norms on innovation are more favorable

[1] This scheme is a modified version of that given in Marketing Science Institute (1967).

in some neighborhoods than in others. They also find that the higher the adoption level in a community, the greater the aggregate use of farming information sources. If the social system norms favor innovation, then the greater the pressure the member presumably will feel to keep up-to-date on farming developments. Also, in areas favorable to innovation, farmers who served as influentials showed higher adoption rates, whereas in areas less favorable to innovation, influentials showed adoption rates similar to other farmers. Group norms, therefore, tend in one case to accelerate change and in the other to retard it.

SOCIAL CLASS

Extent of personal influence may be related to social class. Although it has generally been concluded that the individual is influenced by other people in the same general social class as himself, this does not mean that personal influence necessarily is equally effective at all social class levels. It is reported in the *Workingman's Wife* that the wife of the blue-collar worker has less social contact and is more bound to the "triangle of home, children, and husband" than the middle-class wife (Rainwater, Coleman, and Handel, 1959, p. 40). For example, three out of four middle-class wives belong to clubs, compared to only one out of four working-class wives.

James H. Myers (1964) has conducted research on this issue with the hypothesis that interpersonal communication will be used more by upper-income than lower-income people in finding out about a new product. He found that, in fact, upper-income people (over $8000 per year) were more likely to refer to personal influence than lower-income people (under $5000 per year). He also found that readers of *Time* magazine (presumably middle-class) were more likely to refer to personal influence than nonreaders. These findings are of a preliminary nature, and considerably more research is needed across a range of social classes and at different stages of the purchase decision process to test this hypothesis adequately.

LIFE STYLE

The life style of a given social class also affects what its members value and has a major influence on what innovations they accept. Graham (1956) found that television was accepted better at lower-social class levels, where it was more compatible with the existing interests and form of living. In contrast, canasta was accepted better at higher-social class levels, where it was more compatible with that life style. Alexander (1959) studied the diffusion of new food products among ethnic groupings in greater New York and found that different items had different diffusion rates, depending again on the existing cultural inventories.

The "youth market" (primarily the teenage market) bears certain characteristics which suggest more extensive transfer of personal influence. Consumption is much more specialized—clothing, recreation, entertainment, and cars are the leading items of the cultural inventory—and fads and fashions reflect the desire for newness and to be "in." Personal influence seems to be quite pronounced—a finding in line with the snowball, or interaction, model of diffusion for the rapid acceptance of such fads (Coleman, Katz, and Menzel, 1966). The teen's desire for membership and identification with his fellow teens would seem to be a strong motivation to accept the norms of the youth culture.

SUMMARY

Extent of personal influence is dependent upon product, consumer, group, and social system characteristics. Relevant *product* characteristics include visibility, testability, complexity, and perceived risk. *Consumers* are not equally susceptible to personal influence. Other-directed individuals as well as individuals at transitional life stages may be more persuasible than average. Additional research has related personality characteristics, particularly self-confidence, to persuasibility; and some evidence suggests that anxiety leads to social influence.

Characteristics of the *group* affecting the operation of personal influence include the salience and attractiveness of the group to its members. The individual's social integration and group role also bear upon his susceptibility to group influence. For many purchases, the husband-wife dyad or some other combination of nuclear family members is the decision-making unit. In most purchases, the family is influential either implicitly or explicitly. Factors governing the level of role integration or specialization in family purchases include social class, social mobility, life cycle, presence of children, and status consistency.

Social system attributes also affect the flow and content of personal influence. Level of personal influence may, for example, be less pronounced at lower social class levels, and most pronounced at middle-class levels.

The acceptance of personal influence by the individual is tied directly to need satisfaction. A number of theories assessing the acceptance of personal influence have been presented—notably those of Kelman, Bauer, Weber, and Festinger. Festinger, for example, proposes that to the extent the individual lacks objective nonsocial means to evaluate his opinions, he will turn to other people for advice, information, and comparison. Bauer has suggested that personal influence may be a logical "reality base" and that not all personal influence is due to conformity behavior. Finally, personal influence represents a mix of problem-solving behavior (using information from others as a reference point to solve problems) and *psychosocial* behavior (using information from others to gain group status or reward). There has been a tendency to overstate the frequency of psychosocial behavior in models of personal influence.

CHAPTER 9

AGGREGATE STRATEGIES TO AFFECT PERSONAL INFLUENCE

Before considering strategies to affect the personal influence process, the marketer must determine if personal influence is important for the product being marketed. Because personal influence strategies are difficult to effect, marketing efforts should be concentrated elsewhere, unless personal influence is deemed highly relevant for the product and market.

Many advertising executives and product managers feel that attempting to control personal influence is more expensive than simply advertising to the total potential market. Communication researcher Joseph T. Klapper (1960) states bluntly that "Personal influence may be more effective than persuasive mass communication, but at present mass communication seems the most effective means of stimulating personal influence" (p. 72). Klapper's statement does suggest, however, that mass media can stimulate personal influence, and in this way, some control is gained over the personal influence process.

REACHING INFLUENTIALS AND NONINFLUENTIALS

The most logical and obvious strategy to "control" personal influence would be to reach opinion leaders and to allow them to reach their followers. This deceivingly simple recommendation can even be extended to suggest that a lower advertising budget would be necessary to reach a select group of influentials rather than the entire market. The problem in this strategy is identifying opinion leaders and having them say positive things about the product. The estimated costs of this are generally considerably greater than advertising to everyone and letting personal influence run its natural course.

In line with the revised conceptualization of personal influence in previous chapters, we should recognize that although identifying and appealing to opinion leaders is not as important as originally thought, it is still a valuable strategy if it can be successfully achieved. The finding that recipient-initiated communication (information seeking) may be as common as source-initiated communication suggests that the personal influence process can be affected by appealing to *followers* as well as *leaders*. Furthermore, since the opinion leader is only *relatively more influential*, it may be more appropriate to identify types of consumers who are higher on opinion leadership, than to try to identify specific influentials.

Thus, it may be just as important to reach noninfluentials as influentials. If interest in the product can be stimulated, it may encourage recipient-initiated communication. The noninfluential then would be likely to turn to the influential for further information, or he could be encouraged to do so by promotional efforts. An advertising program which arouses curiosity or is entertaining in its own right, for example, may encourage conversation about the product.

SPECIFIC OPINION LEADER STRATEGIES

IDENTIFYING OPINION LEADERS

At times it is possible to *identify* opinion leaders. This may be the case if the potential market represents a small number of consumers and if the unit price of the product is high. This is sometimes the case in industrial selling, where it may be found that as company X goes, so goes the industry. When this relationship exists, the earliest and strongest promotional efforts should be directed toward this company and later sales appeals should emphasize that company X has already adopted the product. For the consumer goods marketer, locating and identifying opinion leaders very seldom is worth the cost, since this is indeed a difficult and expensive undertaking.

CREATING OPINION LEADERS

Sometimes it is possible to create opinion leaders. An example of this might be the swimming pool company which goes into a new neighborhood and tries to locate a pool near the center of each block. The chosen homeowner is offered the pool "at cost" if he will allow his neighbors to examine it. The company then canvasses the area using the approach that one's neighbors are buying the pool, and it can be seen at a designated address. In effect, the chosen homeowner is being established by the company as an opinion leader for its product. Of course, it is desirable to choose a person possessing attributes conducive to influencing others. The same principle may hold in party-plan selling. The neighbor who holds the party, although often a paid sales agent of the company, may not be perceived in this capacity. Because of the nature of her role, she may be looked to as possessing opinion leader attributes.

Mancuso (1969) presented a method of creating opinion leaders in connection with the pop music market. His technique was to select a group of social leaders, including class presidents, cheerleaders, and sports captains, from various high schools. They were invited to join what they were told was a select panel of judges to evaluate certain records. They were asked to rate the records and encouraged to discuss them with friends. The results of the study, according to Mancuso (but without supporting evidence), were that "several records reached the top ten charts in the trial cities. These hit records did not make the top ten selections in any other cities" (p. 22).

IDENTIFYING INDIVIDUALS HIGH ON OPINION LEADERSHIP

Identifying individuals high on opinion leadership is a much more viable alternative than attempting to identify and approach opinion leaders. As discussed, the opinion leader concept is actually a matter of relative influence. Therefore, instead of trying to identify the most influential people or to create absolute opinion leaders, it is more realistic to identify individuals who are higher than average on opinion leadership. It has been concluded, for example, that innovators are more influential than most other group members. To the extent that innovators can be identified through purchase records, it is possible to appeal directly to them and to encourage them to influence their friends.

Individuals who have high contact with the public may also tend to be higher on opinion leadership. Ford Motor Company, in the introduction of Mustang, had several promotional programs in which disc jockeys, college newspaper editors, and airline stewardesses were loaned Mustangs, to a considerable extent on the theory that they were likely to influence other people.

Upon evaluation, the airline stewardess program was felt to have been unsuccessful, since stewardesses were not looked to as a source of information about automobiles. The other programs were considered successful.

High public contact, however, need not be related to opinion leadership except for products perceived as relevant. Professionals, for example, tend to be opinion leaders for products within their defined fields. Thus, dentists are likely to be influential in product and brand decisions concerning electric toothbrushes and dental hygiene products. They would not, however, be expected to exercise much influence in automobile purchase decisions, although a dentist might be an automobile opinion leader because of attributes other than his professional role.

CHARACTERIZING OPINION LEADERS

The most basic approach toward influencing the personal influence process is not to focus on specific people, but to study the characteristics of opinion leaders, including their media behavior, and then to aim the promotional program in line with this generalized image of the product opinion leader, who, because of selective perception, should receive and process the message. The only problem with this approach is that while reaching opinion leaders, the message may be alienating nonleaders, who conceivably could react adversely to appeals designed for opinion leaders.

PROMOTIONAL TACTICS AND PERSONAL INFLUENCE

If the personal influence process is to be affected to the advantage of the company, the means to do so must reside in already controllable aspects of the firm's communication-persuasion program. This suggests that the marketer must use advertising, personal selling, and sales promotion tactics to achieve its diffusion objectives. The remainder of this chapter will be devoted to an examination of how these promotional methods may affect the flow of personal influence.

ADVERTISING STRATEGIES

Four advertising approaches are relevant in reaching both influentials and noninfluentials and encouraging personal influence: (1) simulating personal influence, (2) stimulating personal influence, (3) monitoring personal influence, and (4) retarding personal influence.

SIMULATING PERSONAL INFLUENCE

It has been suggested by Bourne (1957), that where personal influence is operative, advertising should "stress the kinds of people who buy the product, reinforcing and broadening where possible the existing stereotypes of users" (p. 222). In effect, this strategy may *simulate* the personal influence process. In contrast, where personal influence is not closely related to product and brand purchase, Bourne advises that "advertising should emphasize the product's attributes, intrinsic qualities, price, and advantages over competing products" (p. 222). Defining "the kinds of people who buy the product" may, however, be a formidable task. It is essential not to define the customer profile too narrowly nor to alienate any significant segment of the market.

If personal influence is important for a product, then how should the product buyer be portrayed in advertising? Should he resemble the man next door, or should he represent a more admirable figure? Or, to state it another way, should the appeal to the audience member be that his fellow group members are buying or that members of his aspirational group are buying? It is important to know for each given product just what the relevant group is—either actual or aspirational. It seems—and is confirmed by actual practice—that perfume advertising should emphasize aspirational groups, while refrigerator or washing machine advertising should emphasize membership groups. The choice of the appropriate group emphasis and the portrayal of the most meaningful kinds of situations should increase the effectiveness of advertising.

Since susceptibility to personal influence depends on consumer characteristics, it may be asked whether an appeal focusing on the kind of people who buy the product would be effective with individuals who are not particularly subject to personal influence. This has not been tested, although Kassarjian (1965) has studied differential preference for message types depending upon degree of inner- or other-directedness. Inner-directed message appeals emphasize product attributes and intrinsic merits; a Kodak ad, for example, proclaimed "for a lasting record." Other-directed message appeals focus on a people-oriented approach; another Kodak ad proclaimed, "Share your experiences with friends at home." Kassarjian found that inner-directed people preferred inner-directed ads and other-directed people preferred other-directed ads. Both groups, however, felt that people in general would be more influenced by other-directed ads. And since it is not easy to identify and appeal to these separate groups, an overall other-directed approach seems somewhat more advisable.

Direct mail advertising offers the marketer an opportunity to reach specific groups of individuals and to use appeals appropriate to them. Lists are available, for example, by income level, profession, religion, and geographic location. For products of a high-unit value, direct mail advertising may encourage feelings that the product has group acceptance, since such advertising is directed to the consumer as a group member. This strategy may be considered a form of personal influence simulation. Response rate is found to increase, for example, the more specifically the mailing identifies the consumer. A mailing addressed to "Resident" receives less response than one addressed to "Community Leader," which receives less response than one addressed to "Mr. Conway, Community Leader."

The basic argument then, is that to a certain extent, advertising can simulate personal influence. In effect, advertising may replace or reduce the need for personal influence (Dichter, 1966). By portraying the idea that the consumer's fellow group members buy the product and that this behavior is appropriate for him, can lessen the consumer's need to turn to other people for legitimation. Another very common example of personal influence simulation in advertising is the testimonial by a famous person or the "unsolicited" testimonial by the man in the street. In this case, the marketer may be simulating opinion leadership, since he is setting up these people as opinion leaders.

As in the actual occurrence of personal influence, testimonials are believable only to the extent that the product is subject to personal influence and to the extent that the media "opinion leader" is viewed as a valid information source. Whereas Dean Martin would be a good endorser for liquor products and Arnold Palmer would be a good endorser for golfing products or accessories, it is doubtful that their influence in other areas would be any greater than that of the consumer influential. Much testimonial advertising probably goes astray because the endorser is not seen as a likely source of information.

STIMULATING PERSONAL INFLUENCE

Some advertising campaigns are much more successful than others in *stimulating* personal influence, that is, in getting consumers to talk about the product. Very few agencies pretest advertising for its conversational impact— which is just not commonly recognized as an advertising objective, though it should be. Of course, advertising must encourage dissemination of positive information about the product, and this too would have to be evaluated in advance of the campaign. The important point is that conversational value can be stated by the marketer as an evaluation criterion for new advertising and can be formalized as an objective by the agency's creative department. Advertising creativity seems very much to be related to ensuing word of mouth.

Certain advertising approaches may be much more repeatable by consumers than others. It may be essential that advertising encouraging personal influence use the same kind of language as the average consumer. This type of advertising also has to provide the consumer with enough understandable information to answer questions his friends may ask if he repeats the ad. Entertaining advertising and "teaser campaigns" in advance of new product introductions may possess inherent attributes encouraging a flow of personal influence.

On a more fundamental level, interpersonal communication can be stimulated by encouraging information giving and information seeking. The most likely information giver is a person who has just bought the product. Such people can be advertised to specifically, if purchase records are available (as for cars, appliances, and furniture), using direct mail. Since they may be in a state of cognitive dissonance, these recent purchasers are likely to be quite receptive to product information justifying purchase. The information provided may then place them in a better position to communicate with friends about the product purchase and encourage them to do so. The most likely information seeker is a person who is considering the purchase of a product. Mass media advertising could encourage an "Ask the man who owns one" approach. Such a tactic may meet with more success than a "Tell your friends" approach, since few people, it is assumed, wish to deliberately influence their friends. Again, it is essential to check personal channels to ascertain that they are disseminating positive information *before* instituting such approaches.

It has been tentatively recommended that it also may be possible to reach product opinion leaders or those higher on opinion leadership by means of advertising. If these persons are informed about the product, they will have a higher probability of purchasing it and then will be in a position to influence others should the occasion arise. It is unrealistic to hope to encourage opinion leaders to actively and deliberately influence fellow consumers. The task is formidable enough to reach such people on a selective basis. The marketer may be allowed to pursue this strategy if (1) opinion leader characteristics are definable, and (2) opinion leaders have distinguishable media behavior patterns. The second factor is crucial, since it allows segmented advertising approaches to leaders and nonleaders. It also is possible to use appeals appropriate to opinion leaders if their characteristics are known. Of course, these factors are interrelated because if opinion leaders possess definable characteristics, some measure of media segmentation is generally possible. It could be a risky strategy to appeal openly to opinion leader traits in media reaching mostly nonleaders.

MONITORING PERSONAL INFLUENCE

It is possible to *monitor* personal influence, that is, to find out what people are saying about the product. This may provide valuable information for marketing decision making. For new products, monitoring personal influence may be especially valuable in discovering what product attributes are discussed, what product uses are emphasized, what disadvantages or problems are discussed, and what the overall attitude toward the product is. As sometimes happens, the features being emphasized in advertising may not be perceived as most relevant by consumers. Consumers also find new uses for products. Sometimes, very minor disadvantages of the product may create a negative overall feeling about the product.

Advertising can be used in reacting to what is taking place in the interpersonal communication channels. Thus, if certain positive things are being said about the product, advertising can emphasize these positive aspects to reinforce and encourage such word of mouth. If unpleasant things are being said about the product, advertising may be able to combat such misunderstandings—if they are misunderstandings—by providing more detailed usage information or emphasizing positive aspects of the product. Some adjustments in advertising appeals may be appropriate, for example, if consumers talk about the quietness of a vacuum cleaner while current advertisements stress its efficiency.

RETARDING PERSONAL INFLUENCE

There may be conditions under which it is desirable to *retard* personal influence. This situation would seem most likely when the product is inferior. Katz and Lazarsfeld (1955) suggest that when a movie is bad, its distributors adopt a penetration strategy and rely on mass advertising. The goal seems to be to get in and out of town before people can start telling other people how bad the movie is. In contrast, when a movie is good, a strategy of limited distribution which capitalizes on personal influence is used. It is unlikely that personal influence ever could be retarded for an inferior product except on such a very short-run basis.

The fact that personal influence can be dysfunctional, especially for radically new or complicated products, suggests the need for extensive dissemination of factual material and product demonstrations. Thus, if farmers rely on other farmers for information, adoption may actually be slower because of the communication of misleading information. But, if farmers can readily turn to extension agents or commercial dealers for advice and demonstrations, adoption may be encouraged. Personal influence is retarded in the latter case by the ready availability of other information sources.

Personal influence, therefore, is not always desirable. Opinion leaders communicate negative as well as positive information and can recommend against adoption of the product. In such a case, it could become necessary to neutralize such negative opinion leaders. Perhaps, a two-sided message format would be more effective with opinion leaders and would innoculate them against competing product advertisements. Unfortunately, the concept of negative opinion leadership barely has been researched.

PERSONAL SELLING STRATEGIES

As emphasized in previous chapters, advertising is of most significance to consumers at the earlier stages of the purchase decision process, while personal selling is of most significance at the later stages. The salesman actually may perform some of the same functions for the consumer as friend-and-neighbor information sources, especially to the extent that he sells multiple brands and is perceived as a knowledgeable and not altogether biased source. This may occur particularly in industrial selling where more reliance is placed on the salesman for his technical expertise and where informal personal influence sources are less operative than in the consumer realm. There is an opportunity for the marketer to *simulate* personal influence through the form of the sales agent.

A point deserving emphasis is that the salesman is likely to be considerably less effective if the consumer is not advanced on the purchase decision process. A salesman seldom can take a consumer from unawareness to purchase. Even in cases where he can, having him do so may be an inefficient allocation of resources, since advertising and sales promotion generally can achieve awareness and interest more cheaply. This suggests the necessity of lead-procurement activities so that sales energies will be directed to most likely prospects. It is necessary in some way to evaluate the stage of the purchase decision stage at which an individual is. In insurance selling, for example, the person who responds to an advertisement by sending in a coupon requesting more information generally is quite advanced on the purchase decision process. The probability of a sales outcome is higher with him than with a randomly selected person on the same block.

Influence generally tends to be exchanged among persons of the same general social status and background. An individual tends to interact with people who are fairly like him and who, in many cases, hold the same overall beliefs and attitudes. Only recently in marketing has it been recognized that similarity in characteristics between salesman and customer may improve the probability of a sales outcome. Evans (1963), in a study of life insurance selling, has found that the more alike salesman and consumer, the more likely a sale. This was true for demographic characteristics such as age, education, and income, for physical characteristics such as height, and for belief characteristics such as politics and religion. Although some of these factors are hard to control, advantage can be gained in many cases by a policy of matching salesman and customer characteristics.

GROUP SANCTIONING

It is important to recognize that even in a salesman-customer situation, the customer is still influenced by his peer group. This suggests that if the salesman receives group approval, his selling task will be considerably easier. Or if he receives approval from one member of the group, especially the opinion leader, other group members may be easier to sell. Group sales and referral programs are important strategies which work with personal influence. This suggests that it may be important to

1. Sell within the boundaries of social systems.
2. Sell within groups within social systems.

3. Concentrate initial sales efforts on individuals of higher opinion leadership.
4. Request referrals.
5. Match salesmen characteristics to the characteristics of social system members.

These points now will be developed in turn.

Social System Selling

The more it is possible to sell within the boundaries of specific *social systems*, the more the flow of personal influence will benefit the seller. For example, some airlines establish campus representatives. Because the social system is well defined, the presence of such a representative who stands ready to help students can be made known rather quickly. And because he is a member of the system, there may be a bias toward calling on him. If he provides good service, knowledge of this reputation can disseminate quickly among social system members. (Of course, if he provides poor service, this also can be made known quickly.) Diamond merchants sometimes establish college representatives for many of the same reasons and because the purchase of a diamond is very subject to personal influence, so that favorable word of mouth can quickly spread and yield a sizable pool of potential customers.

Chrysler Corporation has attempted to harness social system influence in at least two cases. In one case, it very deliberately courted doctors as potential Imperial buyers and offered special trial programs. In another case, it offered special inducements for New York City cab owners to buy Plymouths. Since both these groups were viewed as desirable influentials, the company was interested in the effects of personal influence not only within the social system but also beyond it. Doctors may be influentials for prestige cars and taxi drivers for standard cars.

Group Selling

It may also be possible to focus on specific *groups* within the social system. This would tend to maximize any benefits to be obtained from personal influence. Thus, the campus airline representative could approach each living unit in turn. The automobile dealer could approach each medical building or taxi cab company in turn. Perhaps a more meaningful example of the importance of reaching groups of individuals within a company social system can be given from industrial selling.

In calling on an industrial buyer, the seller often finds not a single buyer, but individuals representing several groups involved in the purchase process. First, there may be a purchasing agent for this line of components who is a member of the purchasing group and has a particular set of criteria in mind—cost perhaps predominating. There also may be an engineer who represents the engineering staff and who has a somewhat different set of criteria—quality perhaps being most important. Then there may be a member of the production group, who again implicitly operates with a somewhat different set of criteria—perhaps delivery schedules being most important. In order to sell this account, the salesman has to sell each group representative. This sometimes requires a selling team where an engineer is brought aboard at the critical point in the negotiations to sell the engineering group and a production specialist is introduced to sell the production group.

Opinion Leadership

It is desirable, where possible, to concentrate initial sales efforts on individuals of higher *opinion leadership*. The salesman, unlike the advertiser, has the possibility of studying the social system or the group and determining its formal leaders and sometimes its opinion leaders for his product category. As pointed out, this is more possible in industrial selling where the number of buyers is small and the salesman calls on them over time. He surely will learn which buyers are most important in selling his other customers. He will also learn within each company where the greatest concentration of influence resides for his product category.

When selling within the confines of a group, it may also be possible for the seller of a consumer product or service to identify persons of higher opinion leadership. Formal group leaders, for example, often may exert more influence than nonleaders. Or it might be possible for the salesman to ask for peer report of who is most influential regarding the product being sold. If he can find the person to whom other group members turn, he should sell him first.

Referrals

In order to gain the full impact of personal channels, it is wise, where possible, to request *referrals*. This is a particularly important way of taking advantage of personal influence. The insurance salesman, for example, often relies heavily on referrals which gain him an entree and perhaps a higher level of perceived trustworthiness than might otherwise be the case. Even if the salesman does not use the informant's name in selling, the process of referral is likely to lead to prospects who are more likely to be considering purchase, since this is the usual rationale in requesting referrals.

Implicit referral also may be used as a selling technique. Thus, in calling upon succeeding group members, it may be advantageous to indicate that purchases already have been made by other social system members, especially those higher on opinion leadership. A product or service may be sold on the basis of a special price for group members, as when the rate can be based on occupational "membership."

Matching Characteristics

It also may be desirable to *match the characteristics* of salesmen and clients. Again, in certain industrial selling situations where each client and his characteristics are known, salesman and customer may be matched specifically on what are considered to be the most important attributes. For the most part, however, the marketing manager would think in terms of matching salesmen to aggregate group characteristics. Thus, one publishing company that specializes largely in junior college accounts pursues a policy of hiring former teachers, who it feels are better able to communicate with teachers. An insurance company whose market is blue-collar workers pursues a policy of hiring former blue-collar workers rather than college graduates, as most insurance companies now prefer. It finds that whereas such salesmen are not as familiar with the intricacies of insurance, they are more in tune with the knowledge level and needs of their market.

SALES PROMOTION STRATEGIES

Certain sales promotion techniques may be used advantageously to impart knowledge about the product and to stimulate personal influence. Probably the best way to gain product knowledgeability among consumers is to provide them with actual experience with the product. They are then more likely to communicate accurate information. For relatively inexpensive products, such as food and household cleaning items, free sampling of the product gives consumers product experience and encourages product communication. Couponing functions in much the same manner. Arndt (1967a) found that when housewives in an apartment complex were offered a new coffee at one third the retail price, 42 percent purchased and 34 percent reported *receiving* word-of-mouth communication about the product.

Consumer experience with relatively more expensive products can be encouraged by in-store demonstrations, displays, and, sometimes, by locating the product to encourage consumer contact with it. Thus, considerable knowledge about a new telephone product was gained by consumers actually using it in key locations, such as airports, hotels, and local stores. Car rental agencies receive considerable discounts from automobile companies, who reason that a consumer's driving a particular make of car may encourage him to consider that car when he is again in the buying market.

Arndt (1968) has offered a brief history of how companies in the past could hire "professional rumor managers" (p. 4). He describes how one rumor agency offered services such as "spontaneous" conversations between stooges in subways, elevators, and other high-traffic locations where they would promote the sponsor's product and degrade competing products. Such services seem to have died in recent years. Today's public relations agencies, however, seek to promote the sponsor's product by a variety of means, some of which border on personal influence. One large liquor distributor, for example, held parties throughout his market area to introduce what he termed the "swingers" to his new Vodka line.

SUMMARY

Given that personal influence is important for a company's product, it is possible to institute promotional strategies to influence, although by no means to control, the personal influence process.

Advertising Strategies

Advertising can perform the function, in certain cases, of *simulating* personal influence by replacing or reducing the need for the consumer to turn to other people for advice and information. Advertising may, for example, persuade a consumer that members of his reference group are buying the product and that this is appropriate behavior for him also. Alternatively, opinion leadership may be simulated by the use of testimonial advertising.

Advertising may also be capable of *stimulating* personal influence. "Teaser campaigns," slogans, and entertaining advertising may be means of encouraging consumers to discuss the product message. Strategies to encourage opinion leaders to disseminate product information and to encourage followers to request product information may also be initiated.

Monitoring personal influence can provide information on what consumers are saying about the product. Adjustments in advertising then may be appropriate to reinforce the dissemination of positive information and to focus on product attributes considered most relevant by consumers. Finally, there may be instances where *retarding* personal influence is in order, since personal influence can be dysfunctional. Misleading information about new or complicated products may sometimes be communicated via personal channels, and advertising may have to respond to such conditions by increasing the availability of adequate product and usage information.

Personal Selling Strategies

Personal selling strategies are usually of greater significance at later stages of the purchase decision process and for large ticket items. The salesman may simulate personal influence for the consumer by performing functions similar to those a knowledgeable acquaintance would perform. However, even in a salesman-customer relationship, consumers will still be influenced by peers; hence, *group sanction* may be important to a sales outcome. It may be important, therefore, to (1) sell within social system boundaries, (2) focus on specific groups within social systems, (3) concentrate initial sales efforts on individuals of higher opinion leadership, (4) request referrals, and (5) match the salesman's characteristics with those of social system members. Among the advantages the salesman may have over the advertiser are that he is usually better placed to study the nature and occurrence of personal influence within relevant groups and social systems, to identify opinion leaders, and to employ explicit or implicit referrals as a selling technique.

Sales Promotion Strategies

Sampling, couponing, in-store demonstrations and displays, and selection of key locations may be employed to provide consumers with actual product experience, thereby imparting knowledge and stimulating interpersonal communication of accurate information.

PART THREE

Models of Attitude Change and New Product Marketing

CHAPTER 10

ATTITUDE AND
ATTITUDE CHANGE

The new product marketer is a professional change agent. Adoption of an innovation implies a change in the individual consumer's behavior patterns. The degree of behavioral change required varies with the nature of the innovation, being relatively minor for continuous innovations and often substantial for discontinuous innovations.

The antecedents of behavioral change are awareness of the innovation and

favorable attitude toward the innovation. If the new product is fairly continuous in nature and primary demand is established, attitude creation and
attitude change will be highly brand-specific. If, however, the product is a
relatively discontinuous innovation, attitude creation and change efforts may
have to be directed at existing consumption patterns in order to stimulate
primary demand.

Diffusion theory has not relied extensively on attitude theory, but has
focused instead on a problem-solving and rational communication process.
The implicit model has been the communication of knowledge to relevant
persons under the assumption that adoption logically would follow. Only
recently have diffusion theorists begun to make use of the attitude change
tradition of research, although marketing diffusion researchers, focusing on
diffusion later than researchers in other disciplines, have tended to use whatever literature seems relevant, including literature in the attitude change
tradition.

Attitude change is, therefore, not the only tradition of planned change. But
as the concept is used in this chapter—and as it has been used in recent
marketing literature—it is broad enough to include the problem-solving,
rational change process generally implicit in adoption models. This process
still involves attitudinal change, thus allowing us to posit attitude change as a
general change model.

THE NATURE OF ATTITUDES

Attitude is probably the most prevalent concept in the field of social
psychology and has received increasing attention from marketers in recent
years.[1] The essential nature of the concept is that an *attitude* is an *intervening
variable* posited to account for differences in behavioral response functions.
Most simply, an attitude is a disposition to act in a certain manner.

Either of the following definitions seems to reflect the essential nature of
the attitude concept.

> An *attitude* is a relatively enduring organization of beliefs about an object
> or situation predisposing one to respond in some preferential manner (Rokeach,
> 1966, p. 530).

> As the individual develops, his cognitions, feelings, and action tendencies
> with respect to the various objects in his world become organized into enduring
> *systems* called attitudes (Krech, Crutchfield, and Ballachey, 1962, p. 139).

A growing volume of data supports the viewpoint that a knowledge of
attitudes can be used to predict behavior. As shown in Figure 10.1, Achen-

---

[1] The objective of this book does not to permit a critical evaluation of each of the many
theories of attitude and attitude change. For a more thorough treatment, the reader is
referred to Insko (1967), McGuire (1969 b), and Kiesler, Collins, and Miller (1969).

baum (1966) has found a direct relationship between the following attitudes and product usage:

1. The more favorable the attitude, the higher the incidence of product usage.
2. The less favorable the attitude, the lower the incidence of usage.
3. The more unfavorable people's attitudes are toward a product, the more likely they are to stop using it.
4. The attitudes of people who have never tried a product tend to be distributed around the mean in the shape of a normal distribution (pp. 112 and 114).

Assael and Day (1968) find attitudes to be effective in explaining variance in market shares among brands. They also find that changes in attitude are related to subsequent behavioral change—again on an aggregate market-share basis. This posited link between attitudes and behavior presents the marketer with opportunities to *predict* consumer behavior and to *measure* advertising effectiveness.

Figure 10.1   Relationship between Attitudes and Usage for Selected Brands of Consumer Products: (a) Cigarette (b) Deodorant (c) Gasoline (d) Laxative

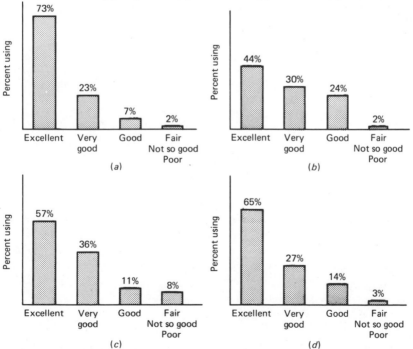

The predictive ability of attitudes may depend upon the length of the repurchase cycle. Day (1970), for example, has found that attitudes are better predictors of brand choice behavior for frequently purchased nondurable items than for infrequently purchased expensive appliances. Day's explanation is that a shorter repurchase cycle lessens the influence of environmental factors because "(1) there is a greater backlog of remembered experience with the brand and the product; (2) there is better prior knowledge of the environmental factors that will be encountered during the shopping process; and (3) the attitudes themselves are more stable and less likely to change under normal circumstances" (p. 36). When the effect of environmental factors is reduced, then initial attitudes provide greater information about subsequent behavior.

In order to understand better the nature of attitudes and how they may be changed, it is important to consider the structural foundations of attitudes, the functions that they serve, and their salience for the individual.

ATTITUDE STRUCTURE

It is common to think of attitudes in terms of their cognitive, feeling, and action tendency components. These components are seen as interdependent and organized into a unified and relatively enduring system. The *cognitive* component refers to the beliefs which the individual holds about an object. Included are knowledge and evaluative beliefs, which attribute qualities to the object such as good or bad, favorable or unfavorable. The *feeling*, or affective, component refers to the individual's emotional range concerning the object, his feelings of liking or disliking, pleasure or displeasure. The *action-tendency* component refers to the individual's readiness to behave overtly toward the object.

Each of these attitude components, according to Krech, Crutchfield, and Ballachey (1962), can be described further in terms of valence and multiplexity. *Valence* is a measure of positiveness or negativeness, or how much the individual's beliefs, feelings, and tendencies to act are for or against an object. Multiplexity is a measure of the number and variety of elements forming an attitude component. Thus, the feeling component may be comprised of a simple like-dislike emotion or a complicated emotional set involving a range of emotions such as love, passion, anger, and regret.

It also is necessary to point out that an attitude generally does not exist in isolation from other attitudes. Attitude components tend to relate to corresponding attitude components. For example, the individual's cognitions about music may tend to relate to his cognitions about entertainment or the arts. Attitudes tend to form *clusters* with other attitudes within the person's total attitudinal *system*.

The structural, or consonance, theory of attitudes maintains that elements of components making up one particular attitude will tend to fit, or be consonant with one another; that attitude components (cognitive, feelings, and action-tendency) will tend to be consonant with one another; and that attitudes within a particular cluster will tend to be consonant with one another.

Although perfect harmony need not exist, beliefs making up the cognitive component of an attitude would be expected to be fairly consistent. Thus, the individual can hardly accept the findings of research linking cigarette smoking to lung disease and believe that cigarette smoking is harmless. Consistency also would be expected to exist among the individual's beliefs, feelings, and action tendencies. Thus, it would seem unusual if the individual believed in new products, liked them better than old products, yet maintained brand loyalty to established products. Finally, attitudes comprising an attitude cluster would be expected to tend toward consistency, although this is not always the case. If a man were a staunch Republican, he would not have been expected to vote for John F. Kennedy in 1960, unless, of course, another cluster, such as his attitudes as a Roman Catholic, was more relevant.

Despite the posited pressure for consistency of attitudes advanced by structural theory, many examples of inconsistency can be found, McGuire (1968) discusses several reasons which reflect both the capriciousness of human nature and the limitations of the human mind. For one, individuals are faced in almost every decision situation with the necessity of drawing a conclusion from insufficient evidence, which may lead to suboptimal decisions and behavioral inconsistencies. McGuire also emphasizes that people experience *gradations* in their attitudes, which explains such apparent illogicalities as X liking Y, and Y liking Z, but X disliking Z. Another explanation of apparent inconsistencies is that human beings are not like computers, "ideal intellectual slaves, experiencing practically no time lag, no loss of memory, and no reluctance to consider all the available evidence. The humans to whom our formulations are meant to apply do unfortunately experience considerable limitations in these regards" (McGuire, 1968, p. 159).

Not all psychologists accept the structural balance theory. Some, in fact, subscribe to its opposite, *variety* theory. Empirical evidence can be cited which shows that people seek variety and new experiences, that novelty produces positive affective responses, and that variety is, in fact, necessary to learning (Maddi, 1968). Consumers can be expected, therefore, to seek risks in certain circumstances (as in fashion purchases) and to act in apparent conflict with attitudinal structures as a means of introducing variety and novelty into their style of life.

THE FUNCTIONS OF ATTITUDES

A few theorists have made the assumption that in order to change attitudes, it is first necessary to know what *type* of attitude the individual holds. This implies gaining some insight into the needs (or functions) that attitudes serve.

Both Smith, Bruner, and White (1956) and Daniel Katz (1960) list four such functions, which show a considerable degree of overlap. The parallel functions from each set are presented below:

Katz	Smith, Bruner, and White
1. Instrumental, adjustive, utilitarian	1. Social adjustment
2. Ego defensive	2. Externalization
3. Knowledge	3. Object appraisal
4. Value-expressive	4. Quality of expressiveness

One of the reasons why these sets do not match perfectly is that the two functional theories often disagree significantly on *how* attitudes are to be categorized. In a critical evaluation of the functional approach, Kiesler, Collins, and Miller (1969) observe that

> This lack of agreement on category boundaries illustrates the arbitrary nature of the functional categories. The lack of convergence on a single set of functional categories reflects gaps in our knowledge and, therefore, is a serious criticism of the functional theories. The problem undoubtedly stems from the lack of empirical research stimulated by the theorist; empirical data would presumably provide insight into the most appropriate category boundaries. On the other hand, it could be argued that the entire taxonomic problem is entirely arbitrary and not dependent on empirical studies (pp. 304–305).

Daniel Katz (1960) is probably the leading proponent of the functional approach and has stimulated a fair amount of research in connection with his theoretical position. His articulation of the functions which attitudes perform for the individual follows:

1. *The adjustment or utilitarian function.* Attitudes acquired to serve this function represent a means for reaching a desired goal or avoiding an undesirable goal. As such, attitudes are the intervening mechanism in the behaviorist's stimulus-response model. They are developed according to their instrumentality in achieving reward or avoiding punishment.
2. *The ego-defensive function.* Attitudes acquired in the service of protecting the individual's ego from his own undesirable impulses serve the ego-defensive function. Racial prejudice, for example, may often be a projection of inferiority feelings on to some visible minority, thus conveniently providing an attitude of superiority to bolster the ego. As such, ego-defensive attitudes tend to arise from within the person as a response to his needs rather than in response to an external stimulus. Mechanisms relating to ego-defensive attitudes include rationalization, projection, and displacement.

3. *The value-expressive function.* These attitudes serve the function of giving *positive* expression to the individual's self-concept; they reflect and confirm his notion of what kind of person he is.
4. *The knowledge function.* Individuals acquire knowledge to provide meaning and order to what would otherwise be a conglomeration of sensations in a chaotic environment. Attitudes in the service of the knowledge function provide structure and standards for responding to what would otherwise be a host of nondifferential stimuli.

This functional framework should assist in our quest to understand why attitudes are formed and how they may be changed. These functions elaborate upon the motivational basis which underlies the acquisition of attitudes. They also provide meaning for the existence of particular attitudes among individuals.

ATTITUDE SALIENCE

Although the individual may hold attitudes on a host of topics, not all of these attitudes will have general salience for him, and the specific salience of attitudes will vary with circumstances. Festinger (1964), for example, has argued that attitude *change* may be inherently unstable unless an environmental or behavioral change occurs to support it. The same phenomenon may also apply for new attitude formation; the attitude may not become an integral part of the individual's attitude system unless it is made salient. Many attitudes toward products and brands may be inherently unstable, since they are not salient enough for the individual. Either they are not tied closely enough to the fulfillment of important needs or functions, or the individual is unwilling to arrive at specific *brand* attitudes and prefers to operate at a *product category* attitude level.

The salience of an attitude is a particularly important variable in Rokeach's model (1966, 1968) of attitude change. As noted earlier, Rokeach defines attitude as "an organization of beliefs"; in examining the structure of individual belief systems, he hypothesizes that

1. Not all beliefs are equally important to the individual; they vary along a central-peripheral dimension and are functionally distinct.
2. The more central a belief, the more it will resist change.
3. Changes in central beliefs will produce greater changes in the rest of the belief system than changes in less central beliefs (Rokeach, 1968, p. 3).

Within this belief system, Rokeach identifies five classes of beliefs along the central-peripheral dimension:

Type A: Primitive Beliefs, 100-percent Consensus. Fundamental, taken-for-granted axioms that are not subject to controversy because we believe, and we believe everyone else believes them; for example, "I believe this is my mother." These beliefs are highly resistant to change and it is extremely upsetting for the individual to have these beliefs questioned.

Type B: Primitive Beliefs, Zero Consensus. Some basic beliefs do not depend on social support or consensus, but arise from deep personal experience; "I believe that I am intelligent." These beliefs are incontrovertible, and we believe them regardless of whether anyone else does. Many represent aspects of self-concept or self-doubts and phobias.

Type C: Authority Beliefs. Beliefs are held about which authorities or reference groups to trust and which not to trust. We look to such authorities for information on how to evaluate things having alternative interpretations or not capable of being personally verified or experienced.

Type D: Derived Beliefs. Belief in the credibility of a particular authority implies an acceptance of other beliefs perceived to emanate from such authority, for example, *The New York Times.* If we know that a person believes in a particular authority, we should be able to deduce many other beliefs of his which emanate or derive from the authorities with which he identifies. Such beliefs can be changed providing (1) the suggestion for change emanates from the person's authority or (2) there is a change in the person's authority.

Type E: Inconsequential Beliefs. Certain beliefs may be intensely held, but a change in them does not alter the total system of beliefs in any significant way. These beliefs may include matters of taste, brand preferences, and so on, but are considered inconsequential because they have few or no connections with other beliefs.

Rokeach's scheme suffers the same drawbacks of categorization as the functional schemes. The classification is arbitrary and not based on empirical research. It is doubtful that these types of belief systems would achieve any consensus among other attitude theorists. However, Rokeach's scheme is conceptually interesting and may advance our understanding, since it recognizes that all attitudes are not of equal salience. Of particular significance is the fact that many brand attitudes may be inconsequential to the individual—depending on his involvement with the product category—and may be changed without disrupting his belief systems. Of course, despite the inconsequential nature of many purchase decisions, strong brand loyalty may exist. And since learning has occurred and the product is not important enough to warrant alternative decision-making, it is much easier to maintain the existing habit pattern.

Rokeach (1966) also makes the distinction between attitudes toward objects and attitudes toward situations. To say that an individual has an attitude toward a particular object does not mean that this attitude will be activated across all situations. Thus, having a generally liberal attitude toward civil rights does not necessarily activate liberal behavior concerning inter-marriage or integrated housing or integrated schools. Similarly, Rokeach argues that a general attitude toward a particular situation will not be activated across all attitude-objects. Salience, then, is a function of the inter-action of *object* and *situation*. A marketing illustration can be seen in the atti-tudes of individuals toward brand names. Marketers often place considerable emphasis on building across-brand identity—generally by the use of a com-pany name. The assumption is that if consumers feel well-disposed towards the company, they will have a favorable opinion of *any* product marketed under its name. However, this may not necessarily be so in practice. A consumer may have a generally favorable attitude towards, say, General Motors, but the same behavior (that is, purchase of the GM brand) will not necessarily be activated for refrigerators as for cars. The characteristics of GM which appeal to the car buyer may not be as relevant or meaningful to him when he is shopping for a refrigerator, for which attributes other than brand name and styling may be more important.

The attempt to build across-brand identity through a company name may be carried to its logical absurdity when the housewife is told that Stouffer frozen foods are a product of Litton Industries and Durkee foods are a product of SCM. If a favorable attitude is associated with Litton's industrial products, this attitude can hardly be expected to carry over to another con-sumer group and product category. The creation of the Bounty brand by the Campbell Soup Company for its canned meat products was in specific recog-nition of the fact that attitudes toward soup were based on different evaluative criteria than would be used for meat products and that the name Campbell's on a canned meat item might have undesirable "watery" associations.

The overall attitude towards a product or brand is the resultant of a number of attitudes toward each of the product *attributes* (for example, price, appearance, flavor, and performance). These and other attributes tend to have varying saliency and, therefore, to contribute in várying degrees to the overall attitude.

Research demonstrates that the attributes relevant in purchase vary from product to product. Thus, styling is a highly salient attribute for cars, but may be less relevant for washing machines; price may be highly salient for bread, but not for salt; and fragrance is highly salient for perfume, but not for gasoline. Attitude change, in order to enhance a brand's consumer appeal, often may be brought about by altering consumer perceptions of the brand's critical attributes.

ATTITUDE CHANGE AND BEHAVIORAL CHANGE

In the course of their persuasive attempts, marketers seek to *create* new attitudes, to *confirm* existing attitudes, or to *change* existing attitudes. Attitude confirmation is the strategy used for most well-established products, whereas attitude creation or attitude change is viewed as the most relevant strategy for new products. Since this book is concerned with new products, the discussion will focus primarily on attitude change and attitude creation.

The attitude change–behavior change relationship has been subject to considerable debate in recent years (as discussed in Chapter 3), and adequate evidence for the relationship has not been found. Festinger's explanation (1964) for this is of particular interest; he suggests that when attitudes are changed on the basis of persuasive communication, this change "is inherently unstable and will disappear or remain isolated unless an environmental or behavioral change can be brought about to support and maintain it" (p. 415). Otherwise, "the same factors that produced the initial opinion and the behavior will continue to operate to nullify the effect of the opinion change" (Festinger, 1964, p. 416). Thus, attitude change may not be a sufficient condition for behavioral change.

Festinger's conclusion and the research which has been done seem to be based on attitudes of a higher order of importance than those attached to most purchase decisions. As noted by Rokeach (1968), *inconsequential* beliefs have few connections with other beliefs and may be changed without significantly affecting the total system of beliefs. An attitude change–behavior change relationship can be expected for most brand decisions, although this may be quite difficult to document, or may be unstable as (1) the time to purchase lengthens, (2) the amount of competing advertising increases, and (3) the importance of the purchase and its relevance to the individual's self-concept increases.

CHANGING THE STRUCTURE OF ATTITUDES

Attitude change, that is, a change in disposition to act toward an object, has been measured most typically as a change in valence from positive to negative or negative to positive. A further useful distinction is between congruent and incongruent attitude change (Krech, Crutchfield, and Ballachey, 1962). *Incongruent change* occurs in the opposite direction of the original attitude, for example, from disliking a person to liking a person. *Congruent change* occurs in the same direction as the original attitude, for example, from disliking a person to disliking him more intensely. It has been argued that congruent change is always easier to elicit than incongruent change. Thus, Republican party workers do not direct their efforts at converting confirmed Democrats, but confront individuals who are independent or leaning toward the Republican cause. Marketers generally do not seek to convert hard-core users of other brands, but seek to persuade new entrants into the market or individuals with brand-switching characteristics.

Certain predictions about attitude change can be made based on a knowledge of (1) attitude dimensions, (2) interactions among attitude components, and (3) attitude clusters.

ATTITUDE DIMENSIONS AND ATTITUDE CHANGE

It generally has been found that the more intense or extreme the *valence* of an attitude, the more difficult it is to change (Tannenbaum, 1956). A person who loves his Volkswagen cannot readily be converted to loving a Chevrolet.

Attitudes of a low degree of *multiplexity* generally are held to be easier to change. Thus, if an infrequent user of coffee has a negative attitude toward freeze-dried coffee simply because he doesn't think it will taste good, it may be possible to change his attitude by having him taste it or by exposing him to advertisements emphasizing that its taste is as good as, or superior to, other coffee products. But a heavy coffee user with a negative attitude based on a complex of factors cannot be converted as readily. Even if he could be convinced that the taste is acceptable, he might maintain his negative attitude on the basis of such factors as cost, habit, and social acceptability.

ATTITUDE-COMPONENT INTERACTION AND ATTITUDE CHANGE

Rosenberg (1960) has presented a structural theory of attitude change based on three propositions:

1. When the affective and cognitive components of an attitude are mutually consistent, the attitude is in a stable state.
2. When these components are mutually inconsistent, to a degree that exceeds the individual's "tolerance limit" for such inconsistency, the attitude is in an unstable state.
3. In such an unstable state the attitude will undergo reorganizing activity until one of three possible outcomes is achieved. These outcomes are: (a) rejection of the communications, or other forces, that engendered the original inconsistency between affect and cognition and thus rendered the attitude unstable, i.e., restoration of the original stable and consistent attitude; (b) "fragmentation" of the attitude through the isolation from each other of the mutually inconsistent affective and cognitive components; (c) accommodation to the original inconsistency-producing change so that a new attitude, consistent with that change, is now stabilized, i.e., attitude change (p. 322).

This statement of a structural model of attitude change assumes that individuals seek congruence between their beliefs and feelings and that attitudes can be changed by modifying either the belief or feeling component. This is not the only attitude change model to operate on the "balance" principle. Osgood and Tannenbaum (1955), for example, have proposed a "principle of congruity" model of attitude change, and Festinger's theory of "cognitive dissonance" (1957) can also be considered in the category of balance models of attitude change.

Alteration of Beliefs

The belief component has been the usual target of communicators seeking attitude change, and communication of information has been relied upon to bring about changes in beliefs which will lead to attitude change. In evaluating such an approach, it is instructive to consider what *kinds* of beliefs are being changed.

Rokeach (1968) employs his framework of classes of beliefs in order to classify "what society's specialized persuaders are trying to do, and which kinds of beliefs they wish most to act upon, to influence and to change" (p. 182). He suggests that advertisers have concentrated mainly on forming or changing inconsequential beliefs; especially to the extent that there is a high degree of competitive advertising within a product class.

The advertiser also may associate higher-order beliefs with inconsequential beliefs in order to achieve attitude change. Rokeach (1968) states:

> Our findings suggest that inconsequential beliefs are generally easier to change than other kinds of beliefs. This does not mean, however, that the consumer will passively yield to others' efforts to change such beliefs. . . . So the advertising man, while he has a psychological advantage over other persuaders specializing in changing more central beliefs, still has to find economical ways of changing the less consequential beliefs he specializes in. . . . He tries to convince the consumer that there are important benefits to be gained by changing brands, that deeper beliefs and needs will perhaps be better satisfied (pp. 183–184).

Rokeach asserts that advertising often associates inconsequential beliefs with authority beliefs (as in testimonials) or with negative self-concept beliefs (as in mouthwash advertising). He attributes this to the influence of behaviorism and psychoanalysis on advertising, but sees an emerging trend toward greater association between inconsequential beliefs and the expression of positive self-conceptions.

Rokeach's analysis and "applications to advertising" reflect subjective evaluations of advertising's focus on particular types of beliefs; and Rokeach's examples are not based on adequate sampling and content analysis. However, his conceptualization makes implicit sense in many ways and may help in understanding the levels of belief upon which advertising may have an impact.

Alteration of beliefs is the most logical means of attitude change open to the marketer, but (as we saw in Chapter 5) its relative success has not been particularly great—which does not suggest that other means will be more successful. Individuals are almost always more resistant to attitude change than to attitude confirmation.

Alteration of Feelings

Structural theory further suggests that alteration of the feeling component can bring about alteration of the belief component as balance is sought. This has been experimentally demonstrated by Rosenberg (1960) and by Rosenberg and Abelson (1960).

For example, a product message may seek to create a certain *mood* and to have the consumer share that mood. Thus, a message may suggest happiness or excitement, which is generally shown to occur as a function of product usage. If the consumer accepts this mood as desirable, he may purchase the product. A considerable amount of advertising operates at this mood or feeling level, and not at the level of beliefs. Similarly, in political advertising, the message is often directed at the feeling component of attitudes. This is exemplified in attempts to build an image of trust or progressiveness for the nominee or to suggest that the opposing candidate is untrustworthy or reactionary.

The difficulty of this message approach is that a favorable mood induced by the advertising *message* need not transfer to the *product*. Thus, a Chevrolet ad suggesting glamor and excitement may place the consumer in a desirable mood, but as a loyal Ford man he may never move to the next step, the conclusion that buying a Chevrolet will make him feel this way.

In an experiment by Axelrod (1963), attitudes toward consumer products were tested before and after exposure to a government documentary which dealt with Nazi war crimes. Significant changes in mood occurred and were found to relate to shifts in the evaluation of moods as goals. More importantly, mood changes were found to systematically influence beliefs which respondents held about the abilities of products to satisfy mood goals. Thus, an increase in depression was related to the belief that the several products would lead to depression; and a decrease in pleasantness was related to a decrease in the belief that these products would produce a mood of pleasantness.

In the dissemination of persuasive marketing messages, it has been assumed further that mood induced by the program or *context* in which a message appears will influence product attitude. Crane (1964), for example, summarizes available results that men's products are best advertised with westerns and that food products fit well with situation comedies, but do poorly in mystery, western, or adventure contexts. In an experimental test of the effect of context on feeling generated toward the product, Crane exposed male and female subjects to television commercials for five products in three different program settings: westerns, situation comedies, and quiz shows. His overall findings were that males based their feelings about commercials primarily on the *product* itself; in contrast, females' ratings were based mainly on the *program* type. Crane reasons that this finding is due to women viewing more television and, therefore, being more "sensitized" to program differences. It could also be due to differences in cognitive style between men and women.

The implication of his study is that mood created by program may be more important in reaching a female than a male audience.

Alteration of Behavior

If the consumer can be induced to change his behavior, attitude change may follow. Herein lies the greatest contribution of Festinger's cognitive dissonance theory (1957) toward an understanding of attitude dynamics. Except for its postdecisional emphasis, cognitive dissonance is equivalent in principle to other balance-theory statements. The basic assumption is that the individual strives for internal consistency. Given commitment to a decision, as in the purchase of many products, the person experiences dissonance because he has foregone one or more alternatives (with generally desirable features) to obtain another. The severity of this dissonance varies with the importance of the purchase, among other factors. Such feelings of dissonance, or inconsistency, being uncomfortable or tension-arousing, lead the individual to seek an equilibrium state.

Among the dissonance reduction means available are (1) revoking the behavior—for example, selling the product if possible; (2) seeking confirming information—for example, reading ads for the product or gaining social support; (3) avoiding dissonance-inducing information—for example, failing to perceive information or ads about the rejected alternatives; (4) distorting information—for example, repressing or changing information about the rejected alternatives; (5) changing attitude about the importance of the purchase; and (6) changing attitude to make it more favorable toward the chosen alternative.

An example will serve to illustrate the implications of this theory for attitude change. A marketer may be successful in gaining new product trial, perhaps by the distribution of product samples. Some triers of the product will have an initially favorable attitude toward it, and others an initially unfavorable attitude. Use of the product by those possessing a favorable attitude is cognitively consistent and should reinforce the already favorable attitude (assuming that the product is, in fact, good).

Use of the product by those possessing an unfavorable attitude suggests a dissonant relationship. The extent of such dissonance will be a function of the importance of the dissonant cognitive element (dislike for the product) compared to the importance of the consonant cognitive element (the behavior is engaged in because the product is free). The experience of dissonance under these conditions can be reduced by revoking the behavior, by minimizing the importance of the trial behavior, or by changing attitude toward the product. If the product is reevaluated and a positive attitude adopted, the new attitude will be consistent with behavior and consonance will be achieved.

It has been reported in experiments by Festinger and Carlsmith (1959) and by Cohen (see Brehm and Cohen, 1962, pp. 73–78) that the smaller the incentive to produce behavior, the greater the dissonance and the greater the change in attitude. This implies that *if it induces behavior*, a ten-cents-off deal is more likely to result in attitude change than a thirty cents-off deal or free sampling of a convenience item. Large inducements, it is reasoned, may lead to rationalization for engaging in the induced behavior; small inducements force the individual to face his behavioral response without a ready excuse. Dissonance reduction is therefore more likely to occur via attitude change under low-inducement conditions. Of course, change in attitude under these conditions of inducement must be balanced against the proportion of behavioral response that will be obtained.

There are a number of other ways to induce behavior inconsistent with existing attitudes in order to encourage attitude change. Role playing is an example. The typical experiment along these lines has subjects take an alien position and argue it, the usual outcome being attitude change in favor of the advocated position. A number of these experiments is summarized in Klapper (1960). This experimental approach, although quite unlike the marketer's, is somewhat equivalent to role playing in advertising. A consumer in a television commercial, for example, may be shown defending his purchase; to the extent that the situation is believable and that the at-home consumer silently role plays while watching, some conversion may be achieved.

A relevant dimension of induced behavior is the range of choice available to the consumer. Cohen (1964) concludes that conforming subjects given a wide range of choice undergo more attitude change than conforming subjects given a narrow range of choice. In an experiment by LoSciuto and Perloff (1967), it was found that subjects required to choose between two highly desirable alternatives showed greater attitude change than subjects required to choose between two alternatives which were not as close in desirability. Those forced to choose between highly desirable alternatives experienced greater dissonance and reduced this dissonance in the postdecisional situation by evaluating the *chosen* alternative more highly than the rejected alternative.

ATTITUDE CLUSTER AND ATTITUDE CHANGE

Change in a single attitude is related to the dynamics of an entire attitude *cluster*. Balance is again a relevant consideration, and the ease of changing a specific attitude is related to the balance or lack of balance within the cluster. Attitudes within balanced clusters are expected to show resistance to change, whereas attitudes within unbalanced clusters may be susceptible to change.

For example, assume a consumer has a balanced set of attitudes regarding food products. Let us further assume that this consumer has favorable attitudes toward General Foods and its coffee brands (+) and an unfavorable attitude toward new coffee products, which she perceives as inferior substitutes (−). General Foods then introduces Maxim freeze-dried coffee, stressing its superiority $(+)$. Under these conditions, attitudinal imbalance is obvious and change is likely. It can be predicted in line with Osgood and Tannenbaum's "principle of congruity" (1955) that when a favorable source makes a favorable assertion about an unfavorable object, attitude toward the source becomes less favorable and attitude toward the object becomes more favorable. This prediction and a number of others are set forth in Table 10.1 (Zajonc, 1960).

Table 10.1   Change of Attitude Toward the Source and the Object when Positive and Negative Assertions Are Made by the Source

Original Attitude Toward the Source	Positive Assertion About an Object Toward Which the Attitude Is		Negative Assertion About an Object Toward Which the Attitude Is	
	Positive	Negative	Positive	Negative
Change of attitude toward the source				
Positive	+	− −	− −	+ +
Negative	+ +	−	−	+
Change of attitude toward the object				
Positive	+	+ +	− −	−
Negative	− −	−	+	+ +

Source: Zajonc (1960, p. 288).

The same balancing principle would be operative for Festinger's cognitive dissonance theory (1957) and for Newcomb's "strain toward symmetry" (1953) in communication. The important conceptual difference in cognitive dissonance theory is that it is postdecisional; the individual has a level of commitment to a certain behavior. The important conceptual difference in Newcomb's symmetry theory is that it is interpersonal and involves attitude change as a result of communication. Newcomb proposes that symmetry in attitudes of two people (A and B) will occur toward an item (x) to which they are mutually oriented and about which they are engaging in communication.

Individuals suscepted to *cross-pressures* represent an interesting case of imbalance in attitude clusters. For example, Lazarsfeld, Berelson, and Gaudet (1948) found in their study of voting behavior that persons under cross-pressure were particularly likely to change their voting intentions. Such cross-pressures could result from disharmony within the family or disharmony in the person's own attitudes toward campaign issues. If attitude change does occur, it may well be unstable since the same cross-pressures are likely to exist pulling the individual back to his original position.

Crane (1965) suggests that attitude change may be gained by changing the *category* in which the consumer places the product. For example, dietetic fruits and vegetables have been demonstrated to sell better in the fruit-and-vegetable aisle (category) of a supermarket than in a special dietetic section. Metrecal achieved far greater success in supermarkets than in drug stores.

Manufacturers face categorizing decisions with many new products, especially those which perform new functions or cross existing categories. In introducing Tang, for example, General Foods had to decide whether it was a breakfast drink and juice substitute or a refreshment and carbonated beverage substitute. Ford Motor Company had to decide whether to fit Mustang into the sports car category, the compact car category, or to create a new specialty car category. Other manufacturers, especially the makers of the Camaro and the Javelin, attempted to associate their cars with Ford's choice of a category by advertising directly against Mustang and mentioning it by name.

It is an interesting question whether a "frontal attack" on existing attitudes, such as an automobile manufacturer mentioning his competition by name, or a "side attack," whereby a new attitude is built, is more effective. In his review of the communication literature, Klapper (1960), finds most evidence favoring a side-attack strategy. He notes that the side attack involves the creation of a new attitude, and that mass media are considerably more effective at this than changing an existing attitude (p. 90). Frontal attack may well invoke the selective processes to resist change, whereas side attack may render the selective processes inoperative. In particular, Klapper notes that "Mass communication is highly effective in creating attitudes on newly risen or newly provoked issues" (p. 53). Klapper's conclusion that side attacks may be more effective cannot be accepted at face value in regard to product advertising, however, because none of the research which he refers to was conducted with products and brands.

A FUNCTIONAL APPROACH TO ATTITUDE CHANGE

If we know why the individual holds the attitudes he does, we may be in a better position to change them. The functional approach to attitude change suggests that the conditions for change vary by the type of attitude. This is illustrated in synopsis form in Table 10.2.

CHANGING UTILITARIAN ATTITUDES

An attitude formed in the service of the utilitarian or adjustment function can be changed if (1) it no longer leads to satisfaction; (2) the acceptance of another attitude can be shown to be more conducive to need satisfaction; or (3) the individual's aspiration level has changed.

The consumer may be aware that his present brand is not offering him complete satisfaction and, as a result, may be susceptible to attitude change

Table 10.2   Determinants of Attitude Formation, Arousal, and Change in Relation to Type of Function

Function	Origin and Dynamics	Arousal Conditions	Change Conditions
Adjustment	Utility of attitudinal object in need satisfaction. Maximizing external rewards and minimizing punishments	1. Activation of needs 2. Salience of cues associated with need satisfaction	1. Need deprivation 2. Creation of new needs and new levels of aspiration 3. Shifting rewards and punishments 4. Emphasis on new and better paths for need satisfaction
Ego defense	Protecting against internal conflicts and external dangers	1. Posing of threats 2. Appeals to hatred and repressed impulses 3. Rise in frustrations 4. Use of authoritarian suggestion	1. Removal of threats 2. Catharsis 3. Development of self-insight
Value expression	Maintaining self identity; enhancing favorable self-image; self-expression and self-determination	1. Salience of cues associated with values 2. Appeals to individual to reassert self-image 3. Ambiguities which threaten self-concept	1. Some degree of dissatisfaction with self 2. Greater appropriateness of new attitude for the self 3. Control of all environmental supports to undermine old values
Knowledge	Need for understanding, for meaningful cognitive organization, for consistency and clarity	1. Reinstatement of cues associated with old problem or of old problem itself	1. Ambiguity created by new information or change in environment 2. More meaningful information about problems

Source: Daniel Katz (1960, p. 192).

in favor of an alternative brand. New brands may possess product advantages which can be shown to be more conducive to need satisfaction. Marketing communications can seek to present a new brand as a superior substitute for existing brands. At times, consumers may actively seek different brands and may be susceptible to attitude change—as when the family head has just secured a promotion and the family's life style is improving.

Much advertising seeks to convince the individual that (1) his needs are not being adequately met by current usage patterns; (2) another product can better fulfill his needs; (3) certain products should be part of his life style; and (4) to heighten or activate certain needs, perhaps not considered until that point.

Attitudes serving the utilitarian function are susceptible to change by the marketer. The easiest form of such change is to offer one product as a superior substitute for another, whereas the most difficult form of such change is to activate dormant needs, or (as many would argue) to "create" needs. The marketer's abilities to create needs are sorely limited, and although the long-run effect of industry advertising may be to make necessities out of what were once luxury products, the individual firm's short-run ability to do this is highly unimpressive. It is always easier to appeal to existing needs than to attempt to activate unspecified or latent needs.

The adoption process for a new product or a product "new" to a particular consumer implies attitude change and may begin with problem perception by the consumer or with his awareness of a need satisfaction alternative as a result of marketer promotional efforts. Thus, the consumer may conclude that his current product preferences are not leading to need fulfillment; and he may be conducive to product alternatives and attitude change, or he may be persuaded to consider another product which the marketer argues will be more conducive to his need fulfillment.

CHANGING EGO-DEFENSIVE ATTITUDES

Attitudes serving the ego-defensive function are not readily changed and are more a task for the clinical psychologist than for the advertising campaign or the sales agent. The difficulty of changing such attitudes is illustrated in an experiment by Cooper and Jahoda (1947) which sought to obtain attitude change by cartoons ridiculing prejudice. One cartoon, for example, ridiculed a "Mr. Biggott" who rejected a blood transfusion from someone who was not 100-percent "American." Instead of changing their attitudes, prejudiced subjects avoided or distorted the meaning implied in the cartoon. Rather than trying to change ego-defensive attitudes, marketers should avoid communications which elicit such attitudes.

CHANGING VALUE-EXPRESSIVE ATTITUDES

Consumption of products and brands is an important aspect of everyday self-presentation. A matching process between what the product represents (whether prestige, conformity, dignity, practicality, or whatever) and what the individual represents or wants to represent is an important explanatory factor of consumer actions. Attitudes held about products can be tied directly to the expression of value-oriented needs. The consumer can favor Ford station wagons as a means of representing the kind of person he is. And one product can serve different value-expressive needs for different people. For example, the Ford station wagon may represent the "family" way of life, the "sporting" way of life, safety, conservatism, or other values.

Change in value-expressive attitudes comes about mainly when an individual is somewhat dissatisfied with his self-concept and strives to portray a more desirable self-concept. Some value-expressive attitudes may be changed by offering a product which better fulfills the person's self-concept. Virginia Slims cigarettes may have offered some women the opportunity to express their femininity in a product category where it previously could not be expressed directly, although this is probably doubtful.

CHANGING KNOWLEDGE FUNCTION ATTITUDES

Attitudes serving the knowledge function may change as the individual finds these attitudes unable to provide a meaningful structure to what he perceives. This failure may result from environmental change or from new information inputs which show the individual that his existing state of knowledge is incomplete or misleading. Deliberate altering of knowledge function attitudes seems to be feasible through the provision of new information. However, the communicator will have to cope with the individual's selective tendency to avoid conflicting information, especially if the person is a simplifier rather than a clarifier.

A simplifier, as conceptualized by Kelman and Cohler (1959), tends to react defensively to ambiguity by avoiding new information, misperceiving it, or challenging its implications. The simplifier achieves cognitive clarity, therefore, by simplifying the environment and avoiding incongruous information. The *clarifier*, in contrast, tends to admit new information and to reduce ambiguity via understanding.

SALIENCE AS A CONSIDERATION IN ATTITUDE CHANGE

Krech, Crutchfield, and Ballachey (1962) suggest that the more central an attitude is in reflecting the individual's values, the more difficult it is to change. This is in line with Rokeach's categorization (1968) of beliefs along a central-peripheral dimension, with the more central beliefs as more resistant to change and a successful change of a central belief having more significant repercussions in the rest of the belief system.

Krugman (1965) found that under low-involvement conditions, behavioral change may occur without *noticeable* intervening attitude change. He suggests, for example, that if we are repeatedly exposed to information on television about a product or brand:

> . . . we will permit significant alterations in the *structure* of our perception of a brand or product, but in ways which may fall short of persuasion

or of attitude change. One way we may do this is by shifting the relative salience of attributes suggested to us by advertising as we organize our perception of brands and products (p. 353).

It seems that less salient attitudes would show greater susceptibility to change than more salient attitudes; and changes in those less salient attitudes might prove more difficult to measure, since the individual might not be aware of them.

An interesting question investigated recently is whether distraction while attending to a message may not actually lead to greater attitude change because either the individual's involvement with the event or the salience of it has decreased. Research findings on the effects of such distraction are somewhat conflicting. They seem to indicate, however, that when the individual's degree of commitment to the message content is high, distraction enhances the persuasive impact of the communication, because the individual's defenses are less active. However, when commitment is relatively low, as in attitudes toward most products and brands, behavioral or visual distraction detracts from the perceptual and cognitive impact of the communication. Venkatesan and Haaland (1968), after researching this issue in relation to television advertising, conclude:

> The implication here is that the concomitant activities of the viewer during the transmission of the message may drastically interfere with the perceptual and cognitive impact of a television commercial. This would imply a strategy of television advertising whereby the initial attraction power of the commercial should hold the viewer's attention and prevent his engaging in any behavioral distraction (p. 66).

The salience of an attitude and therefore its susceptibility to change is also a function of the situation. Rokeach (1966) has distinguished between attitudes toward objects and attitudes toward situations. To say that an individual has an attitude toward a particular object does not mean that the attitude will be activated across all situations. Thus, a generally favorable attitude toward American wines does not indicate that the individual will serve these products at a formal dinner as well as at an informal family supper.

A Los Angeles bottler of a product similar to Seven-Up notes that many consumers favor his product on weekdays, but change to Seven-Up for weekend social affairs. Under such conditions, a firm may be able to broaden the number of situations where a favorable product attitude is likely to be salient. Advertising could, for example, stress the social acceptability of the product for weekend functions.

Finally, as already implied, attitude change can be achieved most productively by focusing on salient product *attributes*. It might, for example, be possible to increase the saliency of the individual attributes on which a brand is favorably evaluated and to decrease the saliency of the attributes on which the brand is weak. Volkswagen has very successfully achieved favorable attitudes among a sizable segment of the population by emphasizing the attributes of cost and economy and deemphasizing the attributes of safety and speed.

SUMMARY

A number of attitudinal theories exist with overlapping implications as to the achievement of attitude change. In the *structural approach*, attitudes are considered in terms of their cognitive, feeling, and action-tendency components. Each of these components is described in terms of valence and degree of multiplexity. This approach maintains that elements of attitude components making up one particular attitude tend to fit, or be consonant with one another, and that attitudes within a particular cluster also tend toward consonance. In the structural approach to attitude change, certain predictions about attitude change can be made on the basis of a posited drive toward consistency among attitude components and within attitude clusters.

The basic assumption of the *functional approach* is that attitudes must be understood in terms of the needs which they serve for the individual. According to Daniel Katz, a leading proponent of the functional approach, there are essentially four functions which attitudes perform: (1) the adjustment, or utilitarian, function; (2) the ego-defensive function; (3) the value-expressive function; and (4) the knowledge function. Change strategies must be designed in line with these functions, and presuppose some knowledge of consumers' needs and motivations.

The *salience approach* posits that, although the individual holds attitudes on a host of topics, not all of them have general salience for him. The more central an attitude is in reflecting the individual's values, the more difficult it is to change. Similarly, product attributes vary in salience for the consumer, and change strategies must focus on the most salient attributes. Thus, some knowledge of how consumers perceive products and brands is necessary in order to focus on attributes of a high degree of salience.

Each of these approaches accounts for some differences in response among consumers. They should be viewed as complementary rather than competing theories. In attempts to market new products, it may be useful to draw to some extent from each approach in order to attract and hold favorable consumer attitudes.

CHAPTER 11

MODELS OF NEW PRODUCT ACCEPTANCE*

INTRODUCTION

A new product is introduced by a company, presumably when a favorable estimate has been made of its future sales and profits. The estimate of a new

* This material was prepared originally by Professor Philip Kotler for his book *Marketing Decision Making: A Model Building Approach* (New York: Holt, Rinehart and Winston, Inc., 1971), and is presented here with modifications with his permission.

product's sales is shaped by many factors, including the size of the potential market, the nature of competition, and the company's marketing plans and resources. As diffusion occurs, the company receives sales data and other types of feedback, leading it to update its sales estimates and possibly to revise its marketing strategy. If sales are disappointing, management may have to consider discontinuing the product.

A number of new product decision models have been developed recently, varying in the number and types of variables considered, the level of aggregation, and the method of solution. All of these models attempt to explain and/or predict the level of sales of a new product over time as a result of behavioral and decision variables characterizing their introduction.

This chapter is divided into two sections. Section 1 examines *first purchase models*, that is, models designed to predict the cumulative number of new product triers over time. These models serve the purpose of forecasting sales for durable goods and novelty items. Section 2 examines *repeat purchase models*, that is, models designed to predict the repeat purchase rates of buyers who have tried the product. Predicting the sales of a repurchasable new product requires joining together an appropriate first purchase model with a repeat purchase model.

A periodic estimate of the new product's future sales is crucial to management planning. The appropriate sales forecasting model, however, varies greatly with the type of new product situation. New product situations can be distinguished according to the degree of *newness* of the product and the degree of product *repurchasability*. Both of these characteristics have implications for the design of the forecasting model.

PRODUCT NEWNESS

The distinction has been made in Chapter 1 that innovations will vary in their effects on established consumption patterns. New products can be characterized, therefore, by degree of "newness," or we can think in terms of a continuum from highly continuous to highly discontinuous innovations. Examples given of continuous innovations were fluoride toothpaste and annual new-model cars; examples given of discontinuous innovations were the computer and the jet aircraft. Marketing considerations for a discontinuous innovation, of course, are different than for a continuous innovation. The company may have to make a substantial investment in consumer learning and in establishing the need for the innovation in order to overcome consumer resistances that might stem from the product's complexity, possible incompatibility with certain cultural or social values, and possible riskiness.

Another categorization scheme for establishing degree of newness is that of *product* versus *brand* versus new *model or size*. The introduction of a new *brand* often represents a new entry into an established product class. Consumers may recognize the brand as part of the established product class, so that the company is not faced with the same investment in consumer learning as for a new *product* introduction. The company's task is to persuade buyers of the superiority of its brand in satisfying their already defined needs. The company must regularly collect information on brand shares and brand switching in order to evaluate its rate of brand acceptance. In the case of a new *model or size* introduction, the item already has established distribution channels and an established image in the minds of buyers. The company's task is to make consumers aware of the item's new attributes. The required introductory marketing effort is small compared to the other two new product situations. Sales forecasting can proceed to a large extent on methods currently in use for the established item.

PRODUCT REPURCHASABILITY

In addition to distinguishing degrees of product newness, it is also helpful to distinguish between products that are likely to be purchased by a consumer only once, occasionally, or frequently. Products that are likely to be purchased only once include extremely expensive goods, one-of-a-kind goods, and certain novelties. In a population of a given size, after all of the potential buyers have purchased the product, there will be no more sales. The sales that can be expected over time for a nonrepurchasable new product are illustrated in Figure 11.1(*a*). Sales rise in each time period initially and later fall until no potential buyers are left. The curve is one version of the familiar product life cycle curve discussed in Chapter 2. If the curve is recast in terms of cumulative sales of the product over time, it would resemble the curve in Figure 11.1(*b*). In this form, the curve can be said to illustrate the rate of market penetration, and it is shown approaching a limiting value representing total possible sales, that is, market potential. If the number of potential buyers is not fixed, then the curves would have to be modified. Thus the market for wedding rings (which in the majority of cases is a one-time purchase) is never really exhausted because people keep getting married.

Products that are purchased occasionally are exemplified by many durable goods such as automobiles, refrigerators, industrial equipment, and certain clothing items. These goods exhibit replacement cycles, dictated either by the physical wearing-out of the product or its psychological obsolescence associated with changing styles and tastes. Most sales forecasting for this category of products consists of separately estimating new sales to first-time buyers and replacement sales. We shall examine methods of forecasting new sales shortly. As for replacement sales, they are estimated from data on the age distribution of existing goods and on product mortality. If the product wears out gradually and the buyer has some discretion as to the replacement date, he will be influenced by the general state of the economy as well as the

Figure 11.1   Sales Life Cycle for a Non-Repurchasable New Product in a Fixed Size Market: (a) noncumulative sales volume, (b) cumulative sales volume

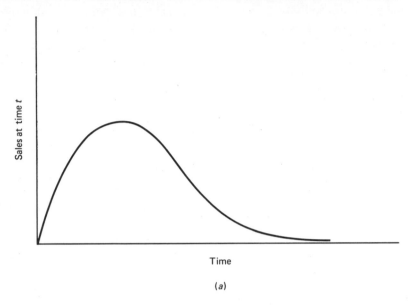

(a)

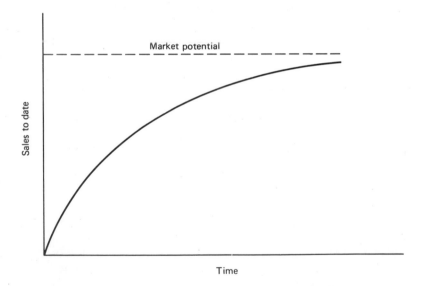

(b)

Figure 11.2   Sales Life Cycle for Infrequently Purchased Products

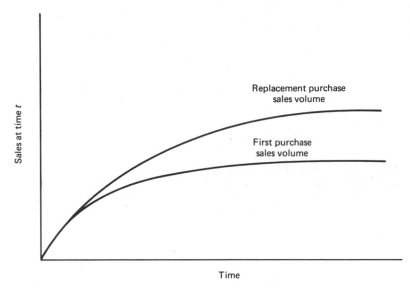

Sales at time t

Replacement purchase
sales volume

First purchase
sales volume

Time

amount of product improvement that has taken place since his last purchase. Figure 11.2 illustrates the sales life cycle of an infrequently purchased product and is composed of new sales and replacement sales.

New products that are likely to be repurchased frequently, such as consumer and industrial nondurables, have a somewhat different-looking sales life cycle as shown in Figure 11.3. The number of persons buying the product for the first time increases initially and then decreases as there are fewer left (assuming a fixed population). Superimposed on the first purchase sales volume is another amount representing repeat purchase sales volume, presuming that the product satisfies some fraction of people and that they become steady customers. The sales curve falls to a plateau representing a level of steady repeat purchase volume, and, by this time, the product may no longer be in the class of new products.

Because all new products, whether they are purchased once, occasionally, or frequently, have in common a first purchase sales volume curve, the discussion will first examine models of first purchase sales volume. The second part of this chapter will then examine repeat purchasing. Models of replacement sales volume will not be specifically considered.

FIRST PURCHASE MODELS

In discussing first purchase models, it will be helpful to think in terms of a relatively discontinuous innovation, although the general principles apply approximately to continuous innovations as well. We shall assume that a firm is preparing to introduce for the first time a new consumer durable (such

Figure 11.3   Sales Life Cycle for Repurchasable New Product

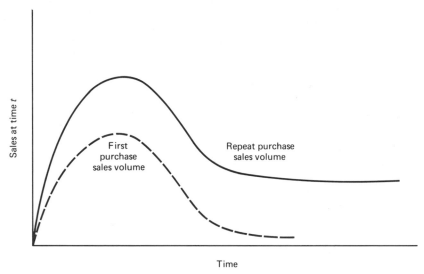

as a television cassette system or an electric dental hygiene product). The firm would like to make an estimate of (1) the market potential, (2) the shape of the likely approach to this potential, and (3) the rate of approach to this potential. Management can resort to one of two analytical frameworks to apply to these questions. It can think about new product sales in terms of the *diffusion process* or in terms of the *adoption process.*

The *diffusion process*, as previously defined, refers to the spread of a new product from its manufacturer to ultimate users or adopters. To model a diffusion process, the analyst works with a few macroparameters that will locate a curve to describe the spread of the innovation over time. These parameters might include the size of the population and its propensity to innovate and imitate. Diffusion process models in the social sciences are often modeled after physical or biological diffusion processes, such as heat transfer and the spread of epidemics.

The *adoption process*, on the other hand, refers to the mental sequence of stages through which a consumer progresses from first awareness of an innovation to final acceptance. Adoption is equivalent to product purchase in the case of nonrepurchasable products. For repurchasable products, adoption represents commitment and continued use of the product over time. Adoption models require a more detailed behavioral rendering of the individual's process of moving toward the trial and use of the new product.

DIFFUSION MODELS

The task of a diffusion model is to produce a definite sales life cycle curve, usually based on a parsimonious set of parameters. The parameters may or may not have definite behavioral content. The presupposition is that they can be estimated either by analogy to the histories of similar new products introduced in the past based on consumer pretests or on analysis of early sales returns as the new product enters the market. In this section four different diffusion models are examined which have been developed by those who have worked on the first purchase forecasting problem. They are the concave models, S-curve models, epidemiological models, and reliability engineering models.

Concave Diffusion Models

One of the earliest market penetration models is the exponential one proposed by Fourt and Woodlock (1960) and tested against several new products. Their retrospective observation of many market penetration curves showed that (1) the cumulative curve approached a limiting penetration level of less than 100 percent of all households, frequently far less, and (2) the successive increments of gain declined. They found that an adequate approximation to these observations was provided by a curve for which "the increments in penetration for equal time periods are proportional to the remaining distance to the limiting 'ceiling' penetration" (p. 32). The increment in penetration for any period is given by

$$Q_t = r\overline{Q}(1 - r)^{t-1} \tag{11.1}$$

where Q_t = increment in cumulative sales (that is, sales at time t) as a fraction of potential sales

   r = rate of penetration of untapped potential (a constant)
   $\overline{Q}$ = potential sales as a fraction of the all buyers
   t = time period

The formula is completely specified by the two parameters, r and $\overline{Q}$. To illustrate how it works, assume that a new product is about to be introduced where it is estimated that 40 percent of all households will eventually try the new product ($\overline{Q} = .4$). Furthermore it is believed that in each period 30 percent of the remaining new buyer potential is penetrated ($r = .3$). Therefore, the increment in new buyer penetration of this market in the first period is

$$Q_1 = r\overline{Q}(1 - r)^{1-1} = r\overline{Q} = .3(.4) = .12 \tag{11.2}$$

The increment in new buyer penetration of this market in the second period is

$$Q_2 = r\overline{Q}(1 - r)^{2-1} = r\overline{Q}(1 - r) = r(\overline{Q} - r\overline{Q}) = .3[.4 - .3(.4)] = .084 \tag{11.3}$$

Note that $r(\overline{Q} - r\overline{Q})$ in (11.3) exactly expresses the essence of this process, that is, the increment in penetration will be the rate of penetration, r, times the untapped potential, which is $\overline{Q} - r\overline{Q}$. The increments in new buyer penetration in the third and fourth periods are

$$Q_3 = r\overline{Q}(1-r)^{3-1} = r\overline{Q}(1-r)^2 = (.3)(.4)(.7^2) = .059 \qquad (11.4)$$

$$Q_4 = r\overline{Q}(1-r)^{4-1} = r\overline{Q}(1-r)^3 = (.3)(.4)(.7^3) = .041 \qquad (11.5)$$

The reader should check that as $t \to \infty$, $dQ/dt \to 0$. This equation (11.1) produces a declining curve of new buyer sales through time. The cumulative sales curve rises monotonically in a concave fashion as illustrated in Figure 11.4(a).

The analyst who wishes to use equation (11.1) in forecasting market penetration for a new product first estimates $\overline{Q}$, the total potential sales volume. Here he may rely on market research studies of the percentage of persons who have expressed a strong desire to buy the new product. The analyst then makes an estimate of r, the penetration rate, on the basis of how fast potential buyers are likely to learn about the product and to seek to purchase it. Once the product has been introduced, and two periods have passed, the analyst can update his estimate of r by finding the ratio of the second period's new buyer increment to the difference between the ceiling level and the first period new buyer increment. In our example, this would be $.084/(.40 - .12) = .3$. Another estimate of r can be made when the third period's results come in. In general, the analyst would probably want to average the past estimates of r as the data come in to determine a current r to use in equation (11.1).

The usefulness of the latest estimated r for predicting next period's sales depends on the continuation of the marketing program and environment that characterized the former periods. Fourt and Woodlock (1960) list five assumptions underlying their forecasting model:

1. Distribution will not shift greatly from the level existing at the end of the first period.
2. Promotional expenditures will not be substantially different in the second period from those during the latter part of the first period.
3. Prices will not change markedly.
4. Neither the product nor the package will be changed.
5. Competitive activity will not differ strikingly (p. 34).

If any of these conditions change, the analyst should reestimate r and possibly $\overline{Q}$ in the expected direction.

The fixity of the assumptions leads to a justified criticism that can be made about Fourt and Woodlock's formula (11.1). Diffusion is seen as a function of time only and the marketing program of the company does not enter explicitly as a variable. It would seem that in its present form (11.1) is there-

Figure 11.4   Increment in New Buyer Penetration: (a) simple model, (b) advanced model

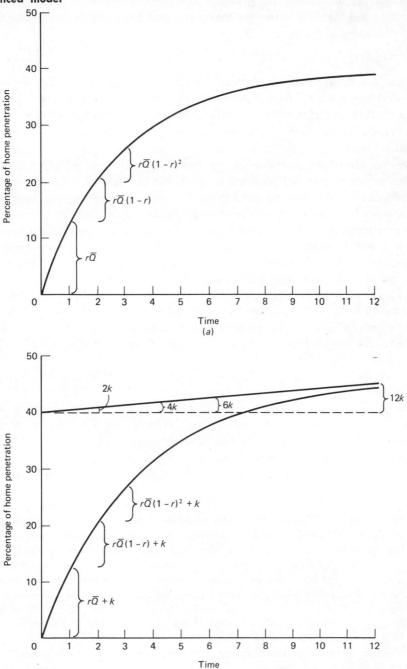

Source: Reprinted from Fourt and Woodlock in the *Journal of Marketing* (1960, pp. 33–34).

fore of little or no help in assisting the company in finding the best marketing strategy for introducing the product. Actually a silght modification of the formula will highlight where the marketing decision variable enters into the determination of sales:

$$Q_t = r(X)\overline{Q}(X)(1 - r(X))^{t-1} \qquad\qquad (11.6)$$

where X is the planned introductory marketing expenditure level for the new product. Equation (11.6) shows that the planned level of marketing expenditures can be expected to influence the level of both r, the penetration rate, and $\overline{Q}$, the potential sales level. For example, if the company adopts a "penetration" marketing strategy, consisting of a low price and substantial expenditures on advertising and distribution, it can be expected to achieve a higher ultimate size market and penetrate it at a faster rate than if it introduces the product at a high price and backs it up with modest advertising and distribution expenditures, that is, a "sales-staging" strategy. The challenge to management is to estimate the functional relationship between a specific marketing plan X and the levels of r and $\overline{Q}$. Once a functional relationship is estimated, management can use (11.6) in conjunction with an appropriate cost equation to determine the marketing plan that would maximize its long-run profits.

Fourt and Woodlock (1960) added one modification to their model which improved its fit to actual data. They found a tendency for the decline in increments of penetration to stretch out and approach a small positive constant, k, rather than zero. This stretch-out effect calls for revising (11.1) to read

$$Q_t = r\overline{Q}(1 - r)^{t-1} + k \qquad\qquad (11.7)$$

and the revised model is illustrated in Figure 11.4(b). They report a rule for estimating k that works out well empirically: let k be one half the increment of new buyers during the fourth average purchase cycle. They report that k is typically a small number, in the order of .002. More interesting is the reason Fourt and Woodlock supply for the observed stretch-out effect:

> . . . consider the fact that different buyers purchase a product class and its individual brands at widely differing rates. Experience shows that, when buyers are grouped by purchase rates into equal thirds, typically the heavy buying third accounts for 65 percent of the total volume, the middle third for 25 percent, and the light third for only 10 percent. This means that, if transaction sizes are equal, heavy buyers make 6.5 purchases for every one of a light buyer, while medium buyers make 2.5, the total averaging 3.3. If the original x, r model is applied to each of these thirds separately, this difference in purchase frequency will be sufficient to induce a remarkable "stretch-out" effect in the decline of increments of penetration for all buyers combined (p. 33).

S-Curve Diffusion Models

The previous concave model of the diffusion process assumes that market penetration is greatest in the first period and declines in every subsequent period. This may be true of new products, such as many grocery products, which have an immediate appeal to the market and are backed by a massive program of promotion and distribution from the very beginning. The cumulative diffusion curve tends to be exponential. In contrast, many products exhibit a diffusion process characterized as S-shaped, or logistic. This is the classic life cycle model of slowly rising sales during *introduction*, followed by a rapid sales *growth* stage, then a leveling-off in sales during *maturity*, and ultimately, a sales *decline* stage as the product is replaced by other new products. The exponential and logistic diffusion patterns are contrasted in Figure 2.2 of Chapter 2.

The logistic curve is given by the following equation:

$$Q_T = \overline{Q}[1 + e^{-(a + bt)}]^{-1} \tag{11.8}$$

where Q_T = the cumulative percentage of adoption by time T
$\quad t$ = time
$\quad \overline{Q}$ = the ceiling or equilibrium level
$\quad a$ = a constant which positions the curve on the time scale
$\quad b$ = rate of growth coefficient

The logistic describes a curve which is asymptotic to zero and $\overline{Q}$ and symmetrical around the inflection point. The rate of growth is proportional to the growth already achieved and to the distance from the ceiling. It is easy to show by algebraic manipulation of (11.8) that

$$ln \; \frac{Q_T}{\overline{Q} - Q_T} = a + bt \tag{11.9}$$

that is, the log of the proportion that has adopted to the proportion that has yet to adopt is a linear function of time. This enables the parameters a and b to be estimated directly by least squares.

Management's task is to estimate $\overline{Q}$, a, and b on the basis of preliminary new product tests and the inferred relationship of any contemplated marketing plan X to Q, a, and b. Presumably more forceful marketing introductions will increase both Q and b. If the new product is tried out with distinct marketing programs in different test markets, it may be possible to derive plausible estimates of the parameters of (11.8) to determine the best plan for the national introduction of the product.

Epidemiological Diffusion Models

A number of investigators have proposed that models of epidemics (sometimes called contagion models) provide a useful analogy to the new product diffusion process. They argue that the passage of a message or idea or product from a knower (company or adopter) to a nonknower (potential adopter) is like passage of a germ from an infective to a susceptible. Admittedly, catching a contagious disease does not involve the human elements of cognition and volition which figure prominently in behavioral models of the adoption process. Modifications of the model may be possible to take these higher-order processes into account. Indeed, quite complicated epidemiological models have been built. Bailey (1957) has classified all of the models into three groups:

1. *Continuous infection models.* Epidemic has a beginning and an end and infection is occurring at all times between.
2. *Chain binomial models.* Infection is limited to a short span of time and during noninfectious periods germs are either latent or incubating.
3. *Recurrent epidemic models.* The infection reaches epidemic proportions at intervals, between which it is always present in less than epidemic proportions (measles).

The last two types could conceivably describe some new product situations, although the most common situation is described by the continuous infection model.

The classic diffusion model of a continuous infection process, cast in terms of the new buyer problem, is given by

$$Q_t = rQ_T(\overline{Q} - Q_T) + p(\overline{Q} - Q_T) \tag{11.10}$$

where Q_t = the number of new adopters in the current period
$\quad\quad Q_T$ = the cumulative number of adopters to date
$\quad\quad r$ = the effect of each adopter on each nonadopter
$\quad\quad \overline{Q}$ = the total number of potential adopters
$\quad\quad p$ = the individual conversion rate in the absence of the adopters' influence

According to (11.10), the time rate of change in the number of adopters is a function of two terms. The first term says that the increment of adopters is a constant proportion, r, of the product of the current number of adopters and nonadopters. The term suggests that diffusion (or infection) is due to the influence (or exposure) of adopters on the nonadopters and implies that each adopter is in contact with all nonadopters (James S. Coleman, 1964).

The second term suggests that nonadopters will be converted into adopters at a constant rate, p, independently of the number of adopters. This could happen by assuming a constant source of influence (for example, advertising) on the nonadopters.

When equation (11.10) is integrated, it leads to an **S**-shaped diffusion process such as discussed earlier. Management's task is to estimate $\overline{Q}$, r, and p in order that the equation is fully specified. Management will be interested especially in the relationship between alternative marketing plans and these parameters. The number of potential adopters, $\overline{Q}$, will be influenced by the product's price and the effectiveness of the promotion in establishing multiple uses for the product. The rate of influence of adopters on nonadopters, r, will be influenced by the product's capacity to stimulate favorable personal influence. The rate of influence of marketer-controlled communications on nonadopters will be influenced by the size and effectiveness of the promotional budget.

Some of the limitations of this epidemiological model should be pointed out. Equation (11.10) does not say anything about the dispersion of differences among people in their readiness to be adopters of this new innovation. It merely assumes there is an average rate of response of potential adopters to various forms of communication. In fact we might argue that p (and possibly r) should decline through time, rather than stay constant, because the remaining potential adopters are less responsive to the product and associated communications.

Equation (11.10) also implies that there is full contact between all members of the social system. In reality, a social system is a complicated network of groups and subgroups based on demographic, geographic, religious, and social affinities and barriers. The probability of any two people coming into contact varies greatly with the characteristics of the two people.

Furthermore, the equation is deterministic, whereas the diffusion process in real life is highly stochastic. The number of people who see a particular advertisement at a point in time or who have a chance conversation about a product is influenced by a great number of random factors. Yet this chance-determined number will greatly influence the rate of subsequent diffusion. If the number of people who talk about the product this week is on the high side, this will increase the number of people who can talk about it next week. Thus the particular cumulative adoption curve that is observed in the real history of the product is like a randomly drawn curve from a population of possible curves that might have been drawn. Yet the deterministic epidemic equation does not suggest this stochastic quality.

A modification of the classic epidemiological model has been developed by Bass (1969) and tested against real data on several new product introductions. Equation (11.10) can be rewritten as

$$Q_t = (p + rQ_T)(\overline{Q} - Q_T) \tag{11.11}$$

This equation says that the time rate of change in the number of adopters is some function $(p + rQ_T)$ of the remaining number of nonadopters. (If

$r = 0$, then [11.11] would be virtually equivalent to the Fourt and Woodlock model.) Bass[1] suggested that the function be modified to read:

$$Q_t = (p + r\frac{Q_T}{\overline{Q}})(\overline{Q} - Q_T) \tag{11.12}$$

According to Bass, p is the coefficient of innovation and r is the coefficient of imitation. In each period, there will be both innovators and imitators buying the product. The innovators are not influenced in their timing of purchase by the number of persons who have already bought, but they may be influenced by the steady flow of marketer-controlled communications. As the process continues, the relative number of innovators will diminish monotonically with time. Imitators, on the other hand, are influenced by the number of previous buyers and grow in relation to the number of innovators as the process continues.

The combined rate of first purchasing of innovators and imitators is given by the first term $(p + \frac{rQ_T}{\overline{Q}})$, and increases through time because Q_T increases through time. In fact, the rate of first purchasing is shown as a linear function of the cumulative number of previous first purchases. But the number of remaining nonadopters, given by $(\overline{Q} - Q_T)$ decreases through time. The shape of the resulting sales curve of new adopters will depend upon the relative rates of these two opposite tendencies. In the case of a successful new product, the coefficient of imitation is likely to exceed the coefficient of innovation, that is, $r > p$, and the sales curve will start at zero, grow to a peak, and then decay. On the other hand, if $r < p$, the sales curve will fall continuously. Figure 11.5 illustrates both cases.

Bass applied his model to the sales time series of eleven major appliance innovations, including room airconditioners, electric refrigerators, home freezers, black-and-white television, and power lawn mowers. In each case, he used annual sales data from the year of the new product's introduction until the year when repeat sales began to be important. The fitting was accomplished through least squares regression after rewriting equation (11.12) as follows:

$$Q_t = p\overline{Q} + (r - p)Q_T - \frac{r}{Q}Q_T^2 \tag{11.14}$$

[1] In Bass's notation (1969, p. 217), the equation is

$$S(T) = \left[p + \frac{q}{m}\int_0^T S(t)\,dt \right]\left[m - \int_0^T S(t)\,dt \right] \tag{11.13}$$

This is equivalent to equation 11.11 given the following definitional identities:

$$Q_t = S(T), p = p, r = q, Q_T = \int_0^T S(t)\,dt, \text{ and } \overline{Q} = m.$$

Figure 11.5   New Buyer Sales Curve—Bass Model: (a) r > p, (b) r ≤ p

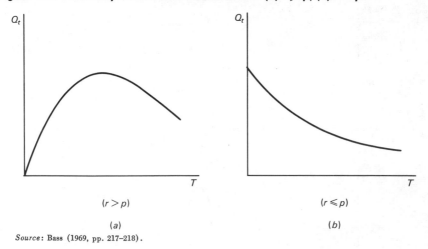

(a)   (b)

Source: Bass (1969, pp. 217–218).

Equation (11.14) is simply a second-degree equation in Q_T, the cumulative sales to time t. It has the form:

$$Q_t = a + bQ_T + cQ_T^2 \qquad\qquad (11.15)$$

letting $a = p\bar{Q}$, $b = (r - p)$, and $c = -\dfrac{r}{\bar{Q}}$. The data consists of time series data on Q_t and Q_T. Equation (11.15) can be estimated as soon as data is available for the first three years of the product's sales, since the parameters, a, b, and c, have to be estimated. After their estimation, it is simple to work back to p, r, and $\bar{Q}$ in equation (11.14). The equation can be reestimated each year as new sales data become available.

The results are illustrated for one of the new products, room airconditioners, in Figure 11.6. The predicted sales match the pattern of actual sales quite well, with a measured coefficient of determination, $R^2 = .92$. This is quite extraordinary when it is remembered that the predicted sales curve is based only on the first three years' data, not the whole time series. The observed deviations of actual sales from predicted sales are largely explainable in terms of short-term variations in national economic activity, for which there is no variable in the model. The estimated parameters of the equation,

$$p = .0104 \qquad r = .4186 \qquad \bar{Q} = 16{,}895{,}000$$

make it possible to predict (1) the time when sales would reach their peak and (2) the magnitude of peak sales.[2] For room air conditioners, the pre-

---

[2] The predicted time of peak is given by $t^* = \dfrac{1}{p + r} \ln\left(\dfrac{r}{p}\right)$ and the predicted magnitude of the peak is given by $Q_{t^*} = \dfrac{\bar{Q}(p + r)^2}{4r}$. These formulas are derived from (11.12) through standard maximization procedures. See Bass (1969, p. 218).

Figure 11.6   Actual Sales and Predicted Sales for Room Air Conditioners—Bass Model

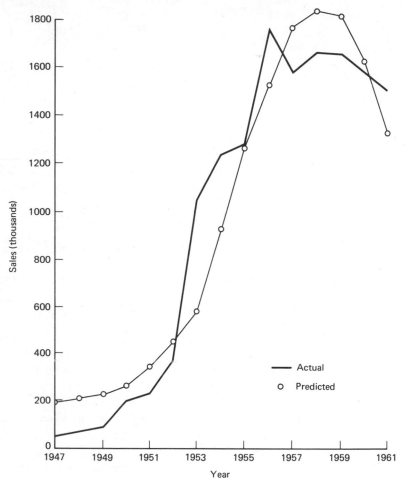

dicted time of peak was 8.6 years as against an actual time of peak of 7 years; the predicted magnitude of peak was 1.8 million as against an actual peak of 1.7 million. This prediction is close, and the Bass model produced reasonably good forecasts for most of the other eleven innovations studied.[3]

The fact that the Bass model has generated good fits to several past innovations makes it an attractive model to use for attempting sales predictions

[3] Bass's model was recently tested against a lognormal model and a Weibull model on seven months of panel data on the introduction of a new detergent product in Lafayette, Indiana. Both the Bass and Weibull models showed up better than the lognormal model with a goodness of fit acceptable at the 0.95 level of significance. See Burger, Bass, and Pessemier (1968).

for current new product introductions. The model can be used both before the new product is introduced extensively and after the new product has been on the market for awhile. In both cases, the parameters p, r, and $\overline{Q}$ have to be estimated.

If it is necessary to estimate p, r, and $\overline{Q}$ before the product is extensively introduced, the following possibilities exist:

1. If the new product is expected to go through the same history as some previous new product in the same product class, then the parameters for the earlier product may be used as an approximation.
2. A study of many past product introductions may reveal predictive relationships between the parameters p, r, and Q, and features of the product class and/or buyer characteristics. If so, these features and characteristics for the new product under consideration are plugged into the predictive equation to find p, r, and $\overline{Q}$.
3. Data that suggest the relative magnitudes of p, r, and Q may be collected from a sample of households either in a laboratory setting, through in-home product usage tests, or in limited test markets.

The resulting equation can then be used for long range forecasting, particularly to predict the time of peak sales and the magnitude of peak sales for the new product. This can be of help in developing long range plans for capacity expansion and financing.[4] It should be recognized, however, that the estimating equation works best before replacement sales occur and during a period of relatively stable population.

Reliability Engineering Diffusion Models

Recently another model, the Weibull model, has been fitted to new product sales data with a fair amount of success. It involves a different point of view of the nature of the diffusion process (Burger, Bass, and Pessemier, 1968). Instead of originating from studies of epidemic diffusion processes, it originated in reliability engineering theory. Applied to consumer behavior, the model assumes that every potential buyer of the new product is bombarded by various stimuli which have random arrival times. The stimuli include seeing the product in a store, hearing about it from an acquaintance, seeing it on television, and so on. If any one of the several stimuli reach the buyer, it is assumed that he makes an initial purchase of the new product. Therefore the issue is how much time is expected to elapse before the buyer receives a stimulus. Now suppose that the arrival time for all the stimuli have an

[4] Bass (1969, pp. 222–226) illustrates this by making a long-range sales forecast for color television using the first three years of sales results after its introduction. His industry sales forecast for color television proved more accurate than many of the manufacturers' published forecasts.

identical gamma probability distribution.[5] We now hypothetically draw an arrival time for each of the stimuli, using the time of arrival of the first stimulus to characterize when the first potential buyer adopted the product. We repeat this simulation for the second, third, . . . , n buyers and end with a distribution of waiting times to first purchase for all the buyers. This will be a Weibull distribution, because this is the form taken by the events in a parallel system of events with identical gamma distributions.[6]

The Weibull distribution supplied a good fit of the data on the diffusion of a new laundry detergent after the product triers were split into two exclusive groups: early buyers and late buyers (Burger, Bass, and Pessemier, 1968). The early buyers (those who bought in the first seventy days after the product's introduction in the market) were found to have a higher response rate to marketing stimuli than the late buyers; and fitting separate Weibull distributions to these populations was necessary to obtain a good fit to the data.

ADOPTION MODELS

Diffusion models, as we have seen, involve postulating a few macro-parameters to locate a relevant curve that might fit or predict the sales for a new product. It is clear that the process of learning about a new product and making a decision to try it is more complicated than the few parameters suggest. Many analysts sacrifice the economy and tractability of a diffusion model for the behavioral richness of an adoption model. An adoption model considers the mental processes through which consumers progress in learning about and deciding to try a new product.

A central characteristic of all adoption process models is the postulation of distinct stages through which the potential purchaser passes before he adopts the new product. As was discussed in Chapter 3, several major schemes have been proposed to describe buyer readiness states, including the AIDA model, the adoption process model, and the hierarchy-of-effects model.

All of these schemes are based on two assumptions. The first assumption is that there is a unidirectional passage through the stages toward the act of purchase. The second assumption is that each stage implies a higher probability that the person will purchase the product than did the preceding stage. A critique of these assumptions has been rendered in Chapter 3 and some

---

[5] The gamma distribution is a two parameter distribution (a, b) given by

$$P(t|a,b) = \frac{1}{b^a \Gamma(a)} t^{a-1} \exp\left(-\frac{t}{b}\right) \text{, where } \Gamma(a) = (a-1)!$$

See Freund (1962, pp. 127–128). The well-known exponential distribution and chi-square distribution are special cases of the gamma distribution.

[6] See Pieruschka (1963). The functional form of the Weibull distribution is

$$P(t|a,b) = \left(\frac{bt^{b-1}}{a}\right) \exp\left(\frac{-t^b}{a}\right)$$

evidence has been presented to show that these assumptions may not *always* hold. However, these assumptions may be considered to *generally* hold and they provide a basis for building models of the adoption process. In this section, four recent examples of quantitative models that deal with the adoption process will be considered.

The DEMON Model

DEMON, an acronym for Decision-Mapping via Optimum GO-NO Networks, was developed under the auspices of the advertising agency Batten, Barton, Durstine and Osborne to aid management in evaluating (1) alternative plans for the introduction of new products and (2) alternative marketing research studies that could shed light on how to improve the product's profitability (Learner, 1968).

The first task is accomplished by the marketing planning framework illustrated in Figure 11.7. Three different company marketing decision variables are shown to affect the number of triers: advertising, sales promotion, and distribution. The effect of advertising on sales is spelled out in the greatest detail, which is not surprising considering that the model was developed for an advertising agency. Some percentage of triers become users and their number, usage rate, and the product's price multiply out to the level of demand in dollars. Presumably a cost model can then be brought in to yield figures that can be netted against revenue to produce a picture of expected profits.

Figure 11.7   Marketing Planning Framework of DEMON

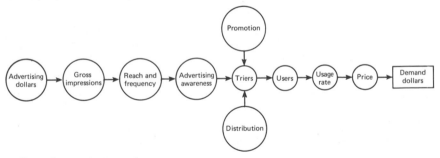

Source: Learner, (1968, p. 153).

The relationship between the rate of trial and the rate of usage will be considered later under repeat purchase models. In the present context, DEMON is of interest in connection with the steps leading from a company decision to spend so many dollars on advertising to its effect on usage rate.

Figure 11.8 shows five functions that are used to trace the effect of a specific advertising expenditure level on the usage rate. The *gross impression function* shows the number of gross impressions (exposures) that the agency can

Figure 11.8   DEMON Marketing Planning Functions

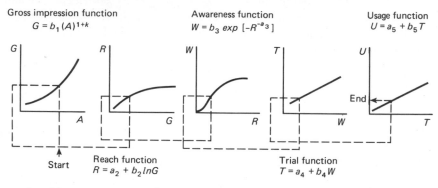

Gross impression function
$$G = b_1 (A)^{1+k}$$

Awareness function
$$W = b_3 \, exp \, [-R^{-a_3}]$$

Usage function
$$U = a_5 + b_5 T$$

Reach function
$$R = a_2 + b_2 \ln G$$

Trial function
$$T = a_4 + b_4 W$$

attain with a certain expenditure of advertising dollars. Since media discounts are available on large-volume purchases, gross impressions increase at an increasing rate with advertising dollars. The *reach function* shows the percentage of the total audience exposed to at least one advertisement. Reach tends to increase at a diminishing rate (represented here by a logarithmic function) because successive media purchases tend to deliver fewer new persons. The *awareness function* shows the fraction of the total audience that can recall the thematic content of the brand advertising. Awareness appears to increase first at an increasing and then at a decreasing rate with reach. The *trial function* shows the fraction of aware persons who try the product at full purchase price; this function appears to be linear. Finally, the *usage function* shows the fraction of triers who go on to become regular users of the product. This function also appears to be linear.

These shapes were determined through least square regression on data available for more than two hundred packaged goods products in sixteen product categories.

Needless to say, the fits of the various functions to the available data varied in quality. The basic question is whether regression equations fitted to a cross-section of products will yield the functions sought for one product. This is known as the identification problem in econometric theory and is illustrated in Figure 11.9 for the case of reach and ad awareness. Five products are shown and the hypothesized **S**-shaped relationship of the awareness function shown in Figure 11.8 is traced. Each product is represented only by the current observation of its reach and ad awareness. It is conceivable that if the awareness functions were known for each product, they might be the nearly horizontal lines shown in Figure 11.9. That is, the response of ad awareness to reach may be relatively unimpressive for each product, although the curve fitted to the cross-section of points observed for the products may give the appearance of a substantial **S**-shaped relationship.

Another criticism is that the model postulates a linked set of two-way

Figure 11.9   Spurious Relationship between Two Variables (Identification Problem)

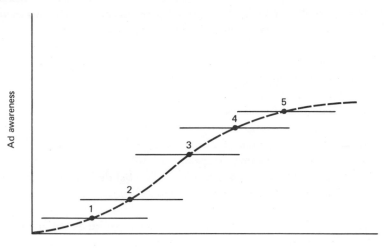

relationships, whereas some of the variables depend upon additional factors. For example, trial depends not only on the amount of awareness but also on such things as advertising frequency, distribution, and price. The usage rate depends not only on the trial rate but also on the amount of product satisfaction. These refinements, of course, can be added to the model as experience is gained.

Once the market planning model is specified, the second task is to develop a *decision model* to find the optimal settings of the controllable factors such as advertising and distribution expenditures, price, and marketing research expenditures. For this purpose, the designers of DEMON developed a model for information collection which presumably leads to a marketing strategy that optimizes the company's objectives. The decision model is oriented toward the idea that a company testing a new product will have to evaluate where it stands after each test. Each evaluation can result in one of three decisions:

GO. The company should begin national marketing because the accumulated evidence indicates that the stated company objectives and requirements will all be met.

NO. The company should discontinue testing and should not market the product.

ON. The company should continue testing because the accumulated evidence is not sufficient to warrant a GO or NO decision.

An ON decision means that the company will undertake to make a particular market study or sequence of studies (product-use tests, TV commercial tests, economic analyses, test markets, and so on). Each alternative study has a certain cost C and is expected to yield a certain improved estimate of demand, Q. The design problem is to find an optimal path through a total information network subject to management-specified instructions:

$m =$ payback period

$n =$ horizon planning period

$Z_G =$ minimum acceptable profits for a GO decision

$Z_0 =$ minimum acceptable profits for an ON decision

$B =$ total marketing research budget

$Pr_G =$ minimum degree of confidence (probability) needed for a GO decision, a chance constraint on Z_G

$Pr_0 =$ minimum degree of confidence (probability) needed for an ON decision, a chance constraint on Z_0.

For example, suppose one constraint is that the expected profit by the end of the payback period should exceed the minimum level for a GO decision; that is,

$$Z_m > Z_G \qquad \text{(condition 1 for GO)} \qquad (11.16)$$

Suppose a second condition is that the probability of achieving this profit within the payback period should exceed the minimum degree of required confidence for a GO decision; that is,

$$Pr\ \{Z_m > Z_G\} > Pr_G \qquad \text{(condition 2 for GO)} \qquad (11.17)$$

These and other constraints delimit further the feasible space of solutions.

The model permits an evaluation to be made of every possible path through alternative marketing studies to reach a GO decision. Each possible sequence of marketing studies involves an estimated cost and an estimated result in terms of the demand estimate. These two can be netted to yield an expected profit and risk for that sequence. The sequence with the best hypothetical profit and risk is found. It may be the sequence ON (product-use test) → ON (test market) → GO. This may appear to be better than an immediate GO decision. The company decides on ON and makes the product-use test. Now it does not make another ON decision (test market) automatically but uses the result of the product-use test to reevaluate the best decision. It may be an immediate GO, NO, or some sequence of ONs.

In one reported application of the DEMON decision system, a drug company launching a new product was advised to spend much less on advertising than it had planned. (It is unusual for a model created by an advertising agency to recommend this.) The company set up two matched markets and spent the planned amount for advertising in one market and the lower amount in the other. When the sales results were in, sales were somewhat lower in the latter market, but profits were higher. Thus the DEMON recommendation appeared vindicated. At the same time, the lower-spending strategy might be bad in the long-run because the company is not building up sales as fast as possible and competitors might move in. Unfortunately, DEMON is not set up to evaluate long-run profit strategies.

The SPRINTER Model

Urban (1968) developed a new product decision model called SPRINTER (Specification of PRofits with INteractions under Trial and Error Response) which, like DEMON, was oriented toward helping management decide between a GO, ON, or NO decision respecting a new product, with the additional capability of considering any relevant interaction of the new product with other products in the company's line. SPRINTER differed from DEMON in utilizing a conventional macroanalytic model of market response instead of a microanalytic formulation. Subsequently, Urban (1969) reported a new model that has a definite microanalytic cast. He postulates five buyer readiness stages in product trial: (1) awareness, (2) intent, (3) search, (4) selection, and (5) postpurchase behavior. The first stage, awareness, is itself divided into four levels, focusing on (a) the brand, (b) its advertisements, (c) specific product appeals, and (d) word-of-mouth recommendation. Each awareness level assumes that all the preceding types of awareness have occurred. And each higher level of awareness is associated with a higher probability of developing an intent to buy, according to the following behavioral rationale:

> The percent of people in a given awareness class who display intent to buy the product will depend upon the perceived compatability and relative advantage of the product to the people who have the specific recall of that class. It would be expected that the percent with intent would be higher in appeal recall classes, since this represents more perception of relative advantage. The highest buying rates might be expected in the awareness class representing receipt of word-of-mouth recommendations, since this group would be one in which the perceived risk is low. After the number of people intending to buy has been determined for each awareness class, they are added to get the total number of people with intent (Urban, 1969, p. 10).

Those who intend to buy the product enter the stage of search. Whether they actually select the brand depends upon its availability and upon in-store stimuli such as price and point-of-purchase displays. The model allows for some customers who enter the store without intent to buy the particular brand to purchase it because of favorable in-store stimuli. They are added to the number of buyers who exercised their intent to find the total number of new brand adopters.

Urban goes on to show how the first-time triers may become word-of-mouth communicators to nontriers. He also shows how triers may move into the class of preferers, preferers into the class of low loyals, and low loyals into the class of high loyals. It might appear that his model is microbehavioral from the description given thus far. Actually, it is microanalytic in that it uses expected values for all the processes, instead of using individual persons going through the stages of the buying process. The model has been tested against a new product and is reported to have produced an unusually accurate forecast of new product acceptance.

Alba's Model

We now turn to two adoption process models that have been formulated along microbehavioral lines. They both estimate new product demand by aggregating the actions of a population of hypothetical but representative consumers who learn about the new product and pass through the several stages of buyer readiness.

The first model was formulated by Alba (1967) to describe the adoption of the new Touch-Tone telephone. He used data collected and analyzed earlier by Robertson (1966) on the diffusion of this innovation in the town of Deerfield, Illinois. The data described seven traits of each adopter (interest polymorphism, venturesomeness, cosmopolitanism, social integration, social mobility, privilegedness, and status concern), each adopter's sources of information about the new phone (personal influence and mass communication), and the date of his adoption. Alba's aim was to see whether he could simulate the adoption process in this community accurately enough to

1. Reproduce the actual number of new adopters each period
2. Reproduce the order in which the 100 households in the sample adopted the Touch-Tone telephone

To do this, he developed the probabilities of each individual being exposed to Touch-Tone telephone advertising and word-of-mouth communications, and, in turn, exposing others. The probabilities were derived from statistical regressions on the traits of individuals. For example, the probability that an individual would be exposed to a Touch-Tone phone advertisement was given by

$$PE_i = .120\left(\frac{VE_i}{7}\right) + .359\left(\frac{IP_i}{7}\right) - .150\left(\frac{CO_i}{7}\right) + .200\left(\frac{SI_i}{7}\right)$$

$$+ .202\left(\frac{SM_i}{7}\right) + .184\left(\frac{PR_i}{7}\right) + .085\left(\frac{SC_i}{7}\right) \tag{11.18}$$

where PE_i = probability that individual i will be exposed to a Touch-Tone advertisement

$VE_i =$ individual i's score on venturesomeness

$IP_i =$ individual i's score on interest polymorphism

$CO_i =$ individual i's score on cosmopolitanism

$SI_i =$ individual i's score on social integration

$SM_i =$ individual i's score on social mobility

$PR_i =$ individual i's score on privilegedness

$SC_i =$ individual i's score on status concern

If an individual scores 7 (the maximum score) on all the traits that cor-related with the tendency to adopt a Touch-Tone telephone, his probability would be 1.00. Otherwise PE_i would be between 0 and 1.

After the individual's PE is determined, a random number is drawn to determine if he saw a persuasive communication in that period. If he did, then another random number is drawn to determine whether he underwent an attitude change. Alba defined an attitude change as tantamount to adopting the phone, although he notes that in most empirical studies (including his data) adoption refers to actual purchase. The probability of an individual undergoing an attitude change is affected by the level of the persuasiveness of the ad. The persuasiveness of the particular ad is rated on the basis of the message, source, transmitter, and content.

The individual who did not adopt the phone might still be exposed to a neighbor who talked about the phone. Alba formulated a model that generated a probability that any two residents of Deerfield would discuss the Touch-Tone phone. The probability varied directly with the degree to which the two residents shared the same traits.

Alba's steps in simulating the word-of-mouth process are shown in Figure 11.10. Alba distinguishes among nonknowers, knower nonadopters, and knower-adopters; and he employs different probabilities of confrontation between any two categories of individuals. As confrontations take place, in those who undergo an attitude change are considered adopters; and the com-puter program totals the number of adopters in each period.

Alba defined a simulation run as covering eight periods, each lasting approximately two months. He replicated the process fifty times and used the mean result to compare with the actual adoption curve. The actual and simu-lated curves are shown in Figure 11.11. The fit is not too satisfactory: Alba's one hundred simulated residents of Deerfield started out slower in their adoption rate and later adopted faster than the actual residents. By period 5, almost all of the simulated residents adopted the phone, although only 60 percent of the real residents did in the sample. These differences were shown to be highly significant in both chi-square and Kolmogorov-Smirnov tests of goodness of fit.

Alba fared better in his predictions concerning the early and later adopters. The rank correlation coefficient (Spearman's rho) for the times of adoption

Figure 11.10   Flow Chart of Adoption Process Model (Alba's Simulation)

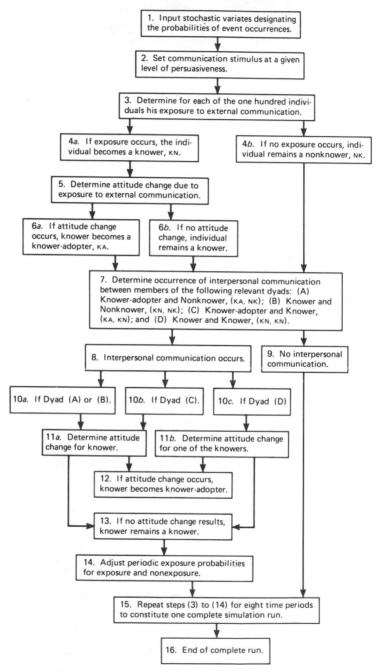

Figure 11.11 Alba's Simulation Results

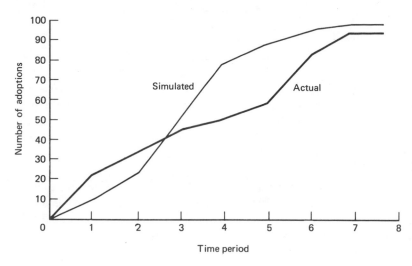

Source: Alba (1967, p. 209).

of the real and simulated residents of Deerfield was high and statistically significant. His model was also able to discriminate accurately between those residents who underwent attitude change because of mass communication influence versus attitude change because of personal influence.

Alba also tested the influence that a higher versus lower level of advertising would have had in accelerating the adoption rate. He found that greater advertising did not increase the rate of adoption significantly.

Alba's simulation of the diffusion of an innovation was a pioneering attempt to determine the relative influence of *social factors*, on the one hand, and *chance*, on the other, in explaining the rate at which a sample population learned about and decided to adopt a new product. Alba worked against the limitations of an existing data bank that was not originally designed for his needs, and yet he managed to develop a complex set of events and generate a plausible set of outputs that matched some of the actual occurrences fairly well. If the data had been originally collected for this project, more would have been gathered on the actual timing of advertisements, the media habits of the sample of residents, and the actual friendship or acquaintance patterns in the area. These data would have permitted the community to be modeled more concretely; and the diffusion process, still a highly stochastic one, could have been modeled more faithfully. Diffusion research has still not adequately documented the relationship between product interest levels, consumer traits, and neighbor interaction patterns and conversations about products. The main contribution of Alba's work is to show that the complex processes of individual and community adoption of new products can be studied insightfully through the medium of microbehavioral simulation.

Amstutz's Model

The most ambitious microbehavioral model of sales determination is that developed by Amstutz (1967). His model is capable of breeding a population of consumers, retailers, salesmen, products, advertisements, and so on, and causing these elements to interact on a stochastic basis to produce the output of ultimate interest—sales. Since it is impossible to describe the behavioral mechanisms of each of Amstutz's submodels, we will present and evaluate perhaps his most unique model—that describing consumer behavior toward a product category.

Amstutz designed a computer program capable of performing four important tasks: (1) breeding a consumer population in any desired number, (2) developing and assigning product and brand awarenesses and attitudes to each individual consumer, (3) putting the consumer through a set of experiences, and (4) updating the consumer's attributes as a result of these experiences.

Figure 11.12 shows the characteristics and experience of one such consumer during a typical simulated week. According to line 2, this person lives in a suburb (su) located in the northeast (ne). He is between twenty-five and thirty-five years of age with an income of $8000 to $10,000 and is college educated. These characteristics could describe an actual person recorded in a sample survey. Alternatively, this person could have been created artificially through a random number generator applied to basic census data. In the latter case, the computer program randomly draws an *age bracket* from an age distribution table stored in its memory, where the chance of drawing a particular age bracket is proportional to its relative frequency in the population. Next, the computer program draws an *income* for the person from a frequency distribution of income within that age bracket. Finally, the computer program randomly draws an *educational level* from an education distribution. In this way, a string of characteristics is generated to create a plausible person. There is no limit to the size of the artificial population that can be bred this way. Furthermore, the population that is bred can be expected to reflect the distribution of characteristics found in the real population.

Turning to line 3, the person owns brand 3 which is now six years old. The product is assumed to be a consumer durable such as an electric floor polisher. Furthermore, the person prefers to deal with retailers 5, 11, and 3, in that order. He also has attitudes toward twelve different product characteristics and twelve different appeals, the attitudes ranging in each case from a —5 (very negative) to a +5 (very positive). The person also has attitudes toward the four brands and the eighteen retailers. Finally, the person has been exposed in the past to a varying number of communications on

Figure 11.12   One Simulated Consumer in Week 117

```
              SIMULATION APP-03 TEST RUN APRIL 4, 1965   1400 HOURS

  -- CONSUMER 0109 NOW BEGINNING WEEK 117  --  FEBRUARY 19, 1962
   - REPORT MONITOR SPECIFIED. TO CANCEL PUSH INTERRUPT.
   - CHARAC - REGION NE SU, AGE 25-35, INCOME 8-10K, EDUCATION COLLEG
   - BRANDS OWN 3, 6 YEARS OLD. RETAILER PREFERENCE 05, 11, 03
   - MEDIA AVAILABLE  1 0 0 1 0 0 0 0 1 1 1 1 0 0 0 0 0 0 0 0 0 0 0
   - ATTITUDES .   1    2    3    4    5    6    7    8    9   10   11   12
     .........................................................
     PROD CHAR .  0  +1  +1   0  -3  -1   0  +5   0  +3   0   0
     APPEALS    . -3   0  +1  +5   0  -3  +3   0   0   0  +5   0
     BRANDS     . +2  +1  +3  +2
     RETAILERS  . +1  -5  +3  +1  +5  -5  -5  +1  -1  -3  +5  +1
                . -3  +1  -1  +3  +1  +1
     AWARENESS .  1   0   0   0
     MEMORY DUMP FOLLOWS.  BRANDS LISTED IN DESCENDING ORDER 1 TO 4
PRODUCT CHARACTERISTIC MEMORY              APPEALS MEMORY

     .  .  .  .  .  .  .  .  .  .  .  .  .  .  .  .  .  .  .  .  .  .  .  .  .
 1   2  3  4  5  6  7  8  9 10 11 12 .  1  2  3  4  5  6  7  8  9 10 11 12
     .  .  .  .  .  .  .  .  .  .  .  .  .  .  .  .  .  .  .  .  .  .  .  .  .
 2   3 15  0  5  5  4 14  8  7  1  3 . 8  9  7  3  1 11  7  4  4  3  9  3
 8   0  6  4  9  5  4 13  0  3  6  7 . 6  8  0  7  0  9  2  4  3 10  3  1
 0   6 15  7  0  3 11  3  5  2  5  7 . 0  4  8 10  9  2 14  3  9  7  9  5
 7   9  3  7  3  2  7  2  6 12 14  2 . 0  9  7  8 13  9 11  6  0  2  5  9
   - MEDIA EXPOSURE INITIATED
      - MEDIUM 003 APPEARS IN WEEK 117 - NO EXPOSURES
      - MEDIUM 004 APPEARS IN WEEK 117
         - EXPOSURE TO AD 013, BRAND 3 -- NO NOTING
         - EXPOSURE TO AD 019, BRAND 4
            - AD 109, BRAND 4 NOTED. CONTENT FOLLOWS
            - PROD. C  11 P = 4,  4 P = 2,
            - APPEALS  5 P = 2,  7 P = 2,  12 P = 2,
      - MEDIUM 007 APPEARS IN WEEK 117 -- NO EXPOSURES
      - MEDIUM 012 APPEARS IN WEEK 117
         - EXPOSURE TO AD 007, BRAND 2
            - AD 007, BRAND 2 NOTED. CONTENT FOLLOWS
            - PROD. C  8 P = 3,  12 P = 1,
            - APPEALS 2 P = 1,  4 P = 1, 6 P = 1, 10 P = 1,
         - EXPOSURE TO AD 013, BRAND 3 -- NO NOTING
         - EXPOSURE TO AD 004, BRAND 1 -- NO NOTING
      - MEDIUM 016 APPEARS IN WEEK 117 -- NO EXPOSURES
      - MEDIUM 023 APPEARS IN WEEK 117 -- NO EXPOSURES
   - WORD OF MOUTH EXPOSURE INITIATED
            - EXPOSURE TO CONSUMER 0093 -- NO NOTING
            - EXPOSURE TO CONSUMER 0104 -- NO NOTING
            - EXPOSURE TO CONSUMER 0117 -- NO NOTING
   - NO PRODUCT USE IN WEEK 117
   - DECISION TO SHOP POSITIVE  --  BRAND 3 HIGH PERCEIVED NEED
                                 -- RETAILER 05 CHOSEN
   - SHOPPING INITIATED
      - CONSUMER DECISION EXPLICIT FOR BRAND 3 -- NO SEARCH
      - PRODUCT EXPOSURE FOR BRAND 3
         - EXPOSURE TO POINT OF SALE 008 FOR BRAND 3
            - POS 008,  BRAND 3 NOTED. CONTENT FOLLOWS
            - PROD. C  3 P = 4,  6 P = 4,
            - APPEALS 5 P = 2,  7 P = 2, 10 P = 2, 11 P = 2,
      - NO SELLING EFFORT EXPOSURE IN RETAILER 05
   - DECISION TO PURCHASE POSITIVE  -  BRAND 3, $ 38.50
      - DELIVERY IMEDAT
      - OWNERSHIP = 3,  AWARENESS WAS 2,  NOW 3
   - WORD OF MOUTH GENERATION INITIATED
      - CONTENT GENERATED, BRAND 3
            - PROD. C  3 P = +15,   8 P = +15,
            - APPEALS 4 P = +50, 11 P = +45
      - FORGETTING INITIATED -- NO FORGETTING
  -- CONSUMER 0109 NOW CONCLUDING WEEK 117 -- FEBRUARY 25, 1962
  -- CONSUMER 0110 NOW BEGINNING WEEK 117 -- FEBRUARY 19, 1962
     QUIT,
     R 11.633+4.750
```

Source: Reprinted from Amstutz (1967, pp. 394–395) by permission of the MIT Press, Cambridge, Massachusetts. Copyright © 1967 by the Massachusetts Institute of Technology.

different product characteristics and appeals for each of the four brands.

How was this information developed? Once again, the information could describe the attitudes, store preference, brands owned, and communication's recall of a real person who was interviewed in a survey. Or these characteristics could have been generated artificially from various frequency distributions compiled in earlier surveys.

Next this consumer passes through a set of events and experiences resembling those which members of the real population might have passed through during that same particular week. Consumer 109 is exposed to media and might or might not note advertisements pertaining to this product; he might be exposed to word-of-mouth influence, use the product during the week, make a decision to shop, deal with a salesman, and decide to purchase. Afterward he might influence others by favorable or unfavorable word of mouth. Some forgetting of his past exposures also would occur.

Each of these events in the consumer's week is regulated by mathematical functions and/or probability distributions. For example, the probability that the consumer shops this week is related to his perceived need, which is an increasing function of his brand-attitude score, opportunity for product use, and time since last purchase; it is also dependent on the level of his income. These factors are combined in a nonlinear mathematical expression.

By generating experiences for each member of the artificial population week after week during the period under study, Amstutz is able to aggregate and summarize their purchases in the form of a simulated time series of brand shares.

Amstutz specified a multilevel validation procedure for his model. *Function level* validation involves two steps: first, a sensitivity analysis indicating the relative sensitivity of total system performance to various functions within the system structure and, second, a chi-square test of the null hypothesis that observed relationships are due to random variation. *Cell level* validation establishes that the behavior of an artificial consumer within the simulated population cannot be differentiated by an expert from that of a similar member of the real world population. *Population level* validation is undertaken to insure that the behavior of members of the simulated population does not differ significantly from corresponding members of the real-world population. Finally, *performance* validation is the ability of the model to duplicate historical real-world population behavior. This level of validation calls for initializing parameter settings in the model to duplicate those existing in the real-world system at a particular point in time and then comparing simulated and actual results.

In a reported application of this methodology to another product area, in this case a pharmaceutical product, Claycamp and Amstutz (1968) indicate that a good fit to the data was obtained. They simulated the prescribing behavior of one hundred simulated doctors toward the ten brands in this product class over a year's time. There was some change in the market share ranks of the ten brands between the beginning and end of the year. Their simulated results correctly predicted all the yearend ranks, as shown in Table 11.1. This table also shows the same data according to market shares, and their average error in predicting yearend values was on the order of 0.7 percent in market share.

The overriding question raised by Amstutz's microbehavioral model is whether the extensive data gathering that this type of model requires produces enough in extra understanding or predictive ability to be worth the cost. There is no question that Amstutz's model allows considerable detail of the consumer buying process to be considered in an interrelated manner, and this can be a real contribution to theory construction. The analyst is challenged to specify the relationships among demographic characteristics, media exposure probabilities, word-of-mouth exposure probabilities, responses to appeals and product characteristics of various kinds, and so forth. These are the kinds of variables which are worth thinking about both by the theorist searching for understanding and by the marketing practitioner searching for clues to promotional strategy. And they are worth thinking about in the operationally defined way required by simulation. But it is a different matter to justify this effort and cost as a route to developing useful forecasting and marketing planning models. In the first place, there is the question of whether the various frequency distribution data on consumer characteristics can be obtained and, if so, at what cost. There is the question of how many consumers should be created for a representative sample population for trying out marketing strategies. Each consumer must be separately processed through many events and many weeks, and the computer cost of maintaining and processing all this detail is high. There is the question of the many types of errors that can creep into the data and program and affect the results without easily being spotted because of the considerable model detail and complexity. There is the question of accurately measuring the marketing actions of competitors with respect to weekly advertising media expenditures and in-store promotions. Competitive intelligence is extremely difficult and costly to collect, and this model demands more detail about competitive behavior than the typical aggregative model. There is the question of validating the many functions used in the model. There are so many possible sensitivity tests that can be performed on different functions in the system that the cost of sensitivity testing can rapidly get out of hand. There is the question of performance validity, and so far only one real application has been made. Here the performance validity appeared good, but more applications are needed before it can be determined whether this was a chance result or an intrinsic accomplishment from this level of model-building.

With respect to performance validity, it must be asked whether a simpler model could have done as well. Amstutz did not test his elaborate model against possible simpler models, though such tests seem desirable. We are not doubting the value of microbehavioral simulation for stimulating theory con-

Table 11.1 Actual and Predicted Brand Shares

Brand Identification	Rank Order Brand Share Comparisons			Absolute Brand Share Comparison			
	Rank as Initialized	Yearend Rank		Initialization Value	Yearend Value		Difference (Magnitude)
		Simulated	Actual		Simulated	Actual	
1—Y	4	2	2	13.7%	15.0%	16.1%	−1.1%
1—0	5	6	6	9.7	9.1	8.7	+ .4
1—X	6	5	5	7.3	9.3	9.0	+ .3
1—+	8	8	8	5.0	3.2	2.8	+ .4
1—□	10	10	10	0	0	0	—
2—□	1	1	1	23.2	27.6	28.8	−1.2
2—0	2	3	3	18.1	13.0	12.7	+ .3
2—X	3	4	4	15.6	13.9	14.4	− .5
2—+	7	7	7	6.2	5.9	5.5	+ .4
2—Y	9	9	9	1.0	2.5	2.0	+ .5
				99.8%	99.5%	100.0%	.7%

Source: Claycamp and Amstutz (1968, p. 148).

struction and firing the imagination of practitioners; we are only raising the question of its promise in the area of practical forecasting and planning. Does Amstutz's microbehavioral model increase the degree of predictability over that of simpler models and, if so, to an extent justifying the substantially larger investment required? It is too early to answer these questions.

REPEAT PURCHASE MODELS

A great many new products that are introduced in the marketplace are of the repurchasable kind. This includes virtually all the nondurables consumed by the household and the factory. The sellers of these products are interested in the repurchase rate even more than the trial rate. A low trial rate could be attributable to poor distribution, promotion, or packaging, all of which are correctable. Trial of a new product can be stimulated by free samples, introductory pricing, and so on. A low repurchase rate may suggest a product that does not meet the consumers' expectations, which is harder to correct. It is a problem that should have been solved at the product development and testing stage. Unfortunately, the early aggregate sales figures do not distinguish between the two rates. A rising sales curve could mean, without further analysis, a high-trying rate with a low-rebuying rate (which would be a bad development) or a low-trying rate with a high-rebuying rate (which might be a good development). If the rebuying rate is nil, to consider an extreme case, the sales curve will turn down to zero immediately after the last trial purchases take place. If the rebuying rate is high, the sales curve will, after the new buyer demand is finished, continue horizontally at a substantial level above zero. In between, the rebuying rate may or may not be sufficient to create a successful product.

The problem facing the marketing analyst is to define and estimate the repurchase rate in advance of the GO decision and to keep track of it as it appears within the early sales figures. The sales taking place in any time period can be decomposed into two parts:

$$S_t = s_{Ft}N_{Ft} + s_{Rt}N_{Rt} \tag{11.19}$$

where S_t = total sales in period t
   s_{Ft} = average purchase volume per period per first-time buyer
   N_{Ft} = number of first-time buyers in period t
   s_{Rt} = average purchase volume per period per repeat buyer
   N_{Rt} = number of repeat buyers in period t

If there is no significant difference in the average purchase volume of trial and repeat buyers, then (11.19) reduces to

$$S_t = s_t(N_{Ft} + N_{Rt}) \tag{11.20}$$

and the analyst can focus his attention on the relative number of the two types of buyers. However most of the evidence indicates that repeat buyers buy larger volumes per period than first-time buyers, that is, $s_{Ft} < s_{Rt}$. First-time buyers tend to buy a smaller quantity in order to sample it. Those who stay with the new product have found satisfaction and tend to become heavier users. Massy's data on a new food product showed the average purchase rate per period rising with the number of repeat purchases, as follows:

Purchase class (number of previous purchases)	Relative number of packages
1	100 (coded)
2	105
3	145
4	153
5	122
6	160
$\geqq 7$	165

Source: Based on Massy (1967).

This last piece of information suggests that equation (11.19) can be usefully expanded to read:

$$S_t = s_{Ft}N_{Ft} + s_{1t}N_{1t} + s_{2t}N_{2t} + S_{3t}N_{3t} + \ldots + s_{it}N_{it} + \ldots \qquad (11.21)$$

where s_{it} = average purchase volume of buyers in the ith repeat purchase class at time t

N_{it} = number of repeat buyers in the ith repeat purchase class at time t

Many analysts have suggested that the seller should study not only the number of first repeat purchasers but also second, third, . . . i^{th} repeat purchasers. For example, Urban (1968) defines a really loyal purchaser as one who has purchased the product at least three times and twice in succession. Fourt and Woodlock (1960) have argued that the success of many products is not clinched by a high ratio of first-repeat purchasers to first-time buyers: the seller should also watch the rate of second- and third-repeat purchasers. Massy (1967) in his STEAM model makes a point of extending Fourt and Woodlock's basic idea of "depth of repeat" analysis:

> The immediate objective in applying a depth of repeat oriented model is to predict the time paths of the cumulative proportions of one time buyers, two time buyers, and so on. These groups are handled separately because of the probable importance of purchase event feedback in the new product context. Effects of feedback are incorporated into the analysis by estimating the model's parameters separately for each depth of trial group (p. 4).

The following pages will describe four different models for defining and estimating repeat purchase sales.

FOURT AND WOODLOCK'S REPEAT PURCHASE MODEL

Basic to Fourt and Woodlock's "depth of repeat" analysis (1960) is the notion of a repeat ratio. The first repeat ratio, for example, is the fraction of initial buyers who make a second purchase. It can be thought of as the probability that a first time buyer will buy a second time. Second, third, and so on, repeat ratios are similarly defined. In terms of the notation in (11.21), these repeat ratios are

$$\frac{N_{1t}}{N_{Ft}}, \frac{N_{2t}}{N_{1t}}, \frac{N_{3t}}{N_{2t}}, \cdots \tag{11.22}$$

If these ratios are all unity, the company can look forward to a remarkably successful product. If successive ratios rapidly fall toward zero, this augurs badly for the product. Fourt and Woodlock calculated the repeat ratios shown in column 1 of Figure 11.13 for a new food product that had just been introduced nationally.[7] These ratios tend to grow larger, the deeper the repeat purchase class, indicating a growing loyalty (or habit) that occurs with use of the product. Fourt and Woodlock used these ratios to predict sales for the next period. First they estimated new buyer sales in the second period to be 8141.[8] This number came from their first purchase model described earlier. They multiplied 8141 by the first repeat ratio of 0.485 to arrive at an estimate of first repeat sales of 3948. Then they multiplied 0.559 by 3948 to estimate second repeat sales, in this case 2207. This was continued for the deeper repeat classes and yielded a prediction of total sales, when summed, of 19,444. The same result is given by the formula

$$S_t = s_{Ft}N_{Ft}(1 + r_1 + r_1r_2 + r_1r_2r_3 + \ldots + r_1r_2r_3r_4r_{5+}) \tag{11.23}$$

where $r_1 = $ first repeat ratio, $\dfrac{N_{1t}}{N_{Ft}}$

$r_2 = $ second repeat ratio, $\dfrac{N_{2t}}{N_{1t}}$; others similarly defined

[7] Consumer panel data are necessary to calculate repeat ratios. First an observation period is chosen, say, a year, and the numbers of new buyers, first repeat buyers, second repeat buyers, and so on are observed. Suppose 6021 new buyer sales and 2170 first repeat sales are observed. Each figure must now be reduced by the number of buyers who just entered the class and did not have a chance, because of the length of the inter-purchase time, to repurchase the product. For example, the average new buyer would not buy again for approximately four months. Therefore, new buyers who bought in the last four months of the observation year are removed, leaving 4472 new buyers. Similarly there are 1932 first repeat buyers instead of 2170 after removing those who came in too late to make another purchase. The first repeat ratio is then calculated as 1932/4472 = .485, the first repeat ratio in Figure 11.13. The other repeat ratios are similarly calculated.

[8] Although Fourt and Woodlock (1960) defined repeat ratios to represent ratios of numbers of buyers in equation (11.22), their example appears to be in terms of the ratios of sales, that is, $s_{1t}N_{1t}/s_{Ft}N_{Ft}$, $s_{2t}N_{2t}/s_{1t}N_{1t}$, and so on. This does not matter much if the average purchase volumes are approximately the same.

Figure 11.13   Using Repeat Ratios to Predict Sales Next Period (Fourt-Woodlock Model)

	Repeat ratios	Estimated number at end of production period (000s)
New buyers		8141
	.485	
First repeat		3948
	.559	
Second repeat		2207
	.645	
Third repeat		1422
	.593	
Fourth repeat		841
	.797	
Fifth repeat		671
	3.300	
Over five		2214
		19,444

The Fourt and Woodlock approach to estimating repeat sales described in (11.23) requires consumer panel data for its implementation. In the absence of such detailed data, a grosser approach to estimating total sales in any period could be derived from a modification of (11.19). Let us assume that a percentage r of new buyers become repeat buyers, that is,

$$N_{Rt} = rN_{Ft} \tag{11.24}$$

Substituting this into (11.19), we get

$$S_t = s_{Ft}N_{Ft} + s_{Rt}rN_{Ft} \tag{11.25}$$

$$\text{or } S_t = (s_{Ft} + s_{Rt}r)N_{Ft} \tag{11.26}$$

In this case, the analyst has to estimate the number of first-time buyers in the next period, N_{Ft} (this comes from his first purchase model), the average sales volume per period of first-time buyers and repeat buyers, s_{Ft} and s_{Rt}, and the percentage of repeat buyers to first time buyers, r. This estimation model in (11.26) is more appropriate for use on a period-to-period basis than as a long-run prediction model. In the long run, the number of new buyers will go to zero, that is, $N_{Ft} \to 0$, and (11.26) could imply that period sales will also go to zero, that is, $S_t \to 0$. In fact, this is prevented because the ratio of repeat buyers to new buyers eventually increases, that is, $r \to \infty$. Yet these tendencies make the formulation in (11.23) or 11.26), which is based on the ever changing and vanishing number of first-time buyers, a tenuous foundation for long-run new product sales forecasting.

PARFITT AND COLLINS'S REPEAT PURCHASE MODEL

As an alternative to tying the repeat purchase rate to the number of new buyers each period, as in the Fourt and Woodlock model, Parfitt and Collins (1968) relate this rate to the cumulative percent of penetration. Their model is designed for long-run share predictions for a new brand being introduced into an established market, rather than for an innovation or a new model. They would like to estimate, on the basis of early consumer panel data, the ultimate market share of a brand. If the forecast ultimate brand share does not appear encouraging, management could consider withdrawing the brand rather than dragging out expected losses.

Parfitt and Collins see ultimate brand share as the product of three factors:

$$s = p \cdot r \cdot b$$

where s = ultimate brand share
   p = ultimate penetration rate of brand (percentage of new buyers of this product class who try this brand)
   r = ultimate repeat purchase rate of brand (percentage of repurchases of this brand to all repurchases by persons who once purchased this brand)
   b = buying rate index of repeat purchase of this brand (average buyer = 1.00)

The definitions of these variables and the working of this formula can best be conveyed through an example. Assume that a company launches a new brand in an established product field. Its share of new buyers in this product field will rise from zero to some ultimate percentage as the weeks pass. Figure 11.14(a) shows the cumulative penetration of a new brand in the toilet soap field. The penetration rate increases at a decreasing rate from time zero. Some weeks after the brand is launched, the analyst can fit a modified exponential curve to the early results (or draw a freehand extrapolation) and predict the ultimate penetration rate, p, that is, the rate that would apply between twelve and eighteen months after the brand is launched.

The analyst will also examine the repeat purchase rate for this brand as the data come in. This rate shows the percent of repurchases of this brand to repurchases of all brands by those who have tried this brand. Figure 11.14(b) shows the repeat purchase rate for the new brand of toilet soap. The repurchase rate is approximately 40 percent in the first four weeks after purchase, that is, four out of ten repurchases of this product were this brand. Figure 11.14(b) shows this rate as falling with the passage of time toward an asymptote of 25 percent. The earlier triers of a new product tend to take to it more than the later triers.

If purchasers of the new brand buy at the average volume of purchasers

Figure 11.14   Brand T: (a) cumulative penetration and (b) repeat-purchase rate (Parfitt and Collins Model)

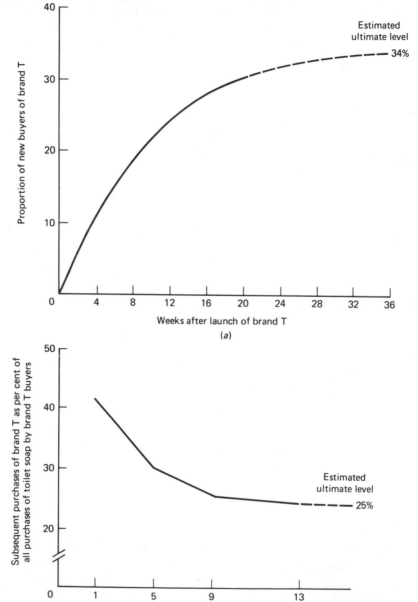

(a)

(b)

Source: Reprinted from Parfitt and Collins in *Journal of Marketing Research* (1968, pp. 132–133).

of all brands in this product class, then $b = 1.00$. We are now ready to predict the ultimate brand share. According to (11.27),

$$s = (.34)(.25)(1.00)$$

$$s = .085$$

That is, if 34 percent of new buyers in this market ultimately try this brand and 25 percent of the triers' subsequent repurchases go to this brand and those buying the brand buy an average quantity, the brand share should settle at an equilibrium level of 8.5 percent. If this brand attracts heavier-than-average buyers, say, with an index of 1.20, then the share prediction would be 10.2 percent $(.34 \times .25 \times 1.20)$; if this brand attracts lighter-than-average buyers, say with an index of .80, then the share prediction would be 6.8 percent $(.34 \times .25 \times .80)$.

The nice feature of this model is that ultimate share prediction can be made as soon as the penetration curve and the repeat purchase curve tend to move toward clear asymptotic values; and this occurs some time before a stable brand share is achieved. By using heavy promotion, the company can achieve faster market penetration and shorten the time required to see where the penetration curve is headed. It is harder for the company to do much to speed its reading of the ultimate repeat purchase rate, as this depends on the average interpurchase time in the product field. The average interpurchase time sets a lower limit to the amount of time that has to elapse before the first share prediction can be made.

The accuracy of the brand share prediction will be affected by whether marketing factors continue into the future in the form and intensity that obtained during the prediction period. If the percentage of retail distribution for the brand is expected to grow significantly in the future, then the ultimate penetration rate will be somewhat higher than currently estimated. If the advertising and promotion of the new brand is expected to change significantly in scale, this will affect the ultimate penetration rate and repeat purchase rate. If the product is expected to be priced at a significantly different level in the future, this may affect all three variables in the basic equation (11.27). Management therefore should make allowances for expected changes in marketing factors in making ultimate brand share predictions.

When the ultimate brand share prediction is discouraging, management should consider whether it can take any action to increase either the penetration rate and/or the repeat purchase rate, before deciding to drop the brand. If management can find a way to increase consumer satisfaction with the brand by altering its features or image, this would be worth considering if its expense would not cancel the value of a higher repeat purchase rate. The easier thing to do is to take steps to increase the penetration rate. But management often acts as if doubling the penetration rate would double the ultimate brand share. This is not necessarily true. Suppose the company runs a price special and this increased the penetration rate, especially by drawing in people who are not devoted to the brand, but who want to take advantage of the value. The higher penetration rate is offset by the lower repeat purchase rate and no gain in ultimate market share need occur. Or suppose the company runs a special advertising campaign which increases the penetration rate. After the campaign is over, the penetration rate falls back to its former level. In this case too, the ultimate brand share is not increased. Management must guard against thinking that increases in the penetration rate will be permanent, or that the repeat purchase rate will remain stable if the penetration rate rises. The ultimate results depend on the marketing approach used to launch the new brand and the satisfaction the product gives to the buyers.

BURGER'S REPEAT PURCHASE MODEL

Still another way to look at the problem of predicting repeat sales and total sales has been proposed by Burger (1968) and represents extensions of earlier work by Chatfield, Ehrenberg, and Goodhart (1966). Burger sees total sales in period T as given by

$$S_t = S_{F,T} + S_{R,T} - S_{R,T-1} \qquad (11.28)$$

where S_t = total sales in period
$\qquad S_{F,T}$ = first purchase sales in period
$\qquad S_{R,T}$ = cumulative repurchases from period 1 to period T
$\qquad S_{R,T-1}$ = cumulative repurchases from period 1 to period $T - 1$

The difference between the last two terms is the expected number of repurchases in period T. The key to estimating this value is to form a model for predicting cumulative repurchases, $S_{R,T}$. (The same model will predict all other summations as well, such as $S_{R,T-1}$).

Cumulative repurchases will depend upon (1) the number of first purchasers in each past period, (2) the proportion of first purchasers who repurchase the product, and (3) the expected number of repurchases per period. The relationship of these variables is exhibited in the following equation:

$$S_{R,T} = \sum_{t=1}^{T} \sum_{k=1}^{\infty} r(t) S_{F,t} \cdot k \cdot p(k = \lambda, T - t) \qquad (11.29)$$

where $\qquad r(t)$ = proportion of first purchasers who are likely to repurchase the product
$\qquad S_{F,t}$ = first purchase sales in period t
$\qquad k$ = number of repurchases in period t (a random variable)
$\qquad p(k = \lambda, T - t)$ = Poisson distribution of the probability of arrival of k repurchases in period t, where λ is expected number of repurchases per period

This equation takes a proportion, r, of the first-time purchases taking place in each period (the proportion is given by $r(t)$, which can change with time, since later triers may show a lower repeat purchase rate than early product triers) and predicts and accumulates the number of repurchases they will make to time T. The number of repurchases they will make to time T depends on the length of time between the time of first purchase, t, and the current period, T. A Poisson distribution is used because it satisfies reasonable underlying assumptions about the distribution of waiting times between repurchases. Information on all of the parameters are derivable from consumer panel data and Burger reports a good fit of this repurchase model in empirical applications.

This ends our review of repeat purchase models. Each model takes a somewhat different approach to estimating repeat purchases and requires different types of data for implementation. A company has to experiment with these models and others in order to determine the one which best fits its data and forecasting needs.

THE NOMMAD MODEL

Herniter, Cook and Norek (1969) set out to design a model that would help explain and predict brand choice behavior toward frequently purchased low-cost consumer products. They wanted a model that would be applicable to pretest market forecasting and planning, test marketing, national introductions, and management of ongoing products. They wanted it to focus on the individual household's behavior and to include several marketing stimuli (advertising, word-of-mouth, and so on) as well as buyer behavioral variables (brand awareness, brand preferences, receptivity to advertising, forgetting, and so on). They wanted the buyer's behavior to be generated by stochastic processes tied to analytical formulations whenever possible. Finally they wanted the model to be data based and verifiable in its component parts and as a whole.

The overall model is diagrammed in Figure 11.15. The figure is divided into three major sections: past purchases, time between purchases, and current purchase. The individual is visualized as having a history of past purchases in this product class. As a result, he also has certain brand preferences, store preferences, and an inherent satisfaction level with the product class. Between purchase occasions, the individual may be exposed to some brand advertising messages and discussions with others about these brands. These have the effect of modifying his brand preference vector. In addition, the individual experiences some forgetting, which also alters his brand preferences. The time of his next purchase is determined probabilistically, as is the individual's store and brand choice.

Herniter, Cook, and Norek employ some very interesting analytical devices to develop the data and relationships. They assume that the individual's past

Figure 11.15   NOMMAD Simulation of Individual Purchase Behavior

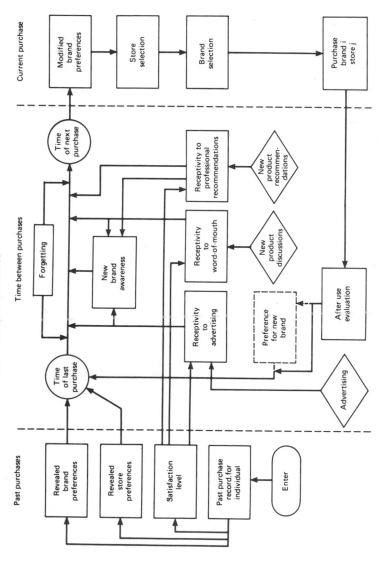

Source: Herniter, Cook, and Norek (1969, p. 31).

purchase history is all that is needed to reveal his brand preferences, store preferences, and satisfaction level. (This is in contrast to using sociodemographic data about the individuals or using direct attitudinal information.) Consider the following twelve past brand purchases by a hypothetical consumer: AABACBDABBBB. Of these twelve purchases, brands A, B, C, and D received respectively 33, 50, 8, and 8 percent of the total. But one would have to believe that the person's relative preference for B would be stronger than 50 percent because the last four purchases were B. Herniter, Cook, and Norek therefore use the sequence of brand choices to modify the raw brand preference percentages. The true revealed brand preference vector is obtained by smoothing geometrically using a constant determined by a least squares fit to some portion of the data according to the authors, although they do not illustrate how this is done.

The individual's store preferences are similarly derived through smoothing past store choices. However, they remain essentially constant over time for the customer. Store preferences are important to introduce because of the strong effect of store selection on brand selection. Since each chain store carries some limited number of brands, the individual's store choice will affect his opportunities for brand choice.

Finally, a measure is also derived of the individual's inherent satisfaction with the product class. This measure is used to determine his receptivity to advertising, word-of-mouth, and professional recommendations. Herniter, Cook, and Norek assume that if the individual has stayed with one brand during the last twelve purchases, his satisfaction is a maximum and he will have very little receptivity to new marketing stimuli. On the other hand, if he has tried all brands equally in the last twelve purchases, it is assumed that his satisfaction is a minimum and he is quite receptive to influences from old and new brands and is more likely to try any new brands. The authors apply an information measure (entropy) to the individual's past purchases to yield a numerical measure of his satisfaction.

Given the individual's initial brand preferences, store preferences, and satisfaction level, he is exposed to various influences which have the effect of modifying his brand preferences. Unfortunately the various mechanisms are too detailed to describe here. Finally, the time of the next purchase by this individual is drawn from an Erlang probability distribution centered on his average purchase frequency. Each buyer is assigned an average purchase frequency such that the distribution of average frequencies duplicates the purchase timings in the original sample.

After the person makes a store and brand choice determined by Monte Carlo procedures, his after-use evaluation is used to modify his brand preference vector.

NOMMAD is capable of processing a population of up to five hundred consumers, ten major brands, ten stores, and fifty time periods. It has been tested on a grocery product and a drug product. Comparisons were made in both product categories of actual and predicted brand purchase sequences, market shares, and trial and repeat purchase rates, and the fittings were reported as most satisfactory. As a result, the authors felt they could use the model to experiment with alternative advertising levels, monthly advertising patterns, and store availabilities. In one experiment they found that a particular company's advertising budget could be cut 20 percent without causing a reduction in sales if the company's seasonal pattern of advertising was revised. In another experiment they found that withdrawing a particular brand from a particular chain did not lead to a significant reduction in its total sales because the preference for this brand was sufficiently strong to lead to changed store preferences. These and other experiments were carried out on the data-based model to predict the effect of alternative brand strategies and events such as a new brand.

The NOMMAD model is a well-conceived total buyer behavior model with several interesting features. As in all models, many questions can and should be raised: Does an individual's past purchase history reveal brand preferences as unambiguously as the authors assume? How about using sociodemographic data and attitudinal data for additional clues to brand preferences? How would multiple brand purchasing behavior be handled in their model? Should variable purchase quantities be introduced? What about the influence of various types and timings of promotions? Is the initialization and computer processing of the behavior of several hundred hypothetical buyers an efficient way to forecast total sales? While these questions can be asked, they in no way should detract from the contributions of this model in suggesting novel analytical formulation and attempting grand theory construction and testing with real data.

SUMMARY

Decision making takes on its most hazardous characteristics in the situation known as new product development and introduction. This is an age when companies must introduce new products to survive, and yet do so in the knowledge that a substantial number of new products will fail.

There has been considerable progress in the area of new product decision models since the days of the simple break-even chart. The variety of current models for new product forecasting and planning reflects to a large extent the variety of new product situations in which companies engage. New product situations can be distinguished according to the degree of newness of the product and the degree of product repurchasability. The latter distinction enables us to separate the analysis of the first-time purchase from repeat purchases, because different factors are involved and total period sales will be made up of the sum of these two sources of sales.

The occurrence of first-time purchases can be analyzed as a diffusion process or as an adoption process. A diffusion process model involves working with a few macroparameters which will locate a curve that describes the spread of the innovation through a population over time. An adoption process, on the other hand, involves modeling in greater detail the behavior of the buyer as he learns and becomes interested in the product.

There are at least four different new product diffusion models which have been proposed. A concave model which assumes that cumulative first purchases approach a limiting penetration level of less than 100 percent of all households and that successive increments of gain decline has been used by Fourt and Woodlock. An S-curve model has been used by a number of investigators to describe the number of adopters over time in a logistic pattern. Other investigators have analogized the spread of an epidemic through a population and accordingly have used one or another of several epidemiological diffusion models. For example, a model by Bass calls for estimating three parameters with the first three years of data on the spread of a new product. His resulting equation has been quite successful in predicting the peak time and magnitude at peak time of future sales. Finally, other investigators have used a Weibull probability distribution coming out of reliability engineering to forecasting the volume of first purchases. The model assumes that the buyer is bombarded by stimuli having random arrival times and he buys the product if any of the stimuli reach him.

Adoption models, in turn, focus on the stages through which the individual progresses to adoption. There is a variety of such buyer readiness paradigms, all of them involving the buyer moving through a cognitive level, affective level, and action level. At least four models have been developed that take the adoption point of view.

The DEMON model views marketing stimuli (advertising, promotion, and distribution) as creating a number of triers, some of whom become users and consume an average quantity that can be multiplied against price to estimate sales. DEMON involves specifying and measuring linked relations between intermediate variables such as advertising dollars, gross impressions, reach and frequency, advertising awareness, and the number of triers.

The SPRINTER model involves several buyer readiness stages leading up to trial, those of awareness (to the brand, the advertisements, the specific product appeals, and word-of-mouth recommendations), intent, search, selection, and postpurchase behavior. Each awareness level assumes that all the preceding types of awareness have occurred, and each higher level of awareness is associated with a higher probability of developing an intent to buy. This model also provides for a certain percentage of triers to be converted into preferers, preferers into low loyals, and low loyals into high loyals. This model requires collecting data through panels and other means and estimating expected values for all of these steps in the buying process.

Alba designed an adoption model using Monte Carlo procedures to duplicate the adoptions of the new Touch-Tone telephone by one hundred households in a suburban community. His households were exposed to the product, mass communications, and word-of-mouth recommendations which influenced their probability of adopting the new product. He considered his model successful if it could reproduce his data on the actual number of new adopters each period and the order in which the one hundred households became adopters.

The most ambitious adoption model is the one developed by Amstutz which breeds a population of consumers, retailers, salesmen, products, and advertisements and causes these elements to interact on a stochastic basis to produce the output of ultimate interest, sales. To use this model, a tremendous amount of data has to be collected and a substantial amount of computer time has to be used to process each hypothetical buyer through a year of exposure to marketing stimuli.

For the case of new frequently purchased products, the forecaster must develop a model to predict repeat purchase volume. An increasing number of analysts are using the concept of depth of repeat purchase because the probability of repeat purchase varies with the household's number of past purchases. Fourt and Woodlock used this notion as the basis of their repeat purchase model. Parfitt and Collins chose to estimate asymptotic levels of ultimate penetration and ultimate repeat purchase rates to forecast the new brand's ultimate market share. Burger sees cumulative repurchases as depending upon the number of first purchasers in each past period, the proportion of first purchasers who repurchase the product, and the expected number of repurchases per period. Herniter, Cook, and Norek assume that the individual's past purchase history is all that is required to reveal his brand choice behavior. Clearly, a variety of models is possible, and their merits will become known only through repeated use and refinement against the hard test of data.

A caution appropriate to all of the models discussed is that they are often based on very tentative assumptions about new product purchase behavior. None of these models is behaviorally rich enough to reflect the most important findings and conclusions of diffusion research discussed throughout this book. But these models do represent significant advances in our sophistication and ability to predict new product success, and the pattern has been to refine these models continually as our knowledge base grows. A most significant development in the marketing field is the behavioral enriching of quantitative models or, as some researchers see it, the quantitative enriching of behavioral models.

REFERENCES

Achenbaum, Alvin A. "Knowledge Is a Thing Called Measurement." In *Attitude Research at Sea*, eds. Lee Adler and Irving Crespi. Chicago: American Marketing Association, 1966, 111–126.

Adams, J. S. "Reduction of Cognitive Dissonance by Seeking Consonant Information." *Journal of Abnormal and Social Psychology*, vol. 62 (1961), 74–78.

Advertest Research, Inc. *Colortown Study No. 1: A Profile of Color Set Owners*. New Brunswick, N.J.: National Broadcasting Company and Batten, Barton, Durstine, and Osborn, Inc., 1958.

Advertising Research Foundation, Inc., *Toward Better Media Comparisons*. New York, 1961.

Alba, Manuel S. "Microanalysis of the Socio-Dynamics of Diffusion of Innovation." Unpublished doctoral dissertation, Northwestern University, 1967.

Alexander, Milton. "The Social Significance of Ethnic Groups In Marketing." In *Perspectives in Consumer Behavior*, eds. Harold H. Kassarjian and Thomas S. Robertson. Glenview, Ill.: Scott, Foresman and Company, 1968, 422–425.

Alexander, Ralph S., James S. Cross, and Richard M. Hill. *Industrial Marketing*. Homewood, Ill.: Richard D. Irwin, Inc., 1961.

Allison, Ralph I., and Kenneth P. Uhl. "Influence of Beer Brand Identification on Taste Perception." *Journal of Marketing Research*, vol. 1 (August 1964), 36–39.

Allvine, Fred C. "Diffusion of a Competitive Innovation." In *Proceedings of the American Marketing Association*, ed. Robert L. King. Chicago: American Marketing Association, 1968, 341–351.

Amstutz, Arnold E. "Development, Validation, and Implementation of Computerized Micro-analytic Simulations of Market Behavior." Paper presented at the Fourth International Conference on Operations Research, Boston, 1966.

Amstutz, Arnold E. *Computer Simulation of Competitive Market Response.* Cambridge, Mass.: MIT Press, 1967.

Andreasen, Alan R. "Attitudes and Consumer Behavior: A Decision Model." In *New Research in Marketing*, ed. Lee E. Preston. Berkeley, Calif.: Institute of Business and Economic Research, University of California, 1965, 1–16.

Andrus, Roman R. "Measures of Consumer Innovative Behavior." Unpublished doctoral dissertation, Columbia University, 1965.

Angelus, Theodore L. "Why Do Most New Products Fail?" *Advertising Age*, vol. 40, (March 24, 1969), 85–86.

Arndt, Johan. "Word of Mouth Advertising: The Role of Product-Related Conversations in the Diffusion of a New Food Product." Unpublished doctoral dissertation, Graduate School of Business Administration, Harvard University, 1966.

Arndt, Johan. "Role of Product-Related Conversations in the Diffusion of a New Product." *Journal of Marketing Research*, vol. 4 (August 1967*a*), 291–295.

Arndt, Johan. *Word of Mouth Advertising.* New York: Advertising Research Foundation, Inc., 1967*b*.

Arndt, Johan. "Profiling Consumer Innovators." In *Insights into Consumer Behavior*, ed. Johan Arndt. Boston: Allyn and Bacon, Inc., 1968, 71–83.

Asch, S. E. "Effects of Group Pressure upon the Modification and Distortion of Judgments." In *Basic Studies in Social Psychology*, eds. H. Proshansky and B. Seidenberg. New York: Holt, Rinehart and Winston, Inc., 1965, 393–401.

Assael, Henry, and George S. Day. "Attitudes and Awareness as Predictors of Market Share." *Journal of Advertising Research*, vol. 8 (December 1968), 3–10.

Atkin, Charles K. "Re-assessing Two Alternative Explanations of De Facto Selective Exposure." Paper presented at the Twenty-fifth Annual Conference of the American Association for Public Opinion Research, May 1970.

Axelrod, Joel N. "Induced Moods and Attitudes toward Products." *Journal of Advertising Research*, vol. 3 (June 1963), 19–24.

Bailey, Norman T. J. *The Mathematical Theory of Epidemics*. New York: Hafner Publishing Company, 1957.

Baker, Norman R. "On Idea Flow." Working paper, Department of Industrial Engineering and Management Science, Northwestern University, 1963.

Bales, Robert F. "Cultural Differences in Rates of Alcoholism." *Quarterly Journal of Studies on Alcohol*, vol. 6 (1946), 480–499.

Barclay, William D. "A Probability Model for Early Prediction of New Product Market Success." *Journal of Marketing*, vol. 27 (January 1963), 63–68.

Barnett, Homer G. *Innovation: The Basis of Cultural Change*. New York: McGraw-Hill, Inc., 1953.

Bass, Frank M. "A New Product Growth Model for Consumer Durables." *Management Science*, January 1969, 215–227.

Bauer, Raymond A. "Consumer Behavior as Risk Taking." In *Proceedings of the American Marketing Association*, ed. R. S. Hancock. Chicago: American Marketing Association, 1960, 389–398.

Bauer, Raymond A. "Risk Handling in Drug Adoption: The Role of Company Preference." *Public Opinion Quarterly*, vol. 25 (Winter 1961), 546–559.

Bauer, Raymond A. "The Initiative of the Audience." *Journal of Advertising Research*, vol. 3 (June 1963a), 2–7.

Bauer, Raymond A. "The Role of the Audience in the Communication Process: Summary." In *Proceedings of the American Marketing Association*, ed. Stephen A. Greyser. Chicago: American Marketing Association, 1963b, 73–82.

Bauer, Raymond A. "The Obstinate Audience: The Influence Process from the Point of View of Social Communication." *American Psychologist*, vol. 19 (May 1964), 319–328.

Bauer, Raymond A. "Attitudes, Verbal Behavior, and Other Behavior." Paper presented at the Bermuda Attitude Research Conference, American Marketing Association, 1966.

Bauer, Raymond A. "Games People and Audiences Play." Paper presented at the Seminar on Communication in Contemporary Society, University of Texas, 1967.

Bauer, Raymond A., and Alice H. Bauer. "America, Mass Society and Mass Media." *The Journal of Social Issues*, vol. 16 (1960), 3–66.

Bauer, Raymond A., and Robert D. Buzzell. "Mating Behavioral Science and Simulation." *Harvard Business Review*, vol. 42 (September–October 1964), 116–124.

Bauer, Raymond A., and Stephen A. Greyser. *Advertising in America: The Consumer View*. Boston: Division of Research, Harvard Business School, 1968.

Bauer, Raymond A., and Gary A. Marple. "Exploring Food Costs and Values."

In *Grocery Manufacturing in the United States*, eds. Gary A. Marple and Harry B. Wissmann. New York: Frederick A. Praeger, Inc., 1968, 310–363.

Bauer, Raymond A., and Lawrence H. Wortzel. "Doctor's Choice: The Physician and His Sources of Information about Drugs." *Journal of Marketing Research*, vol. 3 (February 1966), 40–47.

Beal, George M., and Joe M. Bohlen. *The Diffusion Process*. Ames, Iowa: Iowa Agricultural Extension Service, Special Report no. 18, 1957.

Beal, George M., and Everett M. Rogers. *The Adoption of Two Farm Practices in a Central Iowa Community*. Ames, Iowa: Iowa Agricultural and Home Economics Experiment Station, Special Report no. 26, 1960.

Bell, Gerald D. "Self-Confidence and Persuasion in Car Buying." *Journal of Marketing Research*, vol. 4 (February 1967), 46–53.

Bell, William E. "Consumer Innovators: A Unique Market for Newness." In *Proceedings of the American Marketing Association*, ed. Stephen A. Greyser. Chicago: American Marketing Association, Inc., 1963, 85–95.

Berelson, Bernard. "Communications and Public Opinion." In *Communications in Modern Society*, ed. Wilbur Schramm. Urbana, Ill.: University of Illinois Press, 1948.

Berelson, Bernard, and Gary A. Steiner. *Human Behavior: An Inventory of Scientific Findings*. New York: Harcourt, Brace & Jovanovich, Inc., 1964.

Berey, Lewis A., and Richard W. Pollay. "The Influencing Role of the Child in Family Decision Making." *Journal of Marketing Research*, vol. 5 (February 1968), 70–72.

Berlyne, D. E. *Conflict, Arousal, and Curiosity*. New York: McGraw-Hill, Inc., 1960.

Blau, Peter M. *The Dynamics of Bureaucracy*. Chicago: University of Chicago Press, 1955.

Blau, Peter M., and W. Richard Scott. *Formal Organizations*. San Francisco: Chandler Publishing Company, 1962.

Blood, R. D., Jr., and D. M. Wolfe. *Husbands and Wives: The Dynamics of Married Living*. New York: The Free Press, 1960.

Blum, Milton, and Valentine Appel. "Consumer versus Management Reaction in New Package Development." *Journal of Applied Psychology*, vol. 45 (August 1961), 222–224.

Booz-Allen & Hamilton, Inc. *Management of New Products*. New York, 1965.

Bourne, Francis S. "Group Influence in Marketing and Public Relations." In *Some Applications of Behavioral Research*, eds. Rensis Likert and Samuel P. Hayes, Jr. Paris: UNESCO, 1957, 208–224.

Brehm, Jack W. "Post-decision Changes in the Desirability of Alternatives." *Journal of Abnormal and Social Psychology*, vol. 52 (1956), 384–389.

Brehm, Jack W., and Arthur R. Cohen. *Explorations in Cognitive Dissonance.* New York: John Wiley & Sons, Inc., 1962.

Brody, Robert P., and Scott M. Cunningham. "Personality Variables and the Consumer Decision Process." *Journal of Marketing Research,* vol. 5 (February 1968), 50–57.

Brown, William H. "Innovation in the Machine Tool Industry." *Quarterly Journal of Economics,* vol. 71 (August 1957), 406–425.

Bullock, Henry A. "Consumer Motivations in Black and White." *Harvard Business Review,* vol. 39, pt. i (May–June 1961), 89–104; pt. ii (July–August 1961), 110–124.

Burger, Philip C. "Developing Forecasting Models for New Product Introductions." In *Proceedings of the American Marketing Association,* ed. Robert L. King. Chicago: American Marketing Association, 1968, 112–119.

Burger, Philip C., Frank M. Bass, and Edgar A. Pessemier. "Forecasting New Product Sales." Working paper, Northwestern University, Graduate School of Management, 1968.

Burger, Philip C., Edgar A. Pessemier, and Douglas J. Tigert. "Can New Product Buyers Be Identified?" *Journal of Marketing Research,* vol. 4 (November 1967), 349–354.

Burns, Tom, and G. M. Stalker. *The Management of Innovation.* London: Tavistock Publications, Ltd., 1961.

Business Week. "Research: The Cash Pours Out for Research and Development." May 18, 1968, 72–74.

Buzzell, Robert D. "Competitive Behavior and Product Life Cycles." In *Proceedings of the American Marketing Association,* eds. John S. Wright and Jac L. Goldstucker. Chicago: American Marketing Association, Inc., 1966.

Buzzell, Robert D. "The Product Life-Cycle." In *Grocery Manufacturing in the United States,* eds. Gary A. Marple and Harry B. Wissmann. New York: Frederick A. Praeger, Inc., 1968, 39–83.

Buzzell, Robert D., Victor J. Cook, James R. Peterson, and Paul Hase. "Product Life Cycles." Cambridge, Mass.: Marketing Science Institute, Special Report, November 1969.

Buzzell, Robert D., and Robert E. M. Nourse. *Product Innovation in Food Processing 1954–1964.* Boston: Division of Research, Harvard Business School, 1967.

Bylund, H. Bruce. *Social and Psychological Factors Associated with Acceptance of New Food Products.* University Park, Pa.: Pennsylvania Agricultural Experiment Station, Bulletin no. 708, 1963.

Campbell, Rex R. "A Suggested Paradigm of the Individual Adoption Process." *Rural Sociology,* vol. 31 (December 1966), 458–466.

Cancian, Frank. "Stratification and Risk-Taking: A Theory Tested on Agricultural Innovation." *American Sociological Review*, vol. 32 (December 1967), 912–927.

Carey, James W. "Personality Correlates of Persuasibility." In *Proceedings of the American Marketing Association*, ed. Stephen A. Greyser. Chicago: American Marketing Association, 1963, 30–43.

Carman, James M. "The Fate of Fashion Cycles in Our Modern Society." In *Proceedings of the American Marketing Association*, ed. Raymond M. Haas. Chicago: American Marketing Association, 1966, 722–737.

Carman, James M., and Francesco M. Nicosia. "Analog Experiments with a Model of Consumer Attitude Change." In *Proceedings of the American Marketing Association*, ed. L. George Smith. Chicago: American Marketing Association, 1964, 246–257.

Carter, C. F., and B. R. Williams. *Industry and Technical Progress: Factors Governing the Speed of Application of Science*. New York: Oxford University Press, 1957.

Carter, C. F. and B. R. Williams. "The Characteristics of Technically Progressive Firms." *Journal of Industrial Economics*, (March 1959), 87–104.

Cartwright, Dorwin, and Alvin Zander. *Group Dynamics*, 2nd ed. New York: Harper & Row, Publishers, 1960.

Centers, Richard, and M. Horowitz. "Social Character and Conformity: A Differential in Susceptibility to Social Influence." *Journal of Social Psychology*, vol. 60 (August 1963), 343–349.

Chapanis, N. P., and A. Chapanis. "Cognitive Dissonance: Five Years Later." *Psychological Bulletin*, vol. 61 (January 1964), 1–22.

Charnes, A., W. W. Cooper, J. K. Devoe, and D. B. Learner. "DEMON: A Management Model for Marketing New Products." *California Management Review*, vol. 11 (Fall 1968), 31–46.

Charters, W. W., Jr., and Theodore M. Newcomb. "Some Attitudinal Effects of Experimentally Increased Salience of a Membership Group." In *Readings in Social Psychology*, eds. Guy E. Swanson, Theodore M. Newcomb, and Eugene L. Hartley. New York: Holt, Rinehart and Winston, Inc., 1952.

Chatfield, C., A. S. C. Ehrenberg, and G. J. Goodhart. "Progress on a Simplified Model of Stationary Purchase Behavior." *Journal of the Royal Statistical Society*, ser. A., vol. 129 (1966), 317–360.

Chu, Godwin C. "Impact of Extraneous Anxiety Induction and Reduction on the Persuasiveness of Vague Fear Appeals." Paper presented to the Annual Conference Pacific Chapter, American Association for Public Opinion Research, 1967.

Claycamp, Henry J., and Arnold E. Amstutz. "Simulation Techniques in the Analysis of Marketing Strategy." In *Applications of the Sciences in*

Marketing Management, eds. Frank M. Bass, et al. New York: John Wiley & Sons, Inc., 1968, pp. 113–150.

Cochran, Betty, and G. Clark Thompson. "Why New Products Fail." *The National Industrial Conference Board Record*, vol. 1 (October 1964), 11–18.

Cohen, Arthur R. *Attitude Change and Social Influence*. New York: Basic Books, Inc., 1964.

Coleman, James S. *Introduction to Mathematical Sociology*. New York: The Fress Press, 1964.

Coleman, James S., Elihu Katz, and Herbert Menzel. "The Diffusion of an Innovation among Physicians." *Sociometry*, vol. 20 (December 1957), 253–270.

Coleman, James S., Elihu Katz, and Herbert Menzel. *Medical Innovation: A Diffusion Study*. Indianapolis: The Bobbs-Merrill Company, Inc., 1966.

Coleman, Richard P. "The Significance of Social Stratification in Selling." In *Proceedings of the American Marketing Association*, ed. M. L. Bell. Chicago: American Marketing Association, 1960, 171–184.

Colley, Russell H. *Defining Advertising Goals for Measured Advertising Results*. New York: Association of National Advertisers, Inc., 1961.

Collier, Louis A. "The Difference Must Be Real." In *New Products Marketing*. New York: Duell, Sloan & Pearce–Meredith Press, 1964, 277–290.

Cook, Victor J. "Group Decision, Social Comparison, and Persuasion in Changing Attitudes." *Journal of Advertising Research*, vol. 7 (March 1967), 31–37.

Cook, Victor J. "How Well Does the Life Cycle Work?" In *Product Life Cycles*, ed. Robert D. Buzzell, Cambridge, Mass.: Marketing Science Institute, Special Report, November 1969.

Cook, Victor J., and Jerome D. Herniter. "Preference Measurement in a New Product Demand Simulation." In *Proceedings of the American Marketing Association*, ed. Robert L. King. Chicago: American Marketing Association, 1968, 316–322.

Cook, Victor J., and Jerome D. Herniter. "A Manager's Guide to Model Based Information Systems in Marketing." In *Proceedings of the American Marketing Association*, ed. Bernard A. Morin. Chicago: American Marketing Association, June 1969, 121–128.

Cooper, E., and M. Jahoda. "The Evasion of Propaganda: How Prejudiced People Respond to Anti-Prejudice Propaganda." *Journal of Psychology*, vol. 23 (1947), 15–25.

Copp, James H. *Personal and Social Factors Associated with the Adoption of Recommended Farm Practices among Cattlemen*. Manhattan, Kans.: Kansas Agricultural Experiment Station, Technical Bulletin no. 83, 1956.

Cox, Donald F. "Clues for Advertising Strategists." *Harvard Business Review*, vol. 39, pt. i (September–October 1961), pp. 160–176, pt. ii (November–December 1961), 160–182.

Cox, Donald F. "The Audience as Communicators." In *Proceedings of the American Marketing Association*, ed. Stephen A. Greyser. Chicago: American Marketing Association, 1963, 58–72.

Cox, Donald F., and Raymond A. Bauer. "Self-Confidence and Persuasibility in Women." *Public Opinion Quarterly*, vol. 28 (Fall 1964), 453–466.

Crane, Edgar. *Marketing Communications*. New York: John Wiley & Sons, Inc., 1965.

Crane, Lauren E. "How Product, Appeal, and Program Affect Attitudes toward Commercials." *Journal of Advertising Research*, vol. 4 (March 1964), 15–18.

Crutchfield, Richard S. "Conformity and Character." *American Psychologist*, vol. 10 (1955), 191–198.

Cunningham, Scott M. "Sex Differences in Critical Evaluation." Unpublished working paper, Harvard Business School, 1963.

Cunningham, Scott M. "Perceived Risk as a Factor in the Diffusion of New Product Information." In *Proceedings of the American Marketing Association*, ed. Raymond M. Haas. Chicago: American Marketing Association, 1966, 698–721.

Cunningham, Scott M. "The Major Dimensions of Perceived Risk." In *Risk Taking and Information Handling in Consumer Behavior*, ed. Donald F. Cox. Boston: Division of Research, Harvard Business School, 1967, 82–108.

Curhan, Ronald C. "The Diffusion of Innovation among Consumers and in Retail Distribution." Unpublished working paper, Harvard Business School, 1969.

Day, George S. *Buyer Attitudes and Brand Choice Behavior*. New York: The Free Press, 1970.

Dean, Joel. "Pricing Policies for New Products." *Harvard Business Review*, vol. 28 (November–December 1950), 45–50.

Deutsch, Morton, and H. B. Gerard. "A Study of Normative and Informational Social Influences upon Individual Judgment." *Journal of Abnormal and Social Psychology*, vol. 51 (1955), 629–636.

Dewey, John. *How We Think*. Boston: D. C. Heath and Company, 1910.

Dichter, Ernest. "How Word-of-Mouth Advertising Works." *Harvard Business Review*, vol. 44 (November–December 1966), 147–166.

Drucker, Peter F. *The Practice of Management*. New York: Harper & Row, Publishers, 1954.

Ehrenberg, A. S. C. "A Book Review of *Consumer Decision Processes*, by Francesco M. Nicosia." *Journal of Marketing Research*, vol. 5 (August 1968), 334.

Ehrlich, D., I. Guttmann, P. Schonbach, and J. Mills. "Post-Decision Exposure to Relevant Information." *Journal of Abnormal and Social Psychology*, vol. 54 (1957), 98–102.

Engel, James F., David T. Kollat, and Roger D. Blackwell. *Consumer Behavior.* New York: Holt, Rinehart and Winston, Inc., 1968.

Evans, Franklin B. "Psychological and Objective Factors in the Prediction of Brand Choice: Ford versus Chevrolet." *The Journal of Business*, vol. 32 (October 1959), 340–369.

Evans, Franklin B. "Selling as a Dyadic Relationship: A New Approach." *American Behavioral Scientist*, vol. 6 (May 1963), 76–79.

Federal Trade Commission. "Permissible Period of Time during which New Product May Be Described as 'New.'" *Advisory Opinion Digest*, no. 120, April 15, 1967.

Feldman, Sidney P., and Merlin C. Spencer. "The Effect of Personal Influence in the Selection of Consumer Services." In *Proceedings of the American Marketing Association*, ed. P. D. Bennett. Chicago: American Marketing Association, 1965, 440–452.

Ferber, Robert. "Research on Household Behavior." *American Economic Review*, vol. 52 (March 1962), 19–63.

Festinger, Leon. "Informal Social Communication." *Psychological Review*, vol. 57 (September 1950), 271–282.

Festinger, Leon. "A Theory of Social Comparison Processes." *Human Relations*, vol. 7 (May 1954), 117–140.

Festinger, Leon. *A Theory of Cognitive Dissonance.* Stanford, Calif.: Stanford University Press, 1957.

Festinger, Leon. "Behavioral Support for Opinion Change." *Public Opinion Quarterly*, vol. 28 (Fall 1964), 404–417.

Festinger, Leon, and J. M. Carlsmith. "Cognitive Consequences of Forced Compliance." *Journal of Abnormal and Social Psychology*, vol. 58 (1959), 203–210.

Fishbein, Martin. "An Investigation of the Relationships between Beliefs about an Object and the Attitude toward that Object." *Human Relations*, vol. 16 (August 1963), 233–239.

Fisk, George. "A Conceptual Model for Studying Customer Image." *Journal of Retailing*, vol. 37 (Winter 1961–1962), 1–8, 54.

Fliegel, Frederick C., and Joseph E. Kivlin. "Attributes of Innovations as Factors in Diffusion." *American Journal of Sociology*, vol. 72 (November 1966), 235–248.

Fliegel, Frederick C., Joseph E. Kivlin, and G. S. Sekhon. "A Cross-National Comparison of Farmers' Perceptions of Innovations as Related to Adoption Behavior." Paper presented to the Rural Sociological Society, Boston, 1968.

Foote, Nelson. "The Time Dimension and Consumer Behavior." In *On*

Knowing the Consumer, ed. Joseph W. Newman. New York: John Wiley & Sons, Inc., 1966, 38–46.

Forbes Magazine, "The Coca-Cola Co." vol. 100 (August 1, 1967), 26–34.

Fourt, Louis A., and Joseph W. Woodlock. "Early Prediction of Market Success for New Grocery Products." *Journal of Marketing,* vol. 25 (October 1960), 31–38.

Frank, Ronald E., and William F. Massy. "Innovation and Brand Choice: The Folger's Invasion." In *Proceedings of the American Marketing Association,* ed. Stephen A. Greyser. Chicago: American Marketing Association, 1963, 96–107.

Frank, Ronald E., William F. Massy, and Donald G. Morrison. "The Determinants of Innovative Behavior with Respect to a Branded, Frequently Purchased Food Product." In *Proceedings of the American Marketing Association,* ed. L. George Smith. Chicago: American Marketing Association, 1964, 312–323.

Freedman, J. L., and D. O. Sears. "Selective Exposure." In *Advances in Experimental Social Psychology,* ed. L. Berkowitz. New York: Academic Press, Inc., 1965.

French, Cecil L. "Correlates of Success in Retail Selling." *American Journal of Sociology,* vol. 65 (September 1960), 128–134.

Freund, John E. *Mathematical Statistics.* Englewood Cliffs, N.J.: Prentice-Hall, Inc., 1962.

Fuchs, Douglas A. "Two-Source Effects in Magazine Advertising." *Journal of Marketing Research,* vol. 1 (August 1964), 59–62.

Gardner, Burleigh B., and Sidney J. Levy. "The Product and the Brand." *Harvard Business Review,* vol. 33 (March–April 1955), 33–39.

Gorman, Walter P., III. "Market Acceptance of a Consumer Durable Good Innovation." Unpublished doctoral dissertation, University of Alabama, 1966.

Graham, Saxon. "Cultural Compatibility in the Adoption of Television." *Social Forces,* vol. 33 (1954), 166–170.

Graham, Saxon. "Class and Conservatism in the Adoption of Innovations." *Human Relations,* vol. 9 (1956), 91–100.

Granbois, Donald H. "The Role of Communication in the Family Decision-Making Process." In *Proceedings of the American Marketing Association,* ed. Stephen A. Greyser, Chicago: American Marketing Association, 1963, 44–57.

Granbois, Donald H. "Research Approaches to Decision-Making in the Family." In *The Audience and the Mass Communications Process,* A task-force report. Chicago: American Marketing Association, 1964.

Green, Paul E., and Frank J. Carmone. "The Performance Structure of the Computer Market: A Multivariate Approach." Working paper, Wharton Graduate School of Business, University of Pennsylvania, 1968.

Green, Paul E., and Harry F. Sieber, Jr. "Discriminant Techniques in Adoption Patterns for a New Product." In *Promotional Decisions Using Mathematical Models*, ed. Patrick J. Robinson. Boston: Allyn and Bacon, Inc., 1967, 229–256.

Gross, Irwin. "Toward a General Theory of Product Evolution." Working paper, Cambridge, Mass.: Marketing Science Institute, September 1968.

Gruen, Walter. "Preference for New Products and Its Relationship to Different Measures of Conformity." *Journal of Applied Psychology*, vol. 44 (December 1960), 361–364.

Hagerstrand, Torsten. "A Monte Carlo Approach to Diffusion." *European Journal of Sociology*, vol. 6 (1965), 43–67.

Haines, George H., Jr. "A Theory of Market Behavior after Innovation." *Management Science*, vol. 10 (July 1964), 634–658.

Haines, George H., Jr. "A Study of Why People Purchase New Products." In *Proceedings of the American Marketing Association*, ed. Raymond M. Haas. Chicago: American Marketing Association, 1966, 685–697.

Haines, George H., Jr. "Information and Consumer Behavior." Working paper, College of Business Administration, University of Rochester, 1969.

Hansen, Fleming. "An Attitude Model for Analyzing Consumer Behavior." Unpublished working paper, University of New Hampshire, 1967.

Harding, Murray. "Who Really Makes the Purchasing Decision?" *Industrial Marketing*, vol. 51 (September 1966), 76–82.

Havens, A. Eugene. "A Review of Factors Related to Innovativeness." Columbus, Ohio: Ohio Agricultural Experiment Station, Department of Agricultural Economics and Rural Sociology, Mimeo Bulletin AE 329, 1962.

Havens, A. Eugene. "Increasing the Effectiveness of Predicting Innovativeness." *Rural Sociology*, vol. 30 (1965), 151–165.

Herniter, Jerome D., Victor J. Cook, and Bernard Norek. "Microsimulation of Purchase Behavior for New and Established Products." Paper presented at the University of Chicago Conference on Behavioral and Management Science in Marketing, June 1969.

Hilibrand, Murray. "Source Credibility and the Persuasive Process." Unpublished doctoral dissertation, Graduate School of Business Administration, Harvard University, 1964.

Hollander, E. P. "Competence and Conformity in the Acceptance of Influence." In *Approaches, Contexts, and Problems in Social Psychology*, ed. Edward E. Sampson. Englewood Cliffs, N.J.: Prentice-Hall, Inc., 1964.

Homans, George C. *The Human Group*. New York: Harcourt, Brace & Jovanovich, Inc., 1950.

Homans, George C. "Social Behavior as Exchange." *American Journal of Sociology*, vol. 63 (May 1958), 597–606.

Homans, George C. *Social Behavior: Its Elementary Forms*. New York: Harcourt, Brace & Jovanovich, Inc., 1961.

Hovland, Carl I., Irving L. Janis, and Harold H. Kelley. *Communication and Persuasion*. New Haven, Conn.: Yale University Press, 1953.

Hovland, Carl I., A. A. Lumsdaine, and F. D. Sheffield. *Experiments on Mass Communication*. Princeton, N.J.: Princeton University Press, 1949.

Howard, John A., and Jagdish N. Sheth. "A Theory of Buyer Behavior." In *Perspectives in Consumer Behavior*, eds. Harold H. Kassarjian and Thomas S. Robertson. Glenview, Ill.: Scott, Foresman and Company, 1968, 467–487.

Husband, Richard W., and Jane Godfrey. "An Experimental Study of Cigarette Identification." *Journal of Applied Psychology*, vol. 18 (April 1934), 220–223.

Hyman, Herbert. "Reflections on Reference Groups." *Public Opinion Quarterly*, vol. 24 (Fall 1960), 383–396.

Igoe, Robert. " 'Early Adopters' Analyzed by GE." *Printers Ink*, March 10, 1967, 53–54.

Insko, Chester. *Theories of Attitude Change*. New York: Appleton-Century-Crofts, 1967.

Janis, Irving L. "Personality as a Factor in Susceptibility to Persuasion." In *The Science of Human Communication*, ed. Wilbur Schramm. New York: Basic Books, Inc., 1963, 54–64.

Janis, Irving L., and S. Feshbach. "Effects of Fear-Arousing Communications." *Journal of Abnormal and Social Psychology*, vol. 48 (January 1953), 78–92.

Janis, Irving L., and Leon Mann. "A Conflict-Theory Approach to Attitude Change and Decision-Making." In *Psychological Foundations of Attitudes*, New York: Academic Press, Inc., 1968.

Kassarjian, Harold H. "Social Character and Differential Preference for Mass Communication." *Journal of Marketing Research*, vol. 2 (May 1965), 146–153.

Katona, George. *The Powerful Consumer*. New York: McGraw-Hill, Inc., 1960.

Katona, George, and Eva Mueller. *Consumer Attitudes and Demand: 1950–1952*. Ann Arbor, Mich.: Survey Research Center, University of Michigan, 1954.

Katz, Daniel. "The Functional Approach to the Study of Attitudes." *Public Opinion Quarterly*, vol. 24 (Summer 1960), 163–204.

Katz, Elihu. "The Two-Step Flow of Communication: An Up-to-Date Report on an Hypothesis." *Public Opinion Quarterly*, vol. 21 (Spring 1957), 61–78.

Katz, Elihu. "Communication Research and the Image of Society: Convergence of Two Traditions." *American Journal of Sociology*, vol. 65 (March 1960), 435–440.

Katz, Elihu. "The Social Itinerary of Technical Change: Two Studies on the Diffusion of Innovation." *Human Organization*, vol. 20 (Summer 1961), 70–82.

Katz, Elihu, Herbert Hamilton, and Martin L. Levin. "Traditions of Research on the Diffusion of Innovation." *American Sociological Review*, vol. 28 (April 1963), 237–252.

Katz, Elihu, and Paul F. Lazarsfeld, *Personal Influence*. New York: The Free Press, 1955.

Kelley, Harold H., and Edmund H. Volkart. "The Resistance to Change of Group Anchored Attitudes." *American Sociological Review*, vol. 17 (August 1952), 453–465.

Kelly, Robert. "The Search Component of the Consumer Decision Process: A Theoretical Examination." In *Proceedings of the American Marketing Association*, ed. Robert L. King. Chicago: American Marketing Association, 1968, 273–279.

Kelman, Herbert C. "Processes of Opinion Change." *Public Opinion Quarterly*, vol. 25 (Spring 1961), 57–78.

Kelman, Herbert C., and J. Cohler. "Reactions to Persuasive Communication as a Function of Cognitive Needs and Styles." Paper read at meeting of the Eastern Psychological Association, Atlantic City, 1959.

Kelman, Herbert C., and Carl I. Hovland. "'Reinstatement' of the Communicator in Delayed Measurement of Opinion Change." *Journal of Abnormal and Social Psychology*, vol. 48 (1953), 327–335.

Kenkel, William F. "Family Interaction in Decision-Making on Spending." In *Household Decision-Making*, ed. N. N. Foote. New York: New York University Press, 1961, 140–164.

Kiesler, Charles A., Barry E. Collins, and Norman Miller. *Attitude Change: A Critical Analysis of Theoretical Approaches*. New York: John Wiley & Sons, Inc., 1969.

King, Charles W., Jr. "Fashion Adoption: A Rebuttal to the 'Trickle Down' Theory." *Proceedings of the American Marketing Association*, ed. Stephen A. Greyser. Chicago: American Marketing Association, 1963, 108–125.

King, Charles W., Jr. "A Study of the Innovator and the Influential in the Fashion Adoption Process." Unpublished doctoral dissertation, Graduate School of Business Administration, Harvard University, 1964.

King, Charles W., Jr. "The Innovator in the Fashion Adoption Process." In *Proceedings of the American Marketing Association*, ed. L. George Smith. Chicago: American Marketing Association, 1965, 324–339.

King, Charles W. "Adoption and Diffusion Research in Marketing: An

Overview." In *Proceedings of the American Marketing Association,* ed. Raymond M. Haas. Chicago: American Marketing Association, 1966, 665–684.

King, Charles W., Jr., and John O. Summers. *Interaction Patterns in Interpersonal Communication.* West Lafayette, Ind.: Herman C. Krannert Graduate School of Industrial Administration, Purdue University, Institute for Research in the Behavioral, Economic, and Management Sciences, Paper no. 168, 1967*a*.

King, Charles W., and John O. Summers. *The New Product Adoption Research Project.* West Lafayette, Ind.: Herman C. Krannert Graduate School of Industrial Administration, Purdue University, Institute for Research in the Behavioral, Economic, and Management Science. Paper no. 196, 1967*b*.

King, Charles W., Jr., and John O. Summers. "Technology, Innovation and Consumer Decision Making." In *Proceedings of the American Marketing Association,* ed. Reed Moyer. Chicago: American Marketing Association, 1967*c*, 63–68.

King, Charles W., Jr., and John O. Summers. "Overlap of Opinion Leadership across Consumer Product Categories." *Journal of Marketing Research,* vol. 7 (February 1970), 43–50.

Kirchner, Don. "Anxiety, Cognitive Dissonance and Susceptibility to Personal Influence in Consumer Decision-Making As a Function of Birth Order: A Proposal." Unpublished doctoral thesis, Graduate School of Business Administration, University of California, Los Angeles, 1967.

Klapper, Joseph T. "What We Know about the Effects of Mass Communication: The Brink of Hope." *Public Opinion Quarterly,* vol. 21 (Winter 1957–1958), 453–474.

Klapper, Joseph T. *The Effects of Mass Communication.* New York: The Free Press, 1960.

Klonglan, Gerald E., E. Walter Coward, Jr., and George M. Beal. "Conceptualizing and Measuring Extent of Diffusion: The Concept of Adoption Progress." Paper presented to the Rural Sociological Society, Boston, August 1968.

Komarovsky, Mirra. "Class Difference in Family Decision-Making on Expenditures." In *Household Decision-Making,* ed. N. N. Foote. New York: New York University Press, 1961, 255–265.

Kotler, Philip. "Computer Simulation in the Analysis of New Product Decisions." In *Applications of the Sciences to Marketing Management,* ed. Frank M. Bass, et al., New York: John Wiley & Sons, Inc., 1968.

Krech, David, Richard S. Crutchfield, and Egerton L. Ballachey. *Individual in Society.* New York: McGraw-Hill, Inc., 1962.

Krugman, Herbert E. "The Impact of Television Advertising: Learning without Involvement." *Public Opinion Quarterly*, vol. 29 (Fall 1965), 349–356.

Krugman, Herbert E. "The Measurement of Advertising Involvement." *Public Opinion Quarterly*, vol. 30 (Winter 1966–1967), 583–596.

Krugman, Herbert E. "Electroencephalographic Aspects of Low Involvement: Implications for the McLuhan Hypothesis." Paper presented at the Twenty-fifth Annual Conference, American Association for Public Opinion Research, May 1970.

Langer, Susanne K. *Philosophy in a New Key*. Cambridge, Mass.: Harvard University Press, 1951.

Lavidge, Robert J., and Gary A. Steiner. "A Model for Predictive Measurements of Advertising Effectiveness." *Journal of Marketing*, vol. 25 (October 1961), 59–62.

Lawson, William D., Charles A. Lynch, and John C. Richards. "Corfam: Research Brings Chemistry to Footwear," *Research Management*, vol. 8 (January 1965), 5–26.

Lazarsfeld, Paul F., Bernard Berelson, and Hazel Gaudet. *The People's Choice*, 2nd ed. New York: Columbia University Press, 1948.

Lazer, William, and William E. Bell. "The Communications Process and Innovation." *Journal of Advertising Research*, vol. 6 (September 1966), 2–7.

Learner, David B. "Profit Maximization through New-Product Marketing Planning and Control." In *Applications of the Sciences in Marketing Management*, ed. Frank M. Bass, et al., New York: John Wiley & Sons, Inc., 1968, 151–167.

Lenski, Gerhard E. "Status Crystallization: A Non-Vertical Dimension of Social Status." *American Sociological Review*, vol. 19 (August 1954), 405–413.

Lenski, Gerhard E. "Social Participation and Status Crystallization." *American Sociological Review*, vol. 21 (August 1956), 458–464.

Levitt, Theodore. *Innovation in Marketing*. New York: McGraw-Hill, Inc., 1962.

Levitt, Theodore. "Exploit the Product Life Cycle." *Harvard Business Review*, vol. 43 (November–December 1965), 81–94.

Levy, Sidney J. "Symbols for Sale." *Harvard Business Review*, vol. 37 (July–August 1959), 117–124.

Lewin, Kurt. *Principles of Topological Psychology*. New York: McGraw-Hill, Inc., 1936.

Lewin, Kurt. "Group Decision and Social Change." In *Basic Studies in Social Psychology*, eds. H. Proshansky and B. Seidenberg. New York: Holt, Rinehart and Winston, Inc., 1965, 423–436.

Linton, H., and E. Graham. "Personality Correlates of Persuasability." In

Personality and Persuasability, eds. Carl I. Hovland and Irving L. Janis, New Haven, Conn.: Yale University Press, 1959, 69–101.

Lionberger, Herbert F. *Information Seeking Habits and Characteristics of Farm Operators*. Columbia, Mo.: Missouri Agricultural Experiment Station, Bulletin no. 581, 1955.

Lionberger, Herbert F. *Adoption of New Ideas and Practices*. Ames, Iowa: Iowa State University Press, 1960.

Lionberger, Herbert F. *Legitimation of Decisions To Adopt Farm Practices and Purchase Farm Supplies in Two Missouri Farm Communities: Ozark and Prairie*. Columbia, Mo.: Missouri Agricultural Experiment Station, Research Bulletin no. 826, 1963.

Lionberger, Herbert F., and C. Milton Coughenour. *Social Structure and Diffusion of Farm Information*. Columbia, Mo.: Missouri Agricultural Experiment Station, Research Bulletin no. 631, 1957.

Lipset, Seymour M., and Reinhard Bendix. *Social Mobility in Industrial Society*. Berkeley, Calif.: University of California Press, 1959.

London, P., and H. Lim. "Yielding Reason to Social Pressure: Task Complexity and Expectations in Conformity." *Journal of Personality* (Spring 1964), 75–89.

LoSciuto, Leonard A., and Robert Perloff. "Influence of Product Preference on Dissonance Reduction." *Journal of Marketing Research*, vol. 4 (August 1967), 286–290.

Lynch, Mervin D., and Richard C. Hartman. "Dimensions of Humor in Advertising." *Journal of Advertising Research*, vol. 8 (December 1968), 39–45.

McGuire, William J. "Theory of the Structure of Human Thought." In *Theories of Cognitive Consistency: A Sourcebook*, eds. Robert P. Abelson, et al. Skokie, Ill.: Rand McNally & Company, 1968, 140–162.

McGuire, William J. "An Information-Processing Model of Advertising Effectiveness." Paper presented at the Symposium on Behavioral and Management Science in Marketing, University of Chicago, July, 1969*a*.

McGuire, William J. "The Nature of Attitudes and Attitude Change." In *The Handbook of Social Psychology*, eds. Gardner Lindzey and Elliot Aronson, 2nd ed., vol. 3. Reading, Mass.: Addison-Wesley Publishing Company, Inc., 1969*b*, 136–314.

McLeod, Jack, Scott Ward, and Karen Tancill. "Alienation and Uses of the Mass Media." *Public Opinion Quarterly*, vol. 29 (Winter 1965–1966), 583–594.

Maddi, Salvatore R. "The Pursuit of Consistency and Variety." In *Theories of Cognitive Consistency: A Sourcebook*, ed. Robert P. Abelson, et al., Skokie, Ill.: Rand McNally & Company, 1968, 267–274.

Mancuso, Joseph R. "Why Not Create Opinion Leaders for New Product Introductions?" *Journal of Marketing*, vol. 33 (July 1969), 20–25.

Mansfield, Edwin. "Technical Change and the Rate of Imitation." *Econometrica*, vol. 29 (October 1961), 741–766.

Mansfield, Edwin. "Entry, Gibrat's Law, Innovation, and the Growth of Firms." *American Economic Review*, vol. 52 (December 1962), 1023–1051.

Mansfield, Edwin. "Size of Firm, Market Structure, and Innovation." *Journal of Political Economy*, vol. 71 (December 1963), 556–576.

Mansfield, Edwin. *Industrial Research and Technological Innovation.* New York: W. W. Norton & Company, Inc., 1968.

Marcus, Alan S., and Raymond A. Bauer. "Yes: There Are Generalized Opinion Leaders." *Public Opinion Quarterly*, vol. 28 (Winter 1964), 628–632.

Marketing Science Institute. *Industrial Buying and Creative Marketing.* Boston: Allyn and Bacon, Inc., 1967.

Marsh, C. Paul, and A. Lee Coleman. "Group Influences and Agricultural Innovations: Some Tentative Findings and Hypotheses." *American Journal of Sociology*, vol. 61 (May 1956), 588–594.

Mason, Robert. "An Ordinal Scale for Measuring the Adoption Process." In *Studies of Innovation and of Communication to the Public*, ed. Wilbur Schramm. Stanford, Calif.: Stanford University Institute for Communication Research, 1962.

Mason, Robert. "The Use of Information Sources by Influentials in the Adoption Process." *Public Opinion Quarterly*, vol. 27 (Fall 1963), 455–466.

Massy, William F. "A Stochastic Evolutionary Model for Evaluating New Products." Working paper, Carnegie Institute of Technology, 1967.

Massy, William F. "Forecasting the Demand for New Convenience Products." *Journal of Marketing Research*, vol. 6 (November 1969), 405–413.

Mauser, Ferdinand F. "The Future Challenges Marketing." *Harvard Business Review*, vol. 41 (September–October 1963), 168–188.

Mayer, Martin. *The Intelligent Man's Guide to Sales Measures of Advertising.* New York: Advertising Research Foundation, Inc., 1965.

Mead, George Herbert. *Mind, Self, and Society*, ed. C. W. Morris. Chicago: University of Chicago Press, 1934.

Menzel, Herbert. "Public and Private Conformity under Different Conditions of Acceptance in the Group." *Journal of Abnormal and Social Psychology*, vol. 55 (November 1957), 398–402.

Menzel, Herbert. "Innovation, Integration, and Marginality: A Survey of Physicians." *American Sociological Review*, vol. 25 (October 1960), 704–713.

Menzel, Herbert, and Elihu Katz. "Social Relations and Innovation in the Medical Profession: The Epidemiology of a New Drug." *Public Opinion Quarterly*, vol. 19 (Winter 1956), 337–352.

Merton, Robert K. *Social Theory and Social Structure*, rev. ed. New York: The Free Press, 1957.

Merton, Robert K., Leonard Broom, and Leonard S. Cottrell, Jr., eds. *Sociology Today*. New York: Harper & Row, Publishers, 1959.

Mills, J., E. Aronson, and J. Robinson. "Selectivity in Exposure to Information." *Journal of Abnormal and Social Psychology*, vol. 59 (1959), 250–253.

Montgomery, David B., and Alvin J. Silk. "Patterns of Overlap in Opinion Leadership and Interest for Selected Categories of Purchasing Activity." Working paper, Sloan School of Management, Massachusetts Institute of Technology, July 1969.

Montgomery, David B., and Glen L. Urban. *Management Science in Marketing*. Englewood Cliffs, N.J.: Prentice-Hall, Inc., 1969.

Morrissett, Irving. "Consumer Attitudes, Expectations and Plans." In *Some Applications of Behavioral Research*, eds. Rensis Likert and Samuel P. Hayes, Jr. Paris: UNESCO, 1957, 277–300.

Moscovici, Serge. "Attitudes and Opinions." *Annual Review of Psychology*, Palo Alto, Calif.: Annual Reviews, Inc., vol. 14 (1963), 231–260.

Mueller, Eva. "Effects of Consumer Attitudes on Purchases." *American Economic Review*, vol. 47 (December 1957), 946–965.

Mueller, Eva. "A Look at the American Consumer." In *On Knowing the Consumer*, ed. Joseph W. Newman. New York: John Wiley & Sons, Inc., 1966, 23–37.

Myers, James H. "A Competitive Edge in Marketing Communications." In *Competition in Marketing*, eds. T. W. Meloan and C. M. Whitlo. Los Angeles: University of Southern California, 1964, 23–33.

Myers, James H., and Thomas S. Robertson. "Dimensions of Opinion Leadership." Working paper, University of Southern California, 1970.

Myers, John G. "Patterns of Interpersonal Influence in the Adoption of New Products." In *Proceedings of the American Marketing Association*, ed. Raymond M. Haas. Chicago: American Marketing Association, 1966, 750–757.

Nakanishi, Masao. "A Model of Market Reactions to New Products." Unpub. doctoral dissertation, Graduate School of Business Administration, University of California, Los Angeles, 1968.

National Institute for Economic and Social Research. "The Diffusion of New Technology." *National Institute Economic Review*, no. 48 (May 1969), 40–83.

Newcomb, Theodore M. "Attitude Development as a Function of Reference Groups: The Bennington Study." In *Readings in Social Psychology*, eds. Guy E. Swanson, Theodore M. Newcomb, and Eugene L. Hartley. New York: Holt, Rinehart and Winston, Inc., 1952.

Newcomb, Theodore M. "An Approach to the Study of Communicative Acts." *Psychological Review*, vol. 60 (November 1953), 393–404.

Newman, Joseph W. "On Knowing the Consumer: An Overview." In *On Knowing the Consumer*, ed. Joseph W. Newman. New York: John Wiley & Sons, Inc., 1966, 7–20.

Nicosia, Francesco M. "Opinion Leadership and the Flow of Communication: Some Problems and Prospects." In *Proceedings of the American Marketing Association*, ed. L. George Smith. Chicago: American Marketing Association, 1964, 340–358.

Nicosia, Francesco M. *Consumer Decision Processes*. Englewood Cliffs, N.J.: Prentice-Hall, Inc., 1966.

A. C. Nielsen Company, *Thirty-third Annual Review of Retail Grocery Trends*. Chicago, 1967.

Nisbett, Richard E., and Andrew Gordon. "Self-Esteem and Susceptibility to Social Influence." *Journal of Personality and Social Psychology*, vol. 5 (March 1967), 268–276.

North Central Rural Sociology Subcommittee for the Study of Diffusion of Farm Practices. *How Farm People Accept New Ideas*. Ames, Iowa: Iowa Agricultural Extension Service, Special Report no. 15, 1955.

North Central Rural Sociology Subcommittee for the Study of Diffusion of Farm Practices. *Adopters of New Farm Ideas*. East Lansing, Mich.: North Central Regional Extension Service, Bulletin no. 13, 1961.

Nourse, Robert E. M. "Demand for New Products In Processed Food Industries." Unpublished doctoral dissertation, Graduate School of Business Administration, Harvard University, 1967.

Ogilvy, David. *Confessions of an Advertising Man*. New York: Atheneum Publishers, 1963.

Opinion Research Corporation. *America's Tastemakers*. Research Reports nos. 1 and 2. Princeton, N.J., 1959.

Osgood, Charles, and Percy Tannenbaum. "The Principle of Congruity in the Prediction of Attitude Change." *Psychological Review*, vol. 62 (January 1955), 42–55.

Ostlund, Lyman E. "Product Perceptions and Predispositional Factors as Determinants of Innovative Behavior." Unpublished doctoral dissertation, Graduate School of Business Administration, Harvard University, 1969.

Packard, Vance. *The Waste Makers*. New York: David McKay Company, Inc., 1960.

Paisley, William J. "Researching the Motives of Information-Seeking." Paper presented at Association for Education in Journalism Convention, Syracuse, 1965.

Palda, Kristian S. "The Hypothesis of a Hierarchy of Effects: A Partial

Evaluation." *Journal of Marketing Research,* vol. 3 (February 1966), 13–24.

Papageorgis, Demetrios, and William J. McGuire. "The Generality of Immunity to Persuasion Produced by Pre-Exposure to Weakened Counterarguments." *Journal of Abnormal and Social Psychology,* vol. 62 (May 1961), 475–481.

Parfitt, J. H., and B. J. K. Collins. "The Use of Consumer Panels for Brand-Share Prediction." *Journal of Marketing Research,* vol. 5 (May 1968), 131–146.

Pessemier, Edgar A. *New Product Decisions: An Analytical Approach.* New York: McGraw-Hill, Inc., 1966.

Pessemier, Edgar A., et al. "Using Laboratory Brand Preference Scales To Predict Consumer Brand Purchases." Working paper, Purdue University, September 1967.

Pieruschka, E. *Principles of Reliability.* Englewood Cliffs, N.J.: Prentice-Hall, Inc., 1963.

Politz, Alfred. *A Twelve-Months' Study of* Better Homes and Gardens *Readers.* Des Moines, Iowa: Meredith Publishing Company, 1956.

Polli, Rolando E. "A Test of the Classical Product Life Cycle by Means of Actual Sales Histories." Unpublished doctoral dissertation, University of Pennsylvania, 1968.

Polli, Rolando E., and Victor J. Cook. "Validity of the Product Life Cycle." Working paper, Marketing Science Institute, January 1969.

Polli, Rolando E., and Victor J. Cook. "Product Life Cycle Models: A Review Paper." Working paper, Marketing Science Institute, November 1967.

Popielarz, Donald T. "An Exploration of Perceived Risk and Willingness To Try New Products." *Journal of Marketing Research,* vol. 4 (November 1967), 368–72.

Quaker Oats Company. "The New Item Problem." Chicago, Ill., Publicly available brochure, May 1968.

Radloff, R. "Opinion Evaluation and Affiliation." *Journal of Abnormal and Social Psychology,* vol. 62 (May 1961), 578–585.

Rainwater, Lee, Richard P. Coleman, and Gerald Handel. *Workingman's Wife.* Dobbs Ferry, N.Y.: Oceana Publications, Inc., 1959.

Rarick, G. R. "Effects of Two Components of Communicator Prestige." Paper presented to the Pacific Chapter, American Association for Public Opinion Research, Asilomar, Calif., 1963.

Ray, G. F. "The Diffusion of New Technology." *National Institute Economic Review,* no. 48 (May 1969), 40–83.

Ray, Michael L. "The Refutational Approach in Advertising." Paper presented to the Advertising Division, Association for Education in Journalism, Boulder, Colo., 1967.

Ray, Michael L. "Biases in Selection of Messages Designed To Induce Resistance to Persuasion." *Journal of Personality and Social Psychology,* vol. 9 (July–August 1968), 335–339.

Ray, Michael L. "The Present and Potential Linkages between the Micro-theoretical Notions of Behavioral Science and the Problems of Advertising: A Proposal for a Research System." Paper presented at the Behavioral and Management Science in Marketing Symposium, University of Chicago, July 1969.

Ray, Michael L., and William L. Wilkie. "Fear: The Potential of an Appeal Neglected by Marketing." *Journal of Marketing,* vol. 34 (January 1970), 54–62.

Rich, Stuart U. "Shopping Behavior of Department Store Customers." Unpublished doctoral dissertation, Graduate School of Business Administration, Harvard University, 1963.

Riesman, David. *The Lonely Crowd.* New Haven, Conn.: Yale University Press, 1950.

Robertson, Thomas S. "An Analysis of Innovative Behavior and Its Determinants." Unpublished doctoral dissertation, Northwestern University, 1966.

Robertson, Thomas S. "The Process of Innovation and the Diffusion of Innovation." *Journal of Marketing,* vol. 31 (January 1967*a*), 14–19.

Robertson, Thomas S. "Consumer Innovators: The Key to New Product Success." *California Management Review,* vol. 10 (Winter 1967*b*), 23–30.

Robertson, Thomas S. "Determinants of Innovative Behavior." In *Proceedings of the American Marketing Association,* ed. Reed Moyer. Chicago: American Marketing Association, 1967*c*, 328–332.

Robertson, Thomas S. "Assessing the Influence of the Consumer Innovator." Working paper, University of California, Los Angeles, 1968*a*.

Robertson, Thomas S. "Purchase Sequence Responses: Innovators vs. Non-Innovators." *Journal of Advertising Research,* vol. 8 (March 1968*b*), 47–52.

Robertson, Thomas S. "Response to Innovative Communications: A Theoretical Model." *The Marketer,* vol. 3 (Summer 1968*c*), 14–18.

Robertson, Thomas S. "The Effect of the Informal Group upon Member Innovative Behavior." In *Proceedings of the American Marketing Association,* ed. Robert L. King. Chicago: American Marketing Association, 1968*d*, 334–340.

Robertson, Thomas S. "Group Characteristics and Aggregate Innovative Behavior: Preliminary Report." In *The Consumer and New Products,* ed. Johan Arndt. Boston: Allyn and Bacon, Inc., on press, 1971.

Robertson, Thomas S., and Richard B. Chase. "The Sales Process: An Open Systems Approach." *MSU Business Topics,* vol. 16 (Autumn 1968), 45–52.

Robertson, Thomas S., and James N. Kennedy. "Prediction of Consumer Innovators: Application of Multiple Discriminant Analysis." *Journal of Marketing Research*, vol. 5 (February 1968), 64–69.

Robertson, Thomas S., and James H. Myers. "Personality Correlates of Opinion Leadership and Innovative Buying Behavior." *Journal of Marketing Research*, vol. 6 (May 1969), 164–168.

Rogers, Everett M. "Personality Correlates of the Adoption of Technological Practices." *Rural Sociology*, vol. 22 (September 1957), 267–268.

Rogers, Everett M. "Characteristics of Agricultural Innovators and Other Adopter Categories." In *Studies of Innovation and of Communication to the Public*, ed. Wilbur Schramm. Stanford, Calif.: Stanford University Press, 1962a, 61–98.

Rogers, Everett M. *Diffusion of Innovations*. New York: The Free Press, 1962b.

Rogers, Everett M. *Bibliography on the Diffusion of Innovations*, annual eds. East Lansing, Mich.: Michigan State University, College of Communication Arts, 1966, 1967, and 1968.

Rogers, Everett M. *Modernization among Peasants*. New York: Holt, Rinehart and Winston, Inc., 1969.

Rogers, Everett M., and George M. Beal. "The Importance of Personal Influence in the Adoption of Technological Changes." *Social Forces*, vol. 36 (May 1958), 329–335.

Rogers, Everett M., and D. G. Cartano. "Methods of Measuring Opinion Leadership." *Public Opinion Quarterly*, vol. 26 (Fall 1962), 435–441.

Rogers, Everett M., and L. Edna Rogers. "A Methodological Analysis of Adoption Scales." *Rural Sociology*, vol. 26 (December 1961), 325–336.

Rogers, Everett M., and David J. Stanfield. "Adoption and Diffusion of New Products: Emerging Generalizations and Hypotheses." In *Applications of the Sciences in Marketing Management*, eds. Frank M. Bass, et al. New York: John Wiley & Sons, Inc., 1968, 227–250.

Rokeach, Milton. "Attitude Change and Behavioral Change." *Public Opinion Quarterly*, vol. 30 (Winter 1966), 529–550.

Rokeach, Milton. *Beliefs, Attitudes and Values*. San Francisco: Jossey-Bass, Inc., Publishers, 1968.

Rosenberg, Milton J. "A Structural Theory of Attitude Dynamics." *Public Opinion Quarterly*, vol. 24 (Summer 1960), 319–340.

Rosenberg, Milton J., and Robert P. Abelson. "An Analysis of Cognitive Balancing." In *Attitude Organization and Change*, eds. Carl I. Hovland and Milton J. Rosenberg. New Haven, Conn.: Yale University Press, 1960, 112–163.

Rossiter, John R. "Innovativeness and Opinion Leadership for College Coed Fashions." Unpublished master's thesis, Graduate School of Business Administration, University of California, Los Angeles, 1967.

Rossiter, John R., and Thomas S. Robertson. "Fashion Diffusion: The Inter-play of Innovator and Opinion Leader Roles in College Social Systems." Working paper, Graduate School of Business Administration, University of California, Los Angeles, 1968.

Ryan, Bryce, and Neal C. Gross. "The Diffusion of Hybrid Seed Corn in Two Iowa Communities." *Rural Sociology*, vol. 8 (March 1943), 15–24.

Ryan, Bryce, and Neal C. Gross. *Acceptance and Diffusion of Hybrid Seed Corn in Two Iowa Communities*. Ames, Iowa: Iowa Agricultural Experiment Station, Research Bulletin no. 372, 1950.

Schachter, S. *The Psychology of Affiliation*. Stanford, Calif.: Stanford University Press, 1959.

Schramm, Wilbur. "How Communication Works." In *The Process and Effects of Mass Communication*, ed. Wilbur Schramm. Urbana, Ill.: University of Illinois Press, 1954, 3–26.

Schumpeter, Joseph A. *Business Cycles*, vol. 1. New York: McGraw-Hill, Inc., 1939.

Sears, David O., and Jonathan L. Freedman. "Selective Exposure to Information: A Critical Review." *Public Opinion Quarterly*, vol. 31 (Summer 1967), 194–213.

Sherif, Muzafer. *The Psychology of Social Norms*. New York: Harper & Row, Publishers, 1936.

Sherif, Muzafer. "Formation of Social Norms: The Experimental Paradigm." In *Basic Studies in Social Psychology*, ed. H. Proshansky and B. Seidenberg. New York: Holt, Rinehart and Winston, Inc., 1965, 461–470.

Sheth, Jagdish N. "A Review of Buyer Behavior." *Management Science*, vol. 13 (August 1967), B-718–B-756.

Sheth, Jagdish N. "Perceived Risk and Diffusion of Innovations." In *Insights into Consumer Behavior* ed. Johan Arndt. Boston: Allyn and Bacon, Inc., 1968, 173–188.

Shibutani, Tamotsu. "Reference Groups as Perspectives." *American Journal of Sociology*, vol. 60 (May 1955), 562–569.

Shoaf, F. Robert. "Here's Proof: The Industrial Buyer *Is* Human!" *Industrial Marketing*, vol. 44 (May 1959), 126–128.

Siegel, Alberta Engvall, and Sidney Siegel. "Reference Groups, Membership Groups, and Attitude Change." *Journal of Abnormal and Social Psychology*, vol. 55 (November 1957), 360–364.

Silk, Alvin J. "Overlap among Self-Designated Opinion Leaders: A Study of Selected Dental Products and Services." *Journal of Marketing Research*, vol. 3 (August 1966), 255–259.

Silk, Alvin J. "An Experimental Study of the Effects of Pleasant and Unpleasant Radio Advertising: Hypotheses and Research Design." Unpublished paper, University of Chicago, May 1967.

Silk, Alvin J. "The Use of Preference and Perception Measures in New

Product Development: An Exposition and Review." Working paper, (360–68), Sloan School of Management, Massachusetts Institute of Technology, 1968.

Simmel, Georg. "Fashion." *The American Journal of Sociology*, vol. LXII (May 1957), 541–558.

Simon, Herbert A. "The Architecture of Complexity" *Proceedings of the American Philosophical Society*, December 1962.

Slocum, Kenneth G. "New Flavor at Coke." *Wall Street Journal*, vol. 45 (September 20, 1965), 1, 10.

Smith, M. Brewster, Jerome S. Bruner, and Robert W. White. *Opinions and Personality*. New York: John Wiley & Sons, Inc., 1956.

Stafford, James E. "Effects of Group Influences on Consumer Brand Preferences." *Journal of Marketing Research*, vol. 3 (February 1966), 68–75.

Stafford, James E. "Reference Theory as a Conceptual Framework for Consumer Decisions." In *Proceedings of the American Marketing Association*, ed. Robert L. King, Chicago: American Marketing Association, 1968.

Star, Alvin D. "Adoption of Innovations by Large Retail Firms." Unpublished doctoral dissertation, Northwestern University, 1969.

Stefflre, Volney. "Market Structure Studies: New Products for Old Markets and New Markets (Foreign) for Old Products." In *Applications of the Sciences in Marketing Management*, eds. Frank M. Bass, et al. New York: John Wiley & Sons, Inc., 1968, 251–268.

Stephenson, William. *The Play Theory of Mass Communication*. Chicago: University of Chicago Press, 1967.

Stonequist, Everett V. *The Marginal Man*. New York: Charles Scribner's Sons, 1937.

Summers, John O. "The Identity of the Women's Clothing Fashion Transmitter." Unpublished doctoral dissertation, Purdue University, 1968.

Sutherland, Alister. "The Diffusion of an Innovation in Cotton Spinning." *Journal of Industrial Economics*, vol. 7 (March 1959), 118–126.

Tannenbaum, Percy H. "Initial Attitude toward Source and Concept as Factors in Attitude Change through Communication." *Public Opinion Quarterly*, vol. 20 (Summer 1956), 413–425.

Tarde, Gabriel. *The Laws of Imitation*. New York: Holt, Rinehart and Winston, Inc., 1903.

Thumin, Fred. J. "Identification of Cola Beverages." *Journal of Applied Psychology*, vol. 46 (October 1962), 358–360.

Tigert, Douglas J. "Psychometric Correlates of Opinion Leadership and Innovation." Working paper, Graduate School of Business, University of Chicago, March 1969.

Tosdal, Harry R. *Principles of Personal Selling*. New York: McGraw-Hill, Inc., 1925.

Urban, Glen L. "A New Product Analysis and Decision Model." *Management Science*, (April 1968*a*), 490–517.

Urban, Glen L. "Market Response Models for the Analysis of New Products." In *Proceedings of the American Marketing Association*, ed. Robert L. King. Chicago: American Marketing Association, 1968*b*, 105–111.

Urban, Glen L. "SPRINTER: A Model for the Analysis of New Frequently Purchased Consumer Products." Working paper, Sloan School of Management, Massachusetts Institute of Technology, 1969.

Usher, Abbott Payson. *A History of Mechanical Inventions*. New York: McGraw-Hill, Inc., 1929.

Vavra, Terry G. "Irritation in Radio Advertising: A Study of Affectivity and Effectiveness." Unpublished master's thesis, University of California, Los Angeles, 1967.

Veblen, Thorstein. *The Theory of the Leisure Class*. New York: B. W. Huebsch, 1899.

Venkatesan, M. "Experimental Study of Consumer Behavior Conformity and Independence." *Journal of Marketing Research*, vol. 3 (November 1966), 384–387.

Venkatesan, M., and Gordon A. Haaland. "The Effect of Distraction on the Influence of Persuasive Marketing Communications." In *Insights into Consumer Behavior*, ed. Johan Arndt. Boston: Allyn and Bacon, Inc., 1968, 55–66.

Ward, Scott. "Learning Consumer Roles: Preliminary Results and a Conceptual Framework for Research." Working paper, Marketing Science Institute, April 1970.

Ward, Scott, and David G. Gibson. "Social Influence and Consumer Communication Behavior." Working paper, Marketing Science Institute, 1969.

Wasson, Chester R. "What Is 'New' about a New Product." *Journal of Marketing*, vol. 25 (July 1960), 52–56.

Wasson, Chester R. "How Predictable Are Fashion and Other Product Life Cycles?" *Journal of Marketing*, vol. 32 (July 1968), 36–43.

Weale, Walter B. "Measuring the Customer's Image of a Department Store." *Journal of Retailing*, vol. 37 (Summer 1961), 40–48.

Weber, Max. *The Theory of Social and Economic Organization*, trans. A. M. Henderson and Talcott Parsons, ed. Talcott Parsons. New York: Oxford University Press, 1947.

Webster, Frederick E., Jr. "Word-of-Mouth Communication and Opinion Leadership in Industrial Markets." In *Proceedings of the American Marketing Association*, ed. Robert L. King, Chicago: American Marketing Association, 1968, 455–459.

Webster, Frederick E., Jr. "New Product Adoption in Industrial Markets: A

Framework for Analysis." *Journal of Marketing*, vol. 33 (July 1969), 35–39.

Weiner, Richard. "3M and P&G: A Pair of Triumphs." *Printers' Ink*, vol. 287 (May 29, 1964), 123–124.

Weiss, E. B. "That Malarky About 80 Percent of New Products Failing." *Advertising Age*, vol. 36 (August 2, 1965), 101.

Wells, William D., and Jack M. Chinsky. "Effect of Competing Messages: A Laboratory Simulation." *Journal of Marketing Research*, vol. 2 (May 1965), 141–145.

Westfall, Ralph L. "Psychological Factors in Predicting Product Choice." *Journal of Marketing*, vol. 26 (April 1962), 34–40.

Whyte, William H., Jr. "The Web of Word of Mouth." *Fortune*, vol. 50 (November 1954), 140–143 and 204–212.

Wilding, John. "Problem Solving and Psychosocial Aspects of the Communications Process." Unpublished doctoral dissertation, Graduate School of Business Administration, Harvard University, 1966.

Wilding, John, and Raymond A. Bauer. "Consumer Goals and Reactions to a Communication Source." *Journal of Marketing Research*, vol. 5 (February 1968), 73–77.

Wilkening, E. A. "Roles of Communicating Agents in Technological Change in Agriculture." *Social Forces*, vol. 34 (May 1956), 361–367.

Winick, Charles. "The Diffusion of an Innovation among Physicians in a Large City." *Sociometry*, vol. 24 (December 1961), 384–396.

Wolfe, Harry Deane, James K. Brown, and G. Clark Thompson. *Measuring Advertising Results*. New York: National Industrial Conference Board, Inc., 1962.

Wolgast, E. H. "Do Husbands or Wives Make the Purchasing Decisions?" *Journal of Marketing*, vol. 23 (October 1958), 151–158.

Zajonc, Robert B. "The Concepts of Balance, Congruity, and Dissonance," *Public Opinion Quarterly*, vol. 24 (Summer 1960), 280–296.

Zaltman, Gerald. *Marketing: Contributions from the Behavioral Sciences*. New York: Harcourt, Brace & Jovanovich, Inc., 1965.

Zimmerman, Claire, and Raymond A. Bauer. "The Effects of an Audience upon What Is Remembered." *Public Opinion Quarterly*, vol. 20 (Spring 1956).

Name Index

Subject Index